THE DOCTRINES OF US SECURITY POLICY

An Evaluation under International Law

The practice of outlining principles for the conduct of US security policy in so-called doctrines is a characteristic feature of US foreign policy. From an international lawyer's point of view two aspects of these doctrines are of particular interest. First, to what degree are the criteria for the use of force, as laid down in these doctrines, consistent with the limitations for the use of force in international law? Second, which law-creating effects do these doctrines have? Furthermore, the legal nature of these doctrines remains uncertain. These matters are examined, beginning with the Monroe Doctrine of 1823, taking into account the Stimson Doctrine of 1932, the doctrines of the Cold War period and the Bush Doctrine of 2002. The Bush Doctrine in particular has generated controversies concerning its compatibility with Article 51 of the UN Charter, due to its principle of pre-emptive self-defence.

HEIKO MEIERTÖNS is a Senior Fellow at the Institute for Public International Law and European Law at Humboldt University, Berlin, where he teaches international and constitutional law.

THE DOCTRINES OF US SECURITY POLICY

An Evaluation under International Law

HEIKO MEIERTÖNS

CAMBRIDGE
UNIVERSITY PRESS

CAMBRIDGE
UNIVERSITY PRESS

University Printing House, Cambridge CB2 8BS, United Kingdom

One Liberty Plaza, 20th Floor, New York, NY 10006, USA

477 Williamstown Road, Port Melbourne, VIC 3207, Australia

314-321, 3rd Floor, Plot 3, Splendor Forum, Jasola District Centre, New Delhi - 110025, India

79 Anson Road, #06-04/06, Singapore 079906

Cambridge University Press is part of the University of Cambridge.

It furthers the University's mission by disseminating knowledge in the pursuit of education, learning and research at the highest international levels of excellence.

www.cambridge.org
Information on this title: www.cambridge.org/9780521766487

First published 2010

A catalogue record for this publication is available from the British Library

Library of Congress Cataloging in Publication data
Meiertöns, Heiko.
The doctrines of US security policy : an evaluation under international law / Heiko Meiertöns.
p. cm.
Includes bibliographical references and index.
ISBN 978-0-521-76648-7 (hardback)
1. International law. 2. National security – Law and legislation – United States. 3. International law – United States. 4. United States – Foreign relations – Law and legislation. I. Title.
KZ3410.M447 2010
343.73′01 – dc22 2010006553

ISBN 978-0-521-76648-7 Hardback

CONTENTS

PREFACE AND ACKNOWLEDGEMENTS

The year 2009 will be remembered as the end of eight years of the Bush Administration, with Barack Obama being sworn in as President that January. A legacy of the previous administration, in terms of international law, is the Bush Doctrine of 2002, formulated in reaction to the events of 11 September 2001. It is one of the most striking examples of the generally low opinion in which international law was held by some within the US administration at that time.[1] As one legal adviser from the Pentagon stated in a conversation in 2008, recalling the years 2002 to 2003: 'I wasn't asked a legal question in two years.'

Announced at the height of this generally hostile approach, it seems natural to discuss this doctrine with regard to its impact on the *ius ad bellum*. It also has to be analysed in a broader legal and historical context. The practice of outlining principles for the conduct of US foreign and security policy in so-called doctrines is a characteristic feature of US foreign policy. From an international lawyer's perspective, two questions arise from these doctrines. First, to what degree are the criteria for the use of force laid down in these doctrines consistent with the limitations of the use of force in international law? Second, which law-creating effects do these doctrines have? Furthermore, to date the legal nature of these doctrines remains largely unexplored.

This book examines these matters, beginning with the Monroe Doctrine of 1823. The Stimson Doctrine of 1932 and the doctrines of the Cold War period, like the Truman Doctrine of 1945 are discussed, as is the Bush Doctrine of 2002. The Bush Doctrine in particular generated controversies concerning its compatibility with Article 51 of the UN Charter due to its principle of pre-emptive self-defence.

The question of what effects these doctrines had, and continue to have, on the development of international law is closely connected with matters

1 J. Goldsmith, *The Terror Presidency – Law and Judgment Inside the Bush Administration* (New York: W. W. Norton, 2008), pp. 58–70.

concerning the influence of a sole superpower on the structure of international law. Hence, this book also addresses the questions regarding what influence a hegemonic power can exercise on the development of international law, and whether a 'hegemonic international law' or 'imperial international law' is currently emerging.

A number of issues concerning US foreign policy and their impact on international law have received considerable attention from international lawyers over the last decade. Yet they are rarely placed in the broader context of the history of international law. This book aims to close that gap by providing answers to the two questions outlined above. It places isolated discussions of singular aspects concerning the legality of the use of force in the broader context of the history of international law and also of US security policy.

I have previously thanked those who supported the initial writing of this work in the foreword to the German edition.[2] Now, writing some time later, I would like to thank both those who provided technical support for the writing of the updated English version, and those who provided me with intellectual and spiritual support.

In that broader context I have had the advantage of being able to build on the works of two distinguished scholars of international law and diplomatic history, one German and one American: Herbert Kraus (1884–1965) and Cecil V. Crabb (1924–2003). They devoted a considerable part of their lives to the exploration of doctrines, decades before I set my mind on this subject. I feel a certain closeness to their thoughts and considerations, though – for obvious reasons – I never met them in person. I will, therefore, elaborate briefly on my appreciation of their works. Hence, while working on this topic, I often considered myself fortunate enough to say, as clichéd as this observation may sound: 'If I have seen further it is only by standing on the shoulders of Giants.'[3] I can only hope that this work will satisfy their high standards for the scholarly discussion of doctrines.

The first, Herbert Kraus, founder of the Institute of International Law at the University of Göttingen,[4] laid down a still convincing standard

2 H. Meiertöns, *Die Doktrinen U.S.-amerikanischer Sicherheitspolitik – Völkerrechtliche Bewertung und ihr Einfluss auf das Völkerrecht* (Baden-Baden: Nomos, 2006).

3 Sir Isaac Newton, Letter to Robert Hooke (15 February 1676), quoted in A. Rupert Hall, *Isaac Newton: Adventurer in Thought* (Cambridge University Press, 1996), p. 139.

4 A CV of Herbert Kraus can be found in RdC, 50 (1934-IV), 315; on Herbert Kraus, see further D. Rauschning, 'Herbert Kraus (1884–1965)', in D. Rauschning and D. V. Nerée (eds.), *Die Albertus-Universität zu Königsberg und ihre Professoren* (Berlin: Duncker &

for the positivist legal discussion of an essentially political, even highly politicised, ideological subject such as doctrines. As far back as 1914 Kraus conducted research for his higher doctorate (*habilitation*) on the Monroe Doctrine at Columbia University, New York;[5] a highly unusual place for a German scholar of international law at that point in history. It should not be surprising that I found the work of a German international lawyer (founder of the same institute where I wrote most of this book), who focused on the subject of an American doctrine ninety years before work on this book begun, a great inspiration.[6]

Kraus is a fascinating personality due to a certain fact that sets him apart from most of his contemporaries. After the Nazi seizure of power in 1933, Kraus found himself at a crossroads. Unlike a number of other German scholars of international law, who had at that stage either voiced support for, or opposition to, the National Socialist ideology, or were simply alienated for religious or other reasons,[7] Kraus had remained silent on the issue. His silence itself may be reprehensible, but as a result he was able to choose whether he wanted to endorse or reject this ideology. At exactly the point when others joined the NSDAP in large numbers, decided to remain silent, withdrew to matters of purely academic interest,[8] or continued their work regardless of political changes,[9] he did exactly the opposite. In 1934 he published a text on the crisis of inter-state thought calling the newly elected Chancellor indirectly 'a fool'.[10] A dispute with Carl Schmitt, today regrettably forgotten, on international law and international ethics followed.[11] After a period of forced retirement between 1937 and 1945 he

Humblot, 1994), pp. 371–81; J. Martinez and F. Prill: 'Geschichte der Völkerrechtsforschung und – lehre and der Georg-August-Universität Göttingen', in C. Calliess, G. Nolte and P. Stoll (eds.), *Von der Diplomatie zum kodifizierten Recht – 75 Jahre Institut für Völkerrecht der Universität Göttingen (1930–2005)* (Cologne: Heymanns, 2006).

5 H. Kraus, *Die Monroedoktrin in ihren Beziehungen zur amerikanischen Diplomatie und zum Völkerrecht* (Berlin: Guttentag, 1913).

6 Kraus also happens to be one of the predecessors of the supervisor of this Ph.D. thesis, Georg Nolte as holder of the chair for Public International Law at the University of Göttingen, currently held by Andreas Paulus.

7 On this see D. F. Vagts, 'International Law in the Third Reich', A.J.I.L., 84 (1990), 661–704.

8 M. Stolleis, *History of Public Law in Germany* (Oxford University Press, 2004), pp. 408–31.

9 G. Stuby, *Vom 'Kronjuristen' zum 'Kronzeugen'. Friedrich Wilhelm Gaus: ein Leben im Auswärtigen Amt der Wilhelmstraße* (VSA-Verlag: Hamburg, 2008).

10 H. Kraus, *Die Krise des zwischenstaatlichen Denkens: eine Bilanz* (Göttingen: Vandenhoek & Ruprecht, 1933), p. 26.

11 C. Schmitt, 'Nationalsozialismus und Völkerrecht', *Schriften der Deutschen Hochschule für Politik*, Issue 9, Berlin (1934); H. Kraus, 'Carl Schmitt, Nationalsozialismus und Völkerrecht', N.Z.I.R., 50 (1935), 151–61.

returned to his chair in Göttingen. The fact that after 1945 Kraus – an East Prussian from Kaliningrad/Königsberg – focused on rather unpopular, arcane questions of the legal status of the former eastern territories of the German Reich,[12] may have contributed to the little attention his work received. Yet this cannot diminish his achievements in his early work on the Monroe Doctrine.

The second scholar, Cecil V. Crabb (1924–2003), was Professor of Political Science and Chairman of the Department of Political Science at Louisiana State University from 1968 to 1979. Crabb authored some of the most widely used textbooks on US foreign policy. His textbook on international politics, *Nations in a Multipolar World*, was one of the first to focus on the concept of 'multipolarity' and its implications for the international system.[13] His book, *The Doctrines of American Foreign Policy – Their Meaning role and Future*,[14] was groundbreaking work on the subject of doctrines and provided me with a most valuable and comprehensive analysis and description of doctrines in their historical context.

To a certain degree the English used in the writing of this book remains 'German', and the perspective certainly is. Wherever it was possible, original English texts or translations of texts into English are quoted. However, frequent reference is made to some German scholarly opinions as this work is essentially a product of the German strand of an international discourse. When initially writing this work, this sometimes resulted in a feeling – probably unchanged for 2,000 years, and already known to scholars in the Germanic-Roman province when writing about the Roman Empire – of being unheard. What could have been a better motivation for going ahead with an English version of this text?

The translation of this work began in Göttingen, but it was not before a stay in Paris in late 2007 that I really found the time to work on the translation, still uncertain whether it would ever see the light of day. It was on a cold day in January 2008, having strolled into the Cambridge University Press bookshop on King's Parade, that I made the decision to finalise my work on an English language version. I had never been to Cambridge before; however, the day before I had attended an excellent

12 H. Kraus, *Der völkerrechtliche Status der deutschen Ostgebiete innerhalb der Reichsgrenzen nach dem Stande vom 31. Dezember 1937* (Göttingen: Schwartz, 1964); S. Sharp. 'Review: Herbert Kraus, Osteuropa und der deutsche Osten, vol. I: Die Oder-Neisse-Linie. Eine völkerrechtliche Studie', A.J.I.L., 49 (1955), 284.

13 C. V. Crabb, *Nations in a Multipolar World* (New York: Harper & Row, 1968).

14 C. V. Crabb, *The Doctrines of American Foreign Policy – Their Meaning, Role and Future* (Baton Rouge, LA: Louisiana University Press, 1982).

lecture by Ralph Zacklin, former United Nations Assistant Secretary-General for Legal Affairs at the Lauterpacht Centre.[15] I found it of great comfort that I, holding a Ph.D. from the University of Munich (93 in the *Times Higher Education Supplement*'s ranking of the world's top 100 universities in 2008),[16] felt I could easily relate to scholarly works on international law presented at the University of Cambridge (Rank 3), grasping the references he made. Later that day, standing in the Squire Law Library looking at familiar books, it dawned on me that the German debate on international law was not quite as isolated as I had previously thought.

The English text was finally completed and updated at the Law School of Humboldt University, Berlin, an institution to which I quickly developed strong ties, where work at the chair of Professor Dr Georg Nolte at the Institute for Public International Law and European Law provided me with an ideal working environment to finish this book.

I wish to thank Oscar Rennalls and Mike Giardina for their help with the translation. Research students Felix Ehrhardt, Anika Seemann and Tobias Ross assisted with the format of the footnotes. I thank the anonymous reviewers for their comments on language and style. Errors and omissions, however, are – of course – all mine. I also thank Finola O'Sullivan and Richard Woodham at Cambridge University Press for their guidance throughout the publication process. The participants of the 27th Manfred Wörner Seminar in May 2009 were the ideal conversationalists for discussing the added, updated chapter on the possible emergence of an 'Obama Doctrine'.

Finally, I particularly thank Miriam J. Anderson, Memorial University, St John's for her encouragement, without which I would certainly have never dared to undertake the task of writing an English version of this work. At the time we became acquainted in 2007 she was a Ph.D. candidate at the Centre of International Studies, University of Cambridge and a Visiting Scholar at Columbia University, New York – just like Herbert Kraus more than ninety years before.

Berlin, September 2009
Dr. Heiko Meiertöns, M.Litt.

15 R. Zacklin, 'The UN Secretariat and the Use of Force in a Unipolar World', Hersch Lauterpacht Memorial Lectures, 2007–8, available at: www.lcil.cam.ac.uk/Media/lectures/pdf/2008_Hersch_Lectures/2008_Lecture_3.pdf.

16 www.timeshighereducation.co.uk.

The present book constitutes an updated and revised version of the author's doctoral thesis, which was accepted by the Faculty of Law of the Ludwig-Maximilians-University of Munich, Germany on 2 November 2005 (*summa cum laude*). The thesis was awarded the Helmuth-James-von-Moltke-Preis 2007 by the German Section of the International Society for Military Law and the Law of War for outstanding judicial work in the field of security policy.

ABBREVIATIONS

A.D.	Annual Digest and Reports of Public International Law Cases
AdG	Archiv der Gegenwart
A.F.D.I.	Annuaire Français de Droit International
A.F. & S.	Armed Forces and Society
A.J.I.L.	American Journal of International Law
Am.H.Rev.	American Historical Review
AöR	Archiv des öffentlichen Recht
A.S.I.L.	American Society of International Law
A.U.I.L.Rev.	American University International Law Review
AVR	Archiv des Völkerrechts
B.C.I.C.L.R.	Boston College International & Comparative Law Review
Berk.J.I.L.	Berkeley Journal of International Law
BVerfGE	Entscheidungssammlung des Bundesverfassungsgerichts
B.Y.I.L.	British Yearbook of International Law
Cal.W.I.L.J.	California Western International Law Journal
Cas.W.Res.J.I.L.	Case Western Reserve Journal of International Law
CENTO	Central Treaty Organization
CFR	Council on Foreign Relations
Chin.J.I.L.	Chinese Journal of International Law
C.J.I.L.	Connecticut Journal of International Law
Col.J.T.L.	Columbia Journal of Transnational Law
Cong. Rec.	Congressional Record
Corn.I.L.J.	Cornell International Law Journal
CTS	Consolidated Treaty Series
DGVR	Deutsche Gesellschaft für Völkerrecht
Dipl.Hist.	Diplomatic History
Documents	Documents on International Affairs
D.US.P.I.L.	Digest of US Practice in International Law
EA	Europa Archiv
E.J.I.L.	European Journal of International Law
E.P.I.L.	Encyclopaedia of Public International Law
Eu.GRZ	Europäische Grundrechte-Zeitschrift

Eu.J.I.R.	European Journal of International Relations
For.Aff.	Foreign Affairs
For.Pol.	Foreign Policy
FRUS	Foreign Relations of the United States
FS	Festschrift
GA	General Assembly
G.J.I.C.L.	Georgia Journal of International and Comparative Law
G.L.J.	German Law Journal
G.Y.I.L.	German Yearbook of International Law
Harv.I.L.J.	Harvard International Law Journal
H.J.I.L.	Heidelberg Journal of International Law
H.J.L.P.P.	Harvard Journal of Law & Public Policy
H.L.R.	Harvard Law Review
Hous.J.I.L.	Houston Journal of International Law
Hu.V-I	Humanitäres Völkerrecht–Informationsschrift
ICJ	International Court of Justice
I.C.L.Q.	International and Comparative Law Quarterly
I.Con.	International Conciliation
IISS	International Institute for Strategic Studies
I.J.I.L.	Indian Journal of International Law
I.L.A.Rep.	International Law Association Report Conference held at . . .
ILC	International Law Commission
IMT	International Military Tribunal
Int.Aff.	International Affairs
Int.J.	International Journal
Int.L.	International Lawyer
Int.Org.	International Organisation
Int.Sec.	International Security
I.R.R.C.	International Review of the Red Cross
I.S.P.	International Studies Perspectives
Isr.L.R.	Israel Law Review
I.Y.H.R.	Israel Yearbook on Human Rights
J.C.S.L.	Journal of Conflict and Security Law
J.I.A.	Journal of International Affairs
J.I.L.P.A.C.	Journal of International Law of Peace and Armed Conflict
J.I.P.O.	Journal of International Peace and Organisation (Friedens-Warte)
JöR	Jahrbuch des öffentlichen Rechts
J.Pol.	The Journal of Politics
JZ	Juristenzeitung
K.A.E.V.R.	Kleine Arbeitsreihe zur Europäischen und Vergleichende Rechtsgeschichte

LdR/VR	Lexikon des Rechts/Völkerrecht
L.G.Rev.	Lawyers Guild Review
LNC	League of Nations Covenant
L.N.O.J.	League of Nations Official Journal
LNTS	League of Nations Treaty Series
Louis.L.Rev.	Louisiana Law Review
Mich.J.I.L.	Michigan Journal of International Law
Mich.L.Rev.	Michigan Law Review
Miss.V.H.Rev.	Mississippi Valley Historical Review
Mil.L.Rev.	Military Law Review
M.P.Y.U.N.L.	Max Planck Yearbook of United Nations Law
NATO	North Atlantic Treaty Organization
Natl.Int.	The National Interest
N.D.L.R.	Notre Dame Law Review
N.J.W.	Neue Juristische Wochenschrift
NSS	National Security Strategy
N.Z.I.R.	Niemeyers Zeitschrift für Internationales Recht
OAS	Organization of American States
ÖZöRV	Österreichische Zeitschrift für öffentliches Recht und Völkerrecht
Pac.Aff.	Pacific Affairs
Pace.I.L.R.	Pace International Law Review
P.P.Sci.	Perspectives on Political Science
P.S.Q.	Political Science Quarterly
RBDI	Revue belge de droit international
RdC	Recueil des Courses
Rev.Hell.d.Int.	Revue Hellenique de droit International
RGBl.	Reichsgesetzblatt
R.G.D.I.P.	Revue générale de droit international public
R.I.A.A.	Reports of International Arbitral Awards
R.I.S.	Review of International Studies
R.O.W.	Recht in Ost und West
RuP	Recht und Politik
Rus.P.L.	Russian Politics and Law
SCOR	Security Council Official Record
SEATO	South East Asian Treaty Organization
StanfordJ.I.L.	Stanford Journal of International Law
StanfordL.Rev.	Stanford Law Review
S.S.J.	Schriften der Süddeutschen Juristenzeitung
TempleLQ	Temple Law Quarterly
T.Inq.L.	Theoretical Inquiries in Law
TLCP	Transnational Law & Contemporary Problems
Trans. Grotius Soc.	Transactions of the Grotius Society

UN	United Nations
UNCIO	United Nations Conference on International Organization
UN Doc.	United Nations Document
UN GA	United Nations General Assembly
UN RSC	United Nations Report of the Security Council
UNTS	United Nations Treaty Series
UNO	United Nations Organisation
Va.J.I.L.	Virginia Journal of International Law
Vand.J.T.L.	Vanderbilt Journal of Transnational Law
VBS	Völkerbundssatzung
VCLT	Vienna Convention on the Law of Treaties
VN	Vereinte Nationen
VRÜ	Verfassung und Recht in Übersee
W. & M.L.R.	William & Mary Law Review
Wash.Q.	The Washington Quarterly
WorldP.J.	World Policy Journal
Y.B.WorldAff.	The Year Book of World Affairs
Y.J.I.L.	Yale Journal of International Law
Y.L.J.	Yale Law Journal
ZaöRV	Zeitschrift für ausländisches öffentliches Recht und Völkerrecht
ZdAkDR	Zeitschrift der Akademie für Deutsches Recht
ZfV	Zeitschrift für Völkerrecht
ZRP	Zeitschrift für Rechtspolitik

1

Introduction

'Right' and 'might' are two antagonistic forces representing alternative principles for organising international relations. Considering the interaction between these two forces, one can identify certain features: with regard to questions considered by states as being relevant or having vital importance to their own security international law serves as means of foreign policy, rather than foreign policy serving as a means of fostering international law.[1]

Given the nature of international law as a law of coordination and also the way in which norms are created under it, pre-legal, political questions of power are of far greater importance under international law than they are under domestic law.[2] Despite an increasing codification of international law or even a constitutionalisation,[3] international law lacks a principle which contradicts the assumption that states, based on their own power may act as they wish.[4] In spite of the principle of sovereign equality, the legal relations under international law can be shaped to mirror the distribution of power much more than in domestic law.[5]

1 H. Morgenthau, *Die internationale Rechtspflege, ihr Wesen und ihre Grenzen* (Leipzig: Universitätsverlag Robert Noske, 1929), also: Ph.D. thesis, Leipzig (1929), pp. 98–104; L. Henkin, *How Nations Behave – Law and Foreign Policy* (New York: Praeger, 1968), pp. 84–94.

2 F. Kratochwil, 'Thrasymmachos Revisited: On the Relevance of Norms and the Study of Law for International Relations', J.I.A. 37 (1984), 343–56.

3 J. A. Frowein, 'Konstitutionalisierung des Völkerrechts', *DGVR-Berichte*, 39 (1999), 427–45.

4 N. Krisch, 'Weak as Constraint, Strong as Tool: The Place of International Law in US Foreign Policy', in D. M. Malone and Y. F. Khong (eds.), *Unilateralism and US Foreign Policy* (Boulder, CO: Rienner, 2003), pp. 41–2.

5 In 1910, Max Huber wrote that public international law 'of all laws has the closest connection to its social foundations, and it has to have, because the objective order of law in it is based directly upon the will of the subjects of law, and organs are lacking which would be able to enforce independently a binding effect of the legal order upon the subjects of law.' (Author's translation of: 'von allen Rechten . . . sich am engsten an seinen sozialen Unterbau anschließt und anschließen muß, weil hier die objektive Rechtsordnung unmittelbar auf dem Willen der Rechtssubjekte beruht und weil es hier an Organen fehlt, welche in

The international dominance of the United States since 1991 is a political fact which has implications for the development of international law. This has received considerable attention over recent years, although as an area of study it is still in its infancy.[6] The transformation of political hegemony[7] into international legal structures, on the other hand, is a question which drew attention long before the rise of the United States to superpower status.[8] Wilhelm Grewe has categorised the history of international law into various phases of Spanish, French and English dominance and American–Soviet rivalry.[9] Continuing this categorisation one might consider the current phase of international law as a US-American age.[10]

The political dominance of a single state is not a situation that could be described as unprecedented, but a condition with historically comparable situations – times in which a state with superior power at the same time exercised a predominant role in the development of international law.[11] In spite of that, the legitimacy of singling out the position of a single state and differentiating between the consideration of the legal relations of the most powerful state with the other states, and the legal relations of the states with each other has been questioned. The status of a sole superpower would not create unique relations between the most powerful state and the others, which change the foundations of international law.[12]

der Lage wären, unabhängig vom Willen einzelner Rechtssubjekte die Rechtsordnung zu verwirklichen.') M. Huber, *Die soziologischen Grundlagen des Völkerrechts* (Berlin: Verlag Dr Walther Rothschild, 1928), p. 9.

6 M. Byers and G. Nolte (eds.), *United States Hegemony and the Foundations of International Law* (Cambridge University Press, 2003); J. Murphy, *The United States and the Rule of Law in International Affairs* (Cambridge University Press, 2004); D. Vagts, 'Hegemonic International Law', A.J.I.L., 95 (2001), 843–8; Symposium: 'The New American Hegemony', C.J.I.L., 19 (2004), 231–406.

7 On this term see further: L. Brilmayer, *American Hegemony* (New Haven, CT: Yale University Press, 1997), pp. 14–18. On different concepts of hegemony: P. Minnerop, *Paria-Staaten im Völkerrecht?* (Springer: Berlin, 2004), also Ph.D. thesis, Göttingen, 2003–4, pp. 425 *et seq.*

8 For example, H. Triepel, *Die Hegemonie: ein Buch von führenden Staaten* (Stuttgart: Kohlhammer, 1938), in particular pp. 203–18.

9 W. Grewe, *Epochs of International Law*, trans. Michael Byers (New York: Walter de Gruyter, 2000). On Grewe's work see: B. Fassbender, 'Stories of War and Peace – On Writing the History of International Law in the "Third Reich" and After', E.J.I.L., 13 (2002), 479–512.

10 Similarly see: S. Scott, 'The Impact on International Law of US Noncompliance', in Byers and Nolte (eds.), *United States Hegemony and the Foundations of International Law*, pp. 450–1; S. Scott, 'Is there Room for International Law in Realpolitik?: Accounting for the US "Attitude" Towards International Law', R.I.S., 30 (2004), 87–8.

11 Grewe, *Epochs of International Law*, pp. 19–29; H. Mosler, 'Die Großmachtstellung im Völkerrecht', S.S.J., 8 (1949), 38–45.

12 S. Ratner, 'Comments on Chapter 1 and 2', in Byers and Nolte (eds.), *United States Hegemony and the Foundations of International Law*, pp. 106–8.

With regard to that critique, various commentators have pointed out – correctly – that there seems to be a difference in quality between the meaning of actions and statements of the United States and other states, which tend to acquire a paradigmatic character for the relationship of power and law under the current international legal system.[13]

Since the early days of its existence, the United States has been one of the voices advocating self-restraint and recognition of international law when using force.[14] At a time when the United States was the only nuclear power in the world, it consistently promoted an institutionalised restraint of its predominant position by supporting the foundation of the United Nations.[15] As Alexis de Tocqueville wrote in 1831: 'L'influence de l'esprit légiste s'entend plus loin encore que les limites precises . . . Il n'est presque pas de question politique, aux Etats-Unis, qui ne se resolve tôt ou tard en question judiciaire.'[16] On the other hand, the United States' willingness to accept restrictions on its own course of action through international law has always had its limits with regard to its own security interest. These limits have recently become obvious.[17]

1.1 Doctrines and public international law

Long before it achieved its position of pre-eminence, one characteristic feature of US foreign policy has been the declaration of so-called 'doctrines'. These doctrines have, *inter alia*, the function of setting binding standards for cases when the use of force can serve as a means of US foreign policy. Unlike US-American domestic policy, the leading concepts of which are usually labelled as undogmatic, or even as

13 G. Nolte, 'Conclusion' in: Byers and Nolte (eds.), *United States Hegemony and the Foundations of International Law*, p. 492; M. Byers, 'The Shifting Foundations of International Law: A Decade of Forceful Measures against Iraq', E.J.I.L., 13 (2002), 21–41; Vagts, 'Hegemonic International Law', 843–8; N. Krisch, 'International Law in Times of Hegemony: Unequal Power and the Shaping of the International Legal Order', E.J.I.L., 16 (2005), 369–408.

14 L. Henkin, 'The Use of Force: Law and US Policy', in L. Henkin *et al.* (eds.), *Right v. Might – International Law and the Use of Force*, 2nd edn. (New York: Council on Foreign Relations Press, 1991), pp. 37–69; R. Kagan, *Paradise & Power – America and Europe in the New World Order* (London: Atlantic Books, 2003), pp. 9–11.

15 J. Ikenberry, 'Institutions, Strategic Restraint, and the Persistence of American Postwar Order', Int.Sec., 23/3 (1998/9), 43–78.

16 A. de Tocqueville, *De la Démocratie en Amérique, Oeuvres, papiers et correspondances*, 8th edn. (Paris, Gallimard, 1951), vol. I.I, p. 282.

17 M. Byers, 'Terrorism, the Use of Force and International Law after 11 September', I.C.L.Q., 51 (2002), 401–14.

ideological eclecticism,[18] US foreign policy is full of such declarations of principles.

The declaration of doctrines was a characteristic feature of US foreign policy during the Cold War. Yet the US declared doctrines long before the formation of this so-called bipolar international system of the Cold War,[19] and before the formation of the so-called unipolar system which followed its end.[20] Even though single doctrines have been discussed in depth in political science,[21] little attention has been paid to them in the science of international law. The National Security Strategy (NSS) published in November 2002,[22] the main statements of which are commonly known as the Bush Doctrine,[23] has generated interest not just among the general public and political scientists, but, in contrast to its predecessors, among international lawyers also. Considerable interest has been devoted in particular to the discussion of the legality of the stated criteria for the use of force between states.[24]

Public international law serves as a central instrument of foreign policy, in particular of US foreign policy, especially when it comes to the

18 C. V. Crabb, *The Doctrines of American Foreign Policy* (Baton Rouge, LA: Louisiana State University Press, 1982), pp. 1–2.

19 In general on polarity of the international system see: K. Mingst, *Essentials of International Relations* (New York: W. W. Norton, 1999), pp. 86–91; G. Evans and J. Newnham, *The Penguin Dictionary of International Relations* (London: Penguin, 1998), pp. 52, 340–1, 550–1.

20 C. Krauthammer, 'The Unipolar Moment', For. Aff., 70 (1990/1), 23–33; C. Krauthammer, 'The Unipolar Moment Revisited', Natl.Int., 70 (2002/3), 5–17.

21 For example, E. Rossides (ed.), *The Truman Doctrine of Aid to Greece* (Washington, DC: American Hellenic Institute Foundation, 2001); A. The, *Die Vietnampolitik der USA von der Johnson – zur Nixon-Kissinger-Doktrin* (Frankfurt: Lang, 1979); W. Tucker (ed.), *Intervention & the Reagan Doctrine* (New York: Council on Religion and International Affairs, 1985).

22 The White House, The National Security Strategy of the United States of America, September 2002, available at: www.whitehouse.gov/nsc/nss.html; printed in L. Korb, *A New National Security Strategy* (New York: Council on Foreign Relations, 2003), pp. 99–139.

23 W. Lafeber, 'The Bush Doctrine', Dipl.Hist., 26 (2002), 543–58; F. Heisbourg, 'A Work in Progress: The Bush Doctrine and Its Consequences', Wash.Q., 26/2 (2003), 75–88; G. Nolte, 'Weg in eine andere Rechtsordnung', *Frankfurter Allgemeine Zeitung*, 10 January 2003, p. 8, also printed in D. Lutz and Hans J. Gießmann (eds.), *Die Stärke des Rechts gegen das Recht des Stärkeren* (Baden-Baden: Nomos, 2003), pp. 187–96.

24 T. M. Franck, 'Editorial Comments: Terrorism and the Right of Self-Defense', A.J.I.L., 95 (2001), 839–43; M. E. O'Connell, *The Myth of Preemptive Self-Defense*, ASIL Task Force Papers, Washington, August 2002; F. Mégret, '"War"? Legal Semantics and the Move to Violence', E.J.I.L., 13 (2002), 361–400; S. D. Murphy, 'Contemporary Practice of the United States Relating to International Law, Terrorist Attacks on World Trade Center and Pentagon', A.J.I.L., 96 (2002), 237–55.

implementation of matters of principle.[25] The advancement of a basic political interest may coincide with an interest in furthering the creation of a new legal rule, or a certain interpretation of a legal rule, or it may have that effect.[26] Certain behaviour, of which the conformity with international law may originally have been in doubt, may cause an adjustment of international law to this behaviour and thus may propel a political concept into the realm of legality under international law.[27]

Hence, an examination of the connection between these doctrines and international law seems to be almost an obvious choice for an evaluation under international law.[28] This makes it even more surprising that Cecil V. Crabb's monograph, *The Doctrines of American Foreign Policy – Their Meaning, Role and Future*, is so far the only work which also discusses the subject of doctrines itself.[29] Other works usually offer only an historical description of single US doctrines. However, Cecil V. Crabb wrote from the perspective of diplomatic history and not that of international law,[30] which underlines the fact that the significance of these doctrines is mainly seen as political and not legal.

Along the clearly defined border in international law between 'law' and 'non-law',[31] political doctrines are generally considered as belonging to the realm of non-law.[32] Marcelo Kohen goes as far as to evaluate the relevance

25 Krisch, 'Weak as Constraint, Strong as Tool', pp. 43–53.

26 K. Ipsen *et al.* (eds.), *Völkerrecht*, 5th edn. (Munich: C. H. Beck, 2004), pp. 45 *et seq.*, ch. 1, § 3.I.

27 Within the limits of the principle *ex inuria ius non oritur*, of which the present interpretation has been framed by a US-American doctrine itself, the Stimson Doctrine (see below Chapter 2, section 2.2.2); H. Kelsen, *Principles of International Law*, 2nd edn. (New York: Holt, Rinehart & Winston, 1967), pp. 415–16.

28 W. Nagan and C. Hammer, 'The New Bush National Security Doctrine and the Rule of Law', Berk.J.I.L., 22 (2004), 382, 390: 'To better investigate the National Security issue it would be useful to review an important, often underappreciated aspect of international law: national security doctrines . . . American international lawyers might best deal with the accompanying clashes between international law and international power by examining past American national security doctrines.'

29 See also: C. von Wrede, 'Der Rechtsanspruch der Deutschen Bundesregierung auf völkerrechtliche Alleinvertretung Gesamtdeutschlands und die Hallstein-Doktrin', Ph.D. thesis, Freiburg, Switzerland, 1966, in particular pp. 16–34; R. Watson, C. Gleek and M. Grillo (eds.), *Presidential Doctrines: National Security From Woodrow Wilson to George W. Bush* (New York: Nova Science Publishers, 2003), in particular Watson, 'On the History and Use of Presidential Doctrines', pp. 7–25. However, Watson and his co-workers do not enter into a discussion of the legal and dogmatic aspects of doctrines.

30 Crabb, *The Doctrines of American Foreign Policy*, pp. 1–9

31 P. Kunig, '2. Abschnitt', in Graf Vitzthum (ed.), *Völkerrecht*, p. 148, nos. 165–6.

32 K. Krakau, 'Lateinamerikanische Doktrinen zur Realisierung staatlicher Unabhängigkeit und Integrität', VRÜ, 8 (1975), 117–44.

of doctrines of US security policy as follows: 'little if any insight can be derived from these doctrines which would shed light on the formulation or interpretation of the rules of international law relative to the use of force . . . They primarily demonstrate that law comes after the fact . . . '[33] Yet a classification of doctrines like this does not rule out a discussion and evaluation of doctrines from the perspective of international law.

In addition, the use of the term 'doctrine' is not uniform. In many cases it refers only to a legally irrelevant, journalistic simplification of an explicitly declared or implied principle of American foreign policy.[34] Sometimes organs of state adopt the denomination 'doctrine' for certain principles, although originally used by non-state actors. In part, US presidents have been fully aware of promulgating a doctrine and have used the term themselves.[35] Furthermore, the use of the term 'doctrine' in the English-speaking world with regard to security policy differs widely and refers to different levels of strategic planning.[36] Certain concepts, considered by American strategic planners as 'doctrinal', are considered by British planners as 'operational'. A difference must also be drawn between political doctrines and regulations which are considered 'military doctrine'.[37]

Well-established definitions from the field of strategic studies may contribute to a better basic understanding of doctrines; they do not,

33 M. Kohen, 'The Use of Force by the United States after the End of the Cold War, and its Impacts on International Law', in Byers and Nolte (eds.), *United States Hegemony and the Foundations of International Law*, pp. 197–231. On the other hand, Kohen concedes that doctrines may have a certain legal meaning: 'These policy statements are nevertheless essential starting points to understanding the instances in which the Unites States uses force and how the US government tries to explain its actions from a legal point of view', p. 201.

34 Ernst Reibstein defines a doctrine as a 'formulation of a maxim under international law in the realm of security, respectively, balance' (author's translation of: 'völkerrechtliche Formulierung einer Maxime auf dem Gebiet der Sicherheit bzw. des Gleichgewichts'); E. Reibstein, *Völkerrecht* (Freiburg: Alber, 1963), vol. II, p. 418.

35 While James Monroe was not aware of formulating a doctrine in 1823, Richard Nixon himself called the principles of his speech on 3 November 1969 the Nixon Doctrine. *Cf.* Crabb, *The Doctrines of American Foreign Policy*, p. 304.

36 On the basic division of levels of planning into international politics, grand strategy, theatre strategy, operational, tactical and technical, see: E. N. Luttwak, *Strategy – The Logic of War and Peace*, 2nd edn. (Cambridge, MA: Belknap Press of Harvard University Press, 2001), pp. 87 *et seq.*

37 The definition of 'military doctrine' in *The Oxford Companion to Military History* reads as follows: 'An approved set of principles and methods, intended to provide large military organizations with a common outlook, and a uniform basis for action . . . ' R. Holmes (ed.), *The Oxford Companion to Military History* (Oxford University Press, 2001), pp. 262–3.

however, allow for a sufficiently legally precise classification. Colin S. Gray defines the term doctrine as follows:

> Doctrine teaches what to think and what to do, rather than how to think and how to be prepared to do it. Academic scholars of strategy and war are apt to forget about the vital intermediary function that doctrine plays between ideas and behaviour. Scholars write theory, they do not write doctrine . . . Doctrine *per se* is a box empty of content until organizations decide how much of it they want, and how constraining they wish it to be.[38]

1.2 Objective of this work

The doctrines of US security policy formulate authoritative principles for the use of force which claim validity beyond the area of jurisdiction of the United States. In order to approach these doctrines from a legal perspective, it is necessary to distinguish between doctrines as political guidelines and the legally relevant content of doctrines. Even though doctrines present political guidelines, they are not entirely free of assertions of law.

In this work an evaluation of the United States' so far declared doctrines under international law will be undertaken. The central question in this process is that of the reconcilability of the statements of law and principles for the use of force in US international relations as declared in doctrines with public international law in force at the time. This first requires describing US-American policy and legal opinion with regard to the legality of the use of force, as it can be derived from doctrines. The question of the extent to which US-American statements within doctrines or corollaries contain statements of law is the starting point for the discussion.

Initially, the declaration of a doctrine is merely a unilateral act of state. There are different levels at which unilateral acts of state can be relevant under public international law: they can mark legally non-binding, merely political declarations of principles, or can be a legally recognised type of action (for example, reservations or recognition), of which the legally constitutive effect is not contested in public international law.[39] Unilateral declarations can have a self-binding effect for a state.[40] Furthermore, the

38 C. Gray, *Modern Strategy* (Oxford University Press, 1999), pp. 35–6.

39 See on the meaning of unilateral declarations under international law: A. Rubin, 'The International Legal Effects of Unilateral Declarations', A.J.I.L., 70 (1977), 1–30.

40 *Nuclear Tests* (*New Zealand* v. *France*), judgment, I.C.J. Rep., 1974, pp. 472–3, Nos. 46–8.

quality of unilateral acts as a source of law is in doubt.[41] Within the discussion of the question of legality in cases where force is used as foreseen in doctrines, the question of the legal nature and the quality as a rule of law of certain doctrines will be considered.[42]

Public international law emerges by a transformation of political relations into legal relations. These emerge as pre-legal, political processes transfer their quality from a merely political pattern of behaviour to a legal rule.[43] Thus, the interaction between law and politics is already noticeable during the process of creation of public international law. This interaction also continues once the original process of the creation of public international law with regard to a certain legal rule has been completed. A legal rule of public international law remains connected with politics as far as its interpretation and change are concerned.[44] The United States could have taken actions creating law by declaring certain doctrines. If, for example, the response of other states is limited to *acquiescence*, US behaviour may constitute a change of customary law,[45] a tacit change of a treaty, a changed interpretation of a single legal provision or self-binding behaviour of the United States.

The extent to which doctrines constitute law-creating behaviour, or may have caused such behaviour, is also a subject of this study. The second central question of this work is the question of the extent to which the principles of doctrines continue to have an effect on particular legal rules of public international law. That is, the degree to which a legalisation of these political principles has taken place.[46]

1.3 Course of the inquiry

The answer to these two questions is structured as follows: as a first step, I describe which rules of behaviour each doctrine lays down for the use of force and any statement of law that the United States has made with regard

41 W. Fiedler, 'Unilateral Acts', E.P.I.L., IV (2000), pp. 1018–23.

42 See below, in particular Chapter 2, sections 2.1.3.1 and 2.2.

43 M. Kaplan and N. Katzenbach, *The Political Foundations of International Law* (New York: John Wiley, 1961), pp. 19–29.

44 Ipsen *et al.* (eds.), *Völkerrecht*, ch. 1, § 3.I, nos. 2–4, pp. 45 *et seq.*; I. Brownlie, 'The Reality and Efficacy of International Law', B.Y.I.L., 52 (1981), 1–8.

45 See generally on acquiescence: J. Müller and T. Cottier, 'Acquiescence', E.P.I.L., I (1992), pp. 14–16.

46 For a definition of 'legalization' see: K. Abbott *et al.*, 'The Concept of Legalization', Int.Org., 52 (2000), 401–19.

to the legality of the use of force within the framework of the doctrine presented. I also explore the connections between doctrines and the opinion of public international law held by the respective US administration, as well as the question as to whether the statement constituted an adequate account of the law then in force. Thanks to the distinct accountability of the US executive to Congress with regard to the use of force in international relations, a high number of explanatory statements concerning doctrines exist which deal closely with their meaning and explain the circumstances in which they foresee the use of force.[47]

I shall include possible different legal interpretations under public international law. As a starting point for an evaluation of doctrines under public international law, single questions of law can be used (for example, doctrines and the law of self-defence, doctrines and humanitarian intervention, etc.). Possibly this would require the presentation of the whole law concerning the legality of the use of force and its relation to doctrines. As the regulations on the legality of the use of force have undergone considerable change,[48] a chronologically organised discussion of the doctrines allows one to follow their relationship with the development of international law. It also helps to finally reach an overall conclusion concerning their legal nature.

Additionally, possible questions concerning the legality of the courses of action foreseen in doctrines result from the statements within the doctrines themselves. If the outcome of the description of a doctrine should be that a doctrine does not, for example, proclaim a right of pro-democratic intervention,[49] it would not be necessary to discuss the legality of that type of intervention to evaluate the legality of this particular doctrine under international law.

Furthermore, the influence that these statements of law had on the development of international law with regard to the legality of the use of force will be described. The response to doctrines among the science of

47 M. Glennon, 'The United States: Democracy, Hegemony and Accountability', in C. Ku and H. Jacobson (eds.), *Democratic Accountability and the Use of Force in International Law* (Cambridge University Press, 2003), pp. 323–47; L. Henkin, *Foreign Affairs and the US Constitution*, 2nd edn. (Oxford: Clarendon Press, 1996), pp. 115–28.

48 In general on the development of international law see: I. Brownlie, *International Law and the Use of Force by States* (Oxford: Clarendon Press, 1963), pp. 19 *et seq.*; H. Neuhold, *Internationale Konflikte – verbotene und erlaubte Mittel ihrer Austragung* (Vienna: Springer, 1970), pp. 55 *et seq.*; A. Arend and R. Beck, *International Law and the Use of Force – Beyond the UN Charter Paradigm* (London: Longman, 1993), pp. 15–25.

49 Asserted, for example, with regard to the Reagan Doctrine by M. Reisman, 'Coercion and Self-determination: Construing Charter Art 2(4)', A.J.I.L., 78 (1984), 642–5.

international law is also included in this presentation. Finally, a conclusion with regard to the current status of the respective doctrine – which validity it claims for the current shaping of American security policy, if the doctrine is still valid, to what extent it is in accordance with the current law in force – will be reached. In conclusion, similarities of doctrines is presented, with an examination of whether a uniform classification under international law of the discussed doctrines is possible.

1.4 Historical dynamics of the theme

While texts on international law often deal with doctrines and pronounce a judgement about their legality,[50] they do not often precisely delimit and define the doctrine. This is necessary in order to properly legally evaluate doctrines.

Doctrines on security policy are dynamic matters subject to constant adjustment. An author who is writing, for example, about the Monroe Doctrine, can refer to either the core statements of Monroe's speech of 1823 as an historical term, or to the contents which have been attached to the Monroe Doctrine after certain modifications, changes or interpretations at a later point in time. Likewise, the term can refer to a subsequent practice or to single declarations of principle only.[51]

Ultimately, a direct or indirect link to such a doctrine could be construed for almost the whole of US-American foreign policy over the last 180 years. Furthermore, it is not apparent when a statement is being considered as a doctrine and when a statement is merely considered as a corollary to an already existing doctrine. Doctrines are by their nature in no way static, but are dynamic guidelines for policy because they serve the purpose of determining a course of action for contingencies in the future. As no doctrine can be so comprehensive that it offers a set course of action for all contingencies, a change of the political starting position may result in an adjustment of the doctrine itself.[52]

Hence, due to the dynamics of the subject, a comprehensive and continuous evaluation of doctrines under international law is not possible. It

50 For example, A. Randelzhofer, 'Art. 2(4)', in B. Simma (ed.), *The Charter of the United Nations*, vol. I, p. 129; M. Dixon, *Textbook on International Law*, 6th edn. (Oxford University Press, 2007), p. 328.

51 On different uses of the term 'doctrine' in the literature on international relations see: Evans and Newnham, *The Penguin Dictionary of International Relations*, pp. 57, 61–2, 207–9, 464.

52 Crabb, *The Doctrines of American Foreign Policy*, pp. 394–7.

is only possible to examine essential intermediate states that are representative of phases of a doctrine with regard to their conformity with the law in force at a particular time. This apportionment of a doctrine into phases is not necessarily a legal action, but one that results from the changes of doctrines as political principles. However, changes of the reconcilability of single doctrines with international law also result from fundamental changes of the applicable law on the use of force. Just like doctrines, it is also subject to continuous changes.[53]

Which legally relevant statements in the sense of *opinio iuris* or 'state practice' these doctrines contain, depends again on the rules for the creation of law; the development of these is just as dynamic as that of the rules with regard to the use of force.[54] Thus, in the consideration of doctrines there will be a brief discussion of these rules.

1.5 Dogmatic question und methodology

The outline of a work which surpasses the usual and central question for a jurist of what the law in force is, requires some decisions as to the methodological premises of the work. This choice of methods determines the aspects of the consideration of law and the focus of the work.[55] Beyond any doubt the decisive task with which a jurist is charged in terms of a positivist approach is to answer the question of what the law in force is; thus, the legal obligations of the subjects of international law.[56] An inclusion of the level of 'being', instead of a limitation to the level of 'should', which means leaving a purely normative approach, is considered by representatives of a pure legal doctrine as leaving the discipline of law.[57]

Since the beginning of the confrontation between positivists and adherents of natural law in the seventeenth century, the question has been disputed as to what degree the science of international law may include cognitions which do not result from the study of norms themselves

53 J. Fawcett, 'Intervention in International Law', RdC, 103 (1961-II), 343–423.

54 M. Byers, *Custom, Power and the Power of Rules: International Relations and Customary International Law* (Cambridge University Press, 1999), pp. 133–6, 207–10.

55 K. Larenz, *Methodenlehre*, 3rd edn. (Berlin: Springer, 1975), pp. 165–71.

56 M. Koskenniemi, 'Carl Schmitt, Hans Morgenthau, and the Image of Law in International Relations', in M. Byers (ed.), *The Role of Law in International Politics* (Oxford University Press, 2000), p. 31.

57 H. Kelsen, *General Theory of Law and State*, trans. A. Wedberg (Cambridge, MA: Harvard University Press, 1945), pp. 4–5; H. Kelsen, *Reine Rechtslehre* (Leipzig: Hans Deuticke, 1934), pp. 2, 9–11.

without losing its character as *legal* science.[58] Yet in 1929, Dionisio Anzilotti, a prominent representative of 'voluntaristic' positivism, wrote in his *Textbook of International Law* that the science of international law, on the one hand, has 'to determine and explain the legal rules in force and position them in the logical forms of a system. Secondly . . . it has to strive in connection with other disciplines for a critical evaluation of the law in force and a preparation of future norms.'[59]

This already goes beyond the dogmatic question which would comply with a positivist approach of 'pure legal doctrine'. Alternative methods can be envisaged as to how aspects beyond this approach can be included in a work on public international law.[60]

It would be conceivable to examine the effects of public international law as an instrument within the political process of reaching a decision on the interpretation of norms of public international law. This would have a final aim of deciding how public international law should be designed in order to promote effectively certain values such as a 'free world society' and respect for human beings.[61]

This is basically the starting point of the New Haven School.[62] Even though an indisputable fascination is attached to this basic thought, such a 'policy-oriented approach' has been accused of being merely a means for implementing an ideology. An endangering of public international law may result from an extreme ideologisation, through which a dissolution of law into sequences of decisions is reached resulting in the loss of a quality of a norm.[63] Such a policy-oriented approach is not pursued within this work.

Furthermore, it would be conceivable to examine which political interests fixed in doctrines have been brought to bear in the process of

58 Described in N. Paech and G. Stuby, *Machtpolitik und Völkerrecht in den internationalen Beziehungen* (Baden-Baden: Nomos, 1994), pp. 43–8; 68–70.

59 D. Anzilotti, *Lehrbuch des Völkerrechts* (Berlin: Walter de Gruyter, 1929), pp. 14–15.

60 N. Krisch, *Selbstverteidigung und kollektive Sicherheit* (Berlin: Springer, 2001), also Ph.D. thesis, Heidelberg, 2001, pp. 19–20.

61 M. McDougal, 'International Law, Power and Policy', RdC, 82/1 (1953), 140–1, 180–8.

62 S. Voos, *Die Schule von New Haven: Darstellung und Kritik einer amerikanischen Völkerrechtslehre* (Berlin: Duncker & Humblot, 2000), pp. 98 *et seq.*

63 K. Krakau, *Missionsbewußtsein und Völkerrechtsdoktrin in den Vereinigten Staaten von Amerika* (Metzner, Frankfurt a.M., 1967), pp. 514–18. More drastic is the critique of the 'policy-oriented approach' by Simma, who labels the New Haven School as 'court jurisprudence' (*Hofjuristerei*): B. Simma, 'Völkerrechtswissenschaft und Lehre von den internationalen Beziehungen: Erste Überlegungen zur Interdependenz zweier Disziplinen', ÖZföRV, 23 (1972), 308, n. 53a.

creation and interpretation of particular rules of public international law, and which political questions have thus not become the subject of international law discourse.[64] On this basis, it would be possible to disclose to what degree certain states and jurists assume only a fictional universality and acceptance of norms where their strands of argumentation and use of language are adopted by others as if this was generally accepted public international law. The aim of this approach could be to show differences between real and fictitious expressions of universality and consensus in public international law, and, thus, to 'deconstruct' norms linguistically.[65] This is basically the approach of the Critical Legal Studies School. According to this school, public international law is merely a certain type of discourse about international relations, a certain type of dispute which states have chosen. It is considered as a task of the science of international law to 'deconstruct' this discourse.[66] In doing so, critical legal scholars want to point out that public international law is not politically neutral. They want to achieve this by choosing a method of analysis which focuses on ideologies, interests and structures and create a connection between the theory of public international law and the practice of international law, instead of being limited to the legal discourse itself.[67]

Prima facie this work could, therefore, be attributed to Critical Legal Studies School, because the doctrines of US security policy are by their nature a political subject which constitutes the starting point of the work. Yet in terms of a more traditional, positivist approach, public international law is not treated as a type of discourse about international relations, merely as a type of 'superstructure',[68] but as a binding set of norms. In addition, its historical development only is included in the considerations. Accordingly, no attempt is made in this study to 'deconstruct' norms of public international law. Instead, the possible determination of objective law is assumed. However, different possible interpretations of legal norms will be included. In doing so it is assumed that, despite

64 M. Koskenniemi, *From Apology to Utopia, the Structure of International Legal Argument* (Helsinki: Lakimiesliiton, 1989), pp. 458–501.

65 A. Carty, 'Critical International Law: Recent Trends in the Theory of International Law', E.J.I.L., 2 (1991), 66–96.

66 N. Purvis, 'Critical Legal Studies in Public International Law', Harv.I.L.J., 32 (1991), 81–127, in particular pp. 114–16.

67 D. Kennedy, 'Theses about International Law Discourse', G.Y.I.L., 23 (1980), 353–5.

68 A. Arend, R. Beck and R. Vanderlugt (eds.), *International Rules – Approaches from International Law and International Relations* (Oxford University Press, 1996), pp. 227–9.

judicially conflicting opinions of law, the existence of an objective legal system is possible.[69]

Furthermore, it would be conceivable to examine which design of doctrines of security policy and public international law may be the most sensible in order to achieve certain political aims by connecting methods of law and political science. The interaction between the science of law and political science is a subject which has lately generated considerable attention in the science of public international law.[70]

A comparison often made is that between the importance of international political science (or international relations) for public international law and domestic political science for constitutional law: 'Just as constitutional lawyers study political theory, and political theorists enquire into the nature and substance of constitutions, so too should two disciplines that study the laws of state behaviour seek to learn from one another.'[71] Especially during the 1990s, interdisciplinary works guided by the desire for a better understanding of the connections between public international law and international politics attracted particular attention.[72]

The discussion of doctrines under international law – facts of life capable of legal evaluation, which require a precise determination before they can be evaluated – necessitates a focus on the description of the underlying facts. This constitutes the interdisciplinary element of the work, but it is not the foremost attempt to relate political theory with legal theory.[73] A criterion of analysis, attributed to the theory of political realism, is inserted only marginally into the discussion in the context of doctrines under different polarities of the international system.[74] The

69 On the critics of the critical legal studies approach see: I. Scobbie, 'Towards the Elimination of International Law: Some Radical Scepticism about Sceptical Radicalism', B.Y.I.L., 61 (1990), 339–62, in particular p. 344; M. Byers, 'Response: Taking the Law out of International Law: A Critique of the "Iterative Perspective"', Harv.I.L.J., 38 (1997), 201–5.

70 R. Beck, 'International Law and International Relations: The Prospects for Interdisciplinary Collaboration', in Arend, Beck and Vanderlugt, *International Rules – Approaches from International law and International Relations*, pp. 3–30; K. Abbott, 'Modern International Relations Theory: A Prospectus for International Lawyers', Y.J.I.L., 14 (1989), 335–411.

71 A-M. Slaughter-Burley, 'International Law and International Relations: A Dual Agenda', A.J.I.L., 87 (1993), 205.

72 A-M. Slaughter, A. Tumello and S. Wood, 'International Law and International Relations Theory: a New Generation of Interdisciplinary Scholarship', A.J.I.L., 92 (1998), 367–97; Byers (ed.), *The Role of Law in International Politics – Essays in International Relations and Law*.

73 On this issue see further below, section 1.5.

74 Mingst, *Essentials of International Relations*, pp. 86–91.

work does not constitute an attempt to comply with the requirements of a 'joint discipline', as that term has been explained by Kenneth Abbott, Anne-Marie Slaughter and their co-workers.[75] An attempt will be made rather, as generally proposed by Slaughter, to extend an isolated legal consideration of norms by adding historical–political aspects.

The majority of international lawyers base their activity on a stricter understanding of public international law and the science of international law. They deal with the determination of existence, meaning, range and legal consequences of a legal rule, and only to a lesser extent with understanding the process through which legal norms are created.[76]

As essential and central this question may be for the science of international law, it decouples jurisprudence from its use-oriented actual task: the normative, legal evaluation of facts of life.[77] As Bruno Simma wrote in 1974: 'A scientific method of international law, which limits itself to the mere description of the positive contents of norms, misses in many . . . totally decisive points the international *reality of law*.'[78]

Furthermore, the claim was raised during the debates of the 1970s on methods that the science of public international law should – without losing its characteristics as science of *law* – strive for a further completion of dogmatic–normative work by thoroughly examining public international law in reality. This should be achieved mainly by taking into account the dynamic dimensions of norms, their creation, development and application with regard to 'meta-judicial factors' (*metajuristische Faktoren*).[79] Actions with a double nature are considered as meta-judicial factors. They constitute a social action at the level of 'being' (*Sein*), and at the same time these processes have effects at the level of ideals (*Sollen*), namely that

75 K. Abbott, 'International Law and International Relations Theory: Building Bridges – Elements of a Joint Discipline', ASIL Proceedings, 86th Annual Meeting, 1992, pp. 167–72; Slaughter, Tumello and Wood, *International Law and International Relations Theory*, p. 384.

76 Byers, *Custom, Power and the Power of Rules – International Relations and Customary International Law*, p. 25.

77 P. Mastronardi, *Juristisches Denken. Eine Einführung* (Bern: Haupt, 2001), pp. 1–3; H.-J. Musielak, *Grundkurs BGB*, 7th edn. (Munich: C. H. Beck, 2002), p. 1, no. 1.

78 Author's translation of: 'Eine völkerrechtswissenschaftliche Methode, die ihre Aufgabe im bloßen Beschreiben positivrechtlicher Norminhalte erschöpft sieht, geht in vielen . . . ganz entscheidenden Punkten an der internationalen *Rechtswirklichkeit* vorbei'; B. Simma, 'Völkerrecht und Friedensforschung', Friedens-Warte/J.I.P.O., 57 (1974), 78; already similar in 1929: Morgenthau, *Die internationale Rechtspflege, ihr Wesen und ihre Grenzen*, p. 62.

79 O. Kimminich, 'Der Stand der Friedensforschung', Universitas, 26 (1971), 294–5. Similarly see: H. Mosler, 'Die Großmachtstellung im Völkerrecht', pp. 9–11.

of norms.[80] The target in this process shall be 'to question public international law with more purpose, [and] to advance also into the pre-legal realm, which methodological purists consider as . . . *ultra vires*',[81] without blending syncretically legal norms and facts.

The claim brought forward at the time that the science of international law should 'get rid of the remainders of legal positivism',[82] was quite rightly rejected in order to prevent it from losing its nature as a science of law. If a study wants to satisfy the principles outlined by Simma above without giving in to such a claim, this will need to be done by adding an historical–political dimension to the discussion of norm-related statements in the doctrines of US security policy.[83] The starting point of the work is accordingly a judicial one, which basically matches a positivist method: namely, the question to as to what degree the doctrines of US-American security policy were, and are, in accordance with respective public international law in force.

If, according to the historical–political method of public international law as outlined above, one includes the 'predetermined dimensions of the subject matter of the study',[84] it becomes apparent that a limitation to a presentation of the norm-related content of doctrines of US security policy would not correspond with the subject matter discussed. Such a method would not offer an opportunity for an adequate survey of the subject of cognizance. Thus, the discussion of norms is complemented

80 B. Simma, 'Völkerrechtswissenschaft und Lehre von den internationalen Beziehungen: Erste Überlegungen zur Interdependenz zweier Disziplinen', p. 301. Herbert Kraus argued with regard to this matter that: 'A political principle can very well be at the same time a legal rule of international law or be based on one' (author's translation of: 'Ein politischer Grundsatz kann sehr wohl zugleich inhaltlich ein Völkerrechtssatz sein oder einen solchen zu seiner Grundlage haben'). H. Kraus, *Die Monroedoktrin und ihre Beziehungen zur Amerikanischen Diplomatie und zum Völkerrecht* (Berlin: Guttentag, 1913), p. 353.

81 Own translation of Simma, 'Völkerrecht und Friedensforschung', p. 80: 'das Völkerrecht zielführender zu hinterfragen, [und] auch in jenen vorrechtlichen Bereich vorzudringen, der für den methodologischen Puristen *ultra vires* . . . liegt'.

82 K. Kaiser, 'Völkerrecht und Internationale Beziehungen, Zum Verhältnis zweier Wissenschaften', Friedens-Warte/J.I.P.O., 58 (1976), 199. (Author's translation of 'sich von den Restbeständen des Rechtspositivismus zu trennen'.)

83 Similarly, with regard to the choice of methods, in spite of the obvious differences between the subject and theme of this work see: T. Schweisfurth, *Sozialistisches Völkerrecht? Darstellung – Analyse – Wertung der sowjetmarxistischen Theorie von Völkerrecht 'neuen Typs'* (Berlin: Springer, 1979), p. 42.

84 Author's translation of: 'vorgegebenen Dimensionen [des] Untersuchungsobjekts'; B. Simma, 'Bemerkungen zur Methode der Völkerrechtswissenschaft', in H. von Bonin (ed.), *Festschrift für Ernst Kolb zum 60. Geburtstag* (Innsbruck: Österreichische Kommissionsbuchhandlung, 1971), p. 339.

(with regard to the matter in hand) by attempts to give answers to the questions with regard to the norms of the international law in force, to which answers are expected from a science of public international law which is not limited to a consideration of norms:[85] 'How did they come about? Whose will or interest do they express? What geographical scope or limit do they actually cover? Do they constitute a restraint on the use of state power or do they consecrate a state's liberty of action?'[86]

With regard to doctrines the following questions result from this: which statements of law with regard to the legality of the use of force in international relations have been made within the framework of doctrines?; how have these statements of law, made within the framework of doctrines, been evaluated by the other states?; what connection exists between doctrines and the legal position of the respective US administrations with regard to international law?; to what degree are the principles for the use of force as laid down in doctrines reconcilable with public international law in force at a certain point in time?; what influence did these doctrines have on the development of public international law?; to what degree has a 'legalisation' of these doctrines taken place?; and what is the current status of these doctrines under international law and what is the legal nature of doctrines?

Based on the comprehensive nature of the different aspects of foreign policy with which the doctrines of US security policy deal, and based on the scope of the sets of norms dealing with the legality of the use of force in international relations, a thematic limitation is required. This is achieved through exclusion of a range of topics.

1.6 Limits of this work

This work is limited to the doctrines of US security policy. A generally recognised definition of doctrines of US security policy does not exist – certainly not a legal definition. Thus, in terms of a discussion of public international law as outlined above, it is possible only to attempt to narrow down the object of investigation legally as far as possible, and

85 Simma labels the concept of method as designed by him as 'sociological–political consideration' of international law ('*soziologisch-politische Völkerrechtsbetrachtung*'). B. Simma, 'Völkerrechtswissenschaft und Lehre von den internationalen Beziehungen', p. 311; Similarly see: H. Neuhold, *Internationale Konflikte – verbotene und erlaubte Mittel ihrer Austragung*, pp. 1–16.

86 S. Hoffmann, 'The Study of International Law and the Theory of International Relations', ASIL Proceedings, 57th Annual Meeting, 1963, p. 30.

to complement this judicial limitation with corresponding extra-legal considerations in order to find a definition of doctrines.

Etymologically the term 'doctrine' goes back to the Latin word *doctrina*, which translates as 'teaching'.[87] Within the scope of this work doctrine refers to a declaration of principles, which, in the opinion of the US administration, constitute a binding strategic concept for the use of force in international relations[88] and has been labelled as a doctrine. In order to be able to distinguish between statements which could possibly count as *opinio iuris* and subsequently made rationalisations, the discussion is limited to statements, which in the opinion of the administration, count as doctrine.[89] What in detail may count as *opinio iuris* and its role in the process of customary international law are highly disputed questions.[90]

For the purpose of this work, the minimal standard a statement must meet to be treated as *opinio iuris* is that the claim attempts to articulate a certain right; hence, a certain statement of law ('claim') must be the content of the declaration.[91] No norms of customary international law can be derived from mere patterns of behaviour, but a legal conviction must appear, which necessarily has to be voiced.[92]

87 C. Creifelds (founder), *Rechtswörterbuch*, 18th edn. (Munich: C. H. Beck, 2004), pp. 327–8.

88 Equally, M. Reisman, who describes doctrines as follows: 'In modern International Law, a doctrine – such as Brezhnev, Carter, and Reagan doctrines – consists of a formal and credible statement by a significant international actor of a firm policy and the resolve to implement it upon certain contingencies. Doctrines are positioned at the interface of law and power. They are based on a general right that is theoretically available to other states. By their nature, they constitute a demand for an exception . . . ' M. Reisman, 'Assessing Claims to Revise the Laws of War', A.J.I.L. 97 (2003), 90.

89 For example, the US-American policy of containment as lined out by George F. Kennan in 1947 (G. Kennan, 'The Sources of Soviet Conduct', For.Aff., 25 (1947), 566–82, published under the pseudonym 'X'), later become known as the Kennan Corollary to the Monroe Doctrine. Though its core statements found a way into official US government policy, that is, within the framework of the Report to the National Security Council NSC-68 (*Foreign Relations of the United States 1950*, vol. I, pp. 245–301), at no point in time has it been considered or labelled by US officials as the Kennan Corollary. This label was used the first time in 1984 in the *New York Times Magazine*. Smith, *The Last Years of the Monroe Doctrine*, p. 238.

90 A. E. Roberts, 'Traditional and Modern Approaches to Customary International Law. A Reconciliation', A.J.I.L., 95 (2001), 757–91, in particular pp. 773–88; Byers, *Custom, Power and the Power of Rules*, pp. 147–51; R. M. Walden, 'The Subjective Element in the Formation of Customary International Law', Isr.L.R., 12 (1977), 344–64.

91 Likewise, Byers, *Custom, Power and the Power of Rules*, p. 208; I. C. McGibbon, 'Customary International Law and Acquiescence', B.Y.I.L., 33 (1957), 115–45.

92 M. Akehurst, 'Custom as a Source of International Law', B.Y.I.L., 47 (1974–5), 31–42 at 36–7. See further: A. D'Amato, *The Concept of Custom in International Law* (Ithaca,

Hence, it is not the US practice with regard to the use of force, but hypothetical courses of action (use of force) in line with the principles outlined in doctrines which are decisive. Nevertheless, an interaction between US practice as an expression of doctrines and the reconcilability of doctrines with the international law in force does exist, because a practice based on doctrines may result in an adjustment of international law to these doctrines.[93]

The claims of law and principles for the use of force, made within the frame of these doctrines are a subject matter of this examination. A statement is not only considered as made 'under the scope of a doctrine' if it appears within the text itself, considered as the declaration of the doctrine, but also, if the text is intended as an explanation, specification or adjustment of the concept.

The term 'security policy' requires a closer definition, because of the sporadically advocated inclusion of the so-called 'soft power question' in considerations of security policy[94] as an alternative to a traditional, narrower understanding of 'security policy'.[95] In doing so, a multitude of actions which have an impact on domestic decision making are considered as relevant for the security of a state.[96]

The inclusion of such questions of soft power does not match with the understanding of security which prevails in international law: such a broad understanding of 'security' is alien to the UN Charter, which springs from a more traditional school of thought. The term 'security' in Article 1(1) of the UN Charter is interpreted in a way that includes all activities necessary to maintain peace. 'Peace' is further defined as an absence of the threat or use of force against the territorial integrity or the political independence

NY: Cornell University Press, 1971), pp. 75 *et seq.* According to D'Amato prior explicit information that a single action shall have legal relevance is necessary in order to suggest *opinio iuris.*

93 G. Danilenko, *Law Making in the International Community* (Dordrecht: Martin Nijhoff, 1993), p. 96.

94 J. Nye, *The Paradox of American Power – Why the World's only Superpower Can't go it Alone* (Oxford University Press, 2002), in particular pp. 8–12, 154–63.

95 R. Carey, 'The Contemporary Nature of Security', in T. Salmon (ed.), *Issues in International Relations* (London: Routledge, 2000), pp. 55–75.

96 Nye defines soft power as follows: 'there is also an indirect way to exercise power. A country may obtain the outcomes it wants in world politics because other countries want to follow it, admiring values . . . In this sense, it is just as important to set the agenda in world politics and attract others as it is to force them to change through threat or use of military or economic weapons. The aspect of power – getting others to want what you want – I call soft power.' Nye, *The Paradox of American Power*, pp. 8–9.

of a state.[97] Accordingly, 'security policy' is understood in the context of this work as policy concerning the use of force in international relations between states.

Hence, a 'doctrine of US security policy' is at hand and therefore a declaration of principles with regard to the use of force in international relations, which in the opinion of the US administration is a binding concept in international relations and has been labelled by the administration as a 'doctrine'.

Subsequent rationalisations of US-American security policy, which have been labelled as a 'doctrine' are included in the discussion with regard to statements concerning the legal evaluation of doctrines. Furthermore, the legality of the use of force is an area of law which unites a number of complex issues. Even though doctrines partially contain statements with regard to the way force should be used[98] which is relevant for questions of the *ius in bello*, only questions of the *ius ad bellum* will be discussed. The following questions are of particular importance.

The pre-Charter practice of the United States with regard to collective security expressed itself in doctrines as follows: an attack or a threat against other states constituted a threat to the security of the United States and entitled it to take action.[99] The degree to which such a course of action was legal under international law is questionable and closely connected to the development of the right of self-defence.

It is also questionable whether there is any room left for the use of force which exceeds the mere defence of territorial integrity since the UN Charter entered into force. This touches upon the question of development and interpretation of the prohibition of the use of force and the right of self-defence, respectively, Articles 2(4) and 51 of the UN Charter. Thus, the US-American interpretation of the term "armed attack" within the scope of Article 51 of the UN Charter and the international acceptance of this interpretation are discussed.

This is closely related to the question of whether in connection with single doctrines the prohibition of the use of force has undergone limitations or divergent forms within 'spheres of influence', and if a regionally

97 R. Wolfrum, 'Art. 1', in Simma (ed.), *The Charter of the United Nations*, p. 40, nos. 4–6.

98 For example, the Powell Doctrine and Weinberger Doctrine, occasionally labelled as Powell–Weinberger Doctrine; see C. Stevenson, 'The Evolving Clinton Doctrine on the Use of Force', A.F.&S., 22 (1996), 518. On this see further below, Chapter 4, section 4.1.2.

99 D. W. Bowett, *Self-Defence in International Law* (Manchester University Press, 1958), pp. 207–15.

different understanding of the prohibition of intervention exists resulting in different regulations concerning the legality of the use of force.[100] This question is mostly answered in the negative.[101] Yet the possibility of such differing admissibility of the use of force cannot be denied in principle, as the dissenting opinion of Judge Schwebel to the ICJ judgment in the *Nicaragua* case demonstrates.[102]

It is likewise particularly questionable whether the United States has any obligations to use force under single agreements which have been concluded as an implementation or even a legalisation of doctrines. Likewise, do single doctrines determine different principles for interference in internal conflicts, which are mostly discussed in connection with matters of collective self-defence. Evaluations of the principles of single doctrines with regard to this matter could not differ more: 'The Truman Doctrine had said it should be the policy of the United States to help free people under attack from armed minorities. The Reagan Doctrine said it should be the policy of the United States to assist armed minorities in their attacks on Communist governments.'[103]

The clear-cut delineation of the content of a doctrine may not be as clearly possible as it is sometimes assumed. Depending on the respective school of thought within the discipline of International Relations on which the evaluation of an interpretation of a doctrine is based, its content is sometimes understood differently.[104] For example, Gaddis Smith mentions different possible evaluations of the Monroe Doctrine. According to Smith, realists would consider it in the spirit of Theodore Roosevelt as

100 M. Schweitzer, 'Erleidet das Gewaltverbot Modifikationen im Bereich von Einflußzonen?', in W. Schaumann (ed.), *Völkerrechtliches Gewaltverbot und Friedenssicherung* (Baden-Baden: Nomos, 1971), pp. 219–44; Ipsen *et al.* (eds.), *Völkerrecht*, p. 1083, ch. 15, § 59.II.5, no. 25.

101 G. Nolte, *Eingreifen auf Einladung* (Berlin: Springer, 1999), pp. 571–2 with further evidence.

102 According to this opinion, the general prohibition of intervention under international law, as laid down in Art. 2(1) of the UN Charter and customary law, is more restrictive than the prohibition of intervention resulting from Art. 15 of the OAS Charter; *Military and Paramilitary Activities in and Against Nicaragua* (*Nicaragua* v. *United States of America*), Merits, Judgment. I.C.J. Rep. 1986, p. 295, no. 98; On the sources of the prohibition of intervention see: H. Neuhold, *Internationale Konflikte – verbotene und erlaubte Mittel ihrer Austragung*, pp. 55 *et seq.*

103 Smith, *The Last Years of the Monroe Doctrine*, p. 164.

104 In general, on the different paradigms of international relations theory see: A. Slaughter, 'International Law and International Relations', RdC, 285, (2000), 30–43; Mingst, *Essentials of International Relations*, pp. 57–82.

a sphere of influence, whereas Pan-American, Wilsonian idealists would consider it a special arrangement for regional security.[105]

While realists like Hans Morgenthau would consider doctrines merely as an attempt to rationalise primarily self-interest based aims,[106] commentators who adhere to the liberal school of political theory would understand doctrines as an expression of a sense of mission.[107] The Truman Doctrine, for example, is considered by members of the realist school of thought as merely the ideological cover of a traditional balance-of-power politics.[108]

In 1913, Herbert Kraus defined for his professorial dissertation, *The Monroe Doctrine and its Relations to American Diplomacy and Public International Law* (*Die Monroedoktrin in ihren Beziehungen zur amerikanischen Diplomatie und Völkerrecht*), a standard which today still constitutes a convincing criterion with regard to political assertions: 'In particular, the work at no point makes political statements. Expressing a political opinion about the Monroe Doctrine has been strictly avoided, just as issuing a judgement with regard to its wisdom or "doability", decency, likeliness, possibilities and the like or the contrary has been avoided.'[109]

Even though this standard could be dismissed as simply an expression of its times, this standard is applied to this work. That this claim of 'objectiveness without prejudice' can never be entirely fulfilled because the selection of a certain choice of information already constitutes an evaluation,[110] seems to be a fairly trivial observation. Yet a consideration of what Herbert Kraus labels as the 'doability' (*Tunlichkeit*) of a doctrine, an evaluation of its political value or lack of it, is not a subject of this

105 Smith, *The Last Years of the Monroe Doctrine*, p. 42.

106 H. J. Morgenthau, *Politics among Nations*, 2nd edn. (New York: Alfred Knopf, 1954), pp. 16–19, 39, 53, 172. See further: S. V. Scott, 'Is there Room for International Law in Realpolitik?: Accounting for the US "Attitude" Towards International Law', R.I.S., 30 (2004), 77 *et seq*.

107 K. Krakau, *Missionsbewußtsein und Völkerrechtsdoktrin in den Vereinigten Staaten von Amerika*, pp. 18–19.

108 Unknown author: 'Realism, Liberalism and the War Powers Resolution', Harv.L.R., 102 (1989), 644.

109 Author's translation of: 'Insbesondere gibt die Arbeit in keinem Punkte politische Erörterungen. Es ist streng vermieden worden, eine politische Ansicht über die Monroedoktrin, ein Urteil in Bezug auf Weisheiten oder 'Tunlichkeiten', Anstand, Wahrscheinlichkeiten, Möglichkeiten und der gleichen oder ihr Gegenteil zu äußern', Kraus, *Die Monroedoktrin und ihre Beziehungen zur amerikanischen Diplomatie und zum Völkerrecht*, p. 8.

110 German Federal Constitutional Court, judgment, 28 February 1961, 2/BvG 1, 1/60, BVerfGE 12, 205 (260).

work. Different classifications based on different schools of thought in International Relations as exemplified above, be this the formulation of a doctrine based on idealist, altruistic motives or on self-serving interests, may be significant for the search for a political reason. However, they are of no consequence for the evaluation of the actions foreseen in the doctrines under international law.

Yet in case of doubt, the choice of a school of thought in political theory can influence the determination of the behaviour patterns foreseen in a doctrine. For example: commentators adhering to the school of thought of realism would emphasise the security interests of the United States enshrined in the Monroe Doctrine and derive from that an extension of the doctrine to Canada, whereas commentators adhering to the school of liberalism would make the inclusion of Canada in this doctrine dependent on other criteria such as the form of government there.[111] Hence, only fundamental ideas of doctrines or central features of what a doctrine constitutes can be highlighted, but not borderline cases for which differing conclusions may be reached based on different schools of thought.

The same applies to the delineation of the law in force, which also possesses only in its core area a sufficient degree of unambiguousness, whereas borderline cases may be evaluated differently on the bases of differing interpretations.[112]

In addition, doctrines are closely connected with the question of who is entitled to decide about the legality of the use of force and to interpret the respective rules. As far as it is possible within the scope of this work, alternative possibilities of interpretation of a rule of law are included and related to doctrines. Yet even with regard to the choice of a certain interpretation of a rule of law as an unambiguously determinable core of a rule of law, the jurist depends also on the inclusion of extra-legal criteria and is limited to proposing a certain interpretation.[113] The evaluation of the validity and efficiency of a legal order must be based finally on extra-legal criteria,[114] just as a legal order is based on extra-legal foundations.[115]

111 On the problem of the geographical extent of the Monroe Doctrine see further, Chapter 2, section 2.1.5.

112 See above, Chapter 1, section 1.5.

113 Likewise on the method: Krisch, *Selbstverteidigung und kollektive Sicherheit*, p. 20.

114 I. Brownlie, 'International Law at the Fiftieth Anniversary of the United Nations', RdC, 255 (1995), 30–1, explicitly quoting G. Fitzmaurice, 'The General Principles of International Law', RdC, 92 (1957-II), 36–47.

115 Already in 1899 Heinrich Triepel had written: 'one will always invariably reach the point where a legal explanation of the obligatory character of law becomes impossible itself.

In spite of the changeability of the doctrines of US security policy, these doctrines and the principles for the use of force in international relations outlined within can be determined sufficiently precisely to subject them to an evaluation under international law. This endeavour is undertaken for each doctrine in the following chapters.

The legal basis of the validity of law is extra legal.' (M. Byers' translation of: 'Immer und überall wird man an den Punkt gelangen, an dem eine rechtliche Erklärung der Verbindlichkeit des Rechtes selbst unmöglich wird. Der "Rechtsgrund" der Geltung des Rechts ist kein rechtlicher.') H. Triepel, *Völkerrecht und Landesrecht* (Leipzig: C. L. Hirschfeld, 1899), p. 82 in Byers, *Custom, Power, and the Power of Rules*, p. 7; Kelsen, *Principles of International Law*, pp. 437 *et seq.*

2

The early doctrines

The international system with several influential states as global participants, as it existed prior to the US declaration of independence in 1779 until the beginning of the Cold War in 1945, is generally labelled multipolar. International law was during that period codified only to a low degree. Customary and treaty-based regulations concerning the use of force have formed with increasing clarity over the course of time.[1]

The possibility of forming a balance of power in such a multipolar system, and the consequences of this for the actions of other states with regard to international law is considered to be a decisive factor in the development of international law during this period.[2] However, with regard to the question of polarity of a system of states the respective geographic scope has always to be kept in mind.

2.1 The Monroe Doctrine

On 2 December 1823 the fifth President of the United States of America, James Monroe, in his annual address to Congress described principles of US foreign policy, which in the following period have been considered as points of reference for the long-term orientation of US foreign policy.[3] The term 'Monroe Doctrine' to describe the principles laid down in this speech appeared in a debate in Congress in 1853.[4] Different principles concerning the use of force and different claims of law with regard to the

1 I. Brownlie, *International Law and the Use of Force by States* (Oxford: Clarendon Press, 1963), pp. 19 *et seq.*

2 A. Vagts and D. Vagts, 'Balance of Power in International Law: A History of an Idea', A.J.I.L., 73 (1979), 555–80.

3 Text of Monroe's speech: J. Moore, *A Digest of International Law* (Washington, DC: Government Printing Office, 1906), vol. 6, pp. 401–4, § 396; D. Perkins, *A History of the Monroe Doctrine* (Boston, MA: Little, Brown, 1955), pp. 394–6.

4 Perkins, *A History of the Monroe Doctrine*, p. 99.

legality of the use of force have been put forward within the frame of the Monroe Doctrine.

2.1.1 *Central ideas of the original Monroe Doctrine*

Generally, a bipartite distinction of the basic principles of the original Monroe Doctrine is made. Herbert Kraus distinguishes between the principle of limitation of the political freedom of action of non-American states in America, and the principle of limitation of the political freedom of action of the United States towards Europe.[5] The former principle is split into two sub-principles, referred to in Anglo-American literature as the 'non-colonisation principle' and the 'non-intervention principle'. While the first sub-principle deals with the acquisition of territory, the second deals with the legality of the use of force.[6]

However, the original purpose of James Monroe's speech was not so much the purpose of laying down fundamental guidelines of US foreign policy, but to react to a particular political situation that was perceived as a threat at the time. On the one hand, Monroe's speech was preceded by an exchange of diplomatic notes between the United States and Russia. In these the United States opposed Tsar Alexander's edict (Ukaz) of 16 September 1821, claiming the northwest territory north of 51° to be under Russian jurisdiction. The non-colonisation principle was aimed at that policy. On the other hand, there were fears that Spain with the support of the Holy Alliance could attempt to reoccupy its former colonies, which had been independent since 1810 and were largely recognised by the United States as independent states.[7] The non-intervention principle was aimed at that policy. The two principles can be found in two separate paragraphs in different parts of Monroe's speech.

The phrase in Monroe's speech outlining the 'non-colonisation principle' reads:

5 H. Kraus, *Die Monroedoktrin in ihren Beziehungen zur amerikanischen Diplomatie und zum Völkerrecht* (Berlin: Guttentag, 1913), pp. 66–74. Similarly, see: A. Alvarez, *Droit International Américain* (Paris, A. Pedone, 1910), pp. 133–43; P. Fauchille, *Traité de Droit International Public*, 8th edn. (Paris, Rousseau & Cie, 1922), pp. 592–5; H. Lauterpacht, *Oppenheim's International Law*, 8th edn. (London: Longman Green, 1955), pp. 314–16; J. Whitton, 'La Doctrine de Monroe', R.G.D.I.P., 7 (1933), 5–44, 140–80, 273–325.

6 A. Pearce-Higgins, 'The Monroe Doctrine', B.Y.I.L., 5 (1924), 104.

7 C. Hyde, *International Law – Chiefly as Interpreted and Applied by the United States*, 2nd edn. (Boston, MA: Little, Brown, 1947), vol. III, pp. 286–7.

> the occasion has been judged proper for asserting, as a principle in which the rights and interests of the United States are involved, that the American continents, by the free and independent condition which they have assumed and maintained, are henceforth not to be considered as subjects for future colonization by any European powers.[8]

The territorial extent of this principle as spanning 'the American continents' was later extended and specified as the 'western hemisphere'.[9] The term 'hemisphere' can also be found within the description of the 'non-intervention principle', outlined in the following passage:

> we owe it therefore, to candor and to the amicable relations existing between the United States and those powers to declare that we should consider any attempt on their part to extend their system to any portion of this hemisphere as dangerous to our peace and safety. With existing colonies or dependencies of any European power we have not interfered and shall not interfere. But with the governments who have declared their independence and maintained it, and whose independence we have, on great consideration and on just principles, acknowledged, we could not view any interposition for the purpose of oppressing them, or controlling in any other manner their destiny by any European power, in any other light than the manifestation of an unfriendly disposition towards the United States . . .
>
> It is impossible that the allied powers should extend their political system to any portion of either continent without endangering our peace and happiness; nor can any one believe that our southern brethren, if left to themselves, would adopt it of their own accord. It is equally impossible, therefore, that we should view such interposition in any form with indifference.[10]

As is already clear from this passage, the distinction between the principles in the original text of the speech is blurred. Hence, according to Kraus, elements outlining the second principle of limitation of political freedom of action of the United States towards Europe can be found within this passage. The following phrase from Monroe's speech, which is referred to in literature as the desinteressement principle, highlights this best:[11]

> Our policy in regard to Europe . . . remains the same, which is, not to interfere in the internal concerns of any of its powers.[12]

8 Moore, *A Digest of International Law*, vol. VI, p. 402, § 936.

9 See below, section 2.1.5.

10 Moore, *A Digest of International Law*, vol. VI, pp. 402–3, § 936.

11 H. Kruse, *Monroe-Doktrin*, in H. Schlochauer (ed.), *Wörterbuch des Völkerrechts*, 2nd edn. (Berlin: de Gruyter, 1961), p. 548.

12 Moore, *A Digest of International Law*, vol. VI, p. 403, § 936.

It is a contentious issue among scholars at exactly what point in time the desinteressement principle was abandoned. Partly, it is assumed that this second sub-principle had already been abandoned by the passing of a common resolution by both houses of Congress on 7 July 1898 concerning the annexation of Hawaii.[13] Others argue that the Washington Treaty of 2 December 1899, in which the Samoa dispute was settled, indicates an abandonment of the desinteressement principle;[14] that is if one does not already consider the colonial activity of the United States, such as the participation in the Congress of Berlin in 1884, as a deviation from this principle.[15]

In the statements on the resolution by the Senate of 2 August 1912 in the *Magdalena Bay* case[16] at least the term 'Monroe Doctrine' is used only in connection with the first sub-principle.[17] At the latest the US-American practice fully abandoned this principle with the entry of the United States into the First World War on 6 April 1917 and the deployment of troops to Europe.[18] In spite of recurring appeals within US-American political discussion to revive this principle,[19] this sub-principle has now lacked a ground of validity for a considerable period of time.[20]

For this reason, the sub-principle on the limitation of the United States towards Europe has been exempt from earlier examinations, as since that

13 E. Sauer, *Grundlehre des Völkerrechts*, 2nd edn. (Cologne: Balduin Pick-Verlag, 1948), p. 141.

14 Kraus, *Die Monroedoktrin in ihren Beziehungen zur amerikanischen Diplomatie und zum Völkerrecht*, pp. 339–45.

15 K. Strupp, *Wörterbuch des Völkerrechts und der Diplomatie* (Berlin: de Gruyter, 1925), p. 67.

16 This resolution of the Senate was a reaction to an intended purchase of an area for the construction of port facilities at Magdalena Bay, Mexico by a Japanese firm. G. Hackworth, *Digest of International Law* (Washington, DC: Government Printing Office, 1943), vol. V, pp. 437–8.

17 For example, in the explanations of Senator Henry Cabot Lodge, Sr., Cong. Rec., vol. 48, Pt 10, pp. 10045ff., 2 August 1912. This resolution is sometimes referred to as the Lodge Corollary to the Monroe Doctrine after its initiator; C. V. Crabb, *The Doctrines of American Foreign Policy – Their Meaning, Role and Future*, 3rd edn. (Baton Rouge, LA: Louisiana State University Press, 1990), pp. 40–1.

18 A. F. von Freytag-Loringhoven, *Die Satzung des Völkerbundes* (Berlin: Georg Stilke, 1926), p. 223.

19 Lately in the shape of so-called neo-isolationism. On this see: E. Gholz, D. Press and H. Sapolsky, 'Come Home, America', Int.Sec., 21/4 (1997), 5–48; E. Ravenal, 'The Case for Adjustment', For.Pol., 81 (1990–1), 3–19; P. Buchanan, 'America First – and Second and Third', Natl.Int., 19 (1990) 77–82.

20 J. Whitton, 'Isolation: An Obsolete Principle of the Monroe Doctrine', I.Con., 290 (1933), 211–25.

time it can no longer be counted as a principle of US foreign policy.[21] In addition to this, the United States itself is the addressee of this principle. Likewise, it is the first principle of limitation of political freedom of action of non-American states in America only (as defined by Kraus) that will be discussed here. Yet the two other principles laid down by James Monroe, the non-colonisation principle and the non-intervention principle, have also been subject to considerable modifications during the course of time.

2.1.2 Phases of the Monroe Doctrine

Alejandro Alvarez quotes the *New York Sun* with the statement that 'The Monroe Doctrine is as elastic as India rubber and as comprehensive as all outdoors.'[22] Cecil V. Crabb lists no fewer than ten content-changing interpretations and corollaries to the Monroe Doctrine.[23] Other counts assume more than thirty corollaries.[24] The changes which the Monroe Doctrine has undergone since 1823 cannot be presented in detail in this work and have already been subject to comprehensive historical exploration.[25] According to Dexter Perkins, the history of the development of the Monroe Doctrine can be split into three phases, which will be presented briefly in the following.

21 H. Schatzschneider, *Die neue Phase der Monroedoktrin angesichts der kommunistischen Bedrohung Lateinamerikas – Unter Berücksichtigung des Falles Guatemala vor der Organisation Amerikanischer Staaten und der Vereinten Nationen* (Göttingen: Vandenhoeck & Ruprecht, 1957), p. 7. Kutzner, however, assumes that this principle was never abandoned, as the original principle foresaw only non-participation of the United States in European wars if these concerned purely European matters. G. Kutzner, *Die Organisation Amerikanischer Staaten* (Hamburg: Hansischer Gildenverlag, 1970), p. 20.

22 A. Alvarez, *The Monroe Doctrine: Its Importance in the International Life of States of the New World* (Oxford University Press, 1924), p. 394.

23 Crabb, *The Doctrines of American Foreign Policy*, pp. 33–55.

24 D. Dent, *The Legacy of the Monroe Doctrine* (Westport, CT: Greenwood Press, 1999), pp. 8–13.

25 A detailed description of the historical development of the Monroe Doctrine can be found at D. Perkins, *The Monroe Doctrine, 1823–26* (Cambridge, MA: Harvard University Press, 1927); D. Perkins, *The Monroe Doctrine, 1826–1867* (Baltimore, MD: The Johns Hopkins University Press, 1933); D. Perkins, *The Monroe Doctrine, 1867–1907* (Baltimore, MD: The Johns Hopkins University Press, 1937); D. Perkins, *A History of the Monroe Doctrine* (Boston, MA: Little, Brown, 1955); G. Smith, *The Last Years of the Monroe Doctrine, 1945–1993* (New York: Hill & Wang, 1994); G. Kahle, *Die Rolle der politischen Doktrinen in den Beziehungen zwischen den USA und Lateinamerika 1823–1933*, K.A.E.V.R., 13 (1980).

2.1.2.1 The defensive–isolationist phase of the Monroe Doctrine

The time between 1823 and the beginning of an American desire for hegemony in Latin America during the 1890s can be considered to be the first defensive–isolationist phase of the Monroe Doctrine. Compared with prior principles, this did not constitute an essential change within the policy guidelines of the United States. George Washington had already formulated in his farewell address to Congress a principle which matched, at least to a large extent, the desinteressment principle of Monroe's speech.[26] The principle of the limitation of political activity by European states in America was then added by Monroe's speech.

As the external circumstances of Monroe's speech make clear, the Monroe Doctrine did not aim, at least in its early stages, for the creation or manifestation of a US hegemony in Latin America, but emphasised instead the right of self-preservation of the United States.[27] In this phase, the doctrine did not go beyond a defensive element by asserting pan-American US responsibility for the territorial integrity of Latin American states.[28]

Bowett considers this phase of the Monroe Doctrine, and the pre-charter practice of the United States, as evidence that it considered its security to be so dependent on the security of the whole American continent that, according to American opinion, any attack on any place on the continent would afford to them the right of individual self-defence, as opposed to the later principle of collective self-defence of the whole continent.[29] This orientation of the doctrine, emphasising the principle of limitation of activity of European states in America, has been modified and extended repeatedly. The first clarifications and interpretations of the doctrine partially contained direct references to specific activities of single

26 R. Andrist (ed.), *George Washington, A Biography in His Own Words* (New York: Harper & Row, 1972), p. 373. On US foreign policy prior to Monroe's speech see: Moore, *A Digest of International Law*, vol. VI, pp. 369–401.

27 C. Fenwick, *International Law* (London: Allan & Unwin, 1924), p. 148.

28 Elihu Root on this on 22 December 1912 in a speech to the New England Society of International Law 'The opposition to European control over American territory is not primarily to preserve the integrity of any American state – that may be a result but not a purpose of the Doctrine. The essential idea is to prevent a condition which could menace the national interests of the United States.' Quoted from G. Hackworth, *Digest of International Law* (Washington, DC: Government Printing Office, 1943), vol. V, p. 440.

29 D. W. Bowett, *Self-Defence in International Law* (Manchester University Press, 1958), pp. 209–10.

states in certain territories.[30] Single principles of the doctrine have often been repeated merely in reaction to prior political developments, containing references to the particular situation and have thereby undergone further specification and extension.

An interpretation by President Polk in his annual address to Congress in 1845 has to be particularly emphasised in this context. According to his address, the United States could not accept the transfer of authority or sovereignty ('dominion or sovereignty') over an American territory to England, Spain or any other European power.[31] This principle, also called the 'non-transfer principle', is commonly referred to as the Polk Corollary to the Monroe Doctrine. It extended the Monroe Doctrine to the extent that even activities by European states that did not constitute force would not be accepted by the United States.[32]

President Grant repeated the non-transfer principle in his State of the Union Address on 6 December 1869, but also connected it more generally to any type of legal transfer of territory in America between European states.[33] Yet the basic principle on the use of force is preserved in spite of these variations: that is, the use of military force or an acquisition of territory by European states in America is perceived by the United States as a threat to its security, entitling it to take action, including the use of force if necessary. In this phase, however, the doctrine does not deal with activity of the United States within other American states, even though it attributes to the United States the role of the defender of the whole continent.

The doctrine experienced considerable change during the subsequent phase as an instrument of an American claim of hegemony in the Americas, including the use of force by the United States in Latin America.

30 Among these is a resolution introduced in 1824 by Senator Henry Clay, although not passed by the Senate, which spoke out against a European intervention in Spanish colonies, sometimes labelled as 'Clay Doctrine' (Crabb, *The Doctrines of American Foreign Policy*, p. 34). The interpretation of the Monroe Doctrine referring to Cuba in a speech of 15 March 1826 by President John Quincy Adams (the so-called Adams Doctrine) addressed to Mexico, according to which the United States would not accept a transfer of former Spanish colonies to other states. Crabb, *The Doctrines of American Foreign Policy*, p. 34.

31 For the text of Polk's speech with explicit reference to Monroe's speech in 1823 see Moore, *A Digest of International Law*, vol. 6, pp. 420–1, § 941.

32 Kraus, *Die Monroedoktrin in ihren Beziehungen zur amerikanischen Diplomatie und zum Völkerrecht*, p. 93.

33 Quoted in Ahrens, *Der Karibische Raum als Interessensphäre der Vereinigten Staaten von Amerika*, p. 63.

2.1.2.2 The Monroe Doctrine as an instrument for a US-American claim of hegemony

The defensive–isolationist phase of the Monroe Doctrine was followed by a phase reaching from the 1890s to the 1920s. Single voices go as far as to assume that during this period the Monroe Doctrine became an 'instrument of American imperialism' and 'a symbol of the claim of the United States of hegemony over the middle American area'.[34] A statement in 1895 during the Venezuelan border dispute between Great Britain and Guyana[35] by Secretary of State Olney expressed the intention to understand the Monroe Doctrine not merely as a principle of a defensive-orientation of US security policy in dealing with European States, but rather one of claiming hegemony over the whole American continent:[36]

> Today the United States is practically sovereign on this continent, and its fiat is law upon the subjects of which it confines its interposition.[37]

The Monroe Doctrine experienced the clearest change from a defensive principle towards an attempted justification of US interference in the domestic affairs of Latin American states through the Roosevelt Corollary. This corollary goes back to a speech of President Theodore Roosevelt before the US Congress on 6 December 1904.[38] In reaction to a sea blockade of Venezuela by Great Britain, Germany and Italy in order to enforce certain claims for payments,[39] Theodore Roosevelt expressed in his speech a claim of the United States for being the ordering power

34 Likewise, for example, Schatzschneider, *Die neue Phase der Monroedoktrin*, p. 7. Author's translation of: 'Instrument des amerikanischen Imperialismus' and 'Symbol des Anspruchs der Vereinigten Staaten auf Hegemonie zumindest im mittelamerikanischen Raum.'

35 On the Venezuelan border dispute see: Moore, *A Digest of International Law*, vol. 6, pp. 531–83, § 966; Kraus, *Die Monroedoktrin in ihren Beziehungen zur amerikanischen Diplomatie und zum Völkerrecht*, pp. 142–83.

36 On the geographical extension of the Monroe Doctrine see below, section 2.1.4.

37 Secretary of State Olney to Mr Bayard, Ambassador to Great Britain, in Moore, *A Digest of International Law*, vol. VI, p. 535, § 966.

38 C. Veeser, 'Inventing Dollar Diplomacy: The Roosevelt Corollary to the Monroe Doctrine', Dipl.Hist., 27/3 (2003), 301–26. Some writers assume that the Monroe Doctrine fulfilled the function as an instrument of US-American claim of hegemony in Latin America much earlier. See, for example, F. von Martens, *Völkerrecht* (Berlin: Weidmannsche Buchhandlung, 1883), vol. 1, pp. 303–5. However, an explicit reference to the Monroe Doctrine, as in the case of the Roosevelt Corollary, is missing.

39 On the Venezuelan dispute over debts and its settlement see: Kraus, *Die Monroedoktrin in ihren Beziehungen zur amerikanischen Diplomatie und zum Völkerrecht*, pp. 252–5; Moore, *A Digest of International Law*, pp. 584–94, §967; M. Silagi, 'Preferential Claims Against Nicaragua', E.P.I.L., III (1997), 1098–9.

in America ('the exercise of an international police'). A passage making direct reference to the interpretation of the Monroe Doctrine reads:

> Chronic wrongdoing, or an impotence, which results in a general loosening of the ties of civilized society, may in America, as elsewhere, ultimately require intervention by some civilized nation, and in the Western Hemisphere the adherence of the United States to the Monroe Doctrine may force the United States, however reluctantly, in flagrant cases of such wrongdoing or impotence, to the exercise of international police power.[40]

This general justification of the practice of intervention by the United States during this period goes far beyond the principles of the original Monroe Doctrine. The change of the principles in Monroe's speech resulting from this can be understood as adding 'mission civilisatrice': 'If the United States protected the weaker American States from intervention by European States, then, it could be said, they also had to take care that the conditions in America did not give reason for intervention.'[41]

The first sub-principle of a prohibition of political activity by European states in America was expanded in the so-called Lodge Corollary in connection with the *Magdalena Bay* case of 1912 to a general prohibition of intervention by non-American states.[42] During this phase of the doctrine, the United States was keen to prevent multilateral treaties from limiting their scope of action in the western hemisphere. This became particularly clear during the negotiations on the Hague conventions, the League of Nations Covenant and the Briand–Kellogg Pact, as well as the reservations announced and discussed in connection with these treaties.[43]

Furthermore, the United States was concerned about potential limitations on the political principles of the Monroe Doctrine during the negotiations for the League of Nations Covenant, which resulted in the inclusion of Article 21 into the covenant.[44] A turn away from the political principles laid down in the Roosevelt Corollary can be found in an

40 *Papers Relating to the Foreign Relations of the United States, 1904*, p. XLI.

41 G. Dahm, *Völkerrecht* (Stuttgart: Kohlhammer, 1961), vol. 2, p. 291, Own translation of 'Wenn die Vereinigten Staaten die schwächeren amerikanischen Staaten vor dem Zugriff der europäischen Mächte bewahrten, dann, so ließe sich sagen, hätten sie auch dafür zu sorgen, daß die Verhältnisse in Amerika keinen Anlaß zum Einschreiten böten.'

42 On the *Magdalena Bay* case and the Lodge Corollary see above, section 2.1.1, fnn. 17 and 18.

43 *Papers Relating to the Foreign Relations of the United States, 1928*, vol. 1, p. 36; for details on the reservations see below, section 2.1.3.1

44 S. Kennedy, 'The Monroe Doctrine Clause of the League of Nations Covenant', Graduate Studies Texas Tech University, No. 20, May 1979. On this see further below, section 2.1.3.3.2.

internal memorandum by Undersecretary of State Joshua Reuben Clark in 1928, which however was not published until 1930 as the so-called Clark Memorandum.[45]

One of the reasons for the abandonment of the Roosevelt Corollary was that it was at the centre of critiques of US foreign policy by Latin American states.[46] This was made clear at the Havana Conference in 1928.[47] Clark explained in his memorandum that the Monroe Doctrine did not justify any intervention by the United States in the domestic affairs of Latin American states,[48] and that as a political declaration it could be reconciled entirely with the international law in force (more precisely with the right of self-preservation).[49] This interpretation of the Monroe Doctrine has since been adhered to by the US State Department and has been confirmed repeatedly as correct.[50]

2.1.2.3 The multilateralisation phase of the Monroe Doctrine

The Monroe Doctrine entered the phase referred to as 'multilateralisation',[51] at the beginning of the 1930s. The start of

45 J. Clark, *Memorandum on the Monroe Doctrine: December 17, 1928* (Washington, DC: Government Printing Office, 1930).

46 Perkins, *A History of the Monroe Doctrine*, pp. 341–4.

47 C. Fenwick, *The Organization of American States* (Washington, DC: The Organization of American States, 1963), pp. 54–5.

48 'does not apply to purely inter-American relations. Nor does the declaration purport to lay down any principles that are to govern the inter-relationship of the states of this Western Hemisphere as among themselves. The doctrine states a case of United States vs. Europe, not United States vs. Latin America', Clark, *Memorandum on the Monroe Doctrine*, p. XIX.

49 'the principle [of] "self-preservation" which underlies the Doctrine – which principle, as we shall see is as fully operative without the doctrine as with it – would apply . . . if such aggression challenged our existence . . . the Monroe Doctrine as such might be wiped out and the United States would lose nothing of its broad, international right', Clark, *Memorandum on the Monroe Doctrine*, p. XX.

50 For example, Secretary of State Frank Kellogg, Draft to American diplomatic officers in Latin America, 28 February 1929: 'The Monroe Doctrine has nothing whatever to do with the domestic concerns or policies or the form of government or the international conduct of the peoples of this hemisphere as among themselves. The principles of the Monroe Doctrine become operative only when some European power (either by its own motion or in complicity with an American state) undertakes to subvert or exclude the self-determined form of government of one of these Republics or acquire from them all or a part of their territory . . . The Monroe doctrine is not now and never was an instrument of aggression; it is and always has been a cloak of protection. The Doctrine is not a lance, it is a shield.' *Papers Relating to the Foreign Relations of the United States, 1929*, vol. 1, pp. 698–9.

51 On the term 'multilateralisation' see below, section 2.1.3.3.1. Instead of the term 'multilateralisation' (P. Malaczuk, 'Monroe doctrine', E.P.I.L., III (2000), 462) the terms 'continentalization' (Fenwick, *The Organization of American States*, pp. 61, 63; A. J. Thomas

the process of multilateralisation is mostly said to coincide with the beginning of the 'Good Neighbour Policy'[52] of presidents Herbert Hoover and Franklin D. Roosevelt.[53] To what degree such a multilateralisation of the Monroe Doctrine had taken place in detail will be discussed more closely below in the evaluation of the Monroe Doctrine under international law.

With regard to the historical background it must be noted that at several conferences after 1933 a common responsibility of American states for the defence of the western hemisphere was laid down. The interpretation of the Monroe Doctrine was also considered at these conferences.[54] In 1933 at the 7th Pan-American Conference in Montevideo the convention on the rights and duties of states was adopted. In Article 8 of this convention a mutual prohibition of intervention among American states was laid down. However, the United States declared a reservation against this Article.[55]

The United States also initially refused to join the Saavedra–Lamas Pact of 1933, outlawing 'wars of aggression' in Article 1 and extending the prohibition of war to South America.[56] When joining the pact, the United States declared, just as they had done in the case of the Briand–Kellogg Pact, the reservation of prior rights, which included the right of self-defence and (according to the American understanding) the preservation of the Monroe Doctrine.[57] Finally, a comprehensive prohibition

and A. V. Thomas, *The Organization of American States* (Dallas, TX: Southern Methodist University Press, 1963), pp. 7, 23 *et seq.*; C. Stoetzer, *The Organization of American States*, 2nd edn. (Westport, CT: Praeger, 1993), pp. 22, 267, 294), 'collectivization' (Bowett, *Self-Defence in International Law*, p. 210), 'generalization' (P. Jessup, 'The Generalization of the Monroe Doctrine', A.J.I.L., 29 (1935), 105–9) and 'l'universalisation', (J. Whitton, 'La Doctrine de Monroe', R.G.D.I.P., 7 (1933), VII at 176) are sometimes used.

52 Named after the according formulation by President Franklin D. Roosevelt in his inauguration speech on 4 March 1933. On the 'Good Neighbour Policy' see Evans and Newnham, *The Penguin Dictionary of International Relations*, pp. 205–6.

53 Crabb, *The Doctrines of American Foreign Policy*, pp. 42–5; T. Grant, 'Doctrines (Monroe, Halstein, Brezhnev, Stimson)', in R. Wolfrum (ed.), *The Max Planck Encyclopaedia of Public International Law* (Oxford University Press, 2008), online edition available at: www.mpepil.com, No. 6.

54 K. Weege, *Panamerikanismus und Monroedoktrin (Eine völkerrechtliche und politische Arbeit)* (Schönberg: Lehmann & Bernhard, 1939), Ph.D. thesis, Kiel, 1939, pp. 36–74.

55 H. Friede, 'Die VII. Panamerikanische Konferenz (Montevideo, Dezember 1933)', ZaöRV/H.J.I.L., 4 (1934), 330–9.

56 Anti-War Treaty on Non-aggression and Conciliation, A.J.I.L., 28 (1934), 28, Suppl., 79 *et seq.*

57 The reservation to the Saavedra–Lamas Pact reads: 'In adhering to this treaty the United States does not thereby waive any rights it may have under other treaties, conventions or under international law.' A.J.I.L., 28 (1934), Suppl., 84.

of intervention among American states was enacted at the pan-American conference of Buenos Aires 1936 and accepted by the United States without reservations.[58]

Yet, the Roosevelt Corollary declared by President Theodore Roosevelt had already been abandoned by President Franklin Delano Roosevelt in December 1933. In a speech on 28 December 1933 before the Woodrow Wilson Foundation he announced:

> The definite policy of the United States from now on is one opposed to armed intervention. The maintenance of constitutional government in other nations is not a sacred obligation devolving upon the United States. The maintenance of law and the orderly process of government in this hemisphere is the concern of each individual nation first of all. It is only if and when the failure of orderly process affects the other nations of the continent that it becomes their concern; and the point to stress is that such an event becomes the joint concern of the whole continent in which we are all neighbours.[59]

During the same year on Pan-American Day, 12 April 1933, President Roosevelt had called the Monroe Doctrine a 'Pan-American Doctrine'.[60] The abandonment of the claim of US-American hegemony as proclaimed in the Roosevelt Corollary coincides with the development of a system of collective security of American states, which at first experienced only a vague institutionalisation.

At the Conference of Lima in 1938 certain consultation mechanisms were established, which were to be referred to in the event of interference by non-American states perceived as a threat to American states. A duty of mutual assistance was, however, not included.[61] These mutual guarantees of security were expanded at the conferences of Panama (1939), Havana

58 In the declaration of the Conference of Buenos Aires on 21 December 1936 it is stated, *inter alia*, that: 'Intervention by one State in the internal or external affairs of another state is condemned', quoted in G. Hackworth, *Digest of International Law*, vol. V, p. 463. On this see further: P. Jessup, 'The Inter-American Conference for Maintenance of Peace', A.J.I.L., 31 (1937), 85–91.

59 Quoted in Friede, *Die VII. Panamerikanische Konferenz (Montevideo, Dezember 1933)*, p. 334.

60 'The Monroe Doctrine . . . was and is directed at the maintenance of independence by the peoples of the continent. It was aimed and is aimed against the acquisition in any manner of the control of additional territory in this hemisphere by any non-American power. Hand in hand with this Pan-American doctrine of continental self-defense, the peoples of the American Republics understand more clearly, with the passing years, that the independence of each Republic must recognize the independence of every other Republic.' Hackworth, *Digest of International Law*, vol. V, pp. 455–6.

61 C. Fenwick, 'The Monroe Doctrine and the Declaration of Lima', A.J.I.L., 33 (1939), 257–68.

(1940), Rio de Janeiro (1942) and Mexico (Chapultepec, 1945) against a backdrop of military confrontations in Europe.[62]

On 30 April 1948 the foundation of the Organization of American States (OAS) finally took place, establishing in Articles 3f and 25 of its charter[63] a duty of mutual assistance by American states.[64] This matches the generally recognised definition of collective security.[65] Prior to this a corresponding duty of American states had already been enacted in Article 3(1) of the Rio Pact of 2 September 1947.[66] These obligations were complemented by the American Treaty on the Peaceful Settlement of Disputes, the so-called Bogotá Pact.[67] This complex network of the Rio Pact, the OAS Charter and Bogotá Pact represents the three pillars on which the inter-American system of the post-war period is based.[68]

The question regarding the extent to which the Monroe Doctrine could continue to exist under the UN Charter and be maintained as a political principle, played a central role for the United States during the negotiations for the foundation of the United Nations (UN) in San Francisco.[69] After the foundation of the UN and the OAS, the continued existence of the Monroe Doctrine was announced repeatedly by the United States. For example, John Foster Dulles interpreted the declaration of the 10th American Conference in 1954 in Caracas as a confirmation of the Monroe Doctrine in its multilateralised form.[70]

As late as 1960 the State Department declared[71] in reaction to a statement by Soviet Premier Khrushchev that the principles of the Monroe Doctrine were still valid.[72] However, President Kennedy explicitly rejected

62 In general on this see: Dahm, *Völkerrecht*, pp. 292–3; Fenwick, *The Organization of American States*, pp. 59–74. On the obligations agreed upon at the Conference of Rio de Janeiro see: Fenwick, 'The Third Meeting of Ministers of Foreign Affairs at Rio de Janeiro', A.J.I.L., 36 (1942), 176–7.

63 UNTS, vol. 119, 1951, p. 48.

64 Thomas and Thomas, *The Organization of American States*, pp. 249–60.

65 K. Doehring, 'Kollektive Sicherheit', in R. Wolfrum (ed.), *Handbuch Vereinte Nationen* (Munich: C. H. Beck, 1991), pp. 405–10 with further evidence; J. Delbrück, 'Collective Security', E.P.I.L., I (1992), pp. 646–56; R. Carey, 'The Contemporary Nature of Security', in T. Salmon (ed.), *Issues in International Relations* (London, Routledge, 2000), pp. 55–75; N. Krisch, *Selbstverteidigung und kollektive Sicherheit* (Berlin: Springer, 2001), pp. 45–8.

66 UNTS, vol. 21, 1948, p. 77. 67 UNTS, vol. 30, 1949, p. 55.

68 R. Dolzer, 'Enforcement of International Obligations through Regional Arrangements: Structures an Experience of the OAS', ZaöRV/H.J.I.L., 47 (1987), 113–33.

69 See below, section 2.1.3.4.

70 On the position of Dulles see further below, section 2.1.3.4.

71 'In first place the principles of the Monroe Doctrine are as valid today as they were in 1823, when the Doctrine was proclaimed.' *Department of State Bulletin*, 43 (1960), 170–1.

72 The declaration of Khrushchev of 12 July 1960 is printed in M. Whiteman (ed.), *Digest of International Law* (Washington, DC: Government Printing Office, 1968), vol. V, p. 511:

making reference to the Monroe Doctrine during the Cuban Missile Crisis in October 1962, as had been suggested in a memorandum by the US Department of Justice in order to justify the blockade of Cuba.[73] In his memoirs President Reagan made reference to the spirit of the Monroe Doctrine and saw his actions as a continuation of this doctrine.[74]

Whether one assumes the continued existence of the Monroe Doctrine as a principle of US security policy, or whether one regards it as an abandoned political principle also depends on the question of its inherent ability to be multilateralised. Similarly, the response to the question of whether such a phase of multilateralisation of the Monroe Doctrine is considered to be finalised or still continuing depends on one's understanding of multilaterlisation and of the doctrine. This aspect will be treated in further detail below in the context of the legal evaluation of the Monroe Doctrine.[75]

Later doctrines which could be understood as continuations or modifications of the Monroe Doctrine, such as the so-called Johnson Doctrine and the Reagan Doctrine will be treated separately below.[76]

2.1.3 Evaluation of the Monroe Doctrine under international law

Not only the content attributed to the Monroe Doctrine, but also the legality of the use of force in the law governing international relations has changed since 1823. These changes influenced the reconcilability of the doctrine with the respective law in force. So did changes to the doctrine itself.

2.1.3.1 Evaluation of the Monroe Doctrine under international law until the beginning of the multilateralisation phase

The original principles of the Monroe Doctrine (the non-colonisation principle and the non-intervention principle) as laid down in Monroe's speech and addressed to other states can be reconciled without any

'We consider that the Monroe Doctrine has outlived itself, has died, so to say, a natural death.'

73 A. Chayes, *The Cuban Missile Crisis* (Oxford University Press, 1974), p. 133; On this: W. Grewe, *Spiel der Kräfte in der Weltpolitik* (Düsseldorf: Econ Verlag, 1970), pp. 577–8.

74 R. Reagan, *An American Life* (London: Hutchinson, 1990), pp. 471–4, in particular pp. 471–2: 'the Soviet Union had violated the Monroe Doctrine and gotten away with it twice, first in Cuba, then in Nicaragua'.

75 See below, section 2.1.3.3.1.

76 See below, Chapter 3, sections 3.3 and 3.6.

problems to the international law in force at that point in time.[77] Kraus still argued in 1913 with regard to the original principle of limitation of political freedom of action for non-American states in America that the exclusion of political influence of non-American states in America is not, and was not, *per se* against international law. In principle the United States was permitted to pursue such a political aim without acting against international law by doing so.[78]

Yet it is questionable whether the doctrine foresaw means in accordance with international law for the pursuit of the particular aim laid down by the doctrine. Monroe's speech itself does not contain a threat of force against non-American states. Only later interpretations of the Monroe Doctrine contain a threat of force in case of non-compliance with the prohibition of intervention by non-American states in America.[79] However, such a threat of force was announced by President Polk as early as 2 December 1845 in the so-called Polk Corollary with reference to Monroe's speech.[80] In its moulding by the Roosevelt Corollary a threat of force against the other American states is added to this threat.[81]

This brings up the question: to what extent such a use of force as foreseen in the doctrine and the threat contained in the doctrine were permissible at that point in time prior to the existence of the general prohibition of the use of force. The acquisition of colonies by European states, not then prohibited by international law, would not have constituted an attack on the United States. However, the law then in force (prior to a general prohibition of force) left room for the United States to pursue such a policy to use force. Likewise, the use of force by the United States as a reaction to an intervention by European states in America – against the non-intervention principle – prior to the coming into force of the general prohibition of force would not have been an act against international law.[82]

77 J. Brierly, *The Law of Nations – An Introduction to the International Law of Peace*, 6th edn. (Oxford: Clarendon Press, 1963), pp. 402–4.

78 Kraus, *Die Monroedoktrin in ihren Beziehungen zur amerikanischen Diplomatie und zum Völkerrecht*, p. 354.

79 Kraus, *Die Monroedoktrin in ihren Beziehungen zur amerikanischen Diplomatie und zum Völkerrecht*, pp. 349–50: 'It is . . . a prohibition addressed to the whole non-American world of states, issued by the United States and applying to them with a threat of forcible enforcement in case of non-observance' (author's translation of: 'Sie ist ein.. von den Vereinigten Staaten ausgehendes und ihnen gegenüber bestehendes, unter Androhung gewaltsamer Durchsetzung im Falle seiner Nichtbeachtung erlassenes Verbot an die nichtamerikanische Staatenwelt'); Morgenthau, *Die internationale Rechtspflege, ihr Wesen und ihre Grenzen*, pp. 107–9.

80 Moore, *A Digest of International Law*, vol. VI, pp. 420–1, § 941.

81 See above, section 2.1.2.2.

82 Dahm, *Völkerrecht*, vol. 2, p. 291.

However, with the beginning of the development of a general prohibition on the use of force, the conformity of these principles with international law becomes more and more questionable. Due to generally recognised reservations made by the United States, the principles of the Monroe Doctrine (also in its shaping by the Roosevelt Corollary) were not at odds with the mainly formal limitations of the right to go to war freely which had been established at the Hague Peace Conferences in 1899 and 1907 in the agreements on the peaceful settlement of disputes.[83]

The reservation to the Hague Convention on the Peaceful Settlement of International Disputes on 29 July 1899[84] is the first case in which representatives of the major powers of the time were officially notified of the Monroe Doctrine. However, the reservation does not mention the Monroe Doctrine explicitly, but speaks of 'the tradition of the United States with regard to purely American matters'.[85]

This reservation extended the traditional non-intervention and non-colonisation principles. Thus, the involvement of European states was no longer acceptable, even if it was merely limited to the participation of European states in arbitration procedures. Yet this reservation is primarily an expression of the desinteressement principle, which could already be considered as abandoned at that point in time as outlined above.[86]

The United States made a reservation with the same wording to the Hague Convention on the Peaceful Settlement of Disputes of 1907,[87] as well as to the General Act of the Conference of Algeciras of 7 April 1906.[88]

83 On this subject in general see: H. Wehberg, 'La Contribution des Conférences de la paix de la Haye au progrès du droit international', RdC, 37 (1931-III), 527–667; Y. Dinstein, *War, Aggression and Self-Defence*, 4th edn. (Cambridge University Press, 2005), p. 79.

84 CTS, vol. 187 (1898–9), 410–28.

85 The full wording of this so-called Monroe Reservation to the Hague Convention of 25 July 1899 reads: 'Rien de ce qui est contenu dans cette Convention ne peut être interpreté de facon à obliger les États Unis d´Amérique à se départir de leur politique traditionelle, en vertu de laquelle ils s´abstiennent d´intervenier, de s´ingérer ou de s´immiscer dans les questions politique ou dans la politique ou dans l'administration intérieure d´aucun État étranger. Il est bien etendu également que rien dans la Convention ne pourra être interprété comme impliquant un abandon de par les États-Unis d`Amérique de leur attitude traditionnelle à l`égard des questions purement Américaines.' ('Nothing contained in this Convention shall be interpreted to require the United States of America to abandon their traditional policy, whereby they refrain from intervening or interfering in political issues or policy or internal administration of any foreign state. It is also extended so that nothing in the Convention may be interpreted as implying an abandonment by the United States of America of their traditional attitude towards purely American questions.') CTS, vol. 187 (1898–9), 426–7.

86 See above, section 2.1.1.

87 CTS, vol. 205 (1907), 233–50.

88 RGBl. (1907), pp. 19, 21.

Even though the trigger for making these reservations was a confrontation about certain procedural rules in the treaty,[89] the reservations are worded in such a way as to refer to the entire agreement. In consequence, this means that not a single rule of these treaties was accepted by the United States as binding if considered at odds with the Monroe Doctrine or 'the traditions of the United States with regard to purely American matters'.[90]

The question then arises as to whether the obligations of the United States to take action in case of a violation of the principles of the doctrine by other states can be derived from the doctrine itself. Irrespective of the question regarding the binding nature of unilateral acts in international law, the United States clearly had no intention of binding itself.[91] Secretary of State Clay made it clear in an instruction to the US Chargé d'Affairs in Buenos Aires in 1828, that the original statement of Monroe was not intended to be self-binding for the United States ('the declaration must be regarded as voluntarily made and not as conveying any pledge or obligation').[92]

In reservations to international treaties and other US-American statements, the character of the Monroe Doctrine as a unilateral political declaration of principles without any binding character is also emphasised.[93]

Before the general prohibition on the use of force came into effect, there was less need for justification of its use in international relations.[94] These less stringent requirements of justification resulted mainly from the prohibition of intervention, from which the limits for the use of force in self-defence then resulted.[95] During this phase, however, the Monroe Doctrine was not, as is occasionally claimed, quoted as an isolated justification in international law for single interventions.[96]

89 The starting point for the discussions in the context of the Hague Conventions on the Peaceful Settlement of Disputes were Articles 27 and 48. These clauses regulate the judicial settlement of international conflicts. H. Pohl, 'Der Monroe-Vorbehalt', in Bonner Juristische Fakultät (ed.), *FS-Krüger* (Berlin: Weidmann, 1911), pp. 447 *et seq.*

90 Pohl, *Der Monroe-Vorbehalt*, p. 462.

91 A. Rubin, 'The International Legal Effects of Unilateral Declarations', A.J.I.L., 71 (1977), 1–30 at 10; J. Leutert, *Einseitige Erklärungen im Völkerrecht* (Diessenhoffen: Verlag Rügger, 1979), at pp. 147 *et seq.*

92 Quoted in: Alvarez, *The Monroe Doctrine*, p. 129.

93 On this see further below, section 2.1.3.3.2.

94 Brownlie, *International Law and the Use of Force by States*, pp. 40–9; Neuhold, *Internationale Konflikte – verbotene und erlaubte Mittel ihrer Austragung*, pp. 16–27.

95 P. Winfield, 'The Grounds of Intervention in International Law', B.Y.I.L., 5 (1924), 149–62.

96 B. Ferencz, *Enforcing International Law – A Way to World Peace, A Documentary History and Analysis* (London: Oceana Publications, 1983), vol. II, p. 459; P. Malanczuk, 'Monroe Doctrine', E.P.I.L., III (1997), 462; N. Paech, 'Interventionsimperialismus – Von der

In addition to that, it is a contentious issue as to whether the use of force against non-American states (in the case of their action in America) was covered by the scope of the right of self-defence as it was then recognised if force used by the United States went beyond ensuring the continued existence of the own state. Likewise, it has been contested that the Monroe Doctrine in its moulding as an instrument of an American claim for hegemony (and the use of force against other American states) was covered by a wider customary right of self-preservation.[97]

This has been countered by arguing that as it was up to every state to determine itself when its existence was threatened, interventions by the United States in terms of the Roosevelt Corollary, because 'one could not prohibit an intervention to a state, when according to his opinion his vital interests commanded to do so'.[98]

There is some disagreement within the science of international law about the actual prerequisites and scope of a right of self-preservation and self-defence at that point in time.[99] However, there is agreement that a course of action as foreseen by the Roosevelt Corollary would have been in accordance with international law, if the Monroe Doctrine had constituted an entirely independent rule of law entitling the United States to such a right. The legal nature of the Monroe Doctrine, however, was and remains a contentious issue.

2.1.3.2 The legal nature of the Monroe Doctrine

The central question for international law in connection with the Monroe Doctrine is the question of whether this doctrine is a rule of international law or merely a guiding political principle of the United States. Until now

Monroe – zur Bush-Doktrin', Blätter für deutsche und internationale Politik, 48 (2003), 1261–2.

97 Kraus, *Die Monroedoktrin in ihren Beziehungen zur amerikanischen Diplomatie und zum Völkerrecht*, pp. 369–84, who reaches with reference to the *Caroline* formula (on this see: R. Jennings, 'The Caroline and McLeod Cases' A.J.I.L., 32 (1938), 82–99) the conclusion that action by the United States against non-American states could in principle be justified by a right of self-preservation, yet not an action in terms of the Roosevelt Corollary.

98 Author's translation of: 'man könne einem Staat nicht die Intervention verbieten, wenn nach seiner Meinung sein Lebensinteresse dies gebiete'. H. Wehberg, *Die Monroedoktrin* (Mönchen-Gladbach: Volksvereins-Verlag, 1915), p. 29; Likewise: L. Oppenheim, *International Law* (New York: Longmans, Green, 1905), vol. I, pp. 177–81; A. Nussbaum, *Geschichte des Völkerrechts* (Munich: C. H. Beck, 1960), pp. 209–10.

99 Bowett, *Self-Defence in International Law*, pp. 5 *et seq.*; Brownlie, *International Law and the Use of Force by States*, pp. 5 *et seq.*

this question has not been fully answered by scholars of international law.[100]

2.1.3.2.1 The Monroe Doctrine as a separate rule of international law

It has been assumed by some that the Monroe Doctrine is a separate rule of international law. The argument by Chilean international lawyer, Alejandro Alvarez, has generated special attention in this context. The claim that the Monroe Doctrine has been generally accepted by American states, as illustrated by regular calls for help addressed to the United States, is at the centre of Alvarez's argument:

> tous les États latins du Nouveau Monde sont d'accord avec les États Unis, comme le montrent les déclarations des hommes d'État de l'Amérique, les pactes souscrits dans les congrès internationaux de la première époque, les pactes souscrits par differénts États, les déclarations des Parlements etc. et enfin cette circonstance que chaque fois qu' un des États d'Amérique s'est trouvé dans un des cas compromis dans cette première catégorie, il s'est tourné vers les États Unis pour leur demander aide. (all Latin American states agree with the United States, as declarations by American statesmen, pacts signed during international conferences of the first epoch, pacts signed by different states, declarations of parliaments, etc. and ultimately the matter of fact that every time an American state needs help it turns to the United States to ask for help.)[101]
>
> La doctrine de Monroe est la manifestation des volontés de tout un continent. (The Monroe Doctrine is the manifestation of the will of a whole continent).[102]
>
> . . . la doctrine de Monroe est un principe de droit international américain. (. . . the Monroe Doctrine is a principle of American International Law.)[103]

Alvarez has, however, been accused of making a selective choice of statements by other states on the Monroe Doctrine. Alvarez addressed these criticisms in 1924 with his work, *The Monroe Doctrine – Its Importance in the International Life of the States of the New World*, which contained a comprehensive collection of material.[104]

J. M. Yepes categorised the Monroe Doctrine in the same way: 'il est juste de reconnaître que cette doctrine formula vigoureusement l'un des

100 P. Malanczuk, 'Monroe Doctrine', E.P.I.L., III (1997), 463–4.
101 Alvarez, *Le Droit International Américain*, p. 153.
102 Alvarez, *Le Droit International Américain*, p. 179.
103 Alvarez, *Le Droit International Américain*, p. 180.
104 A. Alvarez, *The Monroe Doctrine – Its Importance in the International Life of the States of the New World* (Oxford University Press, 1924).

principes essentiels de la politique et du droit international en Amérique, à savoir le principe de non-intervention d'un État dans les affaires d'un autre' ('it is correct to consider that this doctrine vigorously states an essential principle of politics and international law in America, namely the principle of non-intervention of one state in the affairs of another').[105] However, what has to be taken into account in particular is that Alvarez and Yepes assumed that the Monroe Doctrine is a legal rule of an 'American international law'. At the time that Alvarez made his claim, it was already being questioned whether an American international law was possible and whether it existed at all. The existence of such an American international law and to what this term referred specifically, were the subject of numerous controversies among international law scholars after 1910 and in the 1920s.[106] Which opinion one follows with regard to the existence of such an American international law influences the response to the question of whether the Monroe Doctrine in its multilateralised version finds expression in the OAS Charter and its relation to the UN Charter.[107]

2.1.3.2.1.1 The evaluation of the Monroe Doctrine, assuming that a separate American international law exists In general Alvarez defined American international law as follows:

> This expression does not mean, as may appear at first sight and as many would have us believe, an international law which is peculiar to the new world and entirely distinct from universal international law, but rather the complex of principles, conventions, customs practices, institutions and doctrines, which are peculiar to the Republics of the New World.[108]

In doing so, it is assumed that American states developed a particularly intense sense of solidarity due to special geographic, historical and social peculiarities. A certain understanding of law which all American states have in common would result from that circumstance.[109] This

105 J. Yepes, 'Problèmes fondamentaux du Droit des Gens en Amérique', RdC, 47 (1934-I), 1–144.

106 M. Savelberg, *Le Problème du Droit International Américain* (S'Gravenhage: A. A. M. Stols, 1946), pp. 1–36.

107 Thomas and Thomas, *The Organization of American States*, pp. 188–99. On this see below, section 2.1.3.5.

108 Dissenting Opinion of Judge Alvarez, *Colombian–Peruvian Asylum* case (*Asylum* case), Judgment, 20 November 1950: I.C.J. Rep. 1950, p. 290.

109 H. Jacobini, *A Study of the Philosophy of International Law as seen in the Works of Latin American Writers* (Westport, CT: Hyperion Press, 1979); Thomas and Thomas *The Organization of American States*, pp. 190–7.

common understanding of law is said to have found in turn an ideal expression in President Monroe's speech of 1823.[110]

In a separate opinion on the *Haya de la Torre Asylum* case between Columbia and Peru in 1950, Alvarez explained the relation between American international law and general international law as follows: 'Such systems of law are not *subordinate* to universal international law but *correlate* to it.'[111]

In this respect, American international law' in terms of Alvarez differs essentially from regional international law.[112] It is without any doubt that the existence of regional international law was also possible at the time when Alvarez formulated this hypothesis.[113] According to this definition, declarations of principle, which would not count as sources of international law according to general international law standards, were counted as sources of American international law. This deviation is stated in a particularly clear way in a definition by the American Institute of International Law (within an expert opinion for the Executive Council of the pan-American Union of 1925), which matches the separate opinion of Alejandro Alvarez: 'By American International Law is understood all of the institutions, principles, rules, doctrines, conventions, customs and practices which, in the domain of international relations, are proper to the republics of the New World.'[114]

Hence, the evaluation that the Monroe Doctrine is a separate rule of international law of an American international law is based on an understanding of possible sources of international law for American states, which differs fundamentally from the generally recognised understanding of the sources of international law. It differs in particular from the recognised understanding of the creation of customary law at

110 Alvarez, *Le Droit International Américain*, pp. 137–8.

111 Dissenting Opinion of Judge Alvarez, *Asylum* case, Judgment, 20 November 1950: I.C.J. Rep. 1950, p. 294 (original emphasis).

112 However, the term 'American international law' is also used with regard to rules regulating the relations between American states, without including elements which do not count under generally recognised principles as sources of law. Besides that the term 'American international system' is used, which includes elements which, according to Alvarez and Yepes, constitute 'American international law'. On these terms see further: J. Barberis, 'International Law, American', E.P.I.L., II (1992), pp. 1179–80.

113 S. Verosta, 'Regionen und Perioden der Geschichte des Völkerrechts', ÖZöRV, 30 (1979), 1–21; Ipsen, *Völkerrecht*, 5th edn., ch. 1, § 2.IV.3, No. 72.

114 Quoted in: Barberis, 'International Law, American', pp. 1179–80.

the point in time when Alvarez came up with his hypothesis of American international law.[115]

2.1.3.2.1.2 The evaluation of the Monroe Doctrine when denying the existence of a separate American international law The existence of a separate American international law has been denied by the majority of scholars of international law, especially by international lawyers from Latin America.[116] If one assumes that there is no such thing as American international law, there is no room for the evaluation of the Monroe Doctrine as a rule of law of American international law. A further-reaching claim – that the Monroe Doctrine constitutes a rule of universal international law – cannot be found in the works of proponents of American international law.

Just like the argument of the proponents of an American international law, the arguments of the opponents of such law starts with the particularities of the development on the American continent. Yet they come to the conclusion that American states never had the desire to develop such a particular system of international law. Rather, they were driven by the desire to become members of the existing community of international law. Though the American states are considered to have had a leading impact on the development of international law, this impact was, however, always within the framework of generally binding law.[117] Hence, the existence of such a particular American international law is considered aptly – in spite of particularities which the historical development on the US-American continent may have had – to be at odds with general international law.[118] Thus, the argument is correct that no particular equal legal order in the shape of American international law exists besides general international law; merely that a particular, regional American international law can exist.[119] Thus, there is no room for the assumption of the Monroe Doctrine as a rule of particular American international law.

115 A. Verdross, 'Entstehungsweisen und Geltungsgrund des universellen völkerrechtlichen Gewohnheitsrechts', ZaöRV/H.J.I.L., 29 (1969), 635–53.

116 M. de Sá Vianna, *De la non-existence d'un droit international américain* (Rio de Janeiro: Figueredo, 1912). Further sources: Jacobini, *A Study of the Philosophy of International Law as seen in the Works of Latin American Writers*, pp. 130–3; O. von Gottberg, 'Die Entwicklung eines amerikanischen Völkerrechts', Ph.D. thesis, Kaliningrad, 1928, pp. 5–6.

117 de Sá Vianna, *De la non-existence d'un droit international américain*, pp. 57 *et seq.*

118 Weege, *Panamerikanismus und Monroedoktrin*, p. 85.

119 von Gottberg, 'Die Entwicklung eines amerikanischen Völkerrechts', p. 7.

2.1.3.2.2 The Monroe Doctrine as expression of a '*Großraumordnung*' in international law Carl Schmitt evaluated the Monroe Doctrine differently. Schmitt considered it a unique precedent and 'so far [the] most successful example of a Großraum Principle in international law' with a 'prohibition of intervention for forces alien to an area'.[120]

Occasionally, this has been considered as the evaluation of the Monroe Doctrine as a principle of law.[121] Arguments considered as evidence for this evaluation are not felt to be sufficient for confirming the status as a rule of law. Neither the mention of a principle in all important textbooks of international law, nor the mention of the doctrine in numerous reservations to international treaties,[122] nor the mention of the Monroe Doctrine in Article 21 of the League of Nations Covenant[123] may suffice in order to establish the quality of the doctrine as a rule of law.[124] In spite of the correctness of this argument that these characteristics do not suffice to elevate the doctrine to the status of a rule of law, it has to be taken into account that Schmitt is merely attempting to prove, by way of these arguments, the 'noteworthiness of the Monroe Doctrine under international law'. Yet he does not consider these arguments as evidence for the status of the doctrine as a rule of law.[125] He considers the question of whether the Monroe Doctrine is a principle of law or a political maxim in itself a 'wrongly put pre-question'. Schmitt even goes as far as to write of a 'pseudo-judicial controversy'. The Monroe Doctrine is considered rather a type of action *sui generis* resisting such a categorisation.[126] However, Schmitt does not discuss the Monroe Doctrine as representing an existing

120 C. Schmitt, *Völkerrechtliche Großraumordnung mit Interventionsverbot für raumfremde Mächte*, 4th edn. (Berlin: Deutscher Rechtsverlag, 1941), p. 13; author's translation of 'bisher erfolgreichstes Beispiel eines völkerrechtlichen Großraumprinzips' and 'Interventionsverbot für raumfremde Mächte'. Schmitt is referring to the three basic principles contained in Monroe's speech of 1823 ('Nicht-Kolonisation . . . ; Nicht-Einmischung . . . ; Nicht-Einmischung Amerikas . . .'). C. Schmitt, 'Großraum gegen Universalismus. Der völkerrechtliche Kampf um die Monroedoktrin', ZAkDR, 6 (1939), 333.

121 L. Gruchmann, 'Nationalsozialistische Großraumordnung – Die Konstruktion einer "deutschen Monroe-Doktrin"', *Schriftenreihe der Vierteljahreshefte für Zeitgeschichte*, No. 4 (Stuttgart, Deutsche Verlags-Anstalt, 1962), p. 146. Gruchmann, however, does not write from the perspective of a lawyer, but includes aspects of international law in considerations of contemporary history.

122 See above, section 2.1.3.1. 123 See below, section 2.1.3.3.2.

124 Gruchmann, *Nationalsozialistische Großraumordnung*, pp. 146–9.

125 Schmitt, *Völkerrechtliche Großraumordnung*, p. 17; author's translation of: 'völkerrechtswissenschaftliche Beachtlichkeit der Monroedoktrin'.

126 Schmitt, *Völkerrechtliche Großraumordnung*, p. 15; author's translation of: 'falsch gestellte Vorfrage' and of 'pseudojuristische[n] Kontroverse', p. 17.

rule of law;[127] the intention is rather 'to expose the justified core of such a thought, namely, the inadmissibility of forces alien to a space governed by an ordering principle'.[128]

Based on this, Schmitt develops the concept of a 'new order of international law', based on '*Großräume*' (large spaces) of international law. These Großräume should have been organised around '*Reiche*' (empires) governing those spaces. According to Schmitt these reichs should have been 'subjects of international law of first order' which 'shall be introduced as specific category of international law into the scholarly discourse'.[129] The legal term '*Raum*' (space) has been added to this.[130]

Schmitt's description of a '*Großraumordnung*' under international law is thus not a description of the law in force *de lege lata*, but a description of a state he considers to be a desirable aim *de lege ferenda* of meaningful legal policy. These considerations of policy of law – in particular the subject of so-called 'hemispheric security' ('*hemisphärischen Sicherheit*') were well-received among German scholars of international law of the Third Reich,[131] who in their considerations made frequent references to the Monroe Doctrine.[132]

127 C. Schmitt, 'Großraum gegen Universalismus. Der völkerrechtliche Kampf um die Monroe-doktrin', ZAkDR, 6 (1939), 333–7; C. Schmitt, *Der Nomos der Erde im Völkerrecht des Ius Publicum Europaeum* (Cologne: Greven Verlag, 1950), pp. 256–70.

128 Schmitt, *Völkerrechtliche Großraumordnung*, p. 21; author's translation of: 'den berechtigten Kerngedanken . . . freizulegen, nämlich . . . die völkerrechtliche Unzulässigkeit von raumfremden Mächten in einem von einem Ordnungsprinzip beherrschten Raum'.

129 Schmitt, *Völkerrechtliche Großraumordnung*, p. 35; author's translation of: 'Völkerrechtssubjekte 1. Ordnung' and 'als spezifische völkerrechtliche Größe in der völkerrechtswissenschaftlichen Erörterung eingeführt werden soll[en]'. On this see further: C. Schmitt, 'Reich und Raum-Elemente eines neuen Völkerrechts', ZAkDR, 6 (1940), 201–3.

130 Schmitt, *Völkerrechtliche Großraumordnung*, pp. 59 *et seq.*; C. Schmitt, 'Raum und Großraum im Völkerrecht', ZfV, 24 (1941), 145–79.

131 On this: P. Steck, *Zwischen Volk und Staat, Das Völkerrechtssubjekt in der deutschen Völkerrechtslehre (1933–1941)* (Baden-Baden: Nomos, 2003), Ph.D. thesis, Mainz, 2001, pp. 230–7.

132 See, for example, U. Scheuner, 'Die Sicherheitszone des amerikanischen Kontinents (Die Erklärung von Panama vom 3. Oktober 1939)', ZfV, 24 (1941), 180–226; U. Scheuner, 'Der Gedanke der Sicherheit Amerikas auf den Konferenzen von Panama und Habana und die Monroedoktrin', ZfV, 24 (1941), 273–92. On this see in detail: M. Schmoeckel, 'Die Großraumtheorie. Ein Beitrag zur Geschichte der Völkerrechtswissenschaft im Dritten Reich, insbesondere der Kriegszeit' (Berlin: Duncker & Humblot, 1994), Ph.D. thesis, Munich, 1993, in particular pp. 64–7; D. Vagts, 'International Law in the Third Reich', A.J.I.L., 84 (1990), 661–704, in particular pp. 689–90.

Yet already the assumption of the Raum as a construction and separate category of international law is a claim of policy of law and not a description of international law in force.[133] In spite of this, the concept and streams of argument based upon it possessed hardly any connecting points with the international law then in force.[134] An in-depth discussion of Schmitt's considerations may be of use for a better understanding of the complex connections between political utopias and political confrontations,[135] but cannot be undertaken within the scope of this study. Furthermore, this question has no impact on the response to the question of the legal nature of the Monroe Doctrine.

This idea of a Großraum, advocated by Schmitt and subsequently by several other German international lawyers, finds its expression in a version of the Monroe Doctrine brought forward by Foreign Secretary von Ribbentrop in 1940. According to this interpretation, non-intervention by European states on the American continent, as prescribed by the Monroe Doctrine, would be legally valid only if American states would in turn abstain from involvement in European affairs.[136] This attempt to equalise the then German policy of expansion with the political principles of the Monroe Doctrine was sharply rejected by Secretary of State Cordell Hull.[137]

The discussion of the Monroe Doctrine among scholars of international law mostly focuses, in contrast to Schmitt, on the categorisation of the

133 Similarly, probably Schmoeckel, who considers Schmitt's reference to the Monroe Doctrine as a precedent of a Großraumordnung merely as an argument of 'rather judicial nature' ('*eher juristischer Natur*'), Schmoeckel, *Die Großraumtheorie*, p. 64; A. Gattini, 'Sense and Quasi-sense of Schmitt's Großraum Theory in International Law: a Rejoinder to Carty's Critique of Liberal International Legal Order', L.J.I.L., 15 (2002), 53–68.

134 Likewise see: N. Paech and G. Stuby, *Machtpolitik und Völkerrecht in den internationalen Beziehungen* (Baden-Baden: Nomos, 1994), pp. 189–91.

135 M. Koskenniemi, *The Gentle Civilizer of Nations: The Rise and Fall of International Law 1870–1960* (Cambridge University Press, 2001), pp. 415–24; A. Carty, 'Schmitt's Critique of Liberal International Legal Order Between 1933 and 1945', L.J.I.L., 14 (2001), 25–76.

136 *Department. of State Bulletin*, 6 July 1940. Berber argued in the same regard, F. Berber, *Der Mythos der Monroe-Doktrin* (Essen: Essener Verlagsanstalt, 1942), pp. 23–4.

137 *Department of State Bulletin*, 6 July 1940. Secretary of State Hull replied to this interpretation of the Monroe Doctrine by Ribbentrop in a diplomatic note: 'It [the Monroe Doctrine] contains within it not the slightest vestige of any implication, much less assumption of hegemony on the part of the United States. It never has resembled, and it does not today resemble, policies which appear to be arising in other geographical areas of the world, which appear to be similar to the Monroe Doctrine but which, instead of resting on the sole policies of self-defense and of respect for existing sovereignties, as does the Monroe Doctrine, would in reality seem to be only the pretext for carrying out conquest by the sword . . .'

Monroe Doctrine as either a declaration of political principle or a rule of law. The focus is less on possible uses of ideas on which the doctrine is based as on a reasoning for desired political constructs of law.[138]

2.1.3.2.3 The Monroe Doctrine as a purely political principle By far the majority of international law scholars agree that the Monroe Doctrine is a purely political principle and oppose dissenting opinions as advocated by Alvarez and Yeps.[139] The rejection of Alvarez's theory is based not only on the rejection of an American international law, but also on the argument that it does not comply with the standards for such an American international law.[140] Besides that, the Monroe Doctrine is considered to lack a sufficiently definable regulatory content, which is indispensable for a rule of law.[141] At least the United States is not willing to consider the doctrine as a rule of law, which would remove it from unilateral interpretation by the United States.[142]

The Olney Corollary of 1895 – 'Today the United States is practically sovereign on this continent, and its fiat is law upon the subjects of which it confines its interposition'[143] – and the statement of President Cleveland to

138 With proximity to Schmitt see, for instance, Ulrich Scheuner (see above, section 2.1.3.2.2., in particular fn. 129). In contrast, rejecting Schmitt see: Herbert Kraus (below, sections 2.1.3.2.3 and 2.1.3.2.5). For a further elaboration of Kraus' critique of Schmitt's understanding of international law see: H. Kraus, 'Carl Schmitt, Nationalsozialismus und Völkerrecht', N.Z.I.R., 50 (1935), 151–61.

139 Fauchille, *Traité de Droit International Public*, p. 646 with further evidence; further sources also at: Kraus, *Die Monroedoktrin in ihren Beziehungen zur amerikanischen Diplomatie und zum Völkerrecht*, p. 356, fn. 1; Schatzschneider, *Die neue Phase der Monroedoktrin angesichts der kommunistischen Bedrohung Lateinamerikas – Unter Berücksichtigung des Falles Guatemala vor der Organisation Amerikanischer Staaten und der Vereinten Nationen* (Göttingen: Vandenhoeck & Ruprecht, 1957), pp. 60 *et seq.*

140 A. Wegner, 'Die Monroedoktrin und ihre Anwendung im 20. Jahrhundert, insbesondere in ihren Beziehungen zur Panamerikanischen Bewegung und zum Schiedsgerichtsbarkeitsgedanken', Ph.D. thesis, Breslau, 1931, pp. 67–71; Kraus, *Die Monroedoktrin in ihren Beziehungen zur amerikanischen Diplomatie und zum Völkerrecht*, pp. 365–7.

141 Kraus, *Die Monroedoktrin in ihren Beziehungen zur amerikanischen Diplomatie und zum Völkerrecht*, pp. 356–7, with explicit reference to the minimum standard laid down in this regard by Dupuis: 'La marque distinctive d'une règle juridique est de fournir des solutions claires précises et identiques pour tous les cas identiques.' C. Dupuis, *Le principe d'équilibre et le concert européen de la paix de Westphalie à l'acte d'Algesiras* (Paris, Perrin, 1900), p. 100.

142 Kraus, *Die Monroedoktrin in ihren Beziehungen zur amerikanischen Diplomatie und zum Völkerrecht*, pp. 358, 356, fn. 1. On this see further below, section 2.1.3.3.2.2. Similarly see: N. Paech, 'Interventionsimperialismus – Von der Monroe – zur Bush-Doktrin', *Blätter für deutsche und internationale Politik*, 48 (2003), 1258–68.

143 Secretary of State Olney to Mr. Bayard, Ambassador to Great Britain, in Moore, *A Digest of International Law*, vol. VI, p. 535, § 966.

Congress in the same year are partially considered as evidence[144] that, in spite of the refusal of European and other states to recognise the Monroe Doctrine as a rule of law,[145] it has been regarded by the United States as a rule of international law.[146] However, multiple opposing statements contradict this claim.[147]

This opinion has been picked up and repeated by succeeding international lawyers, and in doing so the more current respective statements on behalf of the United States with regard to the legal nature of the Monroe Doctrine as a purely political maxim were added.[148] Yet occasionally an acceptance or even adoption of the political principles of the Monroe Doctrine by other states is assumed.[149]

2.1.3.2.4 The Monroe Doctrine as a type of action *sui generis* A further opinion avoids any commitments and assumes that the Monroe Doctrine has (an imprecise as far as a definition is concerned) at least a 'semi-legal character'.[150] Arguing that the Monroe Doctrine resists a clear-cut attribution to either the realm of law or politics, it is considered a phenomenon *sui generis*.[151] The question based on the alternatives of law and

144 Moore, *A Digest of International Law*, vol. VI, pp. 576–9, § 966.

145 That is, in the replying note of Lord Salisbury in the Venezuelan Border Dispute of 26 November 1895: 'But international law is founded on the general consent of nations; and no statesmen, however eminent, and no nation, however powerful, are competent to insert into the code of international law a novel principle which was never recognized before, and which has not been accepted by the Government of any country', Moore, *A Digest of International Law*, vol. VI, p. 563, § 966.

146 A. Desjardins, 'La Doctrine de Monroe', R.G.D.I.P., 3 (1896), 151–2; D. Carto, 'The Monroe Doctrine in the 1980s: International Law, Unilateral Policy, or Atavistic Anachronism?', Cas.W.Res.J.I.L., 13 (1981), 208; H. Bingham, *The Monroe Doctrine: An Obsolete Shibboleth* (New Haven, CT: Yale University Press, 1913), pp. 13–16; B. Hoppenstedt, 'Die Entwicklung des Gewaltverbots in der U.S.-amerikanischen Außenpolitik – Monroe Doktrin, Wilsons 14 Punkte, Kellogg Pakt', in D. Blumenwitz and G. Wehner (eds.), *Schritte in eine neue Rechtsordnung* (Munich: Hans Seidel Stiftung, 2003), p. 62.

147 As an example the statement of President Wilson of 2 February 1916 only has to be mentioned: 'The Monroe doctrine is not part of international law. The Monroe doctrine has never been formally accepted by any international agreement. The Monroe doctrine merely rests upon the statement of the United States that if certain things happen she will do certain things . . .' Quoted in Alvarez, *The Monroe Doctrine*, p. 560.

148 Schatzschneider, *Die neue Phase der Monroedoktrin*, pp. 10 *et seq.*

149 C. Rousseau, *Droit International Public* (Paris: Sirey, 1980), vol. IV, p. 102–3 with further evidence.

150 C. Fenwick, *International Law*, 2nd edn. (New York: Appleton-Century, 1934), p. 178; C. Fenwick, 'The Monroe Doctrine and the Declaration of Lima', A.J.I.L., 33 (1939), 257–68.

151 E. Fraenkel, 'Regionalpakte und Weltfriedensordnung – zur Völkerrechtsentwicklung der Nachkriegszeit', *Vierteljahreshefte für Zeitgeschichte*, 2 (1954), 45. Author's translation of: 'ein Phänomen sui generis'.

politics itself is considered to be a 'violently classifying simplification'.[152] There is a similarity to Schmitt's starting-point for the construction of the Monroe Doctrine as a Großraumordnung in international law.[153] Yet the United States is regarded as having created legally relevant matters of fact when implementing the Monroe Doctrine, or at least has made use of means of international law.

In view of the doctrine in terms of the sharp definitional frontier between law and non-law on which this work is also based,[154] such a categorisation cannot comply with the standard for a legally precise consideration of the Monroe Doctrine.

2.1.3.2.5 Legal nature of the Monroe Doctrine prior to the League of Nations Covenant In 1913 Herbert Kraus came to the following conclusion: 'The Monroe Doctrine is no rule of international law, in particular no rule of an American International Law'.[155] Thus, it was not possible to justify interventions in the spirit of the Roosevelt Corollary by referring to such a rule.[156] Beyond any doubt this statement mirrored the state of historical scholarship and international law scholarship at that time.[157] When considering this result, obviously contradicting the hypothesis of the nature of the Monroe Doctrine as a rule of law, it has to be taken into account, however, that proponents of this hypothesis (like Alvarez and Yepes) and authors rejecting this hypothesis (like Kraus) do not just disagree with regard to the premise of an existing American international law, but also base their evaluation on different understandings of the term Monroe Doctrine.

Alvarez makes a distinction between the Monroe Doctrine and a policy of hegemony ('doctrine de Monroe et la politique d'hégémonie').[158] Whereas the term Monroe Doctrine is used to refer to the principles of Monroe's speech, for which a general acceptance and support of American states is assumed, the policy of hegemony is considered to be a

152 Schatzschneider, *Die neue Phase der Monroedoktrin*, p. 63. Author's translation of: 'gewaltsam-klassifizierende[n] Vereinfachung'.

153 See above, section 2.1.3.2.2.

154 On this see: P. Kunig, '2. Abschnitt', in Vitzthum (ed.), *Völkerrecht*, p. 148, Nos. 165–6.

155 Kraus, *Die Monroedoktrin in ihren Beziehungen zur amerikanischen Diplomatie und zum Völkerrecht*, p. 351. Author's translation of: 'Die Monroedoktrin ist kein Satz des Völkerrechts, insbesondere keiner eines amerikanischen Völkerrechts.'

156 Bingham, *The Monroe Doctrine: An Obsolete Shibboleth*, pp. 54–5; Q. Wright, 'The Outlawry of War', A.J.I.L., 19 (1925), 76–103 at 90–1.

157 Schatzschneider, *Die neue Phase der Monroedoktrin*, p. 61.

158 Alvarez, *Le Droit International Américain*, p. 154.

unilateral policy of the United States ('Cette Politique est personelle aux États Unis').[159] Later content-changing corollaries such as the Roosevelt Corollary are considered to be part of this policy of hegemony. They are seen as a logical consequence of the Monroe Doctrine, but not as constituting a rule of law.[160]

Supporters of the opinion that the Monroe Doctrine is a purely political declaration of principles do not usually use this term in order to refer to the principles of Monroe's original speech, but to the content of the whole doctrine at a certain point in time. In doing so, they include later developments like the Roosevelt Corollary.[161] Kraus, for example, first presents very comprehensively the development of the Monroe Doctrine since 1823, before reaching his conclusion as to what constitutes the current content of the Monroe Doctrine (1913) and afterwards undertakes an evaluation under international law.[162] In this respect, differing evaluations of the Monroe Doctrine under international law are not based on different opinions of law, but on uncertainties of terminology with regard to the use of the term Monroe Doctrine and are thus often less problematic than they may seem at first glance.

It has been claimed that the arguments made by Kraus against the nature of the Monroe Doctrine as a rule of law have been turned upside down due to political developments, making it tenable to assume an international legal character of the doctrine.[163] This argument is based on a comparison of political reality and the state of law with the criteria as laid down by Kraus. Kraus established the following criteria for a respective categorisation of the Monroe Doctrine as a rule of international law:

> In the first place an agreement of the members of the international community in consideration would be necessary for the Monroe Doctrine to turn into a rule of international law.[164]

159 Alvarez, *Le Droit International Américain*, pp. 146, 382. Alvarez also uses the term 'l'imperialisme' alongside, which in contrast to the term 'politique d' Hégémonie' not only refers to action by the United States in the Americas, but also to actions beyond the Americas. Alvarez, *Le Droit International Américain*, p. 175.

160 Alvarez, *Le Droit International Américain*, pp. 180–1.

161 For example, Lauterpacht, *Oppenheim's International Law*, vol. I, pp. 313 *et seq.*; Fauchille, *Traité de Droit International Public*, vol. I.1, pp. 591 *et seq.*; Brownlie, *International Law and the Use of Force by States*, pp. 245–6; Nolte, *Eingreifen auf Einladung*, pp. 59–61.

162 Kraus, *Die Monroedoktrin in ihren Beziehungen zur amerikanischen Diplomatie und zum Völkerrecht*, pp. 75 *et seq.*

163 Schatzschneider, *Die neue Phase der Monroedoktrin*, p. 61.

164 Kraus, *Die Monroedoktrin in ihren Beziehungen zur amerikanischen Diplomatie und zum Völkerrecht*, p. 358. Author's translation of: 'Damit die Monroedoktrin zu einem

> The proof of the claim made by Alvarez [that the Monroe Doctrine is a rule of American International Law] could only be made by showing that the American republics accepted the Monroe Doctrine as a rule standing above them, regulating their conduct in case of an attack on them by European states. The pan-American movement . . . is not suited to show evidence for this. As far as the creation of closer political relations of the American states with each other is under consideration, lasting and real results were not granted to it so far.[165]

A multitude of regulations of international law have been traced back during the last ninety or so years to the pan-American movement.[166] This brings up the question as to what degree the Monroe Doctrine can be considered to be 'multilateralised'.

2.1.3.3 Evaluation of the multilateralisation of the Monroe Doctrine under international law

The Argentinean Foreign Secretary and international law scholar, Drago, had already argued in a note sent during the Venezuelan Debt Dispute on 29 December 1902, that the use of force by European states against an American state (even if merely to collect debt) was at odds with international law *and* the Monroe Doctrine. This position differed from the US-American position, that the European course of action was not at odds with the Monroe Doctrine as long as no territory was acquired.[167] The recognition of this principle of prohibition of the use of force to collect debt, called the Drago Doctrine, was a contentious issue for some time until it found its way into rules of international law.[168] Even though

Völkerrechtssatz werden könnte, wäre vor allem die Zustimmung der in Betracht kommenden Mitglieder der Völkerrechtsgemeinschaft dazu erforderlich.'

165 Kraus, *Die Monroedoktrin in ihren Beziehungen zur amerikanischen Diplomatie und zum Völkerrecht*, p. 366–7. Author's translation of: 'Der Nachweis der von Alvarez aufgestellten Behauptung (daß die Monroedoktrin ein Satz des amerikanischen Völkerrechts sei) könnte nur dadurch geführt werden, daß gezeigt würde, die amerikanischen Republiken wären dazu gelangt, die Monroedoktrin als eine über ihnen stehende Regel für ihr Verhalten europäischen Angriffen gegenüber anzunehmen . . . Die panamerikanische Bewegung . . . ist nicht geeignet hierfür Belege zu geben. Soweit Herstellung engerer politischer Beziehungen der amerikanischen Staaten zueinander in Betracht kommt, sind ihr dauernde und reale Ergebnisse bisher nicht beschieden gewesen.'

166 Fenwick, *The Organization of American States*, pp. 48 *et seq.*

167 *Papers Relating to the Foreign Relations of the United States, 1903*, pp. 1–5 (p. 3 in particular).

168 Brownlie, *International Law and the Use of Force by States*, pp. 225–6; K. Krakau, 'Lateinamerikanische Doktrinen zur Realisierung staatlicher Unabhängigkeit und Integrität', VRÜ, 8 (1975), 131–3.

the Drago Doctrine seems to be the logical continuation of the non-intervention principle according to the original wording of the Monroe Doctrine,[169] Drago's interpretation of the Monroe Doctrine could not prevail.[170] Secretary of State Hay argued in his reply to Drago that in the present case no action by the United States against that type of force against another American state was required, as the Monroe Doctrine did not contain an obligation to protect.[171] Besides being a statement on the legality of the use of force, this also constitutes a claim for the sole authority of the United States to interpret the Monroe Doctrine; which the United States continued to claim.

A statement by Robert Lansing, Counselor of the Department of State, in a memorandum of 11 June 1914 to the then Secretary of State William J. Bryan also makes this clear:

> the Monroe doctrine is exclusively a national policy of the United States and relates to its national safety and national interests... It is manifest from this that the Monroe doctrine is, as has been said a national policy of the United States and also that it is not a Pan-american policy.[172]

Only at a later point in time did the United States accept obligations under international law to lend support to other American states in case of the use of force against them. The American system of regional pacts has been considered a multilateralisation of the Monroe Doctrine and, hence, a legalisation of the unilateral Monroe Doctrine. If, and to what extent, it is apt to talk of such a multilateralisation has been contested repeatedly. Depending on the understanding of the terms multilateralisation and doctrine this question is either answered positively or negatively.

2.1.3.3.1 The term multilateralisation The starting-point for assuming a process of multilateralisation of the Monroe Doctrine is a consideration of the development of a system of regional international law as a multilateral recognition of the doctrine in treaties. This is thus considered a

169 Moulin calls the Drago Doctrine the logical and necessary consequence of the Monroe Doctrine ('la conséquence logique et nécessaire'). H. Moulin, 'La Doctrine de Drago', R.G.D.I.P., 14 (1907), 460 *et seq.*

170 C. Barcia Trelles, 'La Doctrine de Monroe dans son développement historique particulièrement en ce qui concerne les relations inter-américaines', RdC, 34 (1930-II), 521 *et seq.*

171 *Papers Relating to the Foreign Relations of the Unites States, 1903*, pp. 5–6.

172 *Papers Concerning the Foreign Relations of the United States, The Lansing Papers, 1914–1920*, vol. II, p. 461. Similarly, see: E. Root, 'The Real Monroe Doctrine', A.J.I.L., 8 (1914), 431 *et seq.*

'multilateralisation' or 'legalisation' of the unilateral Monroe Doctrine.[173] Bowett considers the Declaration of Lima on 24 December 1938 as the beginning of a gradual transformation of a unilateral Monroe Doctrine to a multilateralised doctrine.[174]

It is ultimately a matter of semantics to what extent one considers the creation of the American system of regional pacts a multilateralisation. The answer to this question depends on different connotations attached to the term Monroe Doctrine. Proponents of the theory that a multilateralisation of the Monroe Doctrine has taken place do not use the term 'Monroe Doctrine' for the Monroe Doctrine in its entirety, but discuss singular fundamental principles which first found expression in the doctrine. If the commitment to the doctrine has been prescribed as legally binding, the question of multilateralisation of the Monroe Doctrine is answered in the affirmative. When Bowett writes about a multilateralisation of the Monroe Doctrine, he is not referring to the doctrine in its entirety as a construct with several sub-principles, but to single principles like that of defending the territorial integrity of America which found entry into international treaties.[175]

It has been argued that such a process of legalisation of the principles of the Monroe Doctrine has taken place, with particular reference to the criteria which have to be fulfilled, according to Herbert Kraus, for the Monroe Doctrine to be considered a rule of international law.[176]

On the other hand, adversaries of this theory of multilateralisation do not draw a distinction between single principles laid down in the doctrine and the doctrine as such. They consider the nature of the doctrine as a unilateral political declaration of principles of central importance. Hence, they accept the term multilateralisation only in the case that together with the principle the unilateral authority of the United States to change this

173 Fenwick, *The Organization of American States*, pp. 61, 63; Thomas and Thomas, *The Organization of American States*, pp. 7, 23 *et seq.*; Fraenkel, *Regionalpakte und Weltfriedensordnung*, p. 52.

174 Bowett, *Self-Defence in International Law*, p. 210. See also: Fenwick, 'The Monroe Doctrine and the Declaration of Lima', p. 266; Fraenkel, *Regionalpakte und Weltfriedensordnung*, p. 52. Individual authors assume a much earlier point in time as the starting point for the multilateralisation of the Monroe Doctrine. Fauchille, for example, considers the treaties of Panama of 1826, 1847, 1856, Lima 1865 and Santiago 1856 at least as an acceptance of the political principles of the US-American Monroe Doctrine by Latin American states. Fauchille, *Traité de Droit International Public*, vol. I.1., pp. 642–3.

175 Bowett, *Self-Defence in International Law*, pp. 208–12.

176 Schatzschneider, *Die neue Phase der Monroedoktrin*, pp. 61–2.

principle is also accepted. Thus, such a multilateralisation is considered to be impossible from the very beginning.[177]

The multilateralisation of the Monroe Doctrine is further denied by arguing that a definition of it would have been necessary for it to be accepted by other American states in a treaty – which would rob the doctrine of its specific characteristics.[178] Kraus assumed a similar understanding of the Monroe Doctrine, when writing: 'According to the remarks made above, it is a defining feature of the Monroe Doctrine that it is a prohibition issued by the United States.'[179]

Thus, multilateralisation is narrowly defined as a state in which the United States cannot alone determine when a threat to the principle (a threat to the American continent) exists. In turn, the unilateral authority to interpret and change the doctrine would be lost. The American system of regional pacts is accordingly considered not as a multilateralisation of the Monroe Doctrine, rather as a *political* process of coordination of the political principles of the United States and Latin America, which, however, does not go together with a *legal* recognition of the Monroe Doctrine by Latin American states. Occasionally, it is even argued that such a process would merge the Monroe Doctrine with the pan-American idea of Bolivar.[180]

177 In this direction, for example, Norman Davis: 'the Monroe doctrine, by its nature, can never entail contractual obligations between nations'. N. Davis, 'Wanted: A Consistent Latin-American Policy', For. Aff., 9 (1931), 567; E. Root, 'The Real Monroe Doctrine', A.J.I.L., 8 (1914), 440; Kutzner, *Die Organisation Amerikanischer Staaten*, p. 63; C. Anderson, 'The Monroe Doctrine Distinguished in Principle From Mutual Protective Pacts', A.J.I.L., 30 (1936), 477–79. Of the same opinion probably also: C. Walter, *Vereinte Nationen und Regionalorganisationen* (Berlin: Springer, 1996), Ph.D. thesis, Heidelberg, 1996, pp. 14–15.

178 Gruchmann, *Nationalsozialistische Großraumordnung*, p. 148.

179 Kraus, *Die Monroedoktrin in ihren Beziehungen zur amerikanischen Diplomatie und zum Völkerrecht*, pp. 349–50. Author's translation of: 'Nach den oben gemachten Bemerkungen gehört es zu den Begriffsmerkmalen der Monroedoktrin, daß sie ein von den Vereinigten Staaten ausgehendes . . . Verbot ist.'

180 Schatzschneider, *Die neue Phase der Monroedoktrin*, p. 8. Author's translation of: 'verschmelzen mit der panamerikanischen Idee Bolivarscher Observanz'. Forty-four years earlier Kraus argued in a very different way: 'the necessary basis for the Monroe Doctrine is a relation of superordination and subordination between the protection power on the one side and the protected powers on the other, formed by the other pan-American republics. The basis of the pan-American movement is in contrast equality' (author's translation of: 'die notwendige Grundlage für die Monroedoktrin ist ein Verhältnis der Überordnung und der Unterordnung, der Schutzmacht und der Schutzobjekte auf der anderen, gebildet durch die übrigen pan-amerikanischen Republiken. Die Grundlage

Even when assuming the doctrine has not been multilateralised, the question arises as to what extent the principles of the doctrine are reflected in regional American rules and general international law and continue to have effects.[181] The Monroe Doctrine is mentioned explicitly in Article 21 of the League of Nations Covenant (LNC). In connection with Article 21 of the LNC it has been argued that this constitutes a tacit recognition of the Monroe Doctrine as a principle of law.[182]

2.1.3.3.2 The Monroe Doctrine and the LNC Even though the United States never joined the League of Nations, they contributed considerably to the formation of the LNC in 1919. The possibility of maintaining the Monroe Doctrine played a central role within the US-American discussion of the principles for the legality of use of force contained in the LNC.[183] Concerns about lacking the ability to maintain the Monroe Doctrine were an important reason for the refusal of the US Senate to ratify the LNC.[184] During the negotiations on the LNC, President Wilson declared that it was the intention of the United States to make the protection of the territorial integrity and political independence of American states (up to that point an 'obligation' of the United States under the Monroe Doctrine) an obligation of all other member states of the League of Nations too.[185] At first the United States suggested that the Monroe Doctrine should be expressed in a reservation to Article 10 of the LNC, in which the

für die pan-amerikanische Bewegung dagegen ist Gleichordnung'). Kraus, *Die Monroedoktrin in ihren Beziehungen zur amerikanischen Diplomatie und zum Völkerrecht*, p. 367.

181 Krakau limits his theory of multilateralisation, by stating that a 'classical Monroe Doctrine' continues to exist alongside with a multilateralised one. K. Krakau, *Die kubanische Revolution und die Monroe-Doktrin: eine Herausforderung der Außenpolitik der Vereinigten Staaten* (Frankfurt a.M.: Alfred Metzner Verlag, 1968), pp. 5–6. Similarly see: Q. Wright, 'The Cuban Quarantine', A.J.I.L., 57 (1963), 552.

182 J. Baratt, 'The Real Monroe Doctrine', Trans. Grotius Soc., 14 (1928), 3 *et seq.* Single voices consider the acceptance of the LNC by Latin American states also as an acceptance of the Monroe Doctrine as 'American international law'. Yet this seems of little consequence after denying prior to this the very existence of that type of law. von Gottberg, 'Die Entwicklung amerikanischen Völkerrechts', p. 72.

183 In detail on the US-American considerations with regard to endangering the Monroe Doctrine by the LNC: S. Kennedy, 'The Monroe Doctrine Clause of the League of Nations Covenant', Graduate Studies, Texas Tech University, 20 (1979), in particular pp. 13–28.

184 L. Gross, 'The Charter of the United Nation and the Lodge Reservation', A.J.I.L., 41 (1947), 535.

185 Speech by Wilson to the US Senate on 22 January 1917, 'I am proposing as it were, that the nations should with one accord adopt the doctrine of President Monroe as doctrine of the World . . .' Quoted in: Hackworth, *Digest of International Law*, p. 442.

member states guarantee each other their territorial integrity, political independence and protection against 'external aggressions'. In doing so, US-American drafts did not at first mention the term 'Monroe Doctrine', but instead described the right of American states to defend, together or alone, their political integrity and independence.[186]

In response to French concerns that the limitations of Article 10 of the LNC were not comprehensive enough, the parties dispensed with such wording.[187] Article 21 of the LNC was added instead, the wording of which is identical to that of the reservation to Article 10 of the LNC[188] discussed above:

> Nothing in this Covenant shall be deemed to affect the validity of international engagements, such as treaties of arbitration or regional understandings like the Monroe doctrine, for securing the maintenance of peace.

This Monroe Doctrine clause in Article 21 of the LNC has been subject to intense scrutiny by scholars of international law, in particular by German scholars during the 1930s and 1940s.[189] What consequences the mention of the Monroe Doctrine may have had under international law has been discussed in connection with a number of problems. In these discussions two questions in particular were raised: if the legal nature of the doctrine had changed, did the doctrine become subject to objective interpretation because the United States had lost the authority to interpret the doctrine unilaterally?; and, second, how should the term 'regional understanding' be understood in connection with the Monroe Doctrine?

2.1.3.3.2.1 Possible change of the legal nature of the Monroe Doctrine due to its mention in Article 21 of the LNC It has been assumed by some that the Monroe Doctrine was elevated to a rule of international law by its being

186 W. Schücking and H. Wehberg, *Die Satzung des Völkerbundes*, 2nd edn. (Berlin: Franz Vahlen, 1924), pp. 670–1.

187 L.N.O.J., vol. I, p. 445.

188 D. Miller, *The Drafting of the Covenant* (New York: Putnam, 1928, reprint 1969), vol. I, pp. 425–7.

189 J. Spencer, 'The Monroe Doctrine and the League Covenant', A.J.I.L., 30 (1936), 400–13; A. Wegner, 'Die Monroedoktrin und ihre Anwendung im 20. Jahrhundert, insbesondere in ihren Beziehungen zur Panamerikanischen Bewegung und zum Schiedsgerichtsbarkeitsgedanke', Ph.D. thesis, Breslau, 1931; A. Kolbeck, *Völkerbund und Monroedoktrin* (Ebersberg: Buch- und Verlagsdruckerei Karl Schmidle, 1933), Ph.D. thesis, Würzburg, 1933; W. Reinhold, *Monroedoktrin und Völkerbundssatzung* (Emsdetten, Westfalen: Dissertationsdruckerei Heinr. & J. Lechte, 1937), Ph.D. thesis, Halle-Wittenberg, 1937; Weege, *Panamerikanismus und Monroedoktrin*.

mentioned in Article 21 of the LNC.[190] This opinion primarily emphasises the difference between the prior US-American practice of describing the Monroe Doctrine merely within a reservation and its inclusion within the text of a treaty.

This claim is met by stating that it becomes clear, when including the history of the creation of Article 21 of the LNC, that the parties to the treaty did not intend to establish the status of the doctrine as a rule of law.[191] As even a precise definition or just sufficient certainty of the Monroe Doctrine (or the principles contained within it) are lacking, this could not be considered to be an elevation to a principle of law.[192]

In the course of the negotiations on the LNC, US-American statements clearly showed that it was a central matter of concern for the United States not to be forced through the LNC to abandon the Monroe Doctrine.[193] However, President Wilson defined the Monroe Doctrine narrowly during the negotiations and assumed that it was limited to the protection of the territorial integrity and political independence of American states by the United States, and that therefore the doctrine did not contradict the principles of the LNC.[194]

On the other hand, statements made during the Senate's debate on the ratification of the LNC make it clear that it was of particular importance to the United States that the Monroe Doctrine was still subject to US-American authored interpretations only.[195] Specifically, the fifth of the Lodge Reservations – named after Senator Henry Cabot Lodge Sr. (Republican, Massachusetts) and after whom the Lodge Corollary to the Monroe Doctrine is also named – made in the debate on the Versailles Peace Treaty makes this clear.[196] This would have suggested the mention

190 Fauchille, *Traité de Droit International Public*, pp. 645–6; in continuation of the categorisation of the doctrine by Fenwick (see above, section 2.1.3.2.3) is sometimes assumed, the doctrine attained by being mentioned in Art. 21 of the LNC a 'quasi-legal' character. Lauterpacht, *Oppenheim's International Law*, p. 316.

191 Spencer, *The Monroe Doctrine and the League Covenant*, p. 406.

192 C. Tower, 'The Origin, Meaning and International Force of the Monroe Doctrine', A.J.I.L., 14 (1920), 24.

193 Miller, *The Drafting of the Covenant*, vol. I, pp. 382–4.

194 Miller, *The Drafting of the Covenant*, vol. I, p. 444.

195 Kennedy, 'The Monroe Doctrine Clause of the League of Nations Covenant', pp. 13 *et seq.*; L. Dunn and W. Kuehl, *Keeping the Covenant – American Internationalists and the League of Nations, 1920–1939* (Kent. OH: Kent State University Press, 1997), p. 45.

196 Cong. Rec., vol. 58, pp. 2541 *et seq.*; D. Fleming, *The United States and the League of Nations 1918–1920* (New York, Russell & Russell, 1968), pp. 424–6. For a summary of the debate in the Senate see: Kennedy, 'The Monroe Doctrine Clause of the League of Nations Covenant', pp. 29–49.

of the Monroe Doctrine within a reservation rather than as a treaty provision.

Yet the sole opinion, expressed only internally, of a state participating in the negotiations cannot be decisive for the interpretation of a multilateral treaty. Rather, the preparation of a treaty can serve only as a supplementary means of interpretation.[197] If the Monroe Doctrine had become a rule of law due to its being mentioned in Article 21 of the LNC, it would have become subject to authentic interpretation by the parties of the treaty. It is, however, disputed who was authorised to interpret the Monroe Doctrine after the coming into force of Article 21 of the LNC. This may serve as a suggestion in regard to the answer to the question of whether the Monroe Doctrine acquired the status of a rule of law due to its inclusion in the LNC.

2.1.3.3.2.2 Possible change of authority to interpret the Monroe Doctrine through its mention in Article 21 of the LNC It is questionable whether the authority to interpret the term 'Monroe Doctrine' under the LNC was no longer solely up to the United States, but extended to other states of the League of Nations or to organs of the League of Nations.

In spite of contradictory statements made by the United States concerning the legal nature of the Monroe Doctrine, it did reserve beyond any doubt the unilateral interpretation of the doctrine prior to the LNC. There are a broad variety of examples within US treaty practice reserving the unilateral authority of the United States to interpret the Monroe Doctrine as a unilateral declaration of principles: the Monroe Doctrine was part of disputes over international treaties, in particular the Hague Convention on the Peaceful Settlement of International Disputes.[198] Yet it was not initially mentioned explicitly and was only brought to attention in vaguely circumscribing words ('tradition of the United States in purely American matters'), leaving no doubt as to the sole authority of the United States to interpret the doctrine. Doubts about the possibility of the United States being the sole interpreter of the term 'Monroe Doctrine' are based on the difference in quality between its mention in a reservation and the text of the treaty itself. Consequences of this authority of interpretation for the legal obligations of the United States are also discussed.[199]

197 I. Brownlie, *Principles of International Law* (Oxford, Clarendon Press, 1998), pp. 633 *et seq.* with further sources.

198 See above, section 2.1.3.1.

199 Schücking and Wehberg, *Die Völkerbundssatzung*, p. 680; P. M. Brown, *The Monroe Doctrine and the League of Nations*, A.J.I.L., 14 (1920), 208.

While the Monroe Doctrine was not mentioned up to that point in the actual text of treaties, but only in reservations to treaties, in which it was not mentioned explicitly by way of descriptions of contained principles, it was, however, mentioned explicitly in Article 21 of the LNC in the text of a treaty. In principle, a provision positively included in the text of a treaty is subject to authentic interpretation. The consensus laid down in the treaty refers to the agreement positively concluded by the treaty.[200] With regard to a reservation there is a consensus between the parties concerning the content of the reservation.[201] However, it is the specific intention of the party declaring the reservation to exclude certain matters from the legal effects of the treaty.[202]

The US-American understanding of its sole authority to interpret the Monroe Doctrine did not change fundamentally after the coming into force of the LNC. The US reservation to the Briand–Kellogg Pact does not show a direct reference to the principles of the doctrine. However, it is considered a clause preserving the Monroe Doctrine,[203] just like the earlier reservations to the Hague Conventions on the Peaceful Settlement of Disputes.[204] A reservation to the Statute of the Permanent International Court of 1926 has exactly the same wording as the reservation declared before the coming into force of the LNC.[205] Numerous contemporary statements further highlight this US-American understanding, according to which the United States also possessed the sole authority to define what the Monroe Doctrine contained under the LNC.[206]

200 Brownlie, *Principles of International Law*, pp. 607–12.

201 A. Aust, *Modern Treaty Law and Practice* (Cambridge University Press, 2000), pp. 100 *et seq*.

202 R. Kühner, *Vorbehalte zu multilateralen Verträgen* (Berlin: Springer, 1986), pp. 12–15.

203 A. von Mandelsloh, 'Die Auslegung des Kelloggpaktes durch den amerikanischen Staatssekretär Stimson', ZaöRV/H.J.I.L., 3.1 (1932/33), 617–27; Schmitt, *Völkerrechtliche Großraumordnung*, p. 16.

204 A note of 23 June 1928 reads: 'There is nothing in the American draft of an anti-war treaty which restricts or impairs in any way the right of self-defense. That right is inherent in every sovereign state and is implicit in every treaty.' Quoted after: Brownlie, *International Law and the Use of Force by States*, p. 235. The United States made a similar reservation to the Saavedra–Lamas Pact, which outlaws in Art. 1 'wars of aggression' and extended the prohibition of war in the Briand–Kellogg Pact to Latin America (A.J.I.L., 28 (1934), 79 *et seq*.). The reservation to the Saavedra–Lamas Pact reads: 'In adhering to this treaty the United States does not thereby waive any rights it may have under other treaties, conventions or under international law' (A.J.I.L., 28 (1934), 84).

205 The reservation reads 'adherence to the said protocol and statute [shall not] be construed to imply a relinquishment by the United States of its traditional attitude toward purely American questions'. Hackworth, *Digest of International Law*, vol. V, p. 453.

206 A statement by Foreign Secretary Charles Evans Hughes on 30 August 1923 to the American Bar Association is mentioned as an example: 'As the policy embodied in the

The authority to authentically interpret the LNC has been attributed in principle to the Council and the Assembly of the League of Nations because of a lack of specific regulations in the covenant.[207] At first glance this contradicts the US-American claim to be sole authorised interpreter of the Monroe Doctrine. However, on 1 September 1928 the President of the League of Nations Council declared (in response to a request by Costa Rica), that an attempt at defining a 'regional understanding' (for which the Monroe Doctrine is mentioned as an example) by the organs of the League of Nations would bear the danger of extending the scope of such understandings. Yet this task would concern only the states having accepted *inter se* such understandings.[208]

Due to the general acceptance of the further existing possibility of unilateral interpretation of the doctrine by the United States, the doctrine cannot be considered as a rule of international law after the coming into force of the LNC.[209] The labelling of the doctrine as an 'international engagement' must hence be considered to be incorrect.[210] This contradicts the opinion that the term 'international engagements' refers only to the term 'treaties of arbitration', but not to the term 'regional understandings' separated by 'or'.[211] This becomes particularly clear in the French version, in which there is a comma between 'arbitrage' and 'et les entents régionales'.[212] Ultimately, however, there is consensus that the Monroe Doctrine does not represent such an 'international engagement'. Furthermore, it has been questioned if it had been correct to call the Monroe Doctrine in Article 21 of the LNC a 'regional understanding'.

Monroe doctrine is distinctively the policy of the United States, the Government of the United States reserves to itself its definition, interpretation and application.' C. Hughes, 'Observations on the Monroe Doctrine', A.J.I.L., 17 (1923), 616; Schatzschneider, *Die neue Phase der Monroedoktrin*, p. 10 with further evidence.

207 Schücking and Wehberg, *Die Völkerbundssatzung*, p. 566.

208 'Such a task was not one for the authors of the Covenant; it only concerns the states having accepted *inter se* engagements of this kind.' L.N.O.J., vol. IX, 1608.

209 C. Barcia Trelles, 'La Doctrine de Monroe dans son développement historique particulièrement en ce qui concerne les relations inter-américaines', RdC, 34 (1930-II), 527 *et seq.*

210 A. von Freytag-Loringhoven, 'Die Regionalverträge', *Schriften der Akademie für Deutsches Recht*, 4 (1937), 27–8; Dahm, *Völkerrecht*, vol. 2, p. 294.

211 J. Spencer, 'The Monroe Doctrine and the League Covenant', A.J.I.L., 30 (1936), 409.

212 The French version of the LNC alters the emphasis in comparison with the English version. In the English wording it is assumed that the Covenant does by no means affect the validity of certain obligations, whereas in the French text it is assumed that international obligations are not at odds with the Covenant. The French version is a translation of the English text. No difference in content has been attributed to this deviation. Schücking and Wehberg, *Die Völkerbundssatzung*, p. 672.

2.1.3.3.2.3 The Monroe Doctrine as a 'regional understanding' Latin American states particularly criticised the labelling of the Monroe Doctrine as a 'regional understanding'. Argentina[213] and Mexico made reservations in which they contested the nature of the Monroe Doctrine as such a regional understanding.[214]

The absurdity of considering the Monroe Doctrine, in its moulding through the Roosevelt Corollary, as a 'regional understanding' among American states becomes clear if one takes into account that (besides an agreement on the doctrine having never been reached) Latin American states would in this case have given the United States a right of intervention. Beyond any doubt there was never that general acceptance without any reservations.[215]

To what extent a rejection of the doctrine by American states is assumed depends once more on the content that one attributes to the term 'Monroe Doctrine', just as it did in connection with the case of multilateralisation. If the doctrine in total is differentiated from the principles contained in the doctrine it would be incorrect to talk of a complete rejection of the Monroe Doctrine by Latin American states. This is also expressed by the wording of the Argentinean reservation, in which the non-intervention principle as a political principle of the Monroe Doctrine is fully accepted. If a simultaneous recognition of the unilateral authority to interpret the doctrine is considered to be a criterion for the acceptance of the Monroe Doctrine, this is merely considered an 'own Monroe Doctrine' of the respective American state, but not as an acceptance of the Monroe Doctrine as interpreted by the United States.[216]

213 The Argentinean reservation reads: 'The Monroe Doctrine mentioned in the article is a political declaration of the United States. The policy expressed or enshrined in this declaration . . . when it was made . . . was by a fortunate coincidence of principles of very great service to us at the beginning of our existence. If would be untrue – it is, in fact – quite untrue – to give, as Article 21 gives, even by way of an example, the name of regional agreement to a unilateral political declaration, which has never, as far as I am aware, been explicitly approved by other American states.' Quoted after: Hackworth, *Digest of International Law*, vol. V, p. 444.

214 P. Brown, 'Mexico and the Monroe Doctrine', A.J.I.L., 26 (1932), 119–21 with further evidence.

215 Weege, *Panamerikanismus und Monroedoktrin*, pp. 84–5; Smith, *The Last Years of the Monroe Doctrine*, p. 31. In single provisions, however, such as in the Platt Amendment, codified in Art. 3 of the Cuban Constitution of 21 February 1901, far-reaching rights of intervention were granted to the United States. This provision was furthermore laid down in a treaty. Ahrens, *Der Karibische Raum als Interessensphäre der Vereinigten Staaten von Amerika*, pp. 76–7.

216 Kraus, *Die Monroedoktrin in ihren Beziehungen zur amerikanischen Diplomatie und zum Völkerrecht*, p. 366.

In order to preserve the labelling of the Monroe Doctrine as a 'regional understanding' the imprecise formulation of Article 21 of the LNC has been used by the United States in particular:[217] with regard to the meaning of the term 'regional understanding' it is already considered to be questionable if this refers to an agreement of certain states of a specific region or to an agreement between geographically distant states with regard to a certain region. As the latter interpretation is considered to be the only logical conclusion, recognition of the Monroe Doctrine by Latin American states is considered to be of no importance.[218] This is a position matching that taken in the Clark Memorandum.[219] Even though this interpretation has not been disputed explicitly, it becomes clear from the LNC negotiations and the fact that only Latin American states made reservations to Article 21 of the LNC, that a 'regional understanding' was understood as an agreement between the states of a region.[220]

According to customary law (in force at the time of the LNC),[221] which has been codified in Article 32 of the VCLT since 1969, the *traveaux préparatoires* play only a supplementary role in interpreting treaties. They may be drawn upon only if no definite result can be reached by using the primary methods of interpretation, or in order to confirm the result which was reached based on these methods.[222]

If one does not dismiss the thought that – based on the ordinary meaning rule according to which a clear wording needs no interpretation[223] – a 'regional understanding' might well be an agreement between geographically distant states, it becomes clear by looking at the statements on the creation of Article 21 of the LNC that the term 'regional understanding' refers to an agreement among states of a region. An amendment suggested by China in 1921 even went as far as to erase the term 'regional understanding' completely and instead to merely codify the reconcilability of the Monroe Doctrine with the LNC.[224]

217 G. Grafton Wilson, 'Regional Understandings', A.J.I.L., 27 (1933), 310–11.

218 Spencer, *The Monroe Doctrine and the League Covenant*, pp. 409–10; J. Whitton, 'La Doctrine de Monroe', R.G.D.I.P., VII (1933), 287–9.

219 See above, section 2.1.2.2; Clark, *Memorandum on the Monroe Doctrine*, pp. XIX–XX.

220 Miller, *The Drafting of the Covenant*, vol. I, pp. 442–51.

221 Whitton, 'La Doctrine de Monroe', R.G.D.I.P., 7 (1933), 208–9.

222 Brownlie, *Principles of Public International Law*, pp. 632–40.

223 ICJ, *Admission of a State to the United Nations (Charter, Art. 4)*, Advisory Opinion: I.C.J. Rep., 1950, p. 8. On this in general see: Brownlie, *Principles of Public International Law*, p. 634 with further sources.

224 On the proposed changes of Art. 21 of the LNC see: Walter, *Vereinte Nationen und Regionalorganisationen*, pp. 15–16.

2.1.3.3.2.4 The reconcilability of the Monroe Doctrine as political principle with the LNC Apart from the question of whether it was apt to classify the Monroe Doctrine as a 'regional understanding', another question arises if inclusion of the Monroe Doctrine in Article 21 of the LNC meant that the League of Nations was entitled to take action only outside the western hemisphere.[225] After the previous conclusion that the mention of the doctrine in Article 21 of the LNC at least did not alter the legal nature of the doctrine nor the sole authority of the United States to interpret the doctrine, another question arises: namely, to what degree the principles attributed to the Monroe Doctrine during the interwar period were reconcilable with the LNC. With regard to the regulations concerning the legality of the use of force, the question of reconcilability of the doctrine with the guarantee of territorial integrity and political independence as laid down in Articles 10 and 11 is of particular interest. Article 11 foresaw an intervention by the League of Nations in the case of war and the threat of war. Also of particular interest is the reconcilability with the obligation of peaceful settlement of disputes contained in Article 13.

However, due to the fact that the United States never became a member of the League of Nations this matter possibly concerned only necessary adjustments of the Monroe Doctrine which might have had to be made in the case of a possible accession.[226] A limited competence of the League of Nations to take action in certain cases was, however, assumed irrespective of the accession of the United States due to Article 21 of the LNC.[227]

Once more, a clear-cut response to these two questions is complicated by the lack of terminological clarity of the term 'Monroe Doctrine'. With regard to this matter Brown came to the very apt conclusion that the reconcilability of the doctrine with the LNC depended on the content attributed to the doctrine; in doing so implying the possibility of an interpretation of the doctrine in a way that was in accordance with the LNC. At least he considered the interpretation of the doctrine advocated by President Wilson as not being contradictory to the principles of the

225 See: E. Fraenkel, 'Regionalpakte und Weltfriedensordnung', *Vierteljahreshefte für Zeitgeschichte*, 2 (1954) 43–4.

226 Kolbeck, *Völkerbund und Monroedoktrin*, in particular pp. 69–71.

227 Schmitt, *Völkerrechtliche Großraumordnung*, p. 17; Whitton, 'La Doctrine de Monroe', R.G.D.I.P., 7 (1933), 29. However, the rule of Art. 21 of the LNC did not prevent the League of Nations from taking action in cases of inter-American conflicts; for example, in 1933 between Colombia and Peru and 1934 between Bolivia and Paraguay. Hackworth, *Digest of International Law*, vol. V, pp. 455 *et seq.*; vol. VI, pp. 50 *et seq.*

LNC.[228] Yet to attribute content to the doctrine in accordance with the covenant is partly considered to be a mere fiction, attributing content quite different from that actually attributed to the doctrine by the United States at that point in time.[229] The specific mention of the Monroe Doctrine in Article 21 of the LNC has been considered as evidence for content then attributed to the Monroe Doctrine going beyond the mere inter-American guarantee of the principles of Article 10 of the LNC, because otherwise a separate mention in Article 21 of the LNC would be purely declarative.[230] Consequently, an irreconcilability of the inclusion of the Monroe Doctrine, including the Roosevelt Corollary, with the LNC is assumed.[231] Yet a categorisation of that type neglects the possible consequences of including the doctrine in Article 21 on the legal obligations of the United States through the LNC. Even though the Monroe Doctrine was not elevated by its inclusion to the status of a rule of law, this can be seen as recognition of the legitimacy of this principle of American policy.[232] When adhering to such an interpretation, this implies that the other members of the League of Nations could no longer decide, based on purely political considerations, whether they would respect its principles in cases where the Monroe Doctrine was considered to be affected but that they were bound by law to comply with its principles.[233] In connection with the US authority to interpret the Monroe Doctrine, for the United States this meant the ability to define its own legal obligations under the LNC, as well as in cases of accession.[234] Carl Schmitt, who considered Article 21 of the LNC to be a prohibition on the other member states to intervene in American affairs, adhered to this view.[235]

228 Brown, 'The Monroe Doctrine and the League of Nations Covenant', pp. 207–10. Similarly, with regard to the interpretation, Wilsons: Schücking and Wehberg, *Die Völkerbundssatzung*, pp. 678–9; Whitton, 'La Doctrine de Monroe', pp. 274–5.

229 Kolbeck, *Völkerbund und Monroedoktrin*, p. 13; Reinhold calls the interpretation of Wilson a 'pseudo-Monroe Doctrine' ('Pseudo-Monroedoktrin') in contrast to 'the real Monroe Doctrine' ('echten Monroedoktrin'). Reinhold, *Monroedoktrin und Völkerbundssatzung*, pp. 27–9.

230 Weege, *Panamerikanismus und Monroedoktrin*, p. 89.

231 Reinhold, *Monroedoktrin und Völkerbundssatzung*, p. 11.

232 Dahm, *Völkerrecht*, vol. 2, p. 294.

233 C. Elliott, 'The Monroe Doctrine Exception in the League of Nations Covenant', I.L.A.Rep., 30 (1921), 74 *et seq.*; Fauchille, *Traité de droit international public*, p. 647; Fraenkel, 'Regionalpakte und Weltfriedensordnung', *Vierteljahreshefte für Zeitgeschichte*, 2 (1954), 42–7; Kutzner, *Die Organisation Amerikanischer Staaten*, p. 48.

234 Hyde, *International Law – Chiefly as Interpreted and Applied by the United States*, vol. I, pp. 314–15; Schücking and Wehberg, *Die Satzung des Völkerbundes*, p. 679; O. Göppert, *Der Völkerbund* (Stuttgart: Kohlhammer, 1938), pp. 58–60 at 314.

235 Schmitt, *Völkerrechtliche Großraumordnung*, pp. 16–17.

Hence, even in case of an accession to the League of Nations, the United States would have been free of the limitations contained in Articles 10, 11 and 12 of the LNC in case these limitations had – according to the sole opinion of the United States – contradicted the Monroe Doctrine.[236] Furthermore, Article 21 of the LNC also resulted in a limitation of the rights of the other member states to take action in America as a consequence of the 'subsidiary validity of the League of Nations Covenant in America' in relation to the Monroe Doctrine.[237]

Just as the retention of the Monroe Doctrine was a primary concern of the United States during the negotiation of the LNC, it was a primary concern during the negotiations of the UN Charter.

2.1.3.4 The Monroe Doctrine and the UN Charter

During the founding conference of the United Nations in San Francisco in 1945, efforts to maintain the Monroe Doctrine made up a considerable part of the work of the US-American delegation and the negotiations in Committee III/4.[238] This matter of concern became particularly clear in a proposed formulation for the right of self-defence in the UN Charter by a member of the US-American delegation, Harold E. Stassen:

> 1. Nothing in this Charter shall be construed as abrogating the inherent right of self-defense against a violator of the Charter.
> 2. In the application of this provision the principles of the Act of Chapultepec and of the Monroe Doctrine are specifically recognized.
> 3. It is also clear that all regions are fully entitled to use all peaceful means of settling disputes without permission of the Security Council.[239]

The question which springs up under the UN Charter is whether a threat or use of force in case of actions by other states in the western

236 Kolbeck, *Völkerbund und Monroedoktrin*, pp. 69–71.

237 Author's translation of: 'subsidiäre[n] Geltung der Völkerbundssatzung in Amerika'; A. Kolbeck, *Völkerbund und Monroedoktrin*, pp. 33–40. In practice, the League of Nations took action with regard to Latin American conflicts in spite of Art. 21 of the LNC, that is, in the Chaco Dispute 1932–5 between Bolivia and Paraguay (on this see: L. Woolsey, 'The Chaco Dispute', A.J.I.L., 28 (1934), 724–9) and in the Leticia Dispute of 1932 between Columbia and Peru (on this see: L. Woolsey, 'Leticia Dispute between Columbia and Peru', A.J.I.L., 27 (1933), 317–24). Action by the League of Nations in these cases did not meet any protest by the United States. Yet no use of force by non-American states was involved. P. Jessup, 'The Generalization of the Monroe Doctrine', A.J.I.L., 29 (1935), 109.

238 *Foreign Relations of the United States, 1945*, vol. I, pp. 301–7, 426 *et seq.*, 589–98, 612 *et seq.*; UNCIO, vol. XII, pp. 690–2, 838–9.

239 *Foreign Relations of the United States, 1945*, vol. I, pp. 659–60.

hemisphere, as foreseen in the Monroe Doctrine, is in accordance with the general prohibition on the use of force in Article 2(4) of the UN Charter. At least, it has been questioned if Article 51 of the UN Charter constitutes a sufficient basis to maintain the traditional political principles of the Monroe Doctrine.[240] Article 51 of the UN Charter justifies the use of force only in cases of self-defence and, in principle, only as reaction to an armed attack.[241] Thus, in principle, there is no room for the use of force in self-defence in reaction to actions of non-American states not constituting an armed attack.

Similarly, the question of the possibility of maintaining the Monroe Doctrine had already come up in connection with the prohibition of war in the Briand–Kellogg Pact.[242] However, the term 'self-defence' was interpreted in such a broad and unspecified way in connection with the Briand–Kellogg Pact that the Monroe Doctrine was considered to fit easily under it.[243] Furthermore, the determination and definition of a situation of self-defence was left at that time to the single states which were parties to the treaty.[244] Also, the Briand–Kellogg Pact did not contain the requirement of an armed attack for an act of self-defence. The original principle of limitation of political freedom of action of non-American states in America did not, however, just prohibit action by forces alien to the hemisphere which constituted an armed attack, but beyond that also activities considered by the United States to be a threat.[245]

240 J. Kunz, 'Individual and Collective Self-Defense in Article 51 of the Charter of the United Nations', A.J.I.L., 41 (1947), 877; L. Goodrich and E. Hambro, *The Charter of the United Nations* 2nd edn. (London: Stevenson & Sons, 1948), pp. 302–3, who call Art. 51 of the UN Charter a 'Safeguard of the Monroe Doctrine'.

241 On the question of whether an armed attack is required and the matter of anticipated self-defense see: Brownlie, *International Law and the Use of Force by States*, pp. 275 *et seq.*; Y. Dinstein, *War, Aggression and Self-Defence*, 4th edn. (Cambridge University Press, 2004), pp. 165 *et seq.*; M. O'Connell, 'The Myth of Preemptive Self-Defense', ASIL Task Force Papers, Washington, 2002. On this see below, Chapter 4, section 4.2.2.

242 B. Roscher, *Der Briand–Kellog-Pakt von 1928* (Baden-Baden: Nomos, 2004), Ph.D. thesis, Hamburg, 2004, pp. 88–92.

243 D. Miller, *The Peace Pact of Paris* (New York: Putnam, 1928), pp. 86, 123; the Senate Foreign Relations Committee declared on 14 January 1929 that the right of self-defence, as it is recognised in the pact, must also contain a right to maintain the Monroe Doctrine. P. Jessup, *International Security – The American Role in Collective Action for Peace* (New York: Council on Foreign Relations, 1935), p. 40.

244 On this see further below, section 2.2.3.2.

245 Kraus, *Die Monroedoktrin in ihren Beziehungen zur amerikanischen Diplomatie und zum Völkerrecht*, p. 82; H. Kelsen, *The Law of the United Nations* (London: Stevens & Sons, 1950), p. 798.

This is the foundation of the obvious tension between the UN Charter and Monroe Doctrine. Once more, the response to the question of reconcilability of the Monroe Doctrine with the UN Charter depends on the content one attributes to the Monroe Doctrine after the coming into force of the UN Charter. Statements by John Foster Dulles, the then legal adviser to the American delegation to the founding conference in San Francisco, before the Senate Committee on Foreign Relations on 13 July 1945 are illuminating with regard to this problem. Asked about the relationship between Monroe Doctrine and UN Charter, Dulles declared:

> The Monroe Doctrine is a Doctrine originally enunciated and pursued as a Doctrine of national self-defense[246] . . . Now, there is nothing whatever in the Charter which impairs a nation's right of self defense . . . So it is my view – and I so expressed it to the United States Delegation – that there is nothing whatsoever in this charter that impairs the Monroe Doctrine as a doctrine of self-defense.[247]

The interpretation of the Monroe Doctrine on which Dulles' statement is based represents a limitation of the Monroe Doctrine not just with regard to the principles of Monroe's speech, but also with regard to the later understanding of the Monroe Doctrine. This interpretation by Dulles of the Monroe Doctrine particularly did not include the principle of limitation of freedom of action of non-American states in America, and did not contain a prohibition on the creation of a 'non-American system' in America. This interpretation reduces the doctrine to its core of defending the United States, as a principle allowing the use of force only in the case of self-defence. In the case of such a narrow interpretation of the Monroe Doctrine in accordance with the UN Charter as undertaken by Dulles little

246 Whiteman, *Digest of International Law*, vol. XII, p. 84; Secretary of State Cordell Hull interpreted the Monroe Doctrine at an earlier point of time in a similarly narrow way. A press statement of the State Department on 5 July 1940 reads: 'The Monroe Doctrine is solely a policy of self-defense, which is intended to preserve the independence and integrity of the Americas . . .', Hackworth, *Digest of International Law*, vol. V, p. 458.

247 Whiteman, *Digest of International Law*, vol. V, p. 977. In response to Senator Millkins question: 'So that there is nothing either in the Act of Chapultepec or in this Charter that impairs the Monroe Doctrine if we should ever have occasion to use it, or put it in another way, if these regional multilateral arrangements should fail or if the Security Council should fail, we have not abandoned the Monroe Doctrine, and it stands there as, I might call it, as a club behind the door, as something that we can use in self-defense if we have to use it, is that correct?' Dulles replied: 'That is correct.': Whiteman, *Digest of International Law*, vol. V, pp. 977–8.

doubt exists about its reconcilability with the charter, just as little doubt existed with regard to the reconcilability of Wilson's interpretation of the Monroe Doctrine with the LNC.[248] Later US-American interpretations of the Monroe Doctrine, however, were only partially limited to a reduction of the Monroe Doctrine as matching with the right of self-defence according to Article 51 of the UN Charter, like Dulles,[249] whereas in other statements the Monroe Doctrine was just as narrowly interpreted.[250]

The degree to which the Monroe Doctrine can be reconciled with the right of self-defence under Article 51 of the UN Charter depends on the interpretation of this Article. The related question of whether the interpretation of Article 51 of the UN Charter leaves room for anticipated self-defence is of particular importance in this context.[251]

A resolution of the 10th Inter-American Conference in Caracas in 1952 is considered to be an interpretation of the Monroe Doctrine – though in its multilateralised form – foreseeing the use of force in cases in which no armed attack occurred.[252] This resolution, titled 'Declaration on Solidarity for the Preservation of Political Integrity of American States against Communist Intervention' reads:

> the domination or control of the political institutions of any American state by international communist movement, extending to this hemisphere the political system of an extracontinental power, would constitute a threat to the sovereignty and political independence of the American states, endangering the peace of America . . .[253]

This has been considered a corollary to the Monroe Doctrine as a political declaration of principles of the same quality as the Roosevelt Corollary, because according to this declaration an intervention in American states is foreseen in certain cases ('domination or control . . . by international

248 Senator Tom Connally, then the Chairman of the Senate Committee on Foreign Relations, displayed probably a similar understanding of the Monroe Doctrine, when assuming that the Monroe Doctrine in its entirety continued to exist under the UN Charter. Senator Milliken, however, expressed that the Monroe Doctrine went beyond self-defence in case of an aggression. Gross, 'The Charter of the United Nation and the Lodge Reservations', p. 536.

249 For example, Reagan, *An American Life*, pp. 471–4.

250 For example, *Department of State Bulletin*, 43 (1960), 170–1.

251 On this in detail see: M. O'Connell, 'The Myth of Preemptive Self-Defense', ASIL Task Force Papers, Washington, 2002.

252 A. J. Thomas and A. V. Thomas, 'The Organization of American States and the Monroe Doctrine – Legal Implications', LA.L.Rev., 30 (1970), 580–1; Schatzschneider, *Die neue Phase der Monroedoktrin*, pp. 54–6.

253 Printed in Schatzschneider, *Die neue Phase der Monroedoktrin*, pp. 52–3.

communist movement').[254] In 1952 Dulles considered it a confirmation of the Monroe Doctrine in its multilateralised form.[255] This thought was also adopted in the so-called (second) Johnson Doctrine, and is discussed more closely in this context.[256] Yet even when interpreting the Monroe Doctrine as narrowly as Dulles did in his declaration of 1945, the question arises as to whether the United States continued to have the ultimate authority to decide about the legality of the use of force in terms of the doctrine as was the case prior to Article 21 of the LNC.[257]

Even though it is disputed if the authority to judge the legality of the use of force in self-defence can be solely exercised by the Security Council, or beyond that by the International Court of Justice (ICJ), it is at least recognised that the categorisation of an action as an act of self-defence is subject to scrutiny.[258] In the *Nicaragua* case the United States also adhered to the opinion that it is up to the organs foreseen by the UN Charter to determine the legality of a claimed act of self-defence.[259] Different from the relation between the Monroe Doctrine and the LNC, which was limited in Article 21 by the doctrine, the doctrine is hence limited by the regulations of Articles 2(4) and 51 of the UN Charter to the extent that it is no longer solely up to the United States to determine when an action in terms of the doctrine is justified.[260]

However, Dulles assumed that beyond that the Monroe Doctrine had been extended by the preceding Act of Chapultepec:[261]

> The Monroe Doctrine has to an extent been enlarged or is in process of enlargement as a result of the Mexico Conference and the declaration of Chapultepec, where the doctrine of self-defense was enlarged to include the doctrine of collective self-defense and where the view was taken that an attack upon any of the republics of this hemisphere was an attack upon all.[262]

254 D. Carto, 'The Monroe Doctrine in the 1980s: International Law, Unilateral Policy, or Atavistic Anachronism?', Cas.W.Res.J.I.L., 13 (1981), 214.
255 P. Malaczuk, 'Monroe Doctrine', E.P.I.L., III (1997), 462.
256 See below, Chapter 3, section 3.3. 257 See below, section 2.1.3.3.2.4.
258 See Dinstein, *War Aggression and Self-Defence*, pp. 185–7.
259 *Military and Paramilitary Activities in and against Nicaragua* (*Nicaragua* v. *United States of America*), Jurisdiction and Admissibility, Judgment, I.C.J. Rep. 1984, p. 436, No. 99.
260 Schatzschneider, *Die neue Phase der Monroedoktrin*, pp. 23–4.
261 Act of Chapultepec, A.J.I.L., 39 (1945), 108 *et seq.*
262 Whiteman, *Digest of International Law*, vol. XII, p. 84.

In connection with the Inter-American system of collective security, the Monroe Doctrine is partially regarded as 'multilateralised'.[263] Whereas Latin American states protested during the negotiation of the LNC against an inclusion of the Monroe Doctrine, they were eager to maintain prior arrangements which may be considered as a multilateralisation of the Monroe Doctrine like the Act of Chapultepec of 3 March 1945 under the Charter.[264] In Dulles' opinion, this desire had been satisfied:

> At San Francisco, one of the things we stood for most stoutly, and which we achieved with the greatest difficulty, was a recognition of the fact that the doctrine of self-defense, enlarged at Chapultepec to be a doctrine of collective self-defense, could stand unimpaired and could function without the approval of the Security Council.[265]

Asked by Senator Austin if the conditions of regional arrangements (like the Act of Chapultepec) would not experience changes through the UN Charter, Dulles replied:

> It changed in one respect only, Senator Austin: Without the Security Council and the new world organization we could have had in this hemisphere a regional organization which was wholly autonomous and which could act on its own initiative to maintain peace in this hemisphere without reference or regard whatsoever to any world organization. As it results from the Charter at San Francisco, the world security organization is given the first opportunity to maintain peace everywhere, using presumably regional organizations which it is invited to do but not absolutely compelled to.[266]

The possibility of the United States relying on these regional arrangements follows as a logical consequence from this, due to the veto in the Security Council attributed to them in Article 27(3) of the UN Charter as the continuation of Dulles' statement makes clear:

> If however the Security Council fails to maintain peace and despite the existence of the Security Council there is an armed outbreak, then the regional organization moves in without regard to the Security Council.[267]

263 See below, sections 2.1.2.3 and 2.1.3.3.1.
264 Fenwick, *The Organization of American States*, pp. 229–31.
265 Whiteman, *Digest of International Law*, vol. XII, p. 85. 266 Whiteman, *ibid.*
267 Whiteman, *ibid.*.

The right of veto for the United States in the Security Council was considered at that time to be an essential prerequisite for the continued existence of the Monroe Doctrine under the UN Charter.[268] Yet in case of a blockade of the Security Council by the US veto, the requirement of an 'armed attack' continues to be a prerequisite for the use of force in self-defence by regional organisations.[269]

2.1.3.5 The Monroe Doctrine and the inter-American system

It is questionable which particular regional agreements enshrine a common responsibility for the principles of the Monroe Doctrine. It is also questionable if these agreements considered partially as a 'multilateralised' doctrine can be reconciled with the UN Charter.

If one distinguishes between the classical Monroe Doctrine and the single principles expressed in the Monroe Doctrine, like Krakau does,[270] it is possible to speak of a legalisation of the Monroe Doctrine without discussing the question of multilateralisation.[271] The matter of interest with regard to the use of force in this context is: to what degree have the non-intervention principle (since the declaration of the Polk Corollary in 1845 reinforced by a possible use of force) and the prohibitions on non-American states becoming active in America and on extending the political system of non-American states become rules in international law?

Several regulations of the inter-American system foresee a general responsibility for the defence of America. According to Article 3 of the Inter-American Treaty of Reciprocal Assistance of 2 September 1947, commonly known as the Rio Pact, an attack on one of the state parties is considered to be an attack on all American states. All state parties shall react to such an attack by exercising their right of self-defence according to the UN Charter. A predecessor of this regulation was Article 5.I. of the Act of Chapultepec.[272]

268 Senator Vandenberg is quoted in this respect with the following statement: 'We have preserved the Monroe Doctrine and the Inter-American system . . . We have retained a complete veto – exclusive in our hands – over any decisions involving external activities.' Quoted in Smith, *The Last Years of the Monroe Doctrine*, p. 55.

269 F. Morrison, 'The Role of Regional Organizations in the Enforcement of International Law', in J. Delbrück (ed.), *Allocation of Law Enforcement Authority in the International System* (Berlin: Duncker & Humblot, 1997), pp. 39–56, in particular pp. 54–6.

270 See below, section 2.1.3.3.1, in particular fn. 177.

271 See below, section 2.1.3.3.

272 Act of Chapultepec, A.J.I.L., 39 (1945), Suppl., p. 109. Furthermore, this rule matches the Brum Doctrine, named after the Uruguayan President, Balthasar Brum, which contains his repeated suggestion that all American states should help each other in case of an

This rule applies irrespective of whether an attack emerges from a non-American state or an American state, which deviates from the content commonly attributed to the Monroe Doctrine for the better part of its existence. Only in its moulding through the Roosevelt Corollary did the Monroe Doctrine also contain a threat of force against other American states, whereas the original message of Monroe addressed only non-American states.[273] Furthermore, the United States also considers the threat contained in Article 3 of the Rio Pact a threat against themselves. This is considered by some as a separate corollary.[274]

Article 6 of the Rio Pact furthermore foresees that in case of a threat to peace such as (not specifically defined) 'aggression which is not an armed attack', an organ of consultation shall meet in order to take measures for the maintenance of peace and security. According to Article 8 of the Rio Pact the use of force is among the measures which this organ of consultation can take in these cases. The OAS Charter of 30 April 1948 repeats the regulation of Article 3 of the Rio Pact in Article 24, and summarises in Article 25 the regulations of Articles 3, 6 and 8 of the Rio Pact:[275]

> If the inviolability or the integrity of the territorial integrity of the territory or the sovereignty or political independence of any American State should be affected by an armed attack or by an act of aggression that is not an armed attack, or by an extra-continental conflict, or by a conflict between two or more American States, or by any other fact or situation that might endanger the peace of America, the American States, in furtherance of the principles of continental solidarity or collective self-defense, shall apply the measures and procedures established in the special treaties on the subject.

Yet it is disputed if this inter-American regulation can be reconciled with the regulations for the legality of the use of force contained in the UN Charter.[276]

2.1.3.6 Normative conflict between the UN Charter and the inter-American system as a multilateralised Monroe Doctrine

The question of the reconcilability of the regulation of Article 6 in connection with Article 8 of the Rio Pact and Article 25 of the OAS Charter

extra-American threat. K. Krakau, 'Lateinamerikanische Doktrinen zur Realisierung staatlicher Unabhängigkeit und Integrität', VRÜ, 8 (1975), 142.

273 Clark, *Memorandum on the Monroe Doctrine*, p. 186.

274 Thomas and Thomas, *The Organization of American States*, pp. 356–7.

275 UNTS, vol. 119, 1952, pp. 3 *et seq.*

276 L. Caflisch, 'Monroe-Doktrin', in I. Seidl-Hohenveldern (ed.), *LdR/VR*, 3rd edn. (Neuwied: Luchterhand, 2001), pp. 285–7.

with Articles 51 and 53 of the UN Charter arises in detail. Judged only by its wording, Article 8 of the Rio Pact opens up the opportunity of reacting to an aggression which is not an armed attack by using force. However, the use of force is only the last in a set of measures foreseen in Article 8 of the Rio Pact. In consideration of the provisions of Article 10 of the Rio Pact and Article 103 of the UN Charter, however (which lay down a precedence of the UN Charter), Article 8 of the Rio Pact can be interpreted to the effect that it allows the use of force only in cases of aggression also constituting an armed attack as foreseen in Article 51 of the UN Charter.[277]

With regard to Article 25 of the OAS Charter it has been argued that this Article is irreconcilable with the UN Charter, as Article 25 of the OAS Charter foresees collective sanctions not only in the case of an armed attack but also in case of political aggressions.[278] Yet action 'in furtherance of the principles of continental solidarity or collective defence' as foreseen in Article 25 of the OAS Charter can also merely refer to cases in which an armed attack occurs. The norms of Article 102 of the OAS Charter and Article 103 of the UN Charter suggest this interpretation.[279] Hence, possible conflicts between Article 6 in connection with Article 8 of the Rio Pact, Article 25 of the OAS Charter and the UN Charter can be resolved by interpreting these Articles as being in accordance with the UN Charter.[280] At least the United States considers the regulations of the Rio Pact as smoothly reconcilable with the UN Charter.[281] In view of the commandment of Article 102 of the OAS Charter to interpret that charter as not impairing the rights and obligations of the member states under the Charter of the United Nations, no changes as to the legality of the use of force result from these regulations in any way. This applies even if one adheres to the opinion that the general prohibition of intervention

277 Schatzschneider, *Die neue Phase der Monroedoktrin*, p. 71; Kutzner, *Die Organisation Amerikanischer Staaten*, p. 193.

278 Schatzschneider, *Die neue Phase der Monroedoktrin*, pp. 70–1.

279 J. Housten, *Latin America in the United Nations* (Westport, CT: Greenwood Press, 1956, reprint 1978), p. 50; Kutzner, *Die Organisation Amerikanischer Staaten*, p. 193, in particular fn. 171.

280 K. Grommes, 'Der Verteidigungsfall im interamerikanischen Bündnissysstem und nach der Satzung der Vereinten Nationen', Ph.D. thesis, Cologne, 1966, p. 133; Kutzner, *Die Organisation Amerikanischer Staaten*, p. 192.

281 M. Ball, 'Recent Developments in Inter American Relations', Y.B.World Aff., 3 (1949), 105–31, in particular pp. 112–17. See also: Fenwick, *The Organization of American States*, pp. 521–2.

of Article 2(1) of the UN Charter may be broader than the prohibition of intervention stated in Article 15 of the OAS Charter.[282]

Furthermore, it is questionable whether the regulations of Article 6 of the Rio Pact in connection with Article 8 of the Rio Pact and Article 25 of the OAS Charter can be reconciled with Article 53 of the UN Charter. According to Article 53 of the UN Charter, enforcement actions based on regional arrangements or coming within their authority require the authorisation of the Security Council. Depending on whether one prefers the possible role of regional organisations to be as large as possible or as small as possible, the term 'enforcement action' is interpreted either narrowly or broadly.[283] If one adheres to a broad interpretation and includes the use of force by regional organisations as one of these measures, the question arises as to what requirements exactly apply for that type of action by regional organisations.

It has been argued by the United States in connection with the blockade of Cuba, which was based on a resolution under Article 8 in connection with Article 6 of the Rio Pact of the consultative body of the OAS of 23 October 1962,[284] that the recommendation of a regional organisation to use force does not constitute an enforcement measure in terms of Article 53(1) of the UN Charter.[285]

Even when admitting that there is a difference in quality between a recommendation and an authorisation (the respective OAS resolutions used the term 'recommends'), this recommendation could, however, constitute an illegal act against the UN Charter. This questions the nature of the requirement and of the authorisation of the Security Council, required by Article 53(1) of the UN Charter for actions by a regional organisation.

The United States also argued in connection with the Cuban Missile Crisis of 1962 that a subsequent acknowledgement by the Security Council

282 *Military and Paramilitary Activities in and against Nicaragua* (*Nicaragua* v. *United States of America*), Merits, Judgment, I.C.J. Rep. 1986, p. 295, No. 98. On the sources of the prohibition of intervention: Neuhold, *Internationale Konflikte – verbotene und erlaubte Mittel ihrer Austragung*, pp. 55 *et seq.*

283 G. Ress and J. Bröhmer, 'Art. 53', in B. Simma (ed.), *The Charter of the United Nations* (Oxford University Press, 2002), pp. 860–1, Nos. 3–7: Kutzner, *Die Organisation Amerikanischer Staaten*, pp. 190–1; H. Koos, 'Völkerrechtliche Würdigung der Blockademaßnahmen der USA gegen Kuba', Ph.D. thesis, Würzburg, 1967, pp. 85–98. In detail on this see: Walter, *Vereinte Nationen und Regionalorganisationen*, pp. 170 *et seq.*

284 *Department. of State Bulletin*, vol. 47 (1962), 598–600.

285 L. Meeker, 'Defensive Quarantine and the Law', A.J.I.L., 57 (1963), 522.

without explicit disapproval would suffice as an authorisation of that kind.[286] 'Authorisation of the Security Council' as mentioned in Article 53 of the UN Charter at least shall not necessarily mean a 'prior authorisation' nor 'express authorisation'.[287] In the final analysis this interpretation of Article 53 of the UN Charter gave the OAS the opportunity to use force based on its own initiative in cases going beyond Article 51 of the UN Charter. The dangers lying in this approach have been rightly pointed out.[288] Yet this interpretation of Article 53 of the UN Charter is considered by some as maintainable.[289]

When using this line of argument there is room for a multilateralised Monroe Doctrine going beyond the interpretation of the doctrine in accordance with the UN Charter as promoted by John Foster Dulles. At least this construct opens up the opportunity of creatively circumnavigating the limitations of the UN Charter for the use of force in the western hemisphere. Yet it is uncertain to which geographic area the Monroe Doctrine exactly applies.

2.1.4 Geographical extent of the Monroe Doctrine

Just as the interpretation of the Monroe Doctrine regarding content has experienced changes, so has the area to which its principles were applied. Several attempts had already been made at defining the geographical extent of the Monroe Doctrine more closely. The original doctrine as stated in James Monroe's speech does not make a particular statement about the geographical extent of the principles laid down in the speech. It mentions only generally 'the Americas' and 'this hemisphere'.[290] The subsequent unilateral declarations do not show any precision, but restrain

286 A. Chayes, 'Law and the Quarantine of Cuba', For.Aff., 40 (1963), 556.

287 Meeker, 'Defensive Quarantine and the Law', 520, with reference to the Soviet request of 8 September 1960 to recognise the measures of the OAS against the Dominican Republic after the event. UNSC/OR, 893rd Meeting, pp. 2 *et seq.*, 522. In detail on the interpretation of the authorisation according to Art. 53 of the UN Charter see: Walter, *Vereinte Nationen und Regionalorganisationen*, pp. 289–319; Arend and Beck use for this stream of argument the term '*not-unauthorized* enforcement action'. Arend and Beck, *International Law and the Use of Force*, p. 62.

288 M. Akehurst, 'Enforcement Action by Regional Agencies with Special Reference to the Organization of American States', B.Y.I.L., 42 (1967), 214; Kutzner, *Die Organisation Amerikanischer Staaten*, p. 191; Koos, *Völkerrechtliche Würdigung der Blockademaßnahmen der USA gegen Kuba*, pp. 94–7, 138–9.

289 Walter, *Vereinte Nationen und Regionalorganisationen*, pp. 293–5.

290 Moore, *A Digest of International Law*, vol. VI, pp. 402–3, § 936.

themselves to a use of these general terms. To what degree later variations of the principles of the doctrine could be interpreted as limiting it to areas on the American continent and in the Caribbean has been seen as inconsistent.[291]

On the part of the United States, attempts were made to reach a more precise determination of the area of application of the Monroe Doctrine as contained in the term 'western hemisphere'.[292] During the course of the Second World War the inclusion of Canada and Greenland was particularly problematic. In doing so, the application of the Monroe Doctrine as a political principle – narrowly understood as a doctrine of self-defence – to this territory was accepted at least partially by other states. In a declaration by President Franklin D. Roosevelt of 18 August 1938 that the United States would not stand idly by if domination of Canadian territory was threatened by another state, an extension of the Monroe Doctrine to Canada was assumed.[293]

To what degree the principles of the Monroe Doctrine, the non-intervention principle in particular, can be related to Canada had already been disputed prior to that statement.[294] Yet this merely constituted the declaration of an already existing political principle, which – no matter if declared separately or in the context of the Monroe Doctrine – did not mean any deviation from the prior US-American policy. However, at the time of its declaration this action was of special political delicacy.[295]

Secretary of State Cordell Hull declared in April 1941 in connection with a debate in the US Congress on the construction of military bases on Greenland, that Greenland was within the area of application of the Monroe Doctrine. Denmark accepted this statement.[296] An internal paper of the US State Department, dated 1947, furthermore suggested making

291 See Kraus, *Die Monroedoktrin in ihren Beziehungen zur amerikanischen Diplomatie und zum Völkerrecht*, pp. 323 *et seq.*

292 On this see: P. Jessup, 'The Monroe Doctrine in 1940', A.J.I.L., 34 (1940), 704–11.

293 Scheuner, *Der Gedanke der Sicherheit Amerikas auf den Konferenzen von Panama und Habana und die Monroedoktrin*, pp. 282–3.

294 The declaration of Franklin D. Roosevelt reads: 'The People of the United States will not stand idly by if domination of Canadian soil is threatened by another Empire.' C. Fenwick, 'Canada and the Monroe Doctrine', A.J.I.L., 32 (1938), 782–5; C. Fenwick, 'The Question of Canadian Participation in Inter-American Conferences', A.J.I..L., 31 (1937), 473–6.

295 L. Laing, 'Does the Monroe Doctrine cover Canada?', A.J.I.L., 32 (1938), 793–6.

296 Secretary of State Hull declared: 'Greenland is within the area embraced by the Monroe doctrine . . .' Whiteman, *Digest of International Law*, vol. V, pp. 1022–4. The British Government also declared that it considered Greenland as within the area of the Monroe Doctrine. A.J.I.L., 34 (1940), 523.

the Monroe Doctrine a basis for handling possible claims for territory in Antarctica.[297] This suggestion can be considered abolished due to the conclusion of the Antarctic Treaty of 1 December 1959.[298]

If one adheres to the fundamental idea that the Monroe Doctrine or the principles it is based upon were multilateralised, the limits of the obligations as fixed in those treaties can also be seen as the limits of the validity of the multilateralised doctrine.[299] Article 4 of the Rio Pact contains the most precise definition and reads as follows: 'The region to which this treaty refers is bound as follows: beginning at the North Pole; thence due south to a point 74 degrees north latitude, 10 degrees west longitude . . .'[300]

2.1.5 The so-called Monroe Doctrines of other states

The unilateral formulation of a claim considering activity of other states in a certain region as inadmissible has been imitated multiple times and is often called the 'Monroe Doctrine' of the respective state.

A passage in a British note to the United States of 19 May 1928 in connection with the conclusion of the Briand–Kellogg Pact is referred to as the 'British Monroe Doctrine'.[301] With an allusion to the Monroe

297 *Foreign Relations of the United States 1947*, vol. I, pp. 1049–50.

298 UNTS, vol. 402, pp. 71–102.

299 Schatzschneider, *Die neue Phase der Monroedoktrin*, p. 1 *et seq.*

300 UNTS, vol. 21, 1948, p. 77. Graphically presented in Kutzner, *Die Organisation Amerikanischer Staaten*, p. 159. The full text of Art. 4 of the Rio Pact reads: 'The region to which this Treaty refers is bounded as follows: beginning at the North Pole; thence due south to a point 74 degrees north latitude, 10 degrees west longitude; thence by a rhumb line to a point 47 degrees 30 minutes north latitude, 50 degrees west longitude; thence by a rhumb line to a point 35 degrees north latitude, 60 degrees west longitude; thence due south to a point in 20 degrees north latitude; thence by a rhumb line to a point 5 degrees north latitude, 24 degrees west longitude; thence due south to the South Pole; thence due north to a point 30 degrees south latitude, 90 degrees west longitude; thence by a rhumb line to a point on the Equator at 97 degrees west longitude; thence by a rhumb line to a point 15 degrees north latitude, 120 degrees west longitude; thence by a rhumb line to a point 50 degrees north latitude, 170 degrees east longitude; thence due north to a point in 54 degrees north latitude; thence by a rhumb line to a point 65 degrees 30 minutes north latitude, 168 degrees 58 minutes 5 seconds west longitude: thence due north to the North Pole.'

301 Lauterpacht, *Oppenheim's International Law*, pp. 318–19. On this see: Roscher, *Der Briand–Kellogg-Pakt von 1928*, pp. 85–8. In detail on the differences between Monroe Doctrine and the 'British Monroe Doctrine' see: J. Shotwell, *War as an Instrument of National Policy* (New York: Harcourt Brace, 1929), pp. 200–8; P. Malanczuk, *Akehurst's Modern Introduction to International Law*, 7th edn. (London: Routledge, 1997), p. 24.

Doctrine (though without mentioning it explicitly), a protest against interventions in territories of the British Empire is formulated.[302] Prime Minister Chamberlain himself used the term 'British Monroe Doctrine' for this principle.[303]

Japan declared on 17 April 1934 after the invasion of Manchuria, that every supporting action of other states against Japan would be politically significant and disapproved of by Japan. This is commonly labelled as the 'Japanese Monroe Doctrine'.[304]

Two principles, mentioned in a speech by the Australian Prime Minister, William Morris Hughes, of 7 April 1921, are occasionally labelled as the 'Australian Monroe Doctrine'. In this speech he laid down that Australia would condone a pact between Great Britain and Japan only if it was not directed against the United States and that no pact must endanger the principle that Australia belongs to the white race.[305]

Finally, a 'German Monroe Doctrine' is occasionally mentioned. Even though individual proponents of the Monroe Doctrine as a Großraumordnung under international law explicitly denied that they were formulating a 'German Monroe Doctrine',[306] this concept was subsequently labelled as such.[307]

As these other 'Monroe Doctrines' demonstrate, it is a common political practice to mantle political claims as law-like doctrines. A comprehensive consideration of these doctrines is beyond the scope of this work. In any event, these doctrines never remotely drew the same attention among

302 'There are certain regions of the world the welfare and integrity of which constitute a special and vital interest for our peace and safety. Their protection against attack is to the British Empire a measure of self-defence. It must be clearly understood that His Majesty's Government in Great Britain accept the new treaty upon the distinct understanding that it does not prejudice their freedom of action to this respect. The Government of the United States have comparable interests any disregard of which by a foreign Power they have declared that they would regard as an unfriendly act.' Documents on International Affairs, 1928, p. 5.

303 J. Brierly, 'Some Implications of the Pact of Paris', B.Y.I.L., 10 (1929), 208–10, in particular 209; F. Faluhelyi, 'Entwicklungslinien des Völkerrechts nach dem Weltkrieg', ZfV, 23 (1939), 400–2. Occasionally the label 'Chamberlain Doctrine' is used for this declaration. C. Bilfinger, *Das wahre Gesicht des Kelloggpaktes, Angelsächsischer Imperialismus im Gewande des Rechts* (Essen: Essener Verlagsanstalt, 1942), p. 19.

304 G. Blakeslee, 'The Japanese Monroe Doctrine', For.Aff., 11 (1933), 671–81; C. Hyde, 'Legal Aspects of the Japanese Pronouncement in Relation to China', A.J.I.L., 28 (1934), 431–43; W. Friede, 'Die Erklärung Japans über seine Politik in Ostasien (17. April–4. Mai 1934) und die Stellungnahme der Mächte', ZaöRV/H.J.I.L., 4 (1934), 597–608.

305 Fauchille, *Traité de Droit International Public*, vol. I.1, p. 37.

306 Schmitt, *Völkerrechtliche Großraumordnung*, p. 21.

307 Gruchmann, *Nationalsozialistische Großraumordnung*, pp. 11 *et seq.*

scientists of international law as did the US-American Monroe Doctrine. A particularity of this doctrine is that it was discussed with regard to its quality as a separate rule of law and that attempts were made to allocate it to international law.

2.1.6 Conclusion

There can be no doubt that prior to the coming into force of the general prohibition on the use of force and the preceding limitations on the use of force, that the Monroe Doctrine was in accordance with international law in force at that time. The enormous flexibility of the term 'Monroe Doctrine' made it possible at least to attribute to the Monroe Doctrine a term in accordance with international law. Hence, it is possible to reconcile the content attributed to the Monroe Doctrine in the post-war period with Article 51 of the UN Charter.[308]

The United States claimed in the Roosevelt Corollary a right to take action in Latin America. In this moulding between 1904 and 1928 the Monroe Doctrine was at odds with the rules for the use of force in existence at that time, consisting of limitations on the exercise of self-defence.

At no point in time was the Monroe Doctrine itself, even though it features some legal implications, an independent rule of international law. The dispute about the legal evaluation and multilateralisation of the Monroe Doctrine can be largely explained as a dispute over the semantic connotation of the term 'Monroe Doctrine'. If the term 'Monroe Doctrine' is equated with single principles expressed in the doctrine, a multilateralisation of the doctrine is assumed. If, however, one makes an acceptance of the entire doctrine a prerequisite for a multiateralisation of the doctrine (and, hence, its unilateral changeability by the United States), this multilateralisation is rejected. According to its nature as a unilateral, changeable, political principle of the United States the doctrine resists legalisation.

Thus, it would be unfounded to consider the Monroe Doctrine itself as 'multilaterlised'. The doctrine itself is still subject to unilateral interpretation of the United States, as already ascertained in preceding inquiries (Kraus 1913, Schatzschneider 1957). However, single regulations in international treaties are an expression of principles of the Monroe Doctrines, making these principles legally binding for the United States and other states. This so-called multilateralised Monroe Doctrine is codified in the

308 See also: J. Moore, 'The Secret War in Central America and the Future of World Order', A.J.I.L., 80 (1986), 116.

regulations of Article 6 in connection with Article 8 of the Rio Pact and Article 25 of the OAS Charter. In spite of the partially assumed conflicts between these regulations and the rules for the legality of the use of force in Articles 2(4) and 51 of the UN Charter, these regulations are consistent with the UN Charter. Yet, in contrast to the LNC, the doctrine has undergone changes due to the UN Charter. As the verifiability of the attribution of an action as an act of self-defence is no longer the sole competency of the United States but of the organs competent to do so under the UN Charter, the United States no longer possesses (as admitted to them in Article 21 of the LNC) the final authority to decide when an action justifies the use of force according to the doctrine.

The US-American interpretation of the interaction between the regulations of the multilateralised Monroe Doctrine and Article 53 of the UN Charter, however, establish in cases when the requirements of Article 51 of the UN Charter are not met the option of the use of force by regional organisations. Whereas the original Monroe Doctrine did not contain an obligation on the United States, the United States have committed themselves since the Conference of Lima in 1938 under international law to the principle of preserving the limitation of freedom of action of non-American sates in America. Yet this principle has taken quite a different shape from that of the original Monroe Doctrine. Indeed, it is in principle at the discretion of the United States to aspire politically to remove these obligations, but the abandonment of this principle would require not just a unilateral political decision by the United States, but at the same time getting rid of legal obligations under international law.

Thus, the Monroe Doctrine as a decisive doctrine of the security policy of the United States with regard to the American continent found recognition in several rules of international law. To what degree the same is true for US doctrines originally referring to Asia will be examined in the Chapter 3.

2.2 The Stimson Doctrine

On 18 September 1931 Japan invaded Manchuria after the so-called Mukden Incident. This incident was an explosion at a railway track near the Chinese city of Mukden, which resulted in an exchange of fire between Japanese and Chinese military units.[309] By early January 1932

309 On the development of the conflict see: R. Langer, *Seizure of Territory – The Stimson Doctrine and Related Principles in Legal Theory and Diplomatic Practice* (Princeton University Press, 1947), pp. 50–66; H. Stimson and M. Bundy, *On Active Service in Peace and*

most parts of Manchuria were under Japanese control.[310] On 1 March 1932 a Japanese-controlled Manchurian administrative council declared Manchuria's independence from China and founded the state Manchukuo ('State of the Manchu'), with the last Chinese emperor from the Manchu dynasty, Pu-Yi, as regent.[311]

The United States had already reacted prior to this, by having then Secretary of State, Henry Lewis Stimson, send identical diplomatic notes to Japan and China on 7 January 1932.[312] In these notes the United States refused to recognise the situation created by the Japanese occupation under international law.[313] The principle of non-recognition of acquisition of territory against international law, as described in these notes, has become known as the Stimson Doctrine.[314] Partially, the term Stimson Doctrine is used less specifically not to refer to this principle, but in order to refer generally to the non-recognition of situations created in violation of international law.[315]

War (London: Hutchinson, 1949), pp. 69–101; H. Stimson, *The Far Eastern Crisis* (New York: Howard Fertig, 1974).

310 H. Wehberg, *Krieg und Eroberung im Wandel des Völkerrechts* (Frankfurt: Metzner, 1953), p. 97.

311 AdG 1932, p. 119; D. Turns, 'The Stimson Doctrine of Non-Recognition: Its Historical Genesis and Influence on Contemporary International Law', Chin.J.I.L., 2 (2003), 105–10.

312 Stimson's note reads: 'in view of the present situation and of its own rights and obligations therein, the American Government deems it to be its duty to notify both the Government of the Chinese Republic and the Imperial Japanese Government that it cannot admit the legality of any situation *de facto* nor does it intend to recognize any treaty or agreement entered into between these governments, or agents thereof, which may impair the treaty rights of the United States or its citizens in China, including those which relate to the sovereignty, the independence or the territorial and administrative integrity of the Republic of China, or to the international policy relative to China, commonly known as the Open Door Policy; and that it does not intend to recognize any situation, treaty or agreement which may be brought about by means contrary to the covenants and obligations of the Pact of Paris of August 27, 1928 to which treaty both China and Japan, as well as the United States are parties.' *Papers Relating to the Foreign Relations of the United States, 1932*, Japan, vol. I, p. 76.

313 For a description of the role of the United States in the so-called Manchurian Crisis see: P. Clyde, 'The Diplomacy of "Playing No Favorites": Secretary Stimson and Manchuria, 1931', Miss.V.H.Rev., 35/2 (1948), 187–202.

314 H. Wehberg, 'Die Stimson-Doktrin', in D. Constantopoulos (ed.), *Grundprobleme des internationalen Rechts*, FS-Spiropoulus (Bonn: Schimmelbusch, 1957), pp. 433–43; W. Meng, 'Stimson Doctrine', E.P.I.L., IV (2000), pp. 690–3.

315 For example, H. Kubitz, *Die Stimson-Doktrin* (Würzburg: Konrad Triltsch, 1938), Ph.D. thesis, Breslau, 1938, pp. 24–9; C. Bilfinger, *Die Stimsondoktrin* (Essen: Essener Verlagsanstalt, 1943), p. 7.

2.2.1 The Stimson Doctrine as doctrine of US security policy

The Stimson Doctrine differs in many ways from other doctrines of US security policy. This becomes obvious if one looks at its evolutionary history: it did not originate in a speech by an American president to Congress, but was initially declared in a diplomatic note. The Stimson Doctrine is also unique because it is the only diplomatic doctrine of the United States considered to be a 'major doctrine' which does not carry the name of a US president (in spite of the efforts by the 31st president, Herbert Hoover, to claim the authorship of the doctrine),[316] but the name of then Secretary of State, Henry Lewis Stimson.[317]

Stimson's notes did not primarily concern the factual prerequisites for legal use of force in terms of an *ius ad bellum*, but the legal consequences of the illegal use of force under international law. It addressed particularly the legality of annexation, hence, the acquisition of territory as a result of the use of force.[318] Thus, it already seems unclear as to what degree the Stimson Doctrine constitutes a doctrine of US security policy as defined in Chapter 1.[319] However, the matter of generally binding standards for legal use of force was at least addressed indirectly in connection with the Stimson Doctrine. Every application of the Stimson Doctrine requires a prior decision on the legality of the preceding use of force.[320]

In the notes of 7 January 1932, the United States declared that it did 'not intend to recognise any situation, treaty or agreement which may be brought about by means contrary to the covenants and obligations of the [Briand–Kellogg] Pact of Paris of August 27, 1928'.[321] China and Japan were parties to this treaty, just like the United States. This general principle raises the question of how the term 'means contrary to the covenants and obligations of the Pact of Paris' was understood in connection with the Stimson Doctrine.

316 H. Hoover, *The Memoirs of Herbert Hoover: The Cabinet and the Presidency, 1920–1933* (New York: Macmillan, 1952), vol. II, pp. 362–79.

317 Crabb, *The Doctrines of American Foreign Policy*, p. 81. In favour of calling the Stimson Doctrine the Hoover Doctrine see: E. Stowell, 'The Stewardship of Secretary Stimson', A.J.I.L., 27 (1933), 103; H. Jahrreiß, *Die Hoover-Doktrin und die Heiligkeit der Verträge* (Leipzig: Robert Noske, 1933). On the quarrel between Hoover and Stimson about the authorship of the doctrine see: R. Current, 'The Stimson Doctrine and the Hoover Doctrine', Am.H.Rev. 59/3 (1954) 513–42; Current argues in favour of the label 'Hoover–Stimson Doctrine' (p. 541).

318 R. Langer, *Seizure of Territory*, pp. 58–66.

319 See above, Chapter 1, section 1.6.

320 Krakau, *Missionsbewußtsein und Völkerrechtsdoktrin in den Vereinigten Staaten von Amerika*, p. 334.

321 *Papers Relating to the Foreign Relations of the United States, 1932*, Japan, vol. I, p. 76.

The interpretation of the Briand–Kellogg Pact and the obligations which may have resulted from it was a contentious issue in connection with the Stimson Doctrine.[322] This constitutes a generally applicable standard for the legality of the use of force. Hence, it lays down a standard for the use of force applicable to the United States. Thus, the Stimson Doctrine can be considered in spite of its particularities as a doctrine of US security policy.

The policy of the United States towards China was determined by diplomatic doctrines already articulated prior to the Stimson Doctrine. Stimson's notes made direct reference to treaty rights of the United States and to the international policy relative to China commonly known as the 'Open Door Principle'.[323]

2.2.2 The Stimson Doctrine within the context of US policy in China: the Open Door Principle

Prior to the declaration of the Stimson Doctrine, attempts were made on the part of the United States to implement US policy with regard to China by means of international law.

Since the mid-nineteenth century the Open Door Principle (or occasionally the Open Door Doctrine), was a central element of US policy towards China.[324] This principle makes equal opportunities for foreign states to trade with China within their respective spheres of influence an aim of US foreign policy. At the same time, it sought to guarantee the territorial integrity of China.[325] As the Open Door Principle, just like the Monroe Doctrine, formulates limitations on actions by other states in a certain region, its was considered to be the Asian counterpart to the Monroe Doctrine.[326]

Even though the labelling of this principle as the Open Door Principle appears only around the year 1900 in connection with notes by Secretary

322 See below, section 2.2.3.2.

323 *Papers Relating to the Foreign Relations of the United States, 1932*, Japan, vol. I, p. 76.

324 See, for example, J. Fairbank, *The United States and China* (New York: Viking, 1958); J. Spencer, 'The Monroe Doctrine and the League Covenant', A.J.I.L., 30 (1936), 403.

325 Evans and Newnham, *The Penguin Dictionary of International Relations*, pp. 402–4; Stimson himself made an attempt to define the Open Door Principle in a letter to Senator Borah of 24 February 1932 (the so-called Borah Letter): '(1) equality of commercial opportunity among all nations dealing with China, and (2) as necessary to that equality the preservation of China's territorial and administrative integrity', ZaöRV/H.J.I.L., 3/1 (1932/33), 595–9.

326 Crabb, *The Doctrines of American Foreign Policy*, p. 58 for further evidence.

of State Hay, the drive to open up opportunities to trade and to avoid the acquisition of territory by other states in China were early principles of US policy towards China. These principles found their way into treaty obligations of the United States. For example, the United States acquired far-reaching unilateral privileges of trade in five Chinese harbours in the Treaty of Wanghia of 3 July 1844.[327]

The Treaty of Wanghia does not, however, contain a statement on the legality of the use of force, just like the other unequal treaties between China and other states.[328] To codify an explicit authority to use sanctions or a threat of sanctions at this point in time would only have been a declaratory statement, because at that point the right to go to war was still considered a natural attribute of a state.[329] In order to limit the activities of other states in China, the United States used fundamentally different actions as opposed to the unilateral declarations they had used for the American continent, such as the Monroe Doctrine. Quite apart from that, the implementation of the Open Door Principle by the United States from the very beginning shows multilateral characteristics.[330] Whereas a negative exclusion of activities by other states in the western hemisphere was promulgated in the Monroe Doctrine, the United States gave positive assurances for the territorial integrity of China and urged other states to give similar guarantees in order to implement the Open Door Principle.

On 6 September 1899 Secretary of State Hay sent identical notes to Germany, Great Britain, Russia and later to France and Japan. In these notes the United States urged other states to treat all other foreign states

327 CTS, vol. 97 (1844), pp. 104–17.

328 The following treaties are called 'Unequal treaties': Treaty between China and Great Britain (Treaty of Nanjing, 29 August 1842, CTS, vol. 93 (1842), pp. 465–83), Treaty between France and China (Treaty of Whampoa, 24 October 1844, CTS, vol. 97 (1844–5), pp. 375–96), Treaty between Russia and China (Treaty of Tientsin, 13 June 1858, CTS, vol. 119 (1858), pp. 113–18), Treaty between the North German Confederation and China (Treaty of Tientsin, 2 September 1861, CTS, vol. 124 (1861), pp. 299–334), Austria-Hungary (Treaty of Beijing, 2 September 1869, CTS, vol. 139 (1869), pp. 477–90) and Japan (Treaty of 30 August 1871, Martens NRG2, vol. 3, pp. 502–12).

329 Grewe, *The Epochs of International Law*, pp. 530 *et seq.*

330 However, the Monroe Doctrine and Hay Doctrine both have in common that a unilateral action of the United States (Monroe's speech, respectively, the sending of Hay's notes) would only be carried out after a failure of attempts to announce the respective principle together with Great Britain. On the parallels of the genesis of these doctrines in this respect see: Krakau, *Missionsbewußtsein und Völkerrechtsdoktrin in den Vereinigten Staaten von Amerika*, pp. 282 *et seq.*

equally when trading in their respective spheres of influence in China.[331] The states to which these notes were addressed declared subsequently that they would adhere to these principles if the other states involved would also recognise this principle.[332] However, no obligations under international law resulted from these notes.[333]

Ten months later in June 1900 the Boxer Rebellion erupted, ending on 14 August with the relief of the fortified legation compound in Beijing by an expeditionary force of the states maintaining spheres of interest in China. China was forced to sign the Boxer Protocol of 7 September 1901. Against the backdrop of the Boxer Rebellion, and due to the fear that the states involved in quelling the rebellion could acquire Chinese territory, Hay sent a second series of notes. In these notes he simply assumed the universal acceptance of the principle.[334]

In the nine-power treaty of 6 February 1922 the parties agreed in Article 1 to respect the sovereignty, independence and territorial and administrative integrity of China.[335] The United States referred to a violation of this treaty in Stimson's diplomatic notes of 7 January 1932. In spite of numerous legal implications, such as deviations from the principle of sovereign equality, the Open Door Principle and the actions taken by the United States to implement this principle possessed hardly any connection with the legality of the use of force.[336] Secretary of State Elihu Root was quoted as saying in 1930 that it 'never entered the head' of American politicians to defend the Open Door Principle militarily.[337]

331 'the Government of the United States would be pleased to see His German Majesty's Government give formal assurances, and lend its cooperation in securing like assurances from the other interested powers, that each within its respective sphere of influence'. *Papers Relating to the Foreign Relations of the United States, 1899*, pp. 129–30.

332 *Papers Relating to the Foreign Relations of the United States, 1899*, pp. 131–42.

333 Krakau, *Missionsbewußtsein und Völkerrechtsdoktrin in den Vereinigten Staaten von Amerika*, p. 283.

334 *Papers Relating to the Foreign Relations of the United States, 1899*, p. 142. Furthermore, the following agreements count as attempts at legalisation of the Open Door Principle: The Root–Takahira Agreement, 30 November 1908 (*Papers Relating to the Foreign Relations of the United States, 1908*, pp. 510–12) and the Lansing–Ishii Agreement, 31 October and 2 November 1917 (*Papers Relating to the Foreign Relations of the United States, 1917*, pp. 264–5, 1922, vol. II, pp. 595–9), in which the general acceptance of the Open Door Principle towards Japan is once more emphasised.

335 LNTS, vol. 38, 1925, pp. 278–84.

336 The Boxer Protocol, 7 September 1901 mentions under section VII merely a right to station troops for the defence of the legations. CTS, vol. 190 (1901), p. 61.

337 Krakau, *Missionsbewußtsein und Völkerrechtsdoktrin in den Vereinigten Staaten von Amerika*, p. 289.

As a specific application of the Open Door Principle as principle of US policy towards China, Stimson sent identical notes to China and Japan in 1932.

2.2.3 *The Stimson Doctrine according to the notes of 7 January 1932*

Regardless of the few opportunities and the lack of intention on the part of the United States to take military action in order to implement the Open Door Principle, Stimson's notes of 7 January 1932 contain statements on the legality of the use of force which can be generalised. When doing so, various questions of law connected with the Stimson Doctrine have to be separated from statements on the *ius ad bellum* in connection with this doctrine.

2.2.3.1 Questions of law connected with the Stimson Doctrine

The principle of non-recognition of situations brought about by the use of force against international law as it results from the Stimson Doctrine, is discussed in connection with several problems of international law. The problems connected with the instrument of non-recognition are manifold.[338] Quincy Wright considered Stimson's note as progress towards the following principles as rules of international law:

(1) the factual conquest of a territory by a state does not entitle a state to acquire this territory;
(2) treaties which violate the rights of third states are void;
(3) treaties brought about by use of force are void.[339]

These developments refer to general rules of international law, not to the legality of use of force. Rather, they cover the acceptance of the consequences of illegal use of force in international law. The decisive passage of Stimson's note reads: 'the American Government . . . does not intend to recognize any situation, treaty or agreement which may be brought about by means contrary to the covenants and obligations of the Pact of Paris of August 27, 1928 . . .'[340]

338 H. Blix, 'Contemporary Aspects of Non-Recognition', RdC, 130 (1970-II), 593–700.
339 Q. Wright, 'The Stimson Note of January 7, 1932', A.J.I.L., 26 (1932), 344.
340 *Papers Relating to the Foreign Relations of the United States, 1932*, Japan, vol. I, p. 76. The resolution of the League of Nations Council, recognising the principles of Stimson's notes, states 'means contrary to the Covenant of the League of Nations or to the Pact of Paris', L.N.O.J. (1932), 383. In detail on the relation between the LNC and the Briand–Kellogg Pact see: E. Geib, 'Das Verhältnis der Völkerbundssatzung zum Kelloggpakt',

This brings up the questions: which particular measures were in accordance with the opinion of the United States contrary to the Briand–Kellogg Pact and how was this pact interpreted in connection with the Stimson Doctrine.

2.2.3.2 The understanding of the Briand–Kellogg Pact on which the Stimson Doctrine is based

The most far-reaching critique of the Briand–Kellogg Pact is that even though it was a ratified treaty under international law, due to its vague wording no specific obligation would result from it. The non-committal formulation of Article I ('condemn', 'renounce') would not contain an obligation not to use force as a means of foreign policy. Article II ('never to seek settlement except by pacific means') in turn would not contain an obligation to make actual use of peaceful means.[341] Furthermore, the Briand–Kellogg Pact did not constitute an 'outlawry of war' in terms of declaring war *eo ipso* as illegal, due to the lack of a mechanism of sanctions.[342] At best it would constitute a non-binding 'renunciation of war' of little consequence to the states party to the treaty.[343]

Not only the common understanding of the wording contradicts the assumption that no obligation results from the Briand–Kellogg Pact,[344] but also the subsequent state practice attributed a greater relevance and binding effect to it.[345] The lack of a mechanism for sanctions is not opposed to a legally binding effect of a norm.[346] The discussion about the Japanese occupation of Manchuria was of particular importance to

Ph.D. thesis, Kiel, 1934, pp. 58–64. On the attempts to integrate the regulations of the pact into the covenant see: W. Schücking, *Die Revision der Völkerbundssatzung im Hinblick auf den Kelloggpakt* (Berlin: Verlag Dr. Emil Ebering, 1931).

341 ASIL Proceedings, 24th Annual Meeting, 1930, pp. 97–9. In detail on the critique of the Briand–Kellogg Pact see: Roscher, *Der Briand–Kellogg-Pakt von 1928*, pp. 105 *et seq.*

342 H. Haßmann, *Der Kellogg-Pakt und seine Vorbehalte* (Würzburg: Werkbundbuchdruckerei, 1930), Ph.D. thesis, Würzburg, 1931, pp. 58–68; Bilfinger, *Das wahre Gesicht des Kelloggpaktes, Angelsächsischer Imperialismus im Gewande des Rechts*, pp. 46–9.

343 On this dispute see: A. Nichols, *Neutralität und amerikanische Waffenausfuhr* (Berlin: Ebering, 1931), Ph.D. thesis, Berlin, 1931, pp. 114–20 for further evidence.

344 Likewise, Stimson in a speech to the Council on Foreign Relations on 8 August 1932, For.Aff., 11 (1932), Special Suppl., pp. iv–v.

345 Described by Brownlie, *International Law and the Use of Force by States*, pp. 74–80.

346 Lauterpacht, *Oppenheim's International Law*, vol. II, p. 191; Q. Wright, 'The Meaning of the Pact of Paris', A.J.I.L., 27 (1933), 41; H. Wehberg, *Krieg und Eroberung im Völkerrecht* (Berlin: Alfred Metzner Verlag, 1953), p. 48.

the development of this state practice,[347] and the Stimson Doctrine was formulated in the context of this confrontation.

The Stimson Doctrine is based on an interpretation of the Briand–Kellogg Pact which differs fundamentally from the interpretation of the pact by its critics described above. Stimson's notes – and thus also the Stimson Doctrine – imply a binding character of the Briand–Kellogg Pact in terms of an 'outlawry of war'. Hence, the Briand–Kellogg Pact accordingly constitutes a rule of international law, in consequence making war *eo ipso* illegal for the parties to the treaty.[348]

The claim of a third state not directly affected by the prior use of force to formulate a general principle of law of non-recognition has been considered the 'moral-missionary characteristic of the Stimson Doctrine'.[349] George F. Kennan condemned the Stimson Doctrine as an expression of a legalistic–moral approach to policy.[350] Regardless of possibly existing motives of this kind, this critique does no justice to the US-American interpretation of the Briand–Kellogg Pact at that time. According to this interpretation a violation of the treaty not only entitles the attacked state to self-defence, but also entitles the other signatories of the treaty to take action. This interpretation, on which the Stimson Doctrine is based, is apparent in a statement delivered by Stimson in a speech to the Council on Foreign Relations on 8 August 1932. In this speech he declared:

> Under the former concept of international law when a conflict occurred, it was usually deemed the concern only of the parties to the conflict . . . but now under the Covenant and the Briand–Kellogg Pact, the conflict becomes a legal concern to everybody connected with the treaty.[351]

The preamble even suggests an interpretation of the Briand–Kellogg Pact in terms of a modern understanding of collective self-defence.[352] Yet in

347 Krisch, *Selbstverteidigung und Kollektive Sicherheit*, pp. 29–30.

348 von Mandelsloh, 'Die Auslegung des Kelloggpaktes durch den amerikanischen Staatssekretär Stimson', p. 617; Wright, 'The Meaning of the Pact of Paris', 40–1; D. Turns, 'The Stimson Doctrine of Non-Recognition: Its Historical Genesis and Influence on Contemporary International Law', Chin.J.I.L., 2 (2003), 115–17.

349 Author's translation of 'moralisch-missionarischen Charakter[s] der Stimson Doktrin', Krakau, *Missionsbewußtsein und Völkerrechtsdoktrin in den Vereinigten Staaten von Amerika*, p. 314.

350 G. Kennan, *American Diplomacy: 1900–1950* (New York: New American Library, 1952), p. 50.

351 Printed in ZaÖRV/H.J.I.L., 3/1 (1932/33), 593.

352 Dinstein, *War, Aggression and Self-Defence*, pp. 83–5. For a similar argument see: Haßmann, *Der Kellogg-Pakt und seine Vorbehalte*, pp. 67–8; D. Miller, *The Peace Pact of Paris* (New York: Putnam, 1928), p. 41.

the same speech Stimson rejected the use of force or economic measures as sanctions in the case of violations of the Briand–Kellogg Pact.[353]

Critics of the Briand–Kellogg Pact additionally assume that the pact does not contain an efficient limitation of the use of force. This is because every conceivable war would be covered by the exceptions to the prohibition of war like the declared reservations on the right of self-defence.[354]

By using the term 'war' ('*guerre*') the opportunity arose to circumvent the limitation of the pact by simply choosing a label for an armed conflict other than 'war'.[355] According to another opinion, advocating a broad interpretation of the Briand–Kellogg Pact, the pact does contain a general prohibition on the use of force. Based on the formula 'pacific means', contained in Article II, and the statement in the preamble to strive for change only by 'pacific means' and that change must be 'the result of a peaceful and orderly process' it is assumed that there is no room under the pact for any kind of use of force not constituting self-defence.[356] However, proponents of this theory also broadly interpret self-defence in this context, so that it includes the use of force in terms of the contemporary Monroe Doctrine.[357]

Another opinion assumes that the Briand–Kellogg Pact leaves room for other types of use of force, as long as they do not constitute a war. As the statement in the preamble referred only to 'changes of relations', there was still room for the enforcement of already existing legal obligations by force. Furthermore, it was considered possible to categorise the use of force as a peaceful means in terms of Article II if it did not constitute

353 ZaöRV/H.J.I.L., 3/1 (1932/33) 591–2. At the instigation of President Hoover, Stimson is said to have abstained from presenting an interpretation of the Briand–Kellogg Pact suggesting a possibility of sanctions by states not directly involved in the conflict. R. Current, 'The Stimson Doctrine and the Hoover Doctrine', Am.H.Rev., 3 (1954), 534–6.

354 E. Borchard, 'The Multilateral Treaty for the Renunciation of War', A.J.I.L., 23 (1929), 118; E. Borchard, 'The Kellogg Treaties Sanction War', ZaöRV/H.J.I.L., 1/1 (1929), 126–31.

355 Neuhold, *Internationale Konflikte – verbotene und erlaubte Mittel ihrer Austragung*, pp. 66–7.

356 Wright, 'The Meaning of the Pact of Paris', pp. 51–54; A. McNair, 'The Stimson Doctrine of Non-Recognition', B.Y.I.L., 14 (1933), 68.

357 Miller *The Peace Pact of Paris*, p. 114, making a limitation with regard to the Monroe Doctrine and the British 'Monroe Doctrine', pp. 122–3; J. Shotwell, *War as an Instrument of National Policy* (New York: Harcourt Brace, 1929), pp. 209–15, 239.

war.[358] State practice in the immediate aftermath of the coming into force of the Briand–Kellogg Pact was evaluated differently by proponents of both theories and was considered as supporting each.[359]

This undeniable uncertainty of terminology of the Briand–Kellogg Pact due to the use of the term 'war' is avoided in Stimson's notes by choosing the imprecise formulation 'means contrary to the Pact'. This formulation in terms of a broad interpretation of the limitations of the Briand–Kellogg Pact makes it possible to apply the doctrine to illegal use of force in general,[360] as happened later.[361] Yet Stimson's notes do not contain a hint as to which of the two interpretations of the Briand–Kellogg Pact presented above the US government was leaning towards, unless the avoidance of the term 'war' is in itself considered a tendency towards a broad interpretation of the doctrine. Besides the general formulation in Stimson's notes, an explicit determination that the preceding Japanese actions were considered to be a violation of the pact can be found in a letter by Stimson to Senator Borah of 23 February 1932, published in order to explain the position of the United States.[362]

Once more Stimson's speech to the Council on Foreign Relations helps to highlight the US-American interpretation of the Briand–Kellogg Pact at that time. Stimson declared in this speech, after making reference to the character of the treaty as a comprehensive prohibition, that it was the aim and purpose of the pact to make self-defence the only permissible use of force under the pact.[363]

Hence, the position of the United States at that point in time matches the first broad interpretation of the limitations of the Briand–Kellogg Pact, no matter which opinion as to the specific understanding of self-defence

358 Lauterpacht, *Oppenheim's International Law*, vol. II, pp. 184–6; Bowett, *Self-Defence in International Law*, pp. 135–6; Wehberg, *Krieg und Eroberung*, pp. 49–50.

359 While Brownlie considers this as evidence for an understanding in terms of a general prohibition of force (Brownlie, *International Law and the Use of Force by States*, pp. 87–92), Lauterpacht considers this as evidence for the continuing legality of the use of force other than war (Lauterpacht, *Oppenheim's International Law*, pp. 185–6).

360 McNair, 'The Stimson Doctrine of Non-Recognition', 68.

361 On this see further section 2.2.3.3, below.

362 ZaöRV/H.J.I.L., 3/1 (1932/33), 595–9. In order to avoid an unwanted reply to this declaration, Stimson opted for an explanation of the position of the United States in a letter to the than Chairman of the Senate Committee on Foreign Relations, Senator William E. Borah (the so-called 'Borah Letter'). Current, *The Stimson Doctrine and the Hoover Doctrine*, p. 529.

363 For.Aff., 11 (1932), Special Suppl., pp. iv–v.

one supports. Besides criticism of the weakness of the limitations of the Briand–Kellogg Pact, the question arose in the context of the pact as to who is authorised to define if the prior use of force raises the entitlement to self-defence: the state exercising it or a central authority?[364]

The reservation of the United States to the Briand–Kellogg Pact, in which they reserved the right of self-defence, further reads:

> Every nation is free at all times and regardless of treaty provisions to defend its territory from attack or invasion and alone is competent to decide whether circumstances require recourse to war in self-defense.[365]

This reservation on the unilateral determination of the right to self-defence is considered the important aspect of the reservation.[366] A determination of a situation entitling self-defence, depending solely on the subjective estimation of the parties to the treaty, excludes judicial review of the illegality of use of force.[367]

The United States deviated gradually from this reservation to the Briand–Kellogg Pact in the context of the Stimson Doctrine. Even though the Briand–Kellogg Pact did not foresee a mechanism or organs for a centralised determination of the aggressor – in this respect a set-back compared with the League of Nations[368] – the possibility of an objective evaluation of an act as legal self-defence, independent of the subjective opinion of states, is at least also considered in Stimson's notes as well as in his speech to the Council on Foreign Relations.[369] Stimson also argued in favour of a consultation of the parties to the treaty in case of a potential violation of the treaty in order to determine the aggressor as a central organ for this determination was lacking.[370]

364 J. Brierly, 'Some Implications of the Pact of Paris', B.Y.I.L., 10 (1929), 208–10.

365 *Papers Relating to the Foreign Relations of the United States of America, 1928*, vol. I, p. 36, A report by the Senate Committee on Foreign Relations of 14 January 1929 interpreted the pact likewise. Quoted at P. Jessup, *International Security – The American Role in Collective Action for Peace* (New York: Council on Foreign Relations, 1935), pp. 40–1.

366 Brierly, 'Some Implications of the Pact of Paris', pp. 208–10.

367 von Mandelsloh, 'Die Auslegung des Kelloggpaktes durch den amerikanischen Staatssekretär Stimson', 619; Bowett, *Self-Defence in International Law*, p. 262, with a hint to the principle *nemo iudex in sua causa*.

368 Krisch, *Selbstverteidigung und kollektive Sicherheit*, p. 36.

369 Roscher, *Der Briand–Kellogg-Pakt von 1928*, pp. 200–1. Similarly, von Mandelsloh, 'Die Auslegung des Kelloggpaktes durch den amerikanischen Staatssekretär Stimson', 621.

370 For.Aff., 11 (1932), Special Suppl., pp. viii–ix.

In the Japanese reply to Stimson's notes a right to unilateral determination is implicitly called upon, in doing so not linking the formulations 'means contrary to the Pact of Paris' to the Japanese attack.[371] Likewise, Japan claimed before the League of Nations Council with reference to the *Caroline* case, that it acted in self-defence when occupying Manchuria. Japan also claimed that the right to judge whether an action is an act of self-defence was still up to the individual state under the Briand–Kellogg Pact.[372]

This contradiction between the US and Japanese opinions raises the question as to what extent the interpretation of the Briand–Kellogg Pact by the United States and the principles of the Stimson Doctrine were accepted by the other states and found their way into regulations of international law.

2.2.3.3 Transformation of the Stimson Doctrine into a rule of law and acceptance of the *ius ad bellum* assumed in the doctrine

As to the legal nature of the principles of non-recognition, did this then constitute a recognised instrument of self-help, like a reprisal or a retorsion?[373]

The transformation of the non-recognition principle into a rule of law has drawn particular interest among scholars, as well as the evaluation of Stimson's notes under international law with regard to the particular case. Initially, these notes were only the declaration of a unilateral principle of US policy which was not even legally binding on the United States.[374] Starting with this unilateral declaration of a non-legally

371 'The Government of Japan were well aware that the Government of the United States could always be relied on to do everything in their power to support Japan's efforts to secure the full and complete fulfillment in every detail of the Kellogg Treaty for the Outlawry of War. They are glad to receive this additional assurance of the fact . . . They take note of the statement by the Government of the United States that the latter cannot admit the legality of matters . . . which might be brought about by means contrary to the treaty of 27 August 1928 . . . as Japan has no intention of adopting improper means, that question does not practically arise.' *Papers Relating to the Foreign Relations of the United States, 1932,* Japan, vol. I, pp. 76–7.

372 For.Aff., 11(1932), 74, Bowett, *Self-Defence in International Law*, p. 32.

373 Kubitz, *Die Stimson-Doktrin*, pp. 24–34, who comes to the conclusion that non-recognition did not constitute under the international law of those days a known means of self-help, but under international law self-help *sui generis*.

374 Wehberg, *Krieg und Eroberung im Völkerrecht*, p. 88.

binding principle, the Stimson Doctrine principle of non-recognition developed (in spite of fierce criticism)[375] first into a rule of regional international law and then into general international law.[376] Today it is considered *ius cogens*.[377] The International Law Commission (ILC) included the Stimson Doctrine in Article 41(2)[378] of its Draft Articles on state responsibility.[379] At the time of the declaration of the Stimson Doctrine, however, the United States did not consider this declaration a development in terms of the creation of a new rule of law,[380] but merely as a clear formulation of an already existing legal obligation resulting from already existing treaties like the Briand–Kellogg Pact and Article 10 of the LNC.[381]

The transformation of the legal principles of non-recognition contained in the Stimson Doctrine into a generally recognised rule of international law, removed from an exclusive American interpretation, has been subject to in-depth research.[382] A resolution of the League of Nations Assembly of 11 March 1932 stated a general legal duty of non-recognition for the member states of the League of Nations. However, non-recognition of illegal acts in the context of this resolution referred not merely to actions against the Briand–Kellogg Pact, but also to actions against the LNC.[383] In Article 2 of the Saavedra–Lamas Pact of 10 October 1933 a duty of non-recognition was codified for the first time as regional international treaty

375 Particularly by German scholars of international law. For example, Jahreiß, *Die Hoover-Doktrin und die Heiligkeit der Verträge*; Bilfinger, *Die Stimsondoktrin*. On this see: B. Roscher, *Der Briand–Kellogg-Pakt von 1928*, pp. 208–9.

376 T. Grant, 'Doctrines (Monroe, Halstein, Brezhnev, Stimson)', in R. Wolfrum (ed.), *The Max Planck Encyclopaedia of Public International Law* (Oxford University Press, 2008) online edition available at: www.mpepil.com, Nos. 13–15. In this sense already: Q. Wright, 'The Legal Foundation of the Stimson Doctrine', Pac.Aff., 8 (1935), 440. Yokota wrote in 1935 of a 'quasi-general-rule': K. Yokota, 'The Recent Development of the Stimson Doctrine', Pac.Aff., 8 (1935), 137.

377 W. Meng, 'Stimson Doctrine', E.P.I.L., IV (2000), 692.

378 'No State shall recognize as lawful a situation created by a serious breach within the meaning of Article 40, nor render aid or assistance in maintaining that situation.' ILC, Report on the Work of its 53rd Session (2001), UN Doc A/56/10.

379 Turns, 'The Stimson Doctrine of Non-Recognition: Its Historical Genesis and Influence on Contemporary International Law', pp. 134–5.

380 So K. Yokota, 'The Recent Development of the Stimson Doctrine', pp. 134–5.

381 Wright, 'The Legal Foundation of the Stimson Doctrine', pp. 439–40. On Wright's opinion in this regard see: Krakau, *Missionsbewußtsein und Völkerrechtsdoktrin in den Vereinigten Staaten von Amerika*, p. 305.

382 Wehberg, *Krieg und Eroberung im Völkerrecht*, pp. 88–116; Langer, *Seizure of Territory*, pp. 50 *et seq.*; Grewe, *The Epochs of International Law*, pp. 601–2 with further evidence.

383 L.N.O.J., Special Suppl., 101 (1932), 87.

law.[384] Even though the existence of such a legal duty of non-recognition was disputed for quite some time,[385] this duty is considered as implicitly recognised in the UN Charter due to the general prohibition of the use of force in Article 2(4) of the UN Charter. This conviction was also expressed in several resolutions of the UN General Assembly.[386] Today, the quality of *ius cogens* is attributed to the principle of non-recognition of the Stimson Doctrine.[387] Besides these statements referring to the legal consequences of the illegal use of force, the degree to which the interpretation of the Briand–Kellogg Pact, on which the Stimson Doctrine is based, has been accepted by other states is questionable.

The scope of these limitations and particularly the subsequent state practice are hotly debated issues.[388] A limitation in terms of a general prohibition of the use of force was attributed to the pact in the Budapest Articles of the International Law Association of September 1934.[389] The Budapest Articles, however, do not constitute an authentic interpretation of the pact, but are regarded as an important doctrinal statement.[390] Nevertheless, it is certain that at least the subsequent development of international law led to a codification of the general prohibition of the use of force in Article 2(4); already implied in the Stimson Doctrine at that time.[391] The gradual abandonment of the unilateral right of a state to determine unilaterally the occurrence of a situation justifying self-defence, as undertaken by Stimson, found its way into rules of international law only with the creation of a centralised possibility for determining the aggressor in the UN Charter.[392]

Yet the commission installed by the League of Nations Council (the so-called Lytton Commission), held itself competent to make a judgement in this regard and classified the Japanese occupation of Manchuria as an

384 LNTS, vol. 163, 1935–6, p. 393. Subsequent treaties repeat this obligation, for example, the Bogotá Pact in Art. 17. UNTS, vol. 30, 1949, p. 55.

385 Brownlie, *International Law and the Use of Force by States*, pp. 418–19; Langer, *Seizure of Territory*, pp. 98 *et seq*. with further evidence

386 'Friendly Relations Declaration', UN GA Res. 2625 (XXV), 24 October 1970 and the 'Definition of Aggression', UN GA Res. 3314 (XXIX), 14 December 1974.

387 K. Doehring, *Völkerrecht*, 2nd edn. (Heidelberg: C. F. Müller, 2004), p. 51, No. 112.

388 Brownlie, *International Law and the Use of Force by States*, pp. 87–92; Lauterpacht, *Oppenheim's International Law*, pp. 185–6.

389 H. Lauterpacht, 'The Pact of Paris and the Budapest Articles of Interpretation', Trans. Grotius Soc., 20 (1934), 178–9.

390 Wright, 'The Legal Foundation of the Stimson Doctrine', p. 440.

391 Krakau, *Missionsbewußtsein und Völkerrechtsdoktrin in den Vereinigten Staaten von Amerika*, p. 315.

392 On this see further section 2.1.3.4, above.

illegal measure of self-defence.[393] The military tribunals at Nuremberg and Tokyo also interpreted the Briand–Kellogg Pact as providing that whether a use of force was justified as an act of self-defence was open to independent scrutiny.[394]

2.2.4 Conclusion

Differing from attempts on the part of the United States to implement the principles of the Monroe Doctrine, efforts to implement the Open Door Principle were characterised by multilateral approaches. In contrast to prior instruments, which the United States made use of to implement the Open Door Principle under international law, the Stimson Doctrine contains a statement on the legality of the use of force.

Initially, the Stimson Doctrine was a unilateral political declaration of the United States. It was a specific application of the Open Door Principle, which aimed to be the Asian counterpart to the Monroe Doctrine for a limitation of the activities of other states in a certain region. In spite of its close linkage to a specific political situation, the Stimson Doctrine influenced the development of a rule of international law. It evolved from a unilateral statement via regionally accepted international law to general international law, and finally became *ius cogens*. By this subsequent development, the United States was deprived of the unilateral changeability of the principles of the doctrine, just as they were in case of the Monroe Doctrine. In consequence, this elevation of a single principle of the doctrine to a rule of law would make it necessary in order for the United States to abandon this principle (originally limited to a specific situation addressed at other states) to get rid of its obligations under international law. This applies not only to the legalised statements of the Stimson Doctrine on the legal consequences of the use of force, but also to the implied understanding of the *ius ad bellum* under the Briand–Kellogg Pact.

The principles concerning the legality of the use of force assumed, and claimed to be, actual law in force and were at that point in time at least not undisputedly recognised as international law. The general prohibition on

393 A. Kuhn, 'The Lytton Report on the Manchurian Crisis', A.J.I.L., 27 (1933), 96–100. The findings of the Lytton Report were in turn accepted unanimously by the League of Nations Assembly: Q. Wright, 'Some Legal Aspects of the Far Eastern Situation', A.J.I.L., 27 (1933), 509–16.

394 IMT Judgment, vol. I, p. 208; *In Re Hirota and Others*, A.D. (1948), 364. On the interpretation of the Briand–Kellogg Pact by the Nuremberg and Tokyo military tribunals see: Bowett, *Self-Defence in International Law*, pp. 138–45. In summary: Dinstein, *War, Aggression and Self-Defence*, pp. 183–5.

the use of force, still disputed at that time under the Briand–Kellogg Pact and only implied within the doctrine as a rule of law, found its way into the subsequent development of international law.

The gradual abandonment of a unilateral right of a state to determine the occurrence of a situation in which it is entitled to use force in self-defence (as undertaken by Stimson) found its way to be a rule of international law in the UN Charter, which foresees the centralised determination of an aggressor. This initially unilateral declaration of the United States was not regarded as the creation of a new rule of law, but merely as the authentic interpretation of already existing obligations.

Doctrines of US security policy, declared under the UN Charter, also concern the interpretation of rules on the legality of use of force. They will be discussed in Chapter 3.

3

The doctrines during the Cold War period

The UN Charter came into force on 26 June 1945 at the beginning of the Cold War. Due to the almost universal effect of the UN Charter and the comprehensive regulation of the legality of the use of force contained in it, every development of the *ius ad bellum* since then has to be viewed in close connection with interpretation of the Charter.[1] At the same time, the political role of the United States changed from that of an actor in a multipolar system to that of a decisive state (one of the two poles) in an international system now considered as bipolar.[2]

3.1 The Truman Doctrine

Just as earlier doctrines, the doctrines of US security policy during the Cold War period are first of all a reaction to a situation perceived by the US as a concrete threat. In the case of the Truman Doctrine it was the developments in the Greek Civil War in 1943–7 which led to the formulation of the doctrine.[3]

Already in October 1943 at a time when large parts of Greece were still under German occupation, armed confrontations between the Peoples' Liberation Army (ELAS), belonging to the communist controlled National Front for Liberation (EAM), and the National Democratic Army (EDES) were taking place. The degree to which EAM/ELAS received support from the Soviet Union and Yugoslavia is still disputed to this day.[4]

1 A. McNair, *Law of Treaties* (Oxford: Clarendon Press, 1961), p. 217; I. Brownlie, *International Law and the Use of Force by States* (Oxford: Clarendon Press, 1963), pp. 112–16.

2 W. Grewe, *Epochs of International Law*, trans. Michael Byers (Berlin: Walter de Gruyter, 2000), pp. 639 *et seq.*

3 C. V. Crabb, *The Doctrines of American Foreign Policy – Their Meaning, Role and Future*, 3rd edn. (Baton Rouge, LA: Louisiana State University Press, 1990), pp. 108–16.

4 D. Merrill (ed.), *Documentary History of the Truman Presidency* (Bethesda, MD: University Publications of America, 1996), vol. VIII, pp. xxv–xxvi.

A British intervention on the side of EDES in December 1944 solved this conflict temporarily.[5]

EAM/ELAS continued its resistance against the British-supported government in the years 1944–7. Maintaining this support caused increasing financial problems for Great Britain.[6] On 21 February 1947 the British Government finally informed the US State Department that it intended to abandon British support for the Greek government. Likewise, Great Britain deemed itself no longer financially able to support Turkey.[7] For these reasons the United States decided in 1947, in response to a Greek request for help,[8] to lend support to the Greek government and Turkey in place of Britain.[9] It was on this occasion that the Truman Doctrine was declared.

3.1.1 The Truman Doctrine according to the speech of 12 March 1947

In a speech before both Houses of Congress on 12 March 1947, President Harry S. Truman stated the principles which came to serve for more than forty years as guiding principles for US foreign policy. The core statement of the Truman Doctrine can be found in the following phrase:

> I believe that it must be the policy of the United States to support free peoples who are resisting attempted subjugation by armed minorities or by outside pressures.[10]

This decisive passage is embedded in an explanation of the underlying conflict and a statement of the general consideration of relations between principles of US foreign policy and the UN Charter:

> nearly every nation must choose between alternative ways of life . . .
>
> One way of life is based upon the will of the majority, and is distinguished by free institutions, representative government, free elections, guarantees of individual liberty, freedom of speech and religion, and freedom from political oppression.

5 W. Churchill, *Memoirs of the Second World War (An Abridgement of the Six Volumes of the Second World War)* (Boston, MA: Houghton Mifflin, 1990), pp. 791–2, 900–7.
6 On the Greek civil war see further: J. Iatrides and J. Rizopoulos, 'The International Dimension of the Greek Civil War', WorldP.J., 17/1 (2000), 87–103.
7 *Foreign Relations of the United States, 1947*, vol. V, pp. 32–7.
8 *Department of State Bulletin*, 19 (1947), Suppl., pp. 827–8.
9 B. Kondis, 'The United States Role in the Greek Civil War', in E. Rossides (ed.), *The Truman Doctrine of Aid to Greece* (Washington, DC: American Hellenic Institute Foundation, 2001), pp. 144–50.
10 *Department of State Bulletin*, 19 (1947), Suppl., p. 831.

> The second way of life is based upon the will of a minority forcibly imposed upon the majority. It relies upon terror and oppression, a controlled press and radio, fixed elections, and the suppression of personal freedoms.
>
> I believe that it must be the policy of the United States to support free peoples who are resisting attempted subjugation by armed minorities or by outside pressures.
>
> I believe that we must assist free people to work out their own destinies in their own way . . .
>
> The world is not static, and the status quo is not sacred. But we cannot allow changes in the status quo in violation of the Charter of the United Nations by such methods as coercion, or by such subterfuges as political infiltration. In helping free and independent nations to maintain their freedom, the United States will be giving effect to the principles of the Charter of the United Nations.[11]

After outlining these principles, President Truman asked Congress to approve US$400 million in support for Greece and Turkey, and to authorise the sending of American civil and military personnel to support reconstruction, supervise financial aid and train Greek personnel.[12] On 15 May 1947 Congress passed a law concerning aid for Greece and Turkey,[13] and treaties about specific aid were subsequently concluded with both states.[14] The aid to Greece and Turkey served as a model for aid to a multitude of states during the Cold War.[15]

3.1.1.1 Statements on the legality of the use of force within the context of the Truman Doctrine

Truman's speech is regarded as one of the authoritative documents on the security policy of the United States in the early Cold War period, along with George F. Kennan's essay, *The Sources of Soviet Conduct*,[16] and the

11 *Department of State Bulletin*, 19 (1947), Suppl., p. 831.

12 *Department of State Bulletin*, 19 (1947), Suppl., pp. 831–2.

13 Public Law 75, 80th Congress, 1st Session, p. 938; US Congress, Senate, Committee on Foreign Relations (ed.), *Legislative Origins of the Truman Doctrine* (New York: Garland Publishing, 1979), p. 203.

14 Treaty between the United States and Greece, 20 June 1947, UNTS, vol. 7 (1947), pp. 267–98; Treaty between the United States and Turkey, 12 July 1947, UNTS, vol. 7 (1947), pp. 299–308. On this see further below, section 3.1.3.

15 C. Woods, 'An Overview of the Military Aspects of Security Assistance', Mil.L.Rev., 128 (1990), 71–113.

16 G. Kennan ('X'), 'The Sources of Soviet Conduct', For.Aff., 25/4 (1947), 566–82.

Report to the National Security Council, NSC-68[17] which elaborated on the implementation of the policy of containment.[18]

By the same token, Truman's speech acquired importance beyond a temporary orientation of US foreign policy. Senator Vandenberg, Chairman of the Senate Committee on Foreign Relations at the time of Truman's speech went as far as to declare the Truman Doctrine the most important declaration on US policy since the Monroe Doctrine.[19] President Truman himself made reference to the declaration of the Monroe Doctrine in his memoirs and considered the declaration of the Truman Doctrine due to prior political developments as just as appropriate a positioning of the United States as Washington's Farewell Address or the Monroe Doctrine.[20]

The Truman Doctrine is quite different from the Monroe Doctrine because it does not make a geographical distinction between states but an ideological distinction: that is, its principles are not limited to a specific region.[21] Because the Truman Doctrine outlines the basic conflict of the Cold War, the United States repeatedly made reference to its principles during the course of this conflict.[22] Even after the end of the Cold War, the principles of the Truman Doctrine are still considered as guidelines for US security policy. For example, President George W. Bush referred to

17 *Foreign Relations of the United States, 1950*, vol. I, pp. 245–301.

18 Merrill (ed.), *Documentary History of the Truman Presidency*, vol. VIII, p. xxvii.

19 *The New York Times*, 23 March 1947, quoted after: G. Smith, *The Last Years of the Monroe Doctrine, 1945–1993* (New York: Hill and Wang, 1994), p. 62. During the hearing on Public Law 75 the Monroe Doctrine and the Open Door Principle were considered predecessors of the Truman Doctrine. US Congress, Senate Committee on Foreign Relations (ed.), *Legislative Origins of the Truman Doctrine*, pp. 107–8; Similarly, D. Constantopoulos, 'The Significance of the Truman Doctrine for Greece and the Free World', *Revue Hellenique de droit International*, 25 (1972), 235.

20 'the policy which I was about to proclaim was indeed as much required by the conditions of my day as was Washington's [Farewell Address] by the situation in his era and Monroe's Doctrine by the circumstances which he then faced . . . ' H. Truman, *Memoirs by Harry S. Truman – Years of Trial and Hope* (New York: Smithmark Publishing, 1996), vol. 2, p. 102.

21 Smith, *The Last Years of the Monroe Doctrine*, p. 62; Crabb, *The Doctrines of American Foreign Policy*, p. 131.

22 *Department of State Bulletin*, 22 (1950), 975; *Department of State Bulletin*, 25 (1951), 175, 812; *Department of State Bulletin*, 26 (1952), 728, 775; *Department of State Bulletin*, 27 (1952), 169, 564; *Department of State Bulletin*, 32 (1955), 292; *Department of State Bulletin*, 36 (1957), 417, 539; *Department of State Bulletin*, 47 (1962), 100–1; *Department of State Bulletin*, 54 (1966), 186, 394–5, 830, 928; *Department of State Bulletin*, 56, (1967), 546–7, 653–6; *Department of State Bulletin*, 58 (1968), 559–60, 606, 657; *Department of State Bulletin*, 59 (1968), 71–2, 501; *Department of State Bulletin*, 66 (1972), 141; *Department of State Bulletin*, 68 (1973), 97; *Department of State Bulletin*, 72 (1975), 530.

the Truman Doctrine in his speech of 1 May 2003 on board USS *Abraham Lincoln*, in which he declared that the war with Iraq was over.[23]

If one limits this discussion to Truman's speech itself and the principles outlined within it, Marcelo Kohen's judgement that 'little if any insight can be derived from these doctrines which would shed light on the formulation or interpretation of the rules of international law relative to the use of force . . . '[24] seems to be very apt. There is no statement of law in Truman's speech itself, nor does the speech contain an explicit threat to use force in certain situations. The core statement of the speech merely contains the imprecise formulations 'to support' and 'assist', and the formula that the United States 'cannot allow changes in the status quo in violation of the Charter of the United Nations'.[25]

However, US opinion with regard to the use of force as a matter of law in the early phase of the UN Charter period becomes clearer by taking a closer look at the means by which the United States chose to implement the principles of the speech in its aid to Greece and Turkey shortly thereafter.

Internal memos on the discussions within the US Government published in 1971 document the rejection of at least some interpretations of the Charter, which were confirmed in subsequent US practice. These internal memos do not constitute *opinio iuris*, because they are not outwardly expressed legal positions and, thus, of no importance for the development of international law.[26] However, they allow a view of the formation of the US-American legal opinion, which in turn acted as a basis for later developments in international law.

This becomes clear in a memorandum by the State Department of 17 July 1947, in which alternative courses of action for the United States to support the Greek Government in connection with the United Nations are discussed. Besides suggesting sending a delegation commissioned and mandated by the Security Council and urging the Security Council to take action under chapter VII, one of the suggested alternatives reads:

23 The White House, 'President Bush Announces Major Combat Operations in Iraq have Ended', available at: www.whitehouse.gov/news/releases/2003/05/iraq/20030501-15.html.

24 M. Kohen, 'The Use of Force by the United States After the End of the Cold War, and its Impacts on International Law', in M. Byers and G. Nolte (eds.), *United States Hegemony and the Foundations of International Law* (Cambridge University Press, 2003), pp. 197–231.

25 *Department of State Bulletin*, 19 (1947), Suppl. 831.

26 Byers, *Custom Power and the Power of Rules: International Relations and Customary International Law* (Cambridge University Press, 1999), pp. 18–20, 129 *et seq.*

> (d) Action under Article 51 of the United Nations Charter pending the taking of effective action by the Security Council. (... In invoking this article, the United States would presumably rely upon the theory that an attack against one member of the United Nations may nearly always be considered as an attack against all.) ...[27]

Even though this interpretation of the UN Charter – deriving a right of all members to take action against a prior violation of the prohibition on the use of force in Article 2(4) in the form of an armed attack – sounds like the earlier interpretation of the Briand–Kellogg Pact by Secretary of State Stimson (giving all states a right to take action, although not to use force in case of a violation),[28] it was not pursued further. Furthermore, this concept of merging the basic principles of collective security and collective self-defence[29] did not find support among scholars.[30]

The United States never adhered to such a broad interpretation of Article 51 of the UN Charter – considering an attack against one state as an attack against all member states. To do so would have also contradicted the later, repeatedly stated opinion of the United States that it could act in self-defence to aid an attacked state even though it had not itself been attacked.[31] Several other options are discussed in the same memorandum. One of these seems to anticipate the development after the declaration of the Bush Doctrine in 2002. It reads as follows:

> Consideration is also being given to other action within the spirit, although not within the procedural framework, of the United Nations Charter. Such action may be in concert with other UN members or simply with the British ...[32]

The claim to act for the benefit of the values and principles of the UN Charter is a recurring feature and has a direct connection with the Truman Doctrine. In an annex to a memorandum by the Representative of the War Department in the Executive Committee on Regulation of Armaments of 30 July 1947 titled, 'Applying the Truman Doctrine to the United

27 *Foreign Relations of the United States*, 1947, vol. V, p. 241.
28 For.Aff., 11 (1932) Special Suppl., pp. viii–ix. On this see further above, Chapter 2, section 2.2.3.2.
29 N. Krisch, *Selbstverteidigung und kollektive Sicherheit* (Berlin: Springer, 2001), pp. 167–70, Ph.D. thesis, Heidelberg, 2001.
30 L. M. Goodrich and E. Hambro, *Charter of the United Nations*, 2nd edn. (London: Stevens & Sons, 1949), pp. 301–2.
31 For example, *Department of State Bulletin*, 54 (1966), 477; *Department of State Bulletin*, 1 (1986), 70; *UN Yearbook 1990*, pp. 194–6.
32 *Foreign Relations of the United States*, 1947, vol. V, p. 241.

Nations', to the Foreign Secretary, War Secretary and Navy Secretary, the Soviet attitude is evaluated as being against the purpose and principles of the UN Charter. Thus, the United States' aim was, *inter alia*, to highlight the violation of the Charter by the Soviets in contrast to US behaviour.[33]

3.1.1.2 Use of force in terms of the Truman Doctrine as a unilateral enforcement of the collective will: 'giving effect to the principles'

The declaration of the Truman Doctrine meant an abandonment of the idea of Roosevelt's so-called 'one world vision' as a political concept in response to the beginning of the Cold War.[34] However, the matter of possible action through the United Nations, avoiding unilateral courses of action, took up a large part of the internal US discussion on Public Law 75 concerning the aid to Greece and Turkey.[35]

These efforts went so far that the United States even undertook to stop aid to these states if the Security Council of the UN General Assembly found that UN measures made the continuation of this aid unnecessary, and to abstain from exercising its veto with regard to decisions touching on these treaty provisions.[36]

Even though the US aid to Greece took the form of factual exercise of supreme command over the Greek forces by a US-American general and the participation of some American soldiers in hostilities,[37] these treaty provisions did not regulate aid in the form of the use of force.[38] Thus, the United States did not authorise the UN Security Council or the General Assembly to decide on the use of force on the part of the United States. In view of the pro-US majority situation in the General Assembly and the Security Council at the time, and the then existing opportunity of a

33 *Foreign Relations of the United States*, 1947, vol. I, p. 580.

34 'Pepper Deplores Truman Doctrine', *Harvard Law Record*, 16 April 1947, pp. 1–3; N. Paech and G. Stuby, *Machtpolitik und Völkerrecht in den internationalen Beziehungen* (Baden-Baden: Nomos, 1994), pp. 199–203.

35 US Congress, Senate Committee on Foreign Relations (ed.), *Legislative Origins of the Truman Doctrine*, pp. 13–19, 22–4, 54, 61–3, 102–3, 106–7, 109–18, 127–8, 169–74, 181.

36 In Article 10 of the treaty with Greece and Article IV(2) of the treaty with Turkey. UNTS, vol. VII (1947), pp. 267–98; UNTS, vol. VII (1947), pp. 299–308.

37 P. Braim, 'General James A. Van Fleet and the U.S. Military Mission to Greece', in Rossides (ed.), *The Truman Doctrine of Aid to Greece*, pp. 117–27, in particular p. 119.

38 The treaties with Turkey and Greece make in Article 1 reference to Public Law 75 and limit the function of military personal to an advisory capacity ('in advisory capacity only . . . ').

'hidden veto',[39] hardly any practical relevance can be attributed to the US waiver of the veto.

In Truman's speech itself and in Congressional hearings, President Truman and Secretary of State Achenson were eager to create a link between the Truman Doctrine and the UN Charter by arguing that the principles of the doctrine served to reassert the principles of the UN Charter.[40] President Truman, in the speech on 12 March 1947 used the following formulation: 'In helping free and independent nations to maintain their freedom, the United States will be giving effect to the principles of the Charter of the United Nations.'[41] Secretary of State Achenson explained before the House Committee on Foreign Relations on Public Law 75 that the aim of the law was to uphold the principles enshrined in the UN Charter.[42] Similarly, the United States declared through their representative to the United Nations that it would act in this spirit.[43]

These (to a large extent) unspecific, very general formulations anticipated in many ways a self-understanding of the United States within international institutions, as advocates of the New Haven School would later suggest, as 'custodian' of the actual principles of the UN Charter.[44] A separate model for the justification of the use of force has been derived from that. From the interaction of the preamble of the UN Charter and Articles 55 and 56 it is concluded that the repeated emphasis on 'common interest in human rights' would result in a 'coordinate responsibility for the active protection of human rights'. For this reason the member states shall be authorised to use force unilaterally in case of a break-down of the Security Council.[45] In this respect it is not surprising that of all people Myres McDougal defended the Truman Doctrine against criticism by Hans Morgenthau and George F. Kennan, who considered the doctrine an expression of a legalistic–moralist policy approach which could be

39 On this see: B. Simma, S. Brunner and H. Kaul, 'Art. 27', in B. Simma (ed.), *The Charter of the United Nations*, 2nd edn. (Oxford University Press, 2002), pp. 514–15, No. 117 *et seq.*

40 W. Brown, Jr. and R. Opie, *American Foreign Assistance* (Washington, DC: The Brookings Institution, 1954), pp. 124–31; D. Constantopoulos, 'The Significance of the Truman Doctrine for Greece and the Free World', Rev.Hell.d.Int., 25 (1972), 242–4.

41 *Department of State Bulletin*, 19 (1947), Suppl., 831.

42 Crabb, *The Doctrines of American Foreign Policy*, pp. 134–5

43 *Department of State Bulletin*, 19 (1947), Suppl., 834.

44 M. Reisman, 'The United States and International Institutions', Survival, 41/4 (1999–2000), 63–80.

45 M. Reisman and M. McDougal, 'Humanitarian Intervention to Protect the Ibos', in R. Lillich (ed.), *Humanitarian Intervention and the United Nations* (Charlottesville, VA: University of Virginia Press, 1973), pp. 172–5.

implemented only inconsequently and contradictorily.[46] In spite of the similarity between the arguments of proponents of the New Haven School and US representatives in close connection with the Truman Doctrine, in which both emphasised the preservation of Charter principles, these arguments were not invoked by the United States as justification for the use of force. Thus, the aforementioned US-American declarations remain elaborations of political motives rather than *opinio iuris*.

3.1.2 Evaluation of the cases of the use of force foreseen in the Truman Doctrine under international law

Just as in the case of the Monroe Doctrine, the legal evaluation of the reconcilability of the means chosen to implement the Truman Doctrine with international law depends on the content one attributes to the doctrine.

3.1.2.1 Criteria of the Truman Doctrine for the use of force

As the Truman Doctrine is the first US doctrine outlining the fundamental conflict of the Cold War, the measures considered to be an implementation of the doctrine changed frequently over the course of the conflict.[47]

These implementing measures contained a broad spectrum of actions of varying relevance for international law, and for the most part did not concern the use of force.[48] The Marshall Plan,[49] for example, was considered by the United States, as well as the Soviet Union, to be an implementation of the Truman Doctrine.[50] Some commentators entirely exclude the use of force from the measures implementing the doctrine.[51]

46 M. McDougal, 'Law and Power', A.J.I.L., 46 (1952), 102–4.

47 On the details of practical implementation of the doctrine see: R. Tucker, *The American Outlook*, in R. Osgood *et al.* (eds.), *America and the World – From the Truman Doctrine to Vietnam* (Baltimore, MD: The Johns Hopkins University Press, 1970), pp. 34–43.

48 See also: A. Sack, 'The Truman Doctrine in International Law', L.G.Rev., 7 (1947), 142–4.

49 On this see: G. Erler, 'Marshallplan', in H. Schlochauer (ed.), *Wörterbuch des Völkerrechts*, 2nd edn. (Berlin: Walter de Gruyter, 1962), vol. II, pp. 480–4.

50 *Department of State Bulletin*, 59 (1968), 71–2; M. Marinin, *Die 'Truman-Doktrin' und der 'Marshall-Plan'* (Berlin: SWA-Verlag, 1947); E. Borchard, 'Intervention – The Truman Doctrine and the Marshall Plan', A.J.I.L., 41 (1947), 885–8.

51 Schlochauer, for example, makes in his entry 'Truman-Doktrin' only a reference to economic assistance agreements (German: '*s. Wirtschaftshilfeabkommen*'), H-J. Schlochauer (ed.), *Wörterbuch des Völkerrechts*, 2nd edn. (Berlin: Walter de Gruyter, 1962), vol. III, p. 460. Similarly, T. Grant, 'Doctrines (Monroe, Halstein, Brezhnev, Stimson)', in R. Wolfrum (ed.), *The Max Planck Encyclopaedia of Public International Law* (Oxford University Press, 2008), online edition available at: www.mpepil.com, Nos. 29–30.

A definition of the Truman Doctrine by the then Undersecretary of State Eugene V. Rostow of 11 October 1968 illustrates the multitude of actions considered as covered by the Truman Doctrine:

> 'It has two principal aspects:
>
> - First, what has been called *containment*, that is, the establishment of a system or systems which could effectively check any further advances by the Soviet Union and other Communist states.
> - Second, reconstruction and development of *assistance*, as typified initially by the Marshall Plan and the Point 4 programs, which in turn brings stability and should gradually make it possible for the nations of the free world to take a major part in their own defense, reducing the United States gradually to the role of junior partner . . .[52]

Hence, to a large extent the means chosen to implement the Truman Doctrine are only indirectly related to the use of force. However, cases of the use of force – even to the point of massive deployment of US armed forces to Vietnam – were considered an expression of the Truman Doctrine.[53] Secretary of Defence Clark Clifford saw a direct link between the doctrine and US engagement in Vietnam:

> I believe deeply in the necessity for our presence in Viet-Nam. We are assisting that brave and beleaguered nation to fight aggression, under the SEATO Treaty – and for the same reasons we extended our aid to Greece and Turkey over 20 years ago. This is in the tradition of the Truman doctrine, which announced 20 years ago that we would help defend the liberty of peoples who wished to defend themselves . . .[54]

Thus, the use of force is also considered by the United States to be an aspect of implementation of the Truman Doctrine.[55] Irrespective of questions over the legality of isolated incidents of the use of force which were considered to be implementations of the Truman Doctrine, which abstract general principles for the use of force can be derived from the Truman Doctrine? The follow-up question arises as to what extent cases of the use of force based on these principles are justified. Particularly

52 *Department of State Bulletin*, 59 (1968), 501.

53 Q. Wright, 'Legal Aspects of the Vietnam Situation', A.J.I.L., 60 (1966), 754–5; G. Evans and J. Newnham, *The Penguin Dictionary of International Relations* (London: Penguin Books, 1998), p. 546.

54 *Department of State Bulletin*, 58 (1968), 606.

55 K. Schwabe, 'The Origins of the United States Engagement in Europe, 1946–1952', in H. Heller and J. Gillingham (eds.), *NATO: The Founding of the Atlantic Alliance and the Integration of Europe* (New York: St Martin's Press, 1992), p. 164.

in connection with the discussion on the legality of the principles of the later Reagan Doctrine, attempts were made to define the criteria for the use of force in the Truman Doctrine. According to Louis Henkin's definition, the doctrine foresees support by the United States given to democratic governments against direct or indirect armed attack or international rebellion.[56] Kirkpatrick and Gerson consider that the Truman Doctrine allows for the use of counter-force and counter-intervention as an *ultima ratio* if an independent government is subject to attacks, which cannot be repelled in any other way.[57]

It follows that, at the least, the undisputed core of the doctrine is that the Truman Doctrine does not foresee first strike unilateral uses of force, but uses of force which support action in international and domestic armed conflicts.

Different possible justifications for military action by another state within the territory of another are conceivable: due to the basic inapplicability of the prohibition on the use of force in Article 2(4) of the UN Charter in internal conflicts, an intervention upon invitation is in principle a possible justification for the presence of foreign troops.[58] Besides, an action in exercise of collective self-defence may be appropriate.

Ian Brownlie, discussing the Truman Doctrine and the understanding of the legality of the use of force in self-defence that it is based on, considers that the Truman Doctrine is an expression of a general tendency in the practice of states since 1945 to justify interventions as collective self-defence against indirect aggressions and as supporting of governments threatened by subversion.[59] The terms 'indirect aggression' or 'indirect military aggression' are generally understood to mean the concealed sending of irregular armed forces into the territory of another state and supporting actions of armed forces acting in the

56 L. Henkin, 'The Use of Force: Law and U.S. Policy', in L. Henkin *et al.* (eds.), *Right v. Might – International Law and the Use of Force*, 2nd edn. (New York: Council on Foreign Relations Press, 1991), p. 61: 'If it proves necessary, the United States should recommit itself to the Truman doctrine: The U.S. is entitled to help secure democracy by assisting an incumbent democratic government against armed attack, direct and indirect, or even against threatened international rebellion.'

57 J. Kirkpatrick and A. Gerson, 'The Reagan Doctrine, Human Rights, and International Law', in Henkin *et al.* (ed.), *Right v. Might. International Law and the Use of Force*, p. 31.

58 G. Nolte, *Eingreifen auf Einladung* (Berlin: Springer, 1999), pp. 208–17. In favour of that kind of justification for the principles of the Truman Doctrine for use of force see: D. Constantopoulos, 'The Significance of the Truman Doctrine for Greece and the Free World', Rev.Hell.d.Int., 25 (1972), 244.

59 Brownlie, *International Law and the Use of Force by States*, p. 325.

territory of another state, such as the supply of arms and other logistical support.[60]

The question of whether those kind of activities constitute an 'armed attack' and thus entitle the targeted state to self-defence and collective self-defence according to Article 51 of the UN Charter has been answered differently.[61] This, of course, presupposes that the occurrence of an 'armed attack' is considered a necessary prerequisite for the exercise of self-defence and is not considered dispensable on the basis of the word 'inherent'.[62]

In connection with the Truman Doctrine the fact of different answers is significant in two respects. On the one hand, it is questionable whether supporting actions which are considered as implementations of the Truman Doctrine can be justified as self-defence under Article 51 of the UN Charter. On the other hand, this brings up the question as to whether these kinds of action in themselves trigger a right of other states to exercise self-defence. The Mutual Defence Assistance Act 1951, for example,[63] in which the US Congress extended the authorisation to help Greece and Turkey beyond two states to all 'friendly nations' was considered by the USSR and Czechoslovakia as an 'aggression'.[64] The second aspect of this question is whether support by the United States, based on the doctrines of the Cold War period, gave other states a right to exercise self-defence against the United States and its allies. This issue was subsequently discussed among scholars of international law particularly in connection with the Reagan Doctrine and will be treated below.[65]

3.1.2.2 The Truman Doctrine and 'indirect aggression'

Use of force by the United States in support of another state according to the Truman Doctrine requires at least the existence of an action by

60 On this see further: P. Zanardi, 'Indirect Military Aggression', in A. Cassese (ed.), *The Current Legal Regulation of the Use of Force* (Dordrecht: Martin Nijhoff, 1986), pp. 111–19.

61 A. J. Thomas and A. V. Thomas, *The Concept of Aggression in International Law* (Dallas, TX: Southern Methodist University Press, 1972), pp. 65 *et seq.*

62 See Goodrich and Hambro, *Charter of the United Nations*, p. 301; D. W. Bowett, *Self-Defence in International Law* (Manchester University Press, 1958), pp. 187–93. On this see further below, Chapter 4, section 4.2.2.2.

63 A.J.I.L., 46 (1952), Suppl., 14–31. On this see: Brown Jr. and Opie, *American Foreign Assistance*, pp. 463–70.

64 UN Doc. UN/A/1968/Rev. I, 22 November 1951; UN Doc. UN/A/2224/Rev. I, 15 October 1952.

65 See below, section 3.6.

another state which can be considered an 'indirect aggression'. Truman also used the term 'indirect aggression' in his speech of 12 March 1947:

> The United Nations is designed to make possible lasting freedom and independence for all its members. We shall not realize our objectives, however, unless we are willing to help free peoples to maintain their free institutions and their national integrity against aggressive movements that seek to impose upon them totalitarian regimes. This is no more than the frank recognition that totalitarian regimes imposed on free peoples, by direct or indirect aggression, undermine the foundations of international peace and security...

The legality of the use of force by helping a third state to defend itself not against the use of force by regular forces of another state, but against irregular force supported by another state depends on the specific shape this indirect force takes.[66] Numerous different types of support are conceivable. Brownlie distinguishes between seven possible types of involvement of states in activities of armed bands.[67]

The Truman Doctrine does not specify what exact shape the prior undermining of a state by another must have taken for the United States to use force in support of the former. In Truman's speech only the general terms 'indirect aggression' and 'attempted subjugation by armed minorities or by outside pressures' are used in this respect.[68] A precise evaluation of the legality of such uses of force is not possible due to the lack of precise determination of the preconditions under which the United States would take supporting actions under the Truman Doctrine. In contrast, it is possible to evaluate the degree to which supporting uses of force by the United States under the Truman Doctrine were legal, in case the preceding undermining support by another state took the form of an indirect aggression.

A fundamental statement with regard to the legality of the use of force can be found in the *Nicaragua* Judgment of 1986. The ICJ considered that the behaviour described in Article 3(g) of the General Assembly in

66 In detail on this see: C. Kreß, *Gewaltverbot und Selbstverteidigung nach der Satzung der Vereinten Nationen bei staatlicher Verwicklung in Gewaltakte Privater* (Berlin: Duncker und Humblot, 1995), Ph.D. thesis, Cologne, 1994. Sack, in contrast, refers to the necessity of a concrete threat for the supporting state and thus considers use of force according to the principles of the Truman Doctrine as illegal. A. Sack, 'The Truman Doctrine in International Law', L.G.Rev., 7 (1947), 166.

67 I. Brownlie, 'International Law and the Activities of Armed Bands', I.C.L.Q., 7 (1958), 712–35.

68 *Department of State Bulletin*, 19 (1947), Suppl., 831–4.

Resolution 3314 (XXIX) is an armed attack and the court considered this resolution to be an expression of customary law.[69] According to this definition, the sending of armed gangs, groups, irregulars or mercenaries constitutes an aggression.[70] At the same time, however, the ICJ made it clear that delivering arms and other supporting actions constitute aggressions but not an armed attack.[71] Hence, according to this opinion, not all supporting actions which could be categorised as an 'indirect aggression' entitle states to exercise military force, but only those types of actions that include the use of armed groups at an operational level amounts to an armed attack.[72] Furthermore, a requirement for the exercise of collective self-defence shall be that the attacked state declared itself a victim of an armed attack.[73]

The sending of armed bands, irregulars or mercenaries was already considered prior to the *Nicaragua* Judgment as an armed attack in terms of Article 51 of the UN Charter by the vast majority of scholars of public international law.[74] The possibility of evaluating the use of force based on the principles of the Truman Doctrine differently and justifying it under Article 51 of the UN Charter arises only if one adheres to the opinion that irregular troops could advance an 'attack' but not an 'armed attack'.[75] This opinion did not catch on. At least the United States considered the sending of irregular troops an 'armed attack'.[76]

Consequently, Articles 2(4) and 51 of the UN Charter leave room for the use of force based on the principles of the Truman Doctrine (even if it is assumed that the occurrence of an armed attack is a necessary prerequisite for the exercise of self-defence), if the prior 'indirect aggression' took the

69 *Military and Paramilitary Activities in and against Nicaragua* (*Nicaragua* v. *United States of America*), Merits, Judgment, I.C.J. Rep. 1986, pp. 93–4, para. 195.

70 UN Doc. A/RES/3314 (XXIX), 14 December 74.

71 *Military and Paramilitary Activities in and against Nicaragua* (*Nicaragua* v. *United States of America*), Merits, Judgment, I.C.J. Rep. 1986, pp. 126–7, para. 247.

72 Kreß, *Gewaltverbot und Selbstverteidigung nach der Satzung der Vereinten Nationen bei staatlicher Verwicklung in Gewaltakte Privater*, pp. 122–7, in particular p. 126.

73 *Military and Paramilitary Activities in and against Nicaragua* (*Nicaragua* v. *United States of America*), Merits, Judgment, I.C.J. Rep. 1986, p. 127, para. 195.

74 P. Zanardi, 'Indirect Military Aggression', in Cassese (ed.), *The Current Legal Regulation of the Use of Force*, p. 112; different see: Q. Wright, 'United States Intervention in the Lebanon', A.J.I.L., 53 (1959), 116. In detail on this contentious issue see: Kreß, *Gewaltverbot und Selbstverteidigung nach der Satzung der Vereinten Nationen bei staatlicher Verwicklung in Gewaltakte Privater*, pp. 143–7 with further material.

75 F. von der Heydte, *Völkerrecht* (Cologne: Kiepenheuer & Wietsch, 1960), vol. II, p. 345; H. Habig, 'Die SEATO und das Völkerrecht', Ph.D. thesis, Würzburg, 1973, pp. 70–1.

76 For example, *Department of State Bulletin*, 54 (1966), 475.

shape of an armed attack. This depends on the form the supporting action has taken.[77]

Uses of force under the Truman Doctrine were subsequently justified by the United States as in exercise of self-defence after a prior armed attack.[78] Thus, it is possible to justify use of force, based on the principles of the doctrine, by invoking Article 51 of the UN Charter and the means chosen to implement the doctrine are open to an interpretation in accordance with the UN Charter.

3.1.3 Legalisation of the Truman Doctrine

As the Cold War conflict is described in basic terms in the Truman Doctrine,[79] it would be possible to link almost every action taken by the United States over its course to the Truman Doctrine by hinting at the paradigmatic character of the Cold War for US foreign policy at this time and the general formulation ('to assist') of the doctrine. Statements on the legalisation of the doctrine based on a broad consideration of the Truman Doctrine would necessarily have to stay unproductive due to the low level of precision of the courses of action foreseen in it.

However, if the Truman Doctrine is discussed more specifically as a doctrine of US security policy in terms of the definition this work is based on,[80] and is reduced to the attribution of the doctrine to the military support of 'free peoples' in reaction to prior use of force, this leads to the question of whether this more limited principle has found its way into rules of international law.

Unlike the Monroe Doctrine or the Open Door Principle, the Truman Doctrine does not formulate an explicit prohibition addressed to other states warning them not to take action in a certain region. It can be interpreted only as an implicit demand on other states to abstain from certain activities in connection with the contrasting descriptions of alternative types of society in the context of the Cold War.[81] However, this demand did not take the form of a law-like formulation of a political principle.

77 Kreß, *Gewaltverbot und Selbstverteidigung nach der Satzung der Vereinten Nationen bei staatlicher Verwicklung in Gewaltakte Privater*, pp. 336–45.

78 For example, *Department of State Bulletin*, 54 (1966), 475.

79 Crabb, *The Doctrines of American Foreign Policy*, pp. 108–17.

80 See above, Chapter 1, section 1.6.

81 D. Graber, 'The Truman and Eisenhower Doctrines in the Light of the Doctrine of Non-Intervention', P.S.Q., 78/3 (1958), 331.

The only addressee of the principle of support of 'free peoples' described in the Truman Doctrine is the United States itself.[82]

Single cases of the use of force which were considered to be implementations of the Truman Doctrine as evidenced by justifications brought forward in connection with them, make it apparent that the Truman Doctrine was interpreted by the US Government as meaning that the doctrine foresees the use of force only in case of a prior armed attack.[83] Thus, self-imposed obligations to give support in the case of an indirect aggression taking the shape of an armed attack under Article 51 of the UN Charter can be considered to be a legalisation of the Truman Doctrine.[84]

In the memos concerning the implementation of the Truman Doctrine in direct connection with supporting Greece and Turkey in 1947 it was suggested that a treaty be concluded which would obligate the parties to provide mutual aid in case of an armed attack under Article 51.[85] The Act of Chapultepec and the Rio Pact – which were considered legalisations of the Monroe Doctrine – are referred to as role models.[86]

It was also implied in these memos, though not explicitly stated, that an armed attack not only possibly entitles all UN member states to take action, but that there might be an obligation under the UN Charter on the member states to provide aid.[87] This resembles the point of view taken by the United States earlier with regard to the Monroe and Stimson Doctrines, that no new obligations are created under these doctrines but merely that those already existing are restated.[88] However, such an obligation was never claimed by the member states and nor did it translate into state practice. It remained an internal US suggestion only.

Instead of creating a universal organisation for the exercise of self-defence, a number of regional pacts of mutual assistance were founded – of which NATO is the largest – and which have been linked repeatedly to the Truman Doctrine.[89]

82 R. Tucker, 'The American Outlook', in Osgood *et al.* (eds.), *America and the World – From the Truman Doctrine to Vietnam*, pp. 27 *et seq.*

83 For example, *Department of State Bulletin*, 59 (1968), 71–2; *Department of State Bulletin*, 72 (1975), 720.

84 A. Goodhart, 'The North Atlantic Treaty of 1949', RdC, 79 (1951-II), 211–14.

85 *Foreign Relations of the United States, 1947*, vol. I, pp. 568–70.

86 On this see further above, Chapter 2, section 2.1.3.5.

87 *Foreign Relations of the United States, 1947*, vol. I, p. 569: 'Such an obligation is today perhaps implicit in the Charter of the United Nations but it is not explicit . . . '

88 See above, Chapter 2, sections 2.1.3.3 and 2.2.3.2.

89 P. Foot, 'America and the Origins of the Atlantic Alliance: a Reappraisal', in J. Smith (ed.), *The Origins of NATO* (University of Exeter Press, 1990), p. 83.

3.1.3.1 The NATO Treaty as legalisation of the Truman Doctrine

In the first sentence of Article 5 of the North Atlantic Treaty (hereafter the NATO Treaty) of 4 April 1949 the parties to the treaty agree that an attack against one of them in Europe or North America shall be considered an attack against all of them and that they will react together to such an attack.[90] Alongside this the NATO Treaty contains a commitment of the member states to the broader term 'security' as distinct from the narrow term 'defence' in the preamble.[91]

In this respect the political principle to support peoples considered by the United States as being 'free peoples' against indirect aggression – as declared in Truman's speech of 12 March 1947 – has taken the shape of a legally-binding obligation on the United States under international law. Yet the NATO Treaty leaves the individual parties to the treaty a considerable margin of appreciation as to the implementation of the obligation in Article 5 of the NATO Treaty.[92] It is up to the alliance members individually to decide on the point of time at which their alliance obligations arise and whether an armed attack has taken place.[93] The common determination of the occurrence of an armed attack by the North Atlantic Council, as occurred for the first time on 12 September 2001, [94] thus, has a merely declaratory meaning. Furthermore, each party to the treaty decides for itself the nature and scope of the means required to defend against an armed attack.[95] Because the NATO Treaty does not necessarily foresee the use of force, no legal duty to use force results from it.[96]

It has been assumed by some that the opinion of the United States as the strongest partner in the alliance was decisive for determining the

90 UNTS, vol. 34 (1949), pp. 243–55.

91 On this distinction see: G. Nolte, 'Die "neuen Aufgaben" von NATO und WEU', ZaöRV/H.J.I.L., 54 (1994) 101–2.

92 K. Kersting, 'Bündnisfall und Verteidigungsfall', Ph.D. thesis, Bochum, 1979, pp. 4–8.

93 E. Brüel, 'Die juristische Bedeutung des Atlantikpaktes', AVR, 4 (1953/4), 288–300 at 295; G. Meier, *Der bewaffnete Angriff* (Munich: Charlotte Schön, 1963), Ph.D. thesis, Göttingen, 1963, p. 168; K. Ipsen, *Rechtsgrundlagen und Institutionalisierung der Atlantisch-Europäischen Verteidigung* (Hamburg: Hanseatischer Gildenverlag, 1967), Ph.D. thesis, Kiel, 1967, p. 43 with further evidence.

94 S. Murphy (ed.), 'Contemporary Practice of the United States Relating to International Law', A.J.I.L., 26 (2002), 244.

95 Ipsen, *Rechtsgrundlagen und Institutionalisierung der Atlantisch-Europäischen Verteidigung*, pp. 44–51.

96 Meier, *Der bewaffnete Angriff*, pp. 169–70.

alliance duties under Article 5, because the efficiency of the regulation contained in Article 5 would depend on the United States' willingness to exercise this obligation in good faith. Article 5 of the NATO Treaty could, hence, assume only the legal force that the United States was willing to attribute to it. Consequently, an interpretation of Article 5 by the United States alone would constitute an adequate judicial interpretation of this norm.[97]

In contrast to this opinion, the wording of the treaty is decisive in determining the obligations under the treaty.[98] Regardless of this, it is only possible to speak of a gradual legalisation of the Truman Doctrine – or the principle to support 'free states' enshrined in the doctrine – due to a lack of legal obligation to use force under the NATO Treaty.

With regard to the United States' sole discretion for interpreting the Truman Doctrine, even the antagonism between the NATO Treaty and the Truman Doctrine is emphasised.[99] The aspect of defending states and peoples considered as 'free' found little translation into the NATO Treaty. The NATO Treaty does not define 'free', but makes reference in its preamble to the 'principles of democracy, individual liberty and the rule of law'. By doing so, it distinguishes between the NATO member states and other states, and extends the purpose of the treaty beyond that of the UN Charter.[100] Article 2 of the NATO Treaty, furthermore, calls for a harmonisation of the political systems of member states and even uses the same formulation as President Truman in the speech of 12 March 1947 ('free institutions'). The strengthening of free institutions is in itself considered a means of accomplishing the objective of peaceful international relations and the other goals mentioned in the preamble. But the treaty does not determine the means which shall be used to accomplish the 'strengthening of free institutions'.[101]

Unlike the universal principle of supporting all free peoples outlined in the Truman Doctrine, NATO constitutes a geographically limited system of security. The limits are described in Article 6 of the NATO Treaty. Concerns were voiced against this geographical limitation as

97 M. Hagemann, 'Der Atlantikpakt und die Satzung der Vereinten Nationen', AVR, 2 (1950), 387.

98 Meier, *Der bewaffnete Angriff*, p. 169.

99 L. Kaplan, 'After Forty Years: Reflection on NATO as a Research Field', in Heller and Gillingham (eds.), *NATO: The Founding of the Atlantic Alliance and the Integration of Europe*, p. 17.

100 A. Goodhart, 'The North Atlantic Treaty of 1949', RdC, 79 (1951-II), 218–19.

101 E. Brüel, 'Die juristische Bedeutung des Atlantikpaktes', AVR, 4 (1953/4), 292–3.

'free' states outside the system would be exposed to a greater danger of attack.[102] This would even contradict the basic idea of the Truman Doctrine. Yet balancing this was the desire to create a system of alliances as comprehensive as possible, which was a characteristic feature of US foreign policy during the Cold War period. The SEATO Treaty is considered the Asiatic counterpart to the North Atlantic Treaty.[103]

3.1.3.2 The SEATO Treaty as legalisation of the Truman Doctrine

The South East Asia Collective Defence Treaty was in force between 19 February 1955 and 30 June 1977. It was signed in Manila on 8 September 1954 – it is also called Manila Treaty – and is the founding document of SEATO.[104] Article 4(I) of the SEATO Treaty commits the state parties to take measures in accordance with their respective constitutional processes in the case of an aggression by means of armed attack against one of the other state parties. Unlike Article 5 of the NATO Treaty, however, the parties to the treaty do not consider an attack as an attack directed against them all, but as endangering the 'peace and safety' of the other parties.[105]

Determining whether an aggression constitutes an armed attack was left to the state parties themselves, just as in case of the NATO Treaty. Which measures in particular ought to be taken in response was also left to the discretion of the individual member states.[106] Only a duty to consult was imposed.[107] Consequently, no obligation on the United States to use force in order to implement the Truman Doctrine resulted from the SEATO Treaty. However, in subsequent cases of the use of force considered to be an implementation of the Truman Doctrine the United States relied on Article 4(I) of the SEATO Treaty.[108] However, at the same time the United States pointed out that no obligation to use force resulted from the SEATO Treaty.[109]

In an explanation by the United States of Article 11 of the SEATO Treaty it was furthermore determined that the term 'aggression' in

102 Hagemann, 'Der Atlantikpakt und die Satzung der Vereinten Nationen', p. 403.

103 Habig, 'Die SEATO und das Völkerrecht', pp. 3–6, 21–30.

104 UNTS, vol. 209 (1955), pp. 23–37.

105 I. Shearer, 'South-East Asia Treaty Organisation', E.P.I.L., IV (2000), 484–5.

106 A. Rubin, 'SEATO and American Legal Obligations Concerning Laos and Cambodia', I.C.L.Q., 20 (1970), 506–12. Rubin furthermore makes a comparison between the SEATO Treaty and the Monroe Doctrine and calls it an 'extension of the modern United States view of the Monroe Doctrine to Southeast Asia', p. 509.

107 Habig, 'Die SEATO und das Völkerrecht', p. 72.

108 *Department of State Bulletin*, 54 (1966), 480–1.

109 *Department of State Bulletin*, 31 (1954), 820–3, particularly p. 822.

Article 4(I) referred solely to communist aggression. The aim of this explanation was to exclude the application of the SEATO Treaty to the India–Pakistan conflict.[110] Just like the NATO Treaty, the SEATO Treaty contained a regional limitation in Article 8. This was a considerable difference compared with the universal approach of the Truman Doctrine.

Article 3 of the SEATO Treaty also contained the same vague reference to free institutions as Article 2 of the NATO Treaty.[111] In addition, the ending of Article 2 made it clear that the duty of mutual assistance applied only to cases of 'subversive activities from without', in order to exclude domestic unrest by indigenous peoples from the coverage of the treaty.[112] Due to the marginal binding effects of the SEATO Treaty it can be considered – just like the NATO Treaty – as being only a gradual legalisation of the Truman Doctrine.

The Baghdad Pact of 24 February 1955, later renamed the CENTO Treaty, contained further regulation with regard to collective exercise of self-defence. Even though the United States was not a party to this treaty, CENTO will be discussed in further detail in the context of the Eisenhower Doctrine.[113]

3.1.4 Conclusion

The Truman Doctrine outlines in basic terms the Cold War conflict and formulates a political duty for the United States to support states, considered by the United States to be free, fighting against aggression by another state.

The means foreseen to implement the doctrine comprised a multitude of actions which do not constitute the use of force. The Truman Doctrine according to the speech of 12 March 1947 does not determine a precise standard for the use of force by the United States. However, the Truman Doctrine does allow for the use of force in cases of prior 'indirect aggression' as an aspect of US foreign policy.

These cases of the use of force in the event of a prior 'indirect aggression' as foreseen by the Truman Doctrine can be justified as an intervention upon invitation, as well as a collective exercise of self-defence. This results from the fact that the doctrine was interpreted as requiring an 'armed attack' as a necessary prerequisite for the use of force under the Truman Doctrine. The flexibility of the doctrine makes it at least possible

110 Habig, 'Die SEATO und das Völkerrecht', p. 73. 111 See above, section 3.1.3.1.
112 Shearer, 'South-East Asia Treaty Organization', p. 484.
113 See below, section 3.2.2.3.

to interpret it in accordance with the UN Charter so that it foresees the use of force only in accordance with the requirement of an armed attack.

Unlike the Monroe and Stimson doctrines, the Truman Doctrine acquired no importance for the emergence of a separate rule of international law. It is usually not discussed with regard to its quality as a separate rule of law. Rather, it deals with the interpretation of rule of the UN Charter, particularly Article 51. Indeed, the United States emphasised that action in the spirit of the principles of the Truman Doctrine was action to give effect to the principles of the UN Charter. This anticipates a paradigm of justification later advocated by proponents of the New Haven School.

The principles of the Truman Doctrine found their way into US treaty obligations. To assume this transformation is only correct if one does not consider the inclusion of a doctrine into international law as *per se* impossible with a view to the unilateral authority to change doctrines. A transformation can be assumed only if one separates the principle of defending 'free peoples' from the unilateral authority to interpret the doctrine. The NATO and SEATO treaties should be emphasised. Yet no legal duty to use force flows from Article 5 of the NATO Treaty. Likewise no such obligation resulted from the SEATO Treaty. Moreover, under these treaties the United States is free to decide unilaterally on the existence of the legal prerequisites for the use of force.

In view of the extent of the obligations of mutual assistance imposed by the NATO Treaty on the United States, it can only be seen as a gradual legalisation of the Truman Doctrine because under the NATO Treaty the United States accepted an international legal obligation to support states considered as 'free'. Yet the shape and form this support may take is at the discretion of the United States.

Indeed, the United States is basically still free to attempt politically to get rid of these obligations, but abandoning this principle would not just require a unilateral political decision by the United States, but also the disposal of binding obligations under international law. Besides the legal obligations the NATO Treaty imposes on the United States, the impact of this treaty (just like the meaning of the Truman Doctrine) is mostly seen in effects outside the sphere of international law. The importance of the treaty is considered to be political rather than legal.[114] The treaty

114 Ipsen, *Rechtsgrundlagen und Institutionalisierung der Atlantisch-Europäischen Verteidigung*, pp. 90–2. On the characteristic feature of the NATO Treaty as a treaty open

leaves sufficient space for this.[115] In accordance with the assumption that communication with the enemy gained importance in the course of the policy of deterrence during the Cold War,[116] the number and frequency of doctrines increased. Almost exactly ten years after the announcement of the Truman Doctrine, President Eisenhower declared the doctrine bearing his name.

3.2 The Eisenhower Doctrine

The declaration of the Eisenhower Doctrine was prompted by the Suez Crisis of 1956. In November 1956 British and French troops occupied the Egyptian territory around the Suez Canal in reaction to the Egyptian nationalisation of the canal.[117] In October 1956 Israeli troops had already started occupying the Sinai Peninsula. British and French troops withdrew from Egypt by late December 1956 due to international pressure supported by the United States as well as the Soviet Union.[118] Against this background, and driven by worries that a power vacuum in the Middle East caused by the loss of influence and prestige of Western states could be filled by the Soviet Union,[119] President Eisenhower asked Congress for approval for far-reaching authorisations for action by the United States in the Middle East. This authorisation included the use of armed force. The core statement of this speech by Eisenhower is called the Eisenhower Doctrine.[120]

to new developments see: BVerfGE, Judgment of the 2nd Senate, 22 November 2001, No. 147.

115 Nolte, 'Die "neuen Aufgaben" von NATO und WEU', pp. 95–123, in particular pp. 98–104; H. Sauer, 'Die NATO und das Verfassungsrecht: neues Konzept – alte Fragen', ZaöRV/H.J.I.L., 62 (2002), 317–46.

116 K. Payne and C. Watson, 'Deterrence in the Post-Cold War World', in J. Baylis *et al.* (eds.), *Strategy in the Contemporary World – An Introduction to Strategic Studies* (Oxford University Press, 2002), pp. 161–82.

117 On this see further: D. Rauschning, *Der Streit um den Suezkanal* (Hamburg: Forschungsstelle für Völkerrecht und Ausländisches Öffentliches Recht, 1956).

118 On the US-American role in the Suez Crisis see: R. Takey, *The Origins of the Eisenhower Doctrine* (New York: St Martin's Press, 2000), pp. 124–41; D. Neff, *Warriors at Suez: Eisenhower takes America into the Middle East* (New York: Linden Press/Simon & Schuster, 1981).

119 D. Eisenhower, *Waging Peace 1956–1961* (Garden City, New York: Doubleday, 1965), p. 178.

120 Crabb, *The Doctrines of American Foreign Policy*, pp. 153 *et seq.*; P. Vincent, *Non-Intervention and International Order* (Princeton University Press, 1974), pp. 208 *et seq.*

Although the US government initially used the term 'American Doctrine for the Middle East',[121] or simply 'the American Doctrine',[122] the label 'Eisenhower Doctrine' had already appeared during his term of office.[123] President Eisenhower himself originally used the term 'Doctrine for the Middle East',[124] but later in his memoirs used the term 'Eisenhower Doctrine'.[125]

3.2.1 The Eisenhower Doctrine according to the speech of 5 January 1957

The core statement of the speech is Eisenhower's request to Congress to authorise the President to support certain states in the Middle East, including by using force:

> It would . . . include the employment of the armed forces of the United States to secure and protect the territorial integrity and political independence of such [Middle Eastern] nations, requesting such aid, against overt armed aggression from any nation controlled by international communism.[126]

This request was introduced by Eisenhower as further particularisation and specification of a prior request to Congress in the same speech to authorise 'military assistance and cooperation with any nation . . . which desires such aid'.[127]

Earlier in the same speech, President Eisenhower had requested authorisation to support economic development in order to preserve national

121 *Department of State Bulletin*, 37 (1957), 17–19, 339, 352; S. Yaqub, *Containing Arab Nationalism – The Eisenhower Doctrine and the Middle East* (Chapel Hill, NC: University of North Carolina Press, 2004), pp. 89–90.

122 *Department of State Bulletin*, 38 (1957), 758. On the part of the Soviet Union the label 'Dulles–Eisenhower Doctrine' was used. L. Focsaneanu, 'La "Doctrine Eisenhower" Pour Le Proche Orient', A.F.D.I. (1958), 34.

123 For example, by Secretary of State Dulles, *Department of State Bulletin*, 37 (1957), 232. See also: *Department of State Bulletin*, 38 (1957), 87–8.

124 *Public Papers of the Presidents, Dwight D. Eisenhower, 1957* (Washington, DC: Government Printing Office, 1958), vol. V, p. 463.

125 Eisenhower, *Waging Peace 1956–1961*, pp. 182 *et seq*. However, Eisenhower used this term in reference to the resolution of Congress of 9 March (Joint Resolution to Promote Peace and Stability in the Middle East, printed in *Department of State Bulletin*, 37 (1957), 481).

126 *Public Papers of the Presidents, Dwight D. Eisenhower*, 1957, vol. V, p. 13.

127 *Public Papers of the Presidents, Dwight D. Eisenhower*, 1957, vol. V, p. 13.

independence.[128] With respect to the use of force, Eisenhower pointed out that an (official) request as well as a prior attack was required for the use of US armed forces: 'Such authority would not be exercised except at the desire of the nation attacked.'[129]

In response to Eisenhower's request, a joint resolution of both Houses of Congress of 9 March 1957 contained multiple authorisations for the President, for the most part not concerning the use of force, but military and economic support. With regard to the use of force, the resolution stated, that 'if the President determines the necessity thereof, the United States is prepared to use armed forces to assist any such nation or group of such nations'.[130]

3.2.2 Principles of the Eisenhower Doctrine for the use of force

The Eisenhower Doctrine is a particularisation of the Truman Doctrine, because the Eisenhower Doctrine also makes a distinction based on ideological reasons. In his speech President Eisenhower turned on states: that is, 'any nation controlled by international communism . . .' announcing a willingness to use force against them.[131] The US Government itself made reference to the obvious similarity of this aspect of the Eisenhower Doctrine to the Truman Doctrine.[132]

The Eisenhower Doctrine thus merely repeats anew the willingness to use force in the Cold War conflict if necessary, but was restricted to the Middle East. The claim to act in the interests of the values and principles of the UN Charter is a recurring feature of practice under the Eisenhower Doctrine,[133] as was the case of the Truman Doctrine.[134]

3.2.2.1 Criteria of the Eisenhower Doctrine for the use of force

As noted above, the bulk of the means foreseen to implement the Eisenhower Doctrine are connected only indirectly with the use of

128 'It would first authorize the United States to cooperate with and assist any nation or group of nations in the general area of the Middle East in the development of economic strength dedicated to the maintenance of national independence . . . ' *Public Papers of the Presidents, Dwight D. Eisenhower, 1957*, vol. V, pp. 12–13.

129 *Public Papers of the Presidents, Dwight D. Eisenhower*, 1957, vol. V, p. 15.

130 Joint Resolution to Promote Peace and Stability in the Middle East, printed in *Department of State Bulletin*, 37 (1957), 481.

131 *Public Papers of the Presidents, Dwight D. Eisenhower, 1957*, vol. V, p. 13.

132 *Department of State Bulletin*, 37 (1957), 354.

133 *Public Papers of the Presidents, Dwight D. Eisenhower, 1957*, vol. V, pp. 13, 15.

134 See above, section 3.1.1.2.

force.[135] However, the deployment of the use of US armed forces is added as a second key element to this.[136]

Particular cases of the use of force such as, for example, the sending of US armed forces to Lebanon, were also considered by President Eisenhower as implementation of the Eisenhower Doctrine.[137] Eisenhower's speech, as well as the resolution of Congress, authorising the President to use force in terms of the Eisenhower Doctrine contain specific limitations for the use of force by US armed forces. Just like the Truman Doctrine, the Eisenhower Doctrine foresees the use of force in reaction to certain behaviour of communist states. Based on certain premises, they are considered a source of threat with regard to the nature of this ideological inclination.[138]

Neither in Eisenhower's speech nor in the subsequent resolution by Congress is it specifically stated what shape or form these prior actions by communist states must take in order to result in the use of force by the United States. The speech mentions only 'overt armed aggression'.[139]

President Eisenhower hinted that cases of use of force in the Middle East would have to be in accordance with US treaty obligations, particularly the UN Charter.[140] And the authorising resolutions of Congress also limit the authorisation of the President to the use of force in accordance with US treaty obligations: 'such employment shall be consonant with treaty obligations of the United States . . . '[141] Furthermore, a request for aid by the respective state is explicitly required as a condition for using force. Like the Truman Doctrine, the Eisenhower Doctrine does not promulgate a unilateral right of the United States to take action, but referred to a right to take action derived from the right of another state to use force. However,

135 Woods, 'An Overview of the Military Aspects of Security Assistance', p. 75; H. Kissinger, *Diplomacy* (New York: Simon & Schuster, 1994), p. 549.

136 A summary by Special Assistant to the President James P. Richards reads: 'To sum up there are two main features of this American Doctrine. The first is the deterrent effect provided by the declared determination of the United States to use armed forces . . . The second is the extension of economic and military aid . . . ' *Department of State Bulletin*, 36 (1957), 972.

137 Eisenhower, *Waging Peace*, pp. 271–2; Wright, 'United States Intervention in the Lebanon', pp. 112–25.

138 Graber, 'The Truman and Eisenhower Doctrines in the Light of the Doctrine of Non-Intervention', p. 323.

139 *Public Papers of the Presidents, Dwight D. Eisenhower*, 1957, vol. V, p. 13.

140 'These measures would have to be consonant with the treaty obligations of the United States, including the United Nations Charter and with any actions or recommendations of the United Nations . . . ' *Department of State Bulletin*, 36 (1957), 86.

141 *Department of State Bulletin*, 36 (1957), 481.

unlike the Truman Doctrine, a request for aid by the attacked state was explicitly required.[142]

An authorisation of the US President limited to cases of the use of force in accordance with the UN Charter has the following consequence for the interpretation of the Eisenhower Doctrine: cases of the use of force under the Eisenhower Doctrine depend on the US-American interpretation of law regarding the legality of the use of force under the UN Charter.

By linking the use of force foreseen under the doctrine with its conformity with the Charter it is left open what is meant by the use of force consonant with the UN Charter. Thus, cases of use of force, considered by the United States as being in accordance with the Eisenhower Doctrine, permit conclusions to be reached as to US opinion on what uses of force are in compliance with the UN Charter. As it depends on the US interpretation of law which cases of the use of force are considered to be in accordance with the doctrine this is a circular argument.

3.2.2.2 Statements on the legality of the use of force within the context of the Eisenhower Doctrine

Neither Eisenhower's speech nor the subsequent resolution of Congress contains a determination of what is meant by measures 'consonant with treaty obligations of the United States'. Internal discussions within the US Government give some insight as to how this formulation ought to be understood.

A suggested abbreviated version of the authorising resolution of Congress[143] was rejected by Secretary of State Dulles not only because it went beyond addressing communist aggression, but because it did not limit the use of force to cases of an armed attack according to Article 51 of the UN Charter. The reconcilability of the types of action foreseen in the abbreviated version with the Charter was thus doubted on the grounds that it could be understood as not being limited to purely reactive use of force.[144]

How the limitation of the Eisenhower Doctrine for the use of force – foreseeing the use of force only in reaction to 'armed aggression' and

142 'nation or group of such nations requesting assistance ...' *Department of State Bulletin*, 36 (1957), 481.

143 The short version reads: 'The United States regards as vital to her interest the preservation of the independence and integrity of the states of the Middle East and, if necessary, will use her armed forces to that end.' *Department of State Bulletin*, 36 (1957), 129.

144 *Department of State Bulletin*, 36 (1957), 129–30.

'armed attack' – was to be understood exactly was also a matter of internal discussions by the US Government. In connection with the Lebanon Crisis of July 1958, Secretary of State Dulles interpreted the term 'armed attack' in a way that did not exclude 'an armed revolution which is fomented abroad, aided and assisted from abroad'. This includes an indirect aggression within the meaning of armed attack. Dulles also made reference in this context to the matching broad interpretation of the term 'armed attack' in Article 5 of the NATO Treaty, which had been advocated earlier by the Senate Foreign Relations Committee.[145] President Eisenhower in his speech on 5 January 1957 again emphasised the limitation of the right of the United States to self-defence once the UN Security Council had taken action.[146] However, he did not determine which collective measures of the Security Council would result in such a limitation.[147]

3.2.2.3 Evaluation of the cases of the use of force foreseen in the Eisenhower Doctrine under international law

Once more the reconcilability of the cases of the use of force foreseen in the Eisenhower Doctrine with the international law in force at the time can only be evaluated depending on the content attributed to the doctrine. Yet the content attributed to the doctrine in turn depends on the use of force considered legal on the part of the United States.

The fact that the Eisenhower Doctrine contains as a starting point a reservation in favour of the UN Charter and other US treaty obligations leads to the result that a use of force according to the doctrine is always considered on the part of the United States as in accordance with international law regulating the use of force. This makes it impossible for potential critics to consider uses of force based on the doctrine as against international law without doubting the US understanding of the law. On the Soviet Union's part, however, the Eisenhower Doctrine was considered *per se* as aggressive due to the mere possibility of the use of force

145 Focsaneanu, 'La "Doctrine Eisenhower" Pour Le Proche Orient', pp. 44–5; Crabb, *The Doctrines of American Foreign Policy*, p. 157.

146 'These measures would have to be consonant with the treaty obligations of the United States, including the United Nations Charter and with any actions or recommendations of the United Nations. They would also, if an armed attack occurs, be subject to overriding authority of the United Nations Security Council . . . ' *Department of State Bulletin*, 36 (1957), 86.

147 On the problem of the required quality of measures by the Security Council see: Krisch, *Selbstverteidigung und kollektive Sicherheit*, pp. 175–205.

that it contained,[148] as the Soviet Union viewed as essentially aggressive in nature the foreign policy of non-communist states.[149]

As outlined above, an indirect aggression was considered by the United States to be a sufficient precondition for the use of force to aid a victim state under the Eisenhower Doctrine.[150] As an indirect aggression alone does not suffice in order to justify the use of force, but has to have acquired the form of an armed attack (as already pointed out in connection with the Truman Doctrine),[151] this raises the question of whether the use of force according to the Eisenhower Doctrine is limited to such cases.

Accordingly, Quincy Wright has pointed out with regard to the Eisenhower Doctrine that self-defence was justified only in cases of an armed attack and not in cases of an indirect aggression, defined as other acts serving the extension of an ideology considered as dangerous. Hence, the use of force could not be justified based on the doctrine itself:

> States may declare such policies and support them by diplomatic representations and other peaceful methods. But such policies do not constitute a part of the 'self' of a state, and do not of themselves justify armed intervention in foreign territory. They justify such intervention only insofar as they are declaratory of the justifications recognised by international law.[152]

Attempts to establish a separate justification for use of force, as claimed in the case of the Roosevelt Corollary to the Monroe Doctrine, cannot be read into the wording of Eisenhower's speech of 5 January 1957 and the subsequent authorising resolution of Congress of 9 March 1957.[153] The limitation of the doctrine in favour of US treaty obligations and the declarations in the Eisenhower Doctrine suggests rather that the doctrine is based on a much more restrictive understanding of the legality of the use of force. The Eisenhower Doctrine is at least open to the interpretation that the term 'aggression', as it is used in Eisenhower's speech, is interpreted narrowly in terms of an armed attack under the UN Charter. That is how the declarations of Secretary of State Dulles on the Eisenhower Doctrine were understood by scholars.[154]

148 Soviet note of 3 September 1957, printed in *Department of State Bulletin*, 37 (1957), 602–3. In detail on the Soviet reaction see: Focsaneanu, 'La "Doctrine Eisenhower" Pour Le Proche Orient', pp. 66–76.

149 Kennan, 'The Sources of Soviet Conduct', pp. 566–82.

150 See above, section 3.2.2.2.

151 See above, section 3.1.2.2.

152 Wright, 'United States Intervention in the Lebanon', p. 117.

153 See above, Chapter 2, section 2.1.3.2.5.

154 R. Falk, 'International Law and the United States Role in the Viet Nam War', Y.L.J., 75 (1966), 1122–60.

Explanations on the legality of use of force in connection with the Eisenhower Doctrine by the State Department, emphasising the requirement of a preceding use of force, also militate in favour of a narrow interpretation.[155] Thus, regardless of whether the occurrence of an armed attack is *absolutely* required in order to justify the use of force in self-defence,[156] the Eisenhower Doctrine can be interpreted as foreseeing use of force only in accordance with international law. This applies even if one adheres to the most restrictive interpretation of self-defence in this respect.

The remaining question is whether the principle of the Eisenhower Doctrine of providing military support to states against 'overt communist aggression' in the Middle East is reflected in treaty provisions on collective self-defence.

3.2.3 Legalisation of the Eisenhower Doctrine

A declaration by the United States, Great Britain and France concerning the Middle East – the so-called Tripartite Declaration of 25 May 1950[157] – is generally regarded as a predecessor of the Eisenhower Doctrine.[158] This declaration does not, however, address the use of force directly, but the limitation of arms exports to this region. Moreover, nothing in this declaration hints that it imposes a legal obligation concerning the use of force.[159]

One possibility for the gradual transformation of the Eisenhower Doctrine into international law could have been an accession of the United States to the so-called Baghdad Pact between Iraq and Turkey, but it never did accede. Great Britain, Iran and Pakistan acceded to this pact in 1955, and it was called the Central Treaty Organization (CENTO) from 1959 until 1979 when it was terminated.[160] A US plan for founding a separate organisation of collective security for the Middle East, the Middle East Defence Organization (MEDO) had been abandoned in 1954.[161]

155 *Department of State Bulletin*, 36 (1957), 86–7; M. Bennouna, *Le consentment a l´ingérence militaire dans les conflits internes* (Paris: Librarie Generale, 1974), p. 149.
156 On this discussion see further below, Chapter 4, section 4.2.2.2.
157 *Department of State Bulletin*, 22 (1950), 886.
158 Crabb, *The Doctrines of American Foreign Policy*, p. 165.
159 G. Petrochilos, 'The Relevance of the Concepts of War and Armed Conflict to the Law of Neutrality', Van.J.T.L., 31 (1998), 585.
160 On this see: C. Rumpf, 'Central Treaty Organization', E.P.I.L., I (1992), 554–5.
161 *Foreign Relations of the United States*, 1952–1954, vol. IX, pp. 182–3, 226–34, 249–52. On this see: B. Yesilboursa, *The Baghdad Pact: Anglo-American Defence Policies in the Middle*

The participation of the United States in meetings of the Military Committee of the Baghdad Pact from on 22 March 1957 onwards can be considered a logical consequence of the Eisenhower Doctrine,[162] but it did not alter the status of the United States as a non-member of the Baghdad Pact, and did not impose any legally-binding obligations on it.[163] Even in the case of membership by the United States of the Baghdad Pact, no obligation to use force under certain preconditions would have resulted from that, because the Baghdad Pact merely hints in its preamble at an accordance of foreseen measures with Article 51 of the UN Charter and does not obligate states to take specific measures. Article 1 referred to further arrangements which could be made in the future between the treaty parties with regard to their cooperation and maintenance of security and defence.[164] A legally-binding duty to use force in case of an armed attack on one of the states party to the treaty did not result from the treaty, just as it did not result from the NATO or SEATO treaties.[165]

Similarly non-committal like the Baghdad Pact are several bilateral treaties which were also considered to be implementations of the Eisenhower Doctrine with Turkey, Iran and Pakistan of 1959.[166] These treaties make reference in their common Article 1 to the joint resolution of Congress of 9 March 1957 and the obligation on the United States contained therein to take the measures foreseen in this resolution, including the use of force in the event of an aggression against these states. These treaties contain regulations on economic and military development aid similar to those in the treaties with Turkey and Greece concluded after the declaration of the Truman Doctrine,[167] but do not contain an explicit obligation to use force. The parties merely emphasise in the perambulatory clauses their readiness to exercise their right to self-defence according to Article 51 of the UN Charter.[168] Due to their low degree of legally-binding obligations, these treaties can be considered only gradual legalisations of the Eisenhower Doctrine. However, the duty of the United States to provide help to individual states in the Middle East, originally a principle of

East, 1950–1959 (London: Frank Cass, 2005), pp. 12 *et seq.*; M. Röder, *Die Eisenhower-Doktrin vom 9. März 1957 und ihre Anwendung im Libanon im Juli 1958*, Master's thesis, University of Hamburg, 1986, available in the Staats- und Universitätsbibliothek Hamburg, pp. 15–19.

162 'Baghdad Pact', Int.Org., 11/3 (1957), 547.

163 Focsaneanu, 'La "Doctrine Eisenhower" Pour Le Proche Orient', pp. 107–8.

164 UNTS, vol. 233 (1956), pp. 200–15.

165 See above, sections 3.1.3 and 3.1.4.

166 *Department of State Bulletin*, 37 (1957), 339–43

167 See above, section 3.2.3.

168 UNTS, vol. 327 (1959), pp. 277–84, 285–92, 293–9.

the doctrine, undergoes a change due to its articulation in these treaties: it is no longer subject to a subjective interpretation of the doctrine as anticipated by the Congress resolution, but becomes a treaty obligation open to an objective interpretation.[169]

3.2.4 Conclusion

The Eisenhower Doctrine merely repeats the principles of the Truman Doctrine with regard to a certain region.[170] Just like the interpretation of the scope of the Monroe Doctrine under the UN Charter,[171] the United States interpreted the Eisenhower Doctrine in a way that foresaw the use of force only in cases that were in accordance with the UN Charter, such as intervention upon invitation or the exercise of self-defence. In contrast to preceding doctrines, the Eisenhower Doctrine contains a reservation in favour of the UN Charter and limits cases of the use of force to cases that are in accordance with it. This apparent limitation of cases of force foreseen by the doctrine is, however, devalued by the fact that the doctrine also announces that it will rely on the United States' own interpretation of international law.

Just like the Truman Doctrine, the Eisenhower Doctrine experienced only a gradual legalisation. The degree of legalisation of the principle of supporting the use of force in favour of certain states in the Middle East by the United States in international law is far lower than the equivalent provisions establishing the Truman Doctrine as a legally-binding obligation in the NATO and SEATO treaties.[172]

A vaguely described legal duty to help can be found in bilateral treaties which do impose legal obligations on the United States to take military action in order to defend single states in the Middle East. However, due to this articulation in a treaty, the duty has become accessible to authentic interpretation.

The demise of the Eisenhower Doctrine as a political principle is attributed to a diminishing acceptance of its principles by states of the Middle East as a result of the US intervention in Lebanon in July–October 1958. This intervention also led to a cessation of requests for aid which

169 I. Brownlie, *Principles of International Law*, 5th edn. (Oxford: Clarendon Press, 1998), pp. 631–2.

170 Likewise: C. Wrede, 'Der Rechtsanspruch der Deutschen Bundesregierung auf völkerrechtliche Alleinvertretung Gesamtdeutschlands und die Hallstein-Doktrin', Ph.D. thesis, Freiburg/Switzerland, 1966, pp. 28–9.

171 See above, Chapter 2, section 2.1.3.4.

172 See above, sections 3.1.3 and 3.2.3.

had been provided for in the Eisenhower Doctrine.[173] Due to its short lifespan the Eisenhower Doctrine is considered a 'minor doctrine'.[174] Yet these principles of US policy were never formally abandoned.

3.3 The so-called Johnson Doctrine

The term 'Johnson Doctrine' refers to a statement by President Lyndon B. Johnson in a public speech of 2 May 1965,[175] made in the context of the US invasion of the Dominican Republic on 28 April 1965. The invasion was the result of US concerns that the escalating confrontation between supporters of the former President Juan Bosch and supporters of the government of Donald Reid y Cabral could lead to successful civil war on the part of communist forces.[176]

President Johnson in his address connected his explanations on intervention in the Dominican Republic with statements of principles concerning US policy in Latin America.

3.3.1 Principles of the Johnson Doctrine according to the speech of 2 May 1965

Just like the Truman Doctrine, the principles of the Johnson Doctrine refer to the Cold War conflict and are related – like the Eisenhower Doctrine – to a certain region, in this case the western hemisphere. In his speech Johnson described the thinking behind these principles:

> The American Nations cannot, must not, and will not permit the establishment of another Communist government in the Western Hemisphere[177] . . . Our goal, in keeping with the great principles of the

173 Yaqub, *Containing Arab Nationalism – The Eisenhower Doctrine and the Middle East*, pp. 237 *et seq.*
174 Crabb, *The Doctrines of American Foreign Policy*, pp. 187–92.
175 Crabb, *The Doctrines of American Foreign Policy*, pp. 235–77.
176 On the justification, put forward by the United States for its intervention in the Dominican Republic in 1965, see: Nolte, *Eingreifen auf Einladung*, pp. 269–71; Department of State, *Legal Basis for United States Actions in the Dominican Republic, May 7, 1965*, printed in A. Chayes, T. Ehrlicher and A. Lowenfeld (eds.), *International Legal Process – Materials for an Introductory Course* (New York: Little, Brown, 1968), pp. 1179–88; L. Meeker, 'The Dominican Situation in the Perspective of International Law', *Department of State Bulletin*, 53 (1965), 60–5.
177 Occasionally the term 'Johnson Doctrine' is used only with regard to this sentence. T. Franck and E. Weisband, 'The Johnson and Brezhnev Doctrines: The Law You Make May be Your Own', Stanford.L.Rev., 22 (1969–70), 1010.

> inter-American system, is to help prevent another communist state in this hemisphere.[178]

Unlike the Truman and Eisenhower doctrines, he abstained from a more detailed description of the Cold War conflict by characterising general differences of '*Weltanschauung*'. President Johnson emphasised, as had the two previous Cold War doctrines, that the doctrine was the expression of a collective will of several states.[179] In particular, he referred to the 'principles of the inter-American system'[180] as contained in a resolution of the consultative body of the Rio Pact passed in Punta del Este on 31 January 1962.[181] Johnson's speech makes only a very general statement on the use of force ('to defend'). However, it offers no specification with regard to the prerequisites for the use of force, but it can be understood as a threat to the use of force: 'We will defend our Nation against all who seek to destroy not only the United States but every free country of this hemisphere . . . ' Hence, for the most part it was a repetition and specification of the principles of prior doctrines. Just as in the case of the Truman and Eisenhower doctrines, it also hinted at existing US treaty obligations, but only very vaguely.[182]

It already seems questionable whether the Johnson Doctrine is a doctrine of US security policy in terms of the definition on which this work is based.[183]

3.3.2 Use of the term 'Johnson Doctrine'

The term 'Johnson Doctrine' is used in literature on international relations[184] and international law to refer to the principles laid down

178 *Public Papers of the Presidents, Lyndon B. Johnson, 1965* (Washington, DC: Government Printing Office, 1966), vol. I, pp. 472–3.

179 See above, sections 3.1.1.2 and 3.2.1.

180 'This was the unanimous view of all the American nations, when, in January 1962, they declared, and I quote: the principles of communism are incompatible with the principles of the inter-American System.' *Public Papers of the Presidents, Lyndon B. Johnson, 1965*, vol. I, p. 472.

181 Printed in A.J.I.L., 56 (1962), 601–5. On the legal nature and the lack of binding effects of resolutions of the OAS Consultative body see: C. Fenwick, *The Organization of American States* (Washington, DC: The Organization of American States, 1963), pp. 155–6.

182 ('We will honour our treaties . . . ') *Public Papers of the Presidents, Lyndon B. Johnson, 1965*, vol. I, p. 474.

183 See above, Chapter 1, section 1.6.

184 Evans and Newnham, *The Penguin Dictionary of International Relations*, pp. 286–7.

in Johnson's speech of 2 May 1965.[185] Some authors also distinguish a 'first Johnson Doctrine', to refer to US policy in southeast Asia, primarily Vietnam, and derive it mainly from the Tonking Gulf Resolution.[186]

However, not only has the label 'first Johnson Doctrine' not been used in the international law literature and only occasionally in international relations literature, it has also never been used by official US sources. Hence, this label merely constitutes an attempt at a subsequent conceptualisation of US foreign policy. The term 'Johnson Doctrine' normally refers to the policy of the Johnson administration with regard to Latin America, as declared in the speech of 2 May 1965.[187] Indeed, only two days after Johnson's speech, the representative of Uruguay used the label 'Johnson Doctrine' for the principles contained in the 2 May speech in a UN Security Council meeting.[188]

The US administration itself has never used the term 'Johnson Doctrine': it can neither be found in the volumes of the *Department of State Bulletin* nor in the volumes of the *Foreign Relations of the United States* covering Johnson's term of office. President Johnson himself even protested explicitly against the labelling of the principles declared by him as the 'Johnson Doctrine', and stated that he was merely repeating the principles contained in prior declarations of the OAS.[189] Hence, the so-called Johnson Doctrine does not constitute a doctrine of US security policy in terms of the definition on which this work is based, in spite of the frequent

185 H. Neuhold, *Internationale Konflikte – verbotene und erlaubte Mittel ihrer Austragung* (Vienna: Springer, 1970), p. 151; W. Verwey, 'Humanitarian Intervention', in Cassese (ed.), *The Current Legal Regulation of the Use of Force*, p. 70; P. Pirrone, 'The Use of Force in the Framework of the Organization of American States', *ibid.*, p. 230; Paech and Stuby, *Machtpolitik und Völkerrecht in den internationalen Beziehungen*, p. 229; M. Bennouna, *Le consentment a l'ingérence militaire dans les conflits internes*, p. 126; C. Joyner and M. Grimaldi, 'The United States and Nicaragua: Reflections on the Lawfulness of Contemporary Intervention', Va.J.I.L., 25 (1985), 678–9.

186 Crabb, *The Doctrines of American Foreign Policy*, pp. 193–221; E. Plischke, *Contemporary U.S. Foreign Policy* (New York: Greenwood Press, 1991), p. 179.

187 Evans and Newham, *The Penguin Dictionary of International Relations*, pp. 286–7.

188 SCOR, 1198th Session, 4 May 1965, p. 5: 'In a message bro[a]dcast on the evening of 2 May 1965, the President of the United States . . . offered what I think was an interpretation of the principles . . . to which he referred as the principles of the inter-American System. This Johnson doctrine – as it is now being called – or if you prefer, this new corollary to the Monroe Doctrine, is not as indeed President Monroe's Doctrine was not, either a strictly legal doctrine or an American Doctrine . . . '

189 'The OAS itself has enunciated it. I merely repeated it . . . ' *Public Papers of the Presidents, Lyndon B. Johnson, 1965*, vol. II, p. 615.

use of the label 'doctrine' for this declaration of principles.[190] Johnson's speech may have been a statement on matters of security policy, but it was not called a 'doctrine' on the part of the US Government and thus constitutes a political 'matter of fact' of another kind.

Similarly, the terms 'Kennedy Doctrine'[191] or 'Kennedy Corollary to the Monroe Doctrine',[192] which refer to speeches by President Kennedy on 8 May 1961[193] and 22 October 1962,[194] do coincide with the common terminology of the US Government. These terms are also merely attempts to label principles of US foreign policy. Thus, the so-called 'Kennedy Doctrine', like the so-called 'Johnson Doctrine' does not fit under the definition of a doctrine of US security policy on which this work is based.

It can be questioned whether the Johnson Doctrine merely marks a new phase in the Monroe Doctrine beginning in 1965.[195] If so, this leads to a different evaluation of the Johnson Doctrine under international law. The principles of Johnson's speech were called an update of the Monroe Doctrine by Cuba and Uruguay in the Security Council debate immediately after his speech.[196] Individual writers also use the term 'Johnson Corollary' to the Monroe Doctrine.[197] Likewise, individual members of Congress considered Johnson's speech of 2 May 1965 to be relevant for the interpretation of the Monroe Doctrine.[198] In the same year, the House of Representatives passed a resolution in which communist subversion was said to be a violation of the Monroe Doctrine.[199]

190 Besides that, the term 'Johnson–Mann Doctrine', appears as a label for the principles declared in Johnson's speech, after then Under Secretary of State for Latin America, Thomas C. Mann. For example, Evans and Newnham, *The Penguin Dictionary of International Relations*, pp. 286–7.

191 L. FitzSimons, *The Kennedy Doctrine* (New York: Random House, 1972); L. Wilson, 'The Monroe Doctrine, Cold War Anachronism: Cuba and the Dominican Republic', J.Pol., 28 (1966), 333.

192 D. Dozer, *The Monroe Doctrine: Its Modern Significance* (New York: Alfred A. Knopf, 1965), p. 33.

193 *Department of State Bulletin*, 44 (1961), 659–61.

194 *Department of State Bulletin*, 47 (1962), 715–20.

195 On the division of doctrines into 'phases' see above, Chapter 1, section 1.4.

196 SCOR, 1198th Session, 4 May 1965, pp. 5, 18.

197 Wilson, 'The Monroe Doctrine, Cold War Anachronism: Cuba and the Dominican Republic', pp. 338–9.

198 Cong. Rec., vol. 111, Pt. 8 (1965), pp. 10290–91, 10664, 11423–4.

199 '(1) any [communist] subversive domination or threat of it violates the principles of the Monroe Doctrine, and of collective security as set forth in the acts and resolutions heretofore adopted by the American Republics . . . ' Cong. Rec., vol. 111, Pt. 16 (1965), p. 24347.

3.3.3 *The Johnson Doctrine as a corollary to the Monroe Doctrine*

Just like the Monroe Doctrine, the Johnson Doctrine deals with the security interests of the United States in the western hemisphere. Unlike the Monroe Doctrine in its original shape according to Monroe's speech of 1823,[200] it is not aimed against activity by European states in the western hemisphere, but against action by communist states. In this respect, like the Eisenhower Doctrine, it repeats the fundamental idea of ideological distinction established in the Truman Doctrine, but with respect to a certain region.[201] Hence, the Johnson Doctrine only constitutes an update of the 'non-intervention principle' of the Monroe Doctrine, which contained a prohibition on European states extending their system 'to any portion of this hemisphere'.

President Johnson's reference to the irreconcilability of a communist-type government with the principles of the American system was based on a resolution passed by the consultative body of the Rio Pact on 31 January 1962 in Punta del Este.[202] This resolution in turn merely elaborated in detail on the principles stated in the 13th Resolution of the 10th Inter-American Conference of 1954 in Caracas. The 13th Resolution was already considered to be decisive in the transformation of the original anti-colonial Monroe Doctrine into a vehicle against communist types of governments in the western hemisphere.[203]

The 13th Resolution of the Inter-American Conference had not been passed by it in its capacity as consultative organ of the Rio Pact as had the Resolution of Punta del Este of 31 January 1962. Nevertheless, both resolutions remained non-binding resolutions.[204] The reconcilability of the principles of this resolution with the principles of the UN Charter, particularly the prohibition on use of force of Article 2(4) has been questioned by scholars.[205]

The reconcilability implies a particular interpretation of the resolution. The starting point for doing so could be the assumption that the

200 See above, Chapter 2, section 2.1.1. 201 See above, section 3.2.2.

202 *Public Papers of the Presidents, Lyndon B. Johnson, 1965*, vol. I, p. 472.

203 H. Schatzschneider, *Die neue Phase der Monroedoktrin angesichts der kommunistischen Bedrohung Lateinamerikas – Unter Berücksichtigung des Falles Guatemala vor der Organisation Amerikanischer Staaten und der Vereinten Nationen* (Göttingen: Vandenhoeck & Ruprecht, 1957), pp. 55–6; Secretary of State Dulles also related this 13th Resolution to the Monroe Doctrine, *Department of State Bulletin*, 30 (1954), 466.

204 Fenwick, *The Organization of American States*, pp. 155–6.

205 R. Higgins, 'The Attitude of Western States Towards Legal Aspects of the Use of Force', in Cassese (ed.), *The Current Legal Regulation of the Use of Force*, p. 439.

resolution constitutes a corollary to the Monroe Doctrine as a political declaration of principles of the same kind as the Roosevelt Corollary to the Monroe Doctrine. It foresees in certain cases – 'domination or control . . . by international communist movement' – a military intervention by the United States in American states for the sake of hemispheric stability.[206] No distinction is made between a communist assumption of power caused by an attack from the outside, a revolutionary movement or a democratic election.[207]

No matter how one evaluates the legality of those types of action, the question is whether such a claim of intervention, comparable to the Roosevelt Corollary, can be found in the 13th Resolution. The wording of the 13th Resolution suggests that, if necessary, a consultative meeting shall be called in order to consider measures in accordance with the treaty obligations. It does not mention force explicitly and does not make a statement on the use of force in certain situations.[208] Rather, the statements of the 13th Resolution are general so that they also fit into an interpretation of the Monroe Doctrine which is in accordance with the UN Charter as seen by the United States. The US view explained by Secretary of State Dulles in connection with a Senate hearing on the UN Charter was that 'there is nothing whatsoever in this charter that impairs the Monroe Doctrine as a doctrine of self-defense'.[209]

Within the principles of his speech of 2 May 1965 (labelled the 'Johnson Doctrine'), President Johnson merely emphasised once more the principles of the 1962 Punta des Este resolution, which in turn only repeated the principles of the Caracas Resolution of 1954. No statement can be found

206 D. Carto, 'The Monroe Doctrine in the 1980s: International Law, Unilateral Policy, or Atavistic Anachronism?', Cas.W.Res.J.I.L., 13 (1981), 213–15. Likewise: R. Higgins, 'The Attitude of Western States Towards Legal Aspects of the Use of Force', in Cassese (ed.), *The Current Legal Regulation of the Use of Force*, p. 439.

207 Franck and Weisband, 'The Johnson and Brezhnev Doctrines: The Law You Make May be Your Own', p. 1008: 'drew no distinction among communist accession by external invasion, internal coup or democratic election, nor among communist influence upon, infiltration into, or control of any revolutionary movement.'; P. Pirrone, 'The Use of Force in the Framework of the Organization of American States', in Cassese (ed.), *The Current Legal Regulation of the Use of Force*, p. 230; Crabb, *The Doctrines of American Foreign Policy*, pp. 276–7.

208 Schatzschneider, *Die neue Phase der Monroedoktrin*, p. 52.

209 'So it is my view – and I so expressed it to the United States Delegation – that there is nothing whatsoever in this charter that impairs the Monroe Doctrine as a doctrine of self-defense.' M. Whiteman (ed.), *Digest of International Law* (Washington, DC: Government Printing Office, 1963–71), vol. V, p. 977. On this see further above, Chapter 2, section 2.1.3.4.

in any of these declarations of the incompatibility of communist forms of government with the inter-American system, which could be interpreted as a claim of a right of forcible intervention.

Interventions by the United States considered to be expressions of the Johnson Doctrine were never justified solely on the basis that a communist form of government was incompatible with the abovementioned resolutions. More traditional justifications were invoked, whether or not they might in individual cases seem problematic or misplaced.[210]

Yet in spite of the invocation by the United States of traditional justifications of the use of force, the Johnson Doctrine was often considered a parallel to the Brezhnev Doctrine of the Soviet Union, which claimed the right to take action in states of the Warsaw Pact.

3.3.4 Parallels of the Johnson Doctrine and Brezhnev Doctrine

Thomas Franck and Edward Weisband have argued that ultimately the Brezhnev Doctrine was only the reciprocal Soviet response to the justification of US policy in the western hemisphere laid down in the Johnson Doctrine.[211] The use of the term 'Brezhnev Doctrine' also differs and is often merely used as a conceptualisation of Soviet foreign and security policy.

The Brezhnev Doctrine, its principles and theoretical foundations have been the subject of detailed description by others.[212] The term 'Brezhnev Doctrine' has been used since the intervention by Warsaw Pact troops in Czechoslovakia on 21 August 1968, and a speech by the then Secretary-General of the Communist Party of the Soviet Union, Leonid Brezhnev, to the Congress of the Polish Communist Party on 12 November 1968.[213]

210 For example, Department of State, *Legal Basis for United States Actions in the Dominican Republic, May 7, 1965*, printed in Chayes, Ehrlicher and Lowenfeld (eds.), *International Legal Process*, pp. 1179–88.

211 T. Franck, 'Who killed Article 2(4)?', A.J.I.L., 64 (1970), 834–35; Franck and Weisband, 'The Johnson and Brezhnev Doctrines: The Law You Make May be Your Own', pp. 979–1014; T. Franck and E. Weisband, 'Regional Interventions by the Superpowers: A Study of Words and Acts as Inchoate Law Making', in M. Nawaz (ed.), *Essays in Honor of Krishna Rao* (Leiden: Sijthoff, 1976), pp. 241–51; R. Russel, 'Review: Intervention and Negotiation', A.J.I.L., 65 (1971), 875.

212 B. Meissner, *Die 'Breshnew-Doktrin' – Das Prinzip des proletarisch-sozialistischen Internationalismus und die Theorie von den 'verschiedenen Wegen zum Sozialismus'* (Köln: Verlag Wissenschaft und Politik, 1969); T. Schweisfurth, *Sozialistisches Völkerrecht?* (Berlin: Springer, 1979), pp. 150–4.

213 S. Glazer, 'The Brezhnev Doctrine', Int.L., 5 (1971), 169–70.

Prior to this, the principles of Brezhnev's speech had been outlined in an article by S. Kowaljow in *Pravda* of 26 September 1968 titled 'Sovereignty and the international obligations of socialist states'.[214] It is disputed in which statement exactly the Brezhnev Doctrine was laid down, but the term refers to repeatedly stated principles.[215] The principles called the Brezhnev Doctrine are not considered to be major changes or innovations compared with the prior so-called Moscow Doctrine and the theory of socialist internationalism developed in the 1950s and 1960s.[216]

The central idea behind the Brezhnev Doctrine was that in case of a 'danger to socialist achievements' by internal or external influences there was not just a right, but a duty to intervene for the other socialist states, including the use of force.[217] Rules of law, including rules of international law, were subordinated to the rules of class struggle and must not be superseded by formal judicial considerations.[218]

The core element of the Brezhnev Doctrine – intervention based on an assumed right of intervention in order to preserve a certain political system – was at the time beyond doubt a violation of existing international law.[219] Treaties giving permanent rights to intervention were, therefore, void due to the violation of the *ius cogens* rule of Article 2(4).[220]

214 Printed in Meissner, *Die 'Breshnew-Doktrin'*, pp. 64–9.

215 H. Schmidt, 'The Brezhnev Doctrine', Survival, 11 (1969), 307.

216 T. Schweisfurth, 'Breschnjew-Doktrin als Norm des Völkerrechts?', Aussenpolitik, 21 (1971) 523; W. Grewe, *Spiel der Kräfte in der Weltpolitik* (Düsseldorf: Econ Verlag, 1970), pp. 388–9.

217 B. Randelzhofer, 'Art. 2(4)', in Simma (ed.) *The Charter of the United Nations*, p. 129.

218 Glazer, 'The Brezhnev Doctrine', pp. 170–1. On this see further: J. Moore and R. F. Turner, *International Law and the Brezhnev Doctrine* (Lanham, MD: University Press of America, 1987), pp. 13–25. This approach matched the description of the Soviet understanding of international law by George F. Kennan in 1947. Kennan, 'The Sources of Soviet Conduct', pp. 571–3.

219 S. Schwebel, 'The Brezhnev Doctrine Repealed and Peaceful Co-Existence Enacted', A.J.I.L., 66 (1972), 816–19; N. Rostow, 'Law and the Use of Force by States: The Brezhnev Doctrine', Y.J.W.P.O., 7 (1981), 209–43, in particular at pp. 239 *et seq.*; Neuhold, *Internationale Konflikte*, p. 151; Schweisfurth, *Sozialistisches Völkerrecht?*, pp. 455–6; R. Kolb, *Ius contra bellum* (Basel: Helbing & Lichtenhahn, 2003), p. 231, No. 556; T. Stein and C. von Buttlar, *Völkerrecht*, 12th edn. (Cologne: Heymanns, 2009), p. 231. On this see further: Randelzhofer, 'Art. 2(4)', in Simma (ed.), *The Charter of the United Nations*, p. 129 with further sources. On the more current matter of pro-democratic intervention see below, section 3.6.2.3.2.

220 M. Schweitzer, 'Erleidet das Gewaltverbot Modifikationen im Bereich von Einflußzonen', in W. Schaumann (ed.), *Völkerrechtliches Gewaltverbot und Friedenssicherung* (Baden-Baden: Nomos, 1971), pp. 243–4; Randelzhofer, 'Art. 2(4)', in Simma (ed.), *The Charter of the United Nations*, p. 129 with further sources.

Against the background of potential parallels between the US intervention in the Dominican Republic in 1965 and the Soviet intervention in Czechoslovakia in 1968 – the motivation stated in both cases was to prevent a certain type of government – the invitation to compare the Johnson Doctrine[221] and the Brezhnev Doctrine was obvious.[222]

By arguing that the Brezhnev Doctrine merely mirrored the pattern by which the United States justified its interventions in Latin America between 1954 and 1965,[223] it implies that almost every concept of the Brezhnev Doctrine can be traced back to an earlier claim of an identical right of the United States to take action in Latin America. Franck and Weisband identify six principles which the Brezhnev Doctrine and the Johnson Doctrine have in common. They consider that the Johnson Doctrine merely repeated the earlier Brezhnev Doctrine. That is, the principle that every socio-economic or political system which, in the opinion of the other states of a regional or ideological community of states, is at odds with the principles of this community constitutes an aggression against this community of states and entitles the other states to use force. The principle also applies to cases in which the population of a state erected that kind of system without external intervention.[224]

The assumption of the similarity between the Johnson Doctrine and the Brezhnev Doctrine is also based on a certain interpretation of the Johnson Doctrine: because the Johnson Doctrine is considered to be the announcement of a claim to a right to intervene in Latin American states, it is equated with the Monroe Doctrine in its moulding through the Roosevelt Corollary.[225] In this regard the Brezhnev Doctrine parallels the Roosevelt Corollary of the Monroe Doctrine, because it connects a right to use force with limitations of sovereignty. The claim of a right to use force in the Roosevelt Corollary was also based on invoking duties flowing

221 Glazer, 'The Brezhnev Doctrine', pp. 176–9; Grant, 'Doctrines (Monroe, Halstein, Brezhnev, Stimson)', in Wolfrum (ed.), *The Max Planck Encyclopedia of Public International Law*.

222 L. Friedmann, 'United States Policy and the Crisis of International Law', A.J.I.L., 59 (1965), 857–71. Friedmann furthermore detects a similarity between the justification for the intervention in the Dominican Republic in 1965 and the concept of a Großraumordnung in international law (on this see above, Chapter 2, section 2.1.3.2.2), p. 869.

223 Franck and Weisband, 'The Johnson and Brezhnev Doctrines: The Law You Make May be Your Own', p. 990.

224 Franck and Weisband, 'The Johnson and Brezhnev Doctrines: The Law You Make May be Your Own', pp. 980, 987.

225 I. Dore, 'The U.S. Invasion of Grenada: Resurrection of the "Johnson Doctrine?"', Stanford J.I.L., 20 (1984), 182. See above, section 3.3.3.

from sovereignty.[226] As shown above, this parallel between the Johnson Doctrine and the threat of intervention of the Roosevelt Corollary can only be drawn to a certain extent and is not a compelling logical conclusion.[227]

Furthermore, when discussing the comparisons of Franck and Weisband it should be noted that they are referring to 'verbal justifications' and not to the justifications under international law or claims of law adhering to the standard of *opinio iuris*. The United States might have justified its actions in the cases considered by Franck and Weisband on the plane of political motives according to the pattern described above. However, beyond that they also made other arguments in order to justify the respective action under international law.[228]

This factor also constitutes the essential difference between the Brezhnev Doctrine and the Johnson Doctrine: whereas the cases of the use of force considered to be expressions of the Johnson Doctrine were based on already known patterns of justification, the Brezhnev Doctrine contains its own pattern of justification of the use of force based on its own theory of a 'socialist international law'.[229]

The parallels between the Soviet and US doctrines thus lie on a level of unspecific 'rules' of the international system, but not that of rules of international law.[230] Thus, in spite of rhetorical similarities there is in legal terms a clear difference in quality between the Brezhnev Doctrine and the Johnson Doctrine. The arguments put forward in the Brezhnev Doctrine were illegal under international law. Yet seen as a matter of fact both doctrines reflect power policy on a hegemonic basis and do not constitute justification under international law.[231]

226 Meissner, *Die 'Breshnew-Doktrin'*, pp. 34–8; D. Schröder, 'Die Idee der kollektiven Regionalintervention – Rechtsvergleichende Betrachtungen zur Breshnew-Doktrin', R.O.W., 13 (1969), 203 *et seq*.

227 See above, section 3.3.3.

228 For example, L. Meeker, 'The Dominican Situation in the Perspective of International Law', *Department of State Bulletin*, 53 (1965), 60–5.

229 G. Tunkin, *Theory of International Law*, trans. W. Butler (London: George Allen & Unwin, 1974), pp. 435–41. On this see further: Schweisfurth, *Sozialistisches Völkerrecht*, pp. 151 *et seq*. Justifications for interventions considered as expressions of the Brezhnev Doctrine (in particular, the intervention in Czechoslovakia 1968) were furthermore also based on other grounds, such as, for example, intervention upon invitation. Nolte, *Eingreifen auf Einladung*, pp. 271–3; R. Mullerson, 'Intervention by Invitation', in L. Damrosh Fisler and D. Scheffer (eds.), *Law and Force in the New International Order* (Boulder, CO: Westwood Press, 1991), pp. 127–34

230 Franck and Weisband, 'The Johnson and Brezhnev Doctrines: The Law You Make May be Your Own', pp. 979–1014, in particular pp. 987 *et seq*.

231 W. Verwey, 'Humanitarian Intervention', in Cassese (ed.), *The Current Legal Regulation of the Use of Force*, p. 70, based on G. von Glahn, *Law Among Nations*, 6th edn. (New

Hence, rigorous legal analyses of the subject aptly mention a 'far-reaching congruence of the scheme of argumentation', and an 'equivalence of the social effects of the Moscow and the Johnson Doctrine',[232] but not an equivalence of the courses of action under international law foreseen by each doctrine.

3.3.5 Conclusion

Neither the Johnson Doctrine nor the Kennedy Doctrine are doctrines of US security policy in the mind of the US Government. Thus, the Johnson Doctrine does not constitute a doctrine of US security policy in terms of the definition on which this study is based. Rather, it is a subsequent academic conceptualisation of US foreign and security policy and, thus, not a doctrine in terms of the sense in which this study evaluates doctrines under international law.[233]

The assumption that the Johnson Doctrine constitutes a corollary to the Monroe Doctrine, which matches the Roosevelt Corollary to the Monroe Doctrine serving as a vehicle for a general claim to intervention, is based on an interpretation of the Johnson Doctrine which cannot be logically derived from the texts considered authoritative for the Johnson Doctrine. Rather, the principles of the Johnson Doctrine are open to an interpretation in accordance with the UN Charter, just as the Monroe Doctrine is under the UN Charter. In this respect the Johnson Doctrine does not change the evaluation of the reconcilability of the Monroe Doctrine with the UN Charter. Interventions by the United States which were considered by academics as expressions of the Johnson Doctrine, for example, the intervention in the Dominican Republic in 1965, were justified by the United States by referring to traditional patterns of justification.[234]

With regard to the often made comparison with the Brezhnev Doctrine, it thus has to be said that the assumption of similarity between the two doctrines is based on an interpretation of the Johnson Doctrine, which is not supported by the text or surrounding statements by the US Government. The essential difference between these two doctrines is that the Brezhnev Doctrine contains an own model of justification besides

York: Macmillan, 1986), pp. 171–2. Probably likewise: G. Levitt, 'Review: International Law and the Superpowers', A.J.I.L., 81 (1987), 498–9.

232 Schweisfurth, *Sozialistisches Völkerrecht?*, p. 568 (author's translations of 'weitgehenden Kongruenz der Argumentationsmuster'; 'Äquivalenz der sozialen Wirkungen der Moskauer – und der "Johnsondoktrin" . . . ').

233 See above, section 3.3.2. 234 See above, section 3.3.3.

claiming already existing justifications for the use of force. This model is rooted in a socialist theory of international law.[235]

Unlike the Johnson Doctrine, the subsequent Nixon Doctrine was expressly called a doctrine by President Nixon and this term was used repeatedly by the US Government.

3.4 The Nixon Doctrine

The US declaration of the Nixon Doctrine coincided with the conflict in Vietnam and, hence, it has to be assessed in close connection with it.[236] In spite of a massive military engagement – by 1969 almost 550,000 US soldiers had been deployed to Vietnam[237] – the United States failed in its support of the South Vietnamese government against North Vietnam and the Viet-Cong movement to get the upper hand in the conflict.[238]

Unlike the several preceding doctrines, the label 'Nixon Doctrine' was used in direct connection with the declaration of certain political principles of US foreign policy. President Nixon himself used the label 'Nixon Doctrine' in a public speech on 3 November 1969.[239] He had already explained the principles outlined in this speech on 25 May 1969[240] in an informal background talk given on the island of Guam so that at first the term 'Guam Doctrine' was used. President Nixon explicitly made reference in his speech of 3 November 1969 to the declaration on Guam. The explicit use of the label 'Nixon Doctrine', is attributed to President Nixon's desire to coin this label for these political principles instead of the until then commonly used label 'Guam Doctrine'.[241]

The term 'Nixon Doctrine' found its way into regular use in the US-American administration.[242] In spite of the continued use of the term, the

235 See above, section 3.3.4.

236 Vincent, *Non-Intervention and International Order*, pp. 227–9.

237 Kissinger, *Diplomacy*, p. 688.

238 On this see further: J. Frowein, 'Völkerrechtliche Aspekte des Vietnam Konflikts', ZaöRV/H.J.I.L., 27 (1967), 1–23.

239 *Public Papers of the Presidents, Richard Nixon, 1969* (Washington, DC: Government Printing Office, 1971), pp. 901–9.

240 *Public Papers of the Presidents, Richard Nixon, 1969*, pp. 544–56.

241 Kissinger, *Diplomacy*, pp. 707–8; Crabb, *The Doctrines of American Foreign Policy*, pp. 303–4.

242 For example, *Department of State Bulletin*, 64 (1971), 136, 161, 323, 716, 834; *Department of State Bulletin*, 68 (1973), 480, 539, 959; *Foreign Relations of the United States, 1969–1976*, vol. I, Docs. 47, 50, 69, 101, 111. Sporadically the labels 'Nixon–Kissinger Doctrine' (A. The, *Die Vietnampolitik der USA – von der Johnson zur Nixon-Kissinger-Doktrin* (Frankfurt a.M: Lang, 1979), pp. 222 *et seq.*) or 'Kissinger–Nixon Doctrine' (W. Nagan,

principles of the Nixon Doctrine are usually considered to be extremely vague.[243]

3.4.1 The Nixon Doctrine according to the speech of 3 November 1969

President Nixon made a distinction between three principles, which he called guidelines for US foreign policy in Asia: first, he generally emphasised that the US would fulfil its treaty obligations ('First, the United States will keep all of its treaty commitments'). Second, he offered to provide a nuclear shield in case of a threat by a nuclear power against an allied state ('Second, we shall provide a shield if a nuclear power threatens the freedom of a nation allied with us, or of a nation whose survival we consider vital to our security').

The third principle – constituting the actual core of the Nixon Doctrine – was that 'in cases involving other types of aggression we shall furnish military and economic assistance when requested in accordance with our treaty commitments. But we shall look to the nation directly threatened to assume the primary responsibility of providing the manpower for its defence.'[244] This declaration was preceded by a description of the US position in Vietnam, which Nixon described in Cold War terms, but added that although the United States would continue to support other states, the modalities and means of support would need to change.[245] These principles were subsequently commented and elaborated on several times.

3.4.2 Principles of the Nixon Doctrine for the use of force

Nixon's speech itself contains neither a precise indication of the circumstances in which the US would use force, nor a precise statement on the legality of the use of force. It merely mentions generally 'military assistance . . . when requested in accordance with our treaty commitments' and a 'shield' in case of a nuclear threat. Some guidance can be derived from subsequent explanations by the administration.

'Nuclear Arsenals, International Lawyers, and the Challenge of the Millennium', Y.J.I.L., 24 (1999), 492–3) are used. Yet these terms do not match the official language of the US Government, but refer to subsequent rationalisations of US foreign policy.

243 E. Ravenal, 'The Nixon Doctrine and our Asian Commitments', For.Aff., 49 (1970–1), 201–17; Crabb, *The Doctrines of American Foreign Policy*, pp. 279–88.

244 *Public Papers of the Presidents, Richard Nixon, 1969*, pp. 905–6.

245 *Public Papers of the Presidents, Richard Nixon, 1969*, pp. 901–5.

3.4.2.1 Criteria of the Nixon Doctrine for the use of force

President Nixon himself provided the first detailed commentary on the speech in his first annual report to Congress on 18 February 1970.[246] The report contains a section entitled 'Peace through Partnership – The Nixon Doctrine'.[247] The core statement emphasised in this section is that the United States would participate in the defence of allied states, but would not carry the main burden when doing so.[248] Nixon considered this principle a gradual turning away from the implementation of the Truman Doctrine, just as the Marshall Plan had been in 1948.[249]

The principles of Nixon's speech of 3 November 1969, which originally referred only to Asia, were later declared general principles of US security policy without regional limitation. The principles of the Nixon Doctrine were subsequently related to US policy in Europe and in particular to the European Community.[250] Another section of the report of 18 February 1970 is titled 'Partnership and the Nixon Doctrine'. It covers in detail US cooperation with states of specific regions and international organisations.[251] The focus of these statements is on allocating the burdens of providing defence; hence, on how force is used and not on the means of the use of force and not on the preconditions for the use of force. Consequently, they deal with the question of 'how' to use force, not 'if' it is to be used.[252] Instead, the Nixon Doctrine makes a statement as to when US force will not be used and gives clear priority to logistical support over the use of force by the United States. This was repeatedly emphasised by President Nixon.[253]

246 R. Nixon, 'U.S. Foreign Policy for the 1970s – A New Strategy for Peace', *Department of State Bulletin*, 62 (1970), 273–332.

247 *Public Papers of the Presidents, Richard Nixon*, 1970, pp. 118–20.

248 'the 'Nixon Doctrine'. Its central thesis is that the 'United States will participate in the defense and development of allies and friends, but that America cannot – and will not – conceive *all* the programs, design *all* the programs, execute *all* the decisions and undertake *all* the defense of the free nations of the world . . . ' *Public Papers of the Presidents, Richard Nixon, 1970*, pp. 118–19.

249 *Public Papers of the Presidents, Richard Nixon*, 1970, p. 118.

250 *Department of State Bulletin*, 68 (1973), 539; L. Kaplan, 'NATO and the Nixon Doctrine Ten Years Later', Orbis, 24 (1980), 149–64.

251 *Public Papers of the Presidents, Richard Nixon, 1970*, pp. 127 *et seq.*

252 Likewise Nixon: 'it does not mean, that our interests have changed. It does mean that our method of contributing to the achievement of those interests has changed. That is where what has been called the Nixon Doctrine comes in.' *Public Papers of the Presidents, Richard Nixon, 1971*, p. 539.

253 *Public Papers of the Presidents, Richard Nixon, 1970*, pp. 486, 554–5 ('the Nixon Doctrine, which provides that the United States rather than sending men will send arms . . . '), *ibid.*, p. 748.

The second annual report to Congress of 25 February 1971 also contains a section entitled 'The Nixon Doctrine', which is based closely on the text of the speech of 3 November 1969[254] adding only an explanation of how the provision of a nuclear shield should be understood. It is stated to include, if required, the use of nuclear weapons in response to a 'conventional aggression' as part of this deterrence.[255] The Nixon Doctrine was the first doctrine of US security policy which explicitly included the threat of the use of nuclear weapons. In spite of these detailed explanations of the principles of the Nixon Doctrine, it was generally considered to be a basic philosophical conviction rather than a detailed plan. Particularly in the case of the Nixon Doctrine, its indeterminableness is increased by the fact that its content in a specific case results from cooperation with other states, thus making its full implementation dependent on contributions by another states.[256] The annual report by the President to Congress that followed repeated, almost word for word, these explanations of the Nixon Doctrine.[257]

If one attempts to limit the principles of the Nixon Doctrine on the use of force, to cases where force was in fact used and which were considered to be an implementation of the Nixon Doctrine, it is remarkable that the use of force by the United States in Cambodia after 1970 was considered by President Nixon an ideal implementation and 'test case' of the Nixon Doctrine.[258] However, it has to be kept in mind that characterising the use of force by the United Sates in Cambodia as an ideal implementation of the Nixon Doctrine does not refer to the justification of this use of force as a matter of international law, but to its scope.[259]

As far as the phrase '*if* force is to be used' is concerned, the Nixon Doctrine contains no statement which foresees the use of force outside the cases covered by the Truman Doctrine.[260] Accordingly, Sir Robert

254 Nixon, 'U.S. Foreign Policy for the 1970s – Building for Peace', *Department of State Bulletin*, 64, (1971), 341–432, in particular pp. 344–8.

255 *Public Papers of the Presidents, Richard Nixon, 1971*, p. 224.

256 *Public Papers of the Presidents, Richard Nixon, 1971*, p. 228.

257 R. Nixon, 'U.S. Foreign Policy for the 1970s – Shaping a Durable Peace', *Department of State Bulletin*, 68 (1973), 772–3.

258 'Cambodia is the Nixon Doctrine in the purest form; Vietnam was in violation of the Nixon Doctrine . . . ' Nixon, *Public Papers of the Presidents, Richard Nixon, 1971*, p. 1108; M. Green, 'The Nixon Doctrine: A Progress Report', *Department of State Bulletin*, 64 (1971), 161–5.

259 *Public Papers of the Presidents, Richard Nixon, 1971*, p. 1108; J. Stevenson, 'United States Military Actions in Cambodia: Questions of International Law', *Department of State Bulletin*, 62 (1970), 767.

260 R. Yon, 'The Nixon Doctrine: A New Approach to the Containment Strategy', in Watson, Gleek and Grillo (eds.), *Presidential Doctrines: National Security From Woodrow Wilson*

Thompson considered the Nixon Doctrine primarily as a confirmation of the Truman Doctrine,[261] because both doctrines dealt with matters of support not amounting to the use of force by the United States.[262]

3.4.2.2 Evaluation of the cases of foreseen use of force according to the Nixon Doctrine under international law

As already stated, the use of force by the United States in Cambodia was considered by scholars to be an ideal implementation of the Nixon Doctrine. The United States considered this use of force as covered by the right to self-defence under Article 51 of the UN Charter. As justification for the use of force in neutral Cambodia, the United States stated that a belligerent state was allowed to take action in the territory of a neutral state in order to prevent incursions by another belligerent state from the territory of the neutral state, provided that these actions were required as acts of self-defence.[263] As the United States was exercising collective self-defence together with South Vietnam, the action in Cambodia was thus justified.[264]

Regardless of whether this justification was apt, this argument makes it clear that the use of force based on the principles of the Nixon Doctrine was considered by the United States at least as being in accordance with Article 51 of the UN Charter. That interpretation is also suggested by the first of the three basic principles of the Nixon Doctrine, which limits implementation of the doctrine to existing treaty obligations of the United States.[265] Furthermore, none of the subsequent explanations of the Nixon Doctrine by the administration can be interpreted in a way that it necessarily includes the proactive use of force without the existence of an armed attack.[266] Hence, it is possible to justify the use of force based

to George W. Bush, pp. 60–75; R. Litwak, *Détente and the Nixon Doctrine* (Cambridge University Press, 1984), pp. 191–3.

261 R. Thompson, *Revolutionary War and World Strategy: 1945–1969* (New York: Taplinger, 1970), pp. 162–3.

262 S. Gibert, 'Implications of the Nixon Doctrine for Military Aid Policy', Orbis, 16 (1972), 660–81.

263 J. Stevenson, 'United States Military Actions in Cambodia: Questions of International Law', *Department of State Bulletin*, 62 (1970), 765–70 at 769. On this see further: J. Moore, 'Legal Dimensions of the Decision to Intercede in Cambodia', A.J.I.L. 65, (1971), 38–75.

264 In detail on this see: L. Meeker, 'The Legality of the United States Participation in the Defense of Viet-Nam', *Department of State Bulletin*, 54 (1966), 474–89.

265 *Public Papers of the Presidents, Richard Nixon, 1969*, pp. 905–6.

266 J. Johnson, 'Just War, The Nixon Doctrine and the Shape of American Military Policy', Y.B.WorldAff. (1975), 141–4.

on the principles of the Nixon Doctrine by applying Article 51 of the UN Charter, as it was the case with the Truman Doctrine.[267]

The limitation of the doctrine to actions in accordance with US treaty obligations, besides the Charter, includes all treaty obligations of the United States.[268] This raises the question as to whether the limitation of aid formulated in the Nixon Doctrine[269] was in accordance with the existing US treaty obligations under alliance treaties such as the SEATO or NATO treaties.

3.4.2.2.1 The Nixon Doctrine and obligations of the United States under alliance treaties The first phrase of Article 5 of the NATO Treaty leaves open the scope of aid required to be given to the individual states parties to the treaty, and does not require the aid to have a certain content or quality. At least it does not contain a duty to carry the main burden of defence of another NATO member state. The individual parties to the treaty decide themselves on the kind and scope of means required to repel an armed attack.[270] Detailed plans of operations and deployments in NATO bodies do not change this, because these plans are not legally-binding recommendations and do not remove the member states' authority to decide on the use of their armed forces.[271] The treaty obligations of a NATO state leave beyond any doubt room for political principles, such as those formulated in the Nixon Doctrine, which limit in advance the scope of military aid. The same applies to the SEATO Treaty and the duty to support in its Article 4(1).[272]

Besides the limitation of US military aid, the Nixon Doctrine also contains the announcement to construct a 'nuclear shield', and use nuclear weapons if necessary in reaction to an unspecified 'conventional aggression'.[273] The degree to which the use of nuclear weapons and a threat of the use of nuclear weapons are in accordance with international law is, however, questionable.

267 See above, section 3.1.2.

268 Crabb, *The Doctrines of American Foreign Policy*, p. 281.

269 On this see further: E. Ravenal, *Large-Scale Foreign Policy: The Nixon Doctrine as History and Portent* (Berkeley, CA: Institute of International Studies, 1989), pp. 30–3.

270 Ipsen, *Rechtsgrundlagen und Institutionalisierung der Atlantisch-Europäischen Verteidigung*, pp. 44–51. On this see further above, section 3.1.3.1.

271 K. Ipsen, 'Die rechtliche Institutionalisierung der Verteidigung des atlantisch-westeuropäischen Raumes', JöR, 21 (1971), 39–42.

272 See above, section 3.1.3.2.

273 *Public Papers of the Presidents, Richard Nixon, 1971*, p. 224.

3.4.2.2.2 The Nixon Doctrine and the prohibition on the threat of force according to Article 2(4) of the UN Charter As the ICJ made clear in its Advisory Opinion on the *Legality of the Threat or Use of Nuclear Weapons* of 8 July 1996, the use of a certain type of weapon cannot be considered *per se* illegal under international law.[274] Hence, the use of force based on the principles of the Nixon Doctrine was not at that time, or later, illegal under international law solely due to the explicit mention of the use of nuclear weapons. But if a state announces the use of force in cases which cannot be reconciled with the UN Charter, this constitutes a threat of force which is contrary to the prohibition of the threat of force laid down in Article 2(4) of the UN Charter.[275] As the right of self-defence under Article 51 of the UN Charter is limited by customary law to necessary and proportionate measures of self-defence,[276] a proclamation to use nuclear weapons can constitute a violation of the prohibition on the threat of force according to Article 2(4) if the foreseen use of nuclear weapons would be disproportionate.[277]

The declarations referring to the Nixon Doctrine did not foresee a fixed use of nuclear weapons for certain situations, hence, it cannot be considered as intending a disproportionate use of force. In fact, it can itself be seen as a commandment to avoid excess when using force. Because it is possible to interpret the Nixon Doctrine in accordance with the UN Charter, it follows that the Nixon Doctrine by itself intends the use of nuclear weapons only if such use would be in accordance with the UN Charter. This is not changed by the circumstance that the use of nuclear weapons according to the Nixon Doctrine[278] would, if necessary, also be aimed against a conventional attack.[279] Asrat assumes, in fact, that the threat of using nuclear weapons – if it can be understood as a threat of mutual destruction – does not violate the prohibition on the threat of force of Article 2(4) of the UN Charter because of a general acceptance of

274 *Legality of the Threat or Use of Nuclear Weapons*, Advisory Opinion, I.C.J. Rep. 1996, p. 244, No. 39.

275 *Legality of the Threat or Use of Nuclear Weapons*, Advisory Opinion, I.C.J. Rep. 1996, p. 246, No. 47.

276 *Military and Paramilitary Activities in and against Nicaragua* (*Nicaragua* v. *United States of America*), Merits, Judgment, I.C.J. Rep. 1986, p. 94, No. 176.

277 *Legality of the Threat or Use of Nuclear Weapons*, Advisory Opinion, I.C.J. Rep. 1996, pp. 246–7, No. 48.

278 *Public Papers of the Presidents, Richard Nixon, 1971*, p. 224.

279 *Legality of the Threat or Use of Nuclear Weapons*, Advisory Opinion, I.C.J. Rep. 1996, p. 245, No. 44.

nuclear deterrence in state practice.[280] The prohibition of force, however, which has the character of *ius cogens*, is not open to that kind of change in state practice.[281]

However, it is possible that the threat to use nuclear weapons outlined in the Nixon Doctrine violates the prohibition on threatening the use of force in Article 2(4) of the UN Charter, because of the higher degree of specification of the threat which goes beyond a mere possession of nuclear weapons for the sake of deterrence. A threat is generally described as an action serving the purpose of causing a state of apprehension, worry or even fear in the person to whom it is addressed and causing that person to change behaviour in terms of the will of the person threatening.[282]

All doctrines discussed so far have in common the latent threat to use force. The question of whether this violates the prohibition on the threat of the use of force thus not only springs up in connection with the Nixon Doctrine, but also with regard to all the other doctrines declared since 1945. The Truman Doctrine and the Eisenhower Doctrine, for example, were both aimed at channelling the behaviour of states to a specific end, connected with the announcement the United States would use force in cases where other states did not comply with US policy.[283]

Nonetheless, the threat is more specific in the case of the Nixon Doctrine than in prior doctrines because not only does it threaten with the use of a certain type force (nuclear weapons), but it also addresses the threat to a far more clearly delineable number of states – states possessing nuclear weapons[284] and having a certain political system.

While the wording of Article 2(4) suggests that behaviour of that kind violates the prohibition on threatening the use of force, it is questionable if that behaviour is sufficiently specific to count as a threat of force in terms of the prohibition in Article 2(4) of the UN Charter as interpreted by commentators. It is understood as the announcement by a state to use

280 B. Asrat, *Prohibition of Force Under the UN Charter, A Study of Art. 2(4)* (Uppsala: Iustus Verlag, 1991), pp. 143–4.

281 *Military and Paramilitary Activities in and against Nicaragua* (*Nicaragua* v. *United States of America*), Merits, Judgment, I.C.J. Rep. 1986, p. 100, No. 190; Gray, *International Law and the Use of Force*, pp. 30–2.

282 R. Sadurska, 'Threats of Force', A.J.I.L., 82 (1988), 241.

283 See above, sections 3.2.1 and 3.2.2.1.

284 At the time the Nixon Doctrine was declared, four states besides the United States possessed nuclear weapons: the Soviet Union; the United Kingdom; France; and Israel. IISS, *Military Balance*, 1969–70 (Basingstoke: Taylor and Francis, 1970).

force if a certain demand of that state is not fulfilled.[285] The demand to abstain from a certain type of action – 'communist aggression' – can be found in the Nixon Doctrine. In order to count as a threat of force in terms of Article 2(4) of the UN Charter, this demand would have to be aimed at bringing about a specific reaction by the threatened state.[286]

It seems at least questionable if such a general formulation is sufficiently precise to count as a threat. The connection of certain actions foreseen in doctrines to particular states or regions usually only results from the historical situation or the political context in which the doctrine was declared. It cannot usually be found in the doctrine itself. The question of whether a sufficient precision of the required course of action can be derived from the Nixon Doctrine is, however, not decisive. Moreover, a certain degree of temporary proximity of the threatened use of force is required by Article 2(4).[287] However, the use of force threatened in the Nixon Doctrine refers to unspecified situations which may possibly arise in the future, but the emergence of these situations is hoped to be avoided by declaring the doctrine. For this reason the Nixon Doctrine does not constitute a violation of the prohibition on the threat of force in Article 2(4) of the UN Charter. The same is true for the cases of the threat of force in the other doctrines since 1945, which contain even less specific threats than the Nixon Doctrine.

Shortly after the Nixon Doctrine, President Ford declared the so-called 'New Pacific Doctrine', which also deals with US foreign policy in Asia. This so-called doctrine also shows little precision with regard to determining specific patterns of action.

3.4.3 The 'New Pacific Doctrine' or Ford Doctrine

In a speech on 7 December 1975 at the University of Hawaii in Honolulu, President Gerald Ford announced principles for US foreign policy which he called the 'New Pacific Doctrine'.[288] The label 'Ford Doctrine' is also used for these principles.[289] Ford emphasised in the six subsections in

285 Brownlie, *International Law and the Use of Force by States*, p. 364; O. Schachter, 'International Law: The Right of States to Use Armed Force', Mich.L.Rev., 82 (1984), 1625.

286 Randelzhofer, 'Art 2(4)', in Simma (ed.), *The Charter of the United Nations*, p. 124, No. 38.

287 R. Sadurska, 'Threats of Force', A.J.I.L., 82 (1988), 242–3; N. Stürchler, *The Threat of Force in International Law* (Cambridge University Press, 2007), pp. 273–4.

288 *Public Papers of the Presidents, Gerald Ford, 1975-II*, pp. 1950–5.

289 Plischke, *Contemporary U.S. Foreign Policy: Documents and Commentary*, pp. 198–9.

which he arranged this 'doctrine' the special importance of stability in this area of the Pacific for the security of the United States. He considered that maintaining the sovereignty of states in Asia allied with the United States, particularly Japan, normalisation of the relations of the United States with China and economic cooperation with states in the Pacific were all of particular importance.

This declaration did not contain a statement dealing more closely with the use of force – only a general interest in security is mentioned.[290] Thus, the Ford Doctrine does not constitute a doctrine in terms of the definition of a doctrine of US security policy on which this work is based.[291] Whereas the Johnson Doctrine is not considered a doctrine on part of the United States,[292] the Ford Doctrine – although called a doctrine – lacks a statement on a strategic concept for the use of force in international relations, unlike the Nixon Doctrine.

3.4.4 Conclusion

Unlike the Eisenhower Doctrine and the so-called Johnson Doctrine, the Nixon Doctrine is the first comprehensive doctrine of US security policy since the Truman Doctrine that was not regionally limited.[293]

Since the Nixon Doctrine as a political concept – far more than its predecessors – did not try to predetermine precise patterns of actions, but was understood by the United States as a basic political attitude rather than as a detailed concept for US foreign policy, it is far less simple to capture in legal terms. It does not address circumstances in which the United States will use force, but the scope that the specific use of force will have. Just like the Truman and Eisenhower doctrines, only the general term 'aggression' is used in order to describe the situation in which US force will be used. In this respect it only repeats the principles of the Truman Doctrine. Just like the latter, the principles of the Nixon Doctrine are open to an interpretation in accordance with the UN Charter as intending the use of force only if it is justified under Article 51.[294] The limitation of the scope of military aid in the doctrine is in accordance with the existing treaty duties of the United States.[295]

290 'A fourth principle of our Pacific policy is our continuing stake in stability and security in Southeast Asia . . . " *Public Papers of the Presidents, Gerald Ford, 1975-II,* pp. 1951–4.

291 See above, Chapter 1, section 1.6.

292 See above, section 3.3.2.

293 Litwak, *Détente and the Nixon Doctrine,* pp. 191–8.

294 See above, section 3.4.2.2.

295 See above, section 3.4.2.2.1.

Despite its vagueness, the Nixon Doctrine contains an explicit threat to use nuclear weapons. This threat does not violate the prohibition on the threat of force in Article 2(4) of the UN Charter, as the threat contained in the doctrine is not aimed at coercing a sufficiently designated addressee to undertake a sufficiently defined action in the near future. It refers instead to uncertain situations in the future.[296] Whether the Nixon Doctrine caused an increased likelihood of the use of nuclear weapons as is assumed by some,[297] or caused US involvement in conflicts it actually should have helped to avoid[298] are contentious issues.

Herbert Kraus would categorise these matters as going to the 'doability' of this political principle,[299] which is not addressed in this study.[300] The consequences of the Carter Doctrine, discussed in the subsequent chapter, are regarded as just as controversial.

3.5 The so-called Carter Doctrine

In contrast to the Nixon Doctrine, the so-called Carter Doctrine is limited to a specific region. The Soviet intervention in Afghanistan after 27 December 1980 is considered to be the reason for the declaration of the Carter Doctrine.[301] Together with the prior attack on the US embassy in Teheran and the taking hostage of US personnel there on 4 November 1979 following the Iranian revolution in spring 1979, the Soviet intervention was considered as endangering the US-American position in the Gulf region.[302]

President Jimmy Carter declared the doctrine before the US Congress in his annual State of the Union Address on 23 January 1980 as follows:

296 See above, section 3.4.2.2.2.

297 Johnson, 'Just War, the Nixon Doctrine and the Future Shape of American Military Policy', p. 150.

298 Kissinger, *Diplomacy*, p. 709.

299 Kraus, *Die Monroedoktrin und ihre Beziehungen zur amerikanischen Diplomatie und zum Völkerrecht*, p. 8.

300 See above, Chapter 1, section 1.6.

301 J. Wyllie, *The Influence of British Arms – An Analysis of British Military Intervention since 1956* (London: George Allen & Unwin, 1984), p. 107; B. Kuniholm, 'The Carter Doctrine, the Reagan Corollary and the Prospects for United States Policy in Southwest Asia', Int.J., 41 (1984), 342–61.

302 M. Buehler, 'The Carter Doctrine and National Security: An Examination of American Idealism', in Watson, Gleek and Grillo (eds.), *Presidential Doctrines: National Security From Woodrow Wilson to George W. Bush*, pp. 83–5; Evans and Newnham, *The Penguin Dictionary of International Relations*, pp. 61–2.

> An attempt by any outside force to gain control of the Persian Gulf Region will be regarded as an assault on the vital interests of the United States of America and such an assault will be repelled by any means necessary, including force.[303]

The label 'Carter Doctrine' is used for this declared principle.[304] Occasionally, its legality under international law is disputed by scholars. The similarity between the Carter Doctrine and other doctrines, such as the Monroe Doctrine, is that it asserts that force will be used in reaction to actions in a certain region.[305]

Michael Reisman uses the term 'Critical Defense Zone' for such regions. In doing so, he differentiates between these zones and a 'Sphere of Influence', in which a state reserves the right to exercise direct control over a territory. Reisman considers the principle of the 'Carter Doctrine' to be legal, because it is limited to using force in cases of external aggression.[306] Furthermore, he considers declaring such zones to be an accepted practice. Yet Reisman primarily addresses the legality of declaring such Critical Defense Zones with regard to the right of self-determination of the people of states within this zone.[307] If, however, the principle of the Carter Doctrine is regarded as the promulgation of a general claim of predominance, and the enforcement of it is not limited to certain means in certain situations, a far more critical view emerges of the Carter Doctrine.[308] For the most part, however, statements on the Carter Doctrine refer to the political utility of this principle, even when these statements are undertaken in a legal context.[309]

It is unclear whether the label 'Carter Doctrine' is only a subsequent rationalisation of US foreign policy, which was used by the US administration only after being coined by others. Also in the case of earlier doctrines, like the Monroe Doctrine, the labelling of a political principle

303 *Public Papers of the Presidents, Jimmy Carter, 1980–81*, vol. I, p. 197.

304 C. Krauthammer, 'The Reagan Doctrine', in R. Tucker (ed.), *Intervention & the Reagan Doctrine* (New York: Council on Religion and International Affairs, 1985) pp. 19–20; Crabb, *The Doctrines of American Foreign Policy*, pp. 325 *et seq.*; Plischke, *Contemporary U.S. Foreign Policy: Documents and Commentary*, pp. 180 *et seq.*

305 M. Reisman, 'Critical Defense Zones and International Law: The Reagan Codicil', A.J.I.L., 76 (1982), 589; ASIL Proceedings, 75th Annual Meeting, 1981, pp. 111, 120, On this aspect of the Monroe Doctrine see: Bowett, *Self-Defence in International Law*, pp. 208–15.

306 Reisman, 'Critical Defense Zones and International Law: The Reagan Codicil', p. 590.

307 M. Reisman, *Remarks*, ASIL Proceedings, 81st Annual Meeting, 1987, p. 565.

308 Paech and Stuby, *Machtpolitik und Völkerrecht in den internationalen Beziehungen*, pp. 234–5.

309 Vgl. ASIL Proceedings, 75th Annual Meeting, 1981, pp. 272–3.

as a doctrine only occurred after its announcement and was then later adopted by the administration. Detailed consideration of the content and meaning only occurred afterwards in the case of earlier doctrines.[310]

Yet in case of the Carter Doctrine, those kinds of considerations by the administration on the content of the doctrine are absent. By contrast, in spite of a detailed consideration of the policy of the United States with regard to the Gulf region, the term 'Carter Doctrine' was not used by the administration in this process.[311] President Carter himself did not use the term 'Carter Doctrine' in any public statement for the rest of his term of office.[312] Nor did this term find entry into the general use of language by the US government. Though the label 'Carter Doctrine' was used at a later point in time in official statements, it was used in these cases in order to refer to a subsequent rationalisation of the foreign policy of the Carter administration with regard to the Gulf region.[313] The term 'Carter Doctrine' is not used in connection with considerations of the admissibility of such a declaration, nor in connection with the admissibility of cases of use of force based on the principles of Carter's speech of 23 January 1980.[314]

Hence, the Carter Doctrine, just like the Johnson Doctrine, is not a doctrine of US security policy in terms of the definition on which this work is based,[315] but a political statement of another kind.

The label 'Reagan Codicil to the Carter Doctrine'[316] or 'Reagan Corollary'[317] is used for a later declaration by President Reagan of 1 October 1981.[318] In this declaration he stated that the United States would also oppose internal subversion of states in the Gulf region. This statement, however, can be seen as merely a regionally limited anticipation of the subsequent Reagan Doctrine.

310 See above, Chapter 2, sections 2.1–2.2.

311 For example, *Department of State Bulletin*, 80/2038 (1980), 17–19, 63–7.

312 *Public Papers of the Presidents, Jimmy Carter, 1980–81*, vol. III, pp. A1–146.

313 A. Prados, *Saudi Arabia: Current Issues and U.S. Relations* (Washington, DC: Congressional Research Service, 2002), p. 14.

314 D.US.P.I.L., VIII (1980), 1046–55.

315 See above Chap.3.C.II..

316 Reisman, 'Critical Defense Zones and International Law: The Reagan Codicil', p. 590; ASIL Proceedings, 81st Annual Meeting, 1987, p. 565; ASIL Proceedings, 79th Annual Meeting, 1985, p. 218.

317 B. Kuniholm, 'The Carter Doctrine, the Reagan Corollary and the Prospects for United States Policy in Southwest Asia', pp. 342 *et seq.*

318 'There's no way that we could stand by [and see Saudi Arabia] taken over by anyone that would shut off vital interest to the United States.' Quoted after: Prados, *Saudi Arabia: Current Issues and U.S. Relations*, p. 14.

3.6 The Reagan Doctrine

Unlike other doctrines, the declaration of the Reagan Doctrine is generally not considered to be a reaction to a single political event. Instead, it is considered to serve the purpose of countering a perceived general loss of power in relation to the Soviet Union which was expressed in a series of single events.[319] In particular, the installation of several communist regimes in, for example, South Vietnam, Cambodia, Laos, Mozambique, Angola and Ethiopia in the years prior to Reagan's election in 1981 is considered a trigger for the declaration of the Reagan Doctrine.[320] But the Reagan Doctrine is also closely related to US policy in South America, in particular in Nicaragua.[321]

The term 'Reagan Doctrine' was initially coined by the American author, Charles Krauthammer, who used the term in several articles.[322] In doing so he used the term to refer to Reagan's State of the Union Address of 6 February 1985.[323] The term 'Reagan Doctrine' was also used in order to describe principles which were perceived by scholars as characteristic features of the practice of US foreign policy during the Reagan administration – that is a subsequent characterisation.[324]

The US government adopted this term and its content was repeatedly explained in depth, in particular by the then US ambassador to the United Nations, Jeane Kirkpatrick.[325] President Reagan himself initially did not use the term,[326] but later adopted the label for the principles of his

319 Evans and Newnham, *The Penguin Dictionary of International Relations*, p. 464.

320 Kirkpatrick and Gerson, 'The Reagan Doctrine, Human Rights and International Law', in Henkin *et al.* (ed.), *Right v. Might. International Law and the Use of Force*, p. 23.

321 Tucker, 'Intervention & the Reagan Doctrine', in Tucker (ed.), *Intervention & the Reagan Doctrine*, p. 4.

322 Krauthammer, 'The Reagan Doctrine', in Tucker (ed.), *Intervention & the Reagan Doctrine*, pp. 19–24; C. Krauthammer, 'The Poverty of Realism: The Newest Challenge of the Reagan Doctrine', *The New Republic*, 17 February 1986, pp. 14–22.

323 Krauthammer, 'The Reagan Doctrine', in Tucker (ed.), *Intervention & the Reagan Doctrine*, pp. 19–20.

324 J. Scott, *Deciding to Intervene – The Reagan Doctrine and American Foreign Policy* (Durham, NC: Duke University Press, 1996), pp. 1–13; M. Lagon, *The Reagan Doctrine – Sources of American Conduct in the Cold War's Last Chapter* (Westport, CT: Frederick A. Praeger, 1994), pp. 1–4.

325 Kirkpatrick and Gerson, 'The Reagan Doctrine, Human Rights and International Law', in Henkin *et al.* (ed.), *Right v. Might. International Law and the Use of Force*, pp. 19–36; J. Kirkpatrick, *Legitimacy and Force* (New Brunswick, NJ: Transaction Books, 1988), vol. I, pp. 422–46.

326 S. Rosenfeld, 'The Guns of July', For.Aff., 64/2 (1986), 701.

foreign policy.[327] Whereas, one single declaration was usually considered to be a decisive outline for the preceding doctrines, several statements of President Reagan are considered together to make up this doctrine.[328]

3.6.1 The Reagan Doctrine according to the speech of 6 February 1985

A statement in President Reagan's State of the Union Address of 6 February 1985 is one of the clearest explanations of the principles of the Reagan Doctrine.[329] After talking mainly about matters of domestic policy and the US 'mission' to defend freedom and democracy, President Reagan declared that the United States:

> must not break faith with those who are risking their lives – on every continent from Afghanistan to Nicaragua – to defy Soviet-supported aggression and secure rights which have been ours from birth.[330]

After making references to the conflict in Nicaragua and the armed resistance against the Sandinista government, Reagan continued stating that 'support for freedom fighters is self-defence and totally consistent with the OAS and UN Charters'.[331]

Reagan then requested that Congress support that policy. Earlier statements by Reagan concerning individual, regionally limited conflicts also contain hints of similar principles.[332] The principle of supporting 'freedom fighters' was repeated in statements by President Reagan after the 6 February 1985 speech.[333] The principle is also repeated in the National

327 Reagan, *An American Life*, p. 552: 'I also tried to send out a signal that the United States intended to support people fighting for their freedom against communism wherever they were – a policy some writers later described as "Reagan Doctrine"...'

328 Scott, *Deciding to Intervene – The Reagan Doctrine and American Foreign Policy*, pp. 19–24.

329 Kohen, 'The Use of Force by the United States After the End of the Cold War, and its Impacts on International Law'; in Byers and Nolte (eds.), *United States Hegemony and the Foundations of International Law*, p. 199; N. Berry, 'The Conflict between United States Intervention and Promoting Democracy in the Third World', TempleL.Q., 60 (1987), 1015–21.

330 State of the Union Address, 6 February 1985, *Public Papers of the Presidents of the United States, Ronald Reagan, 1985*, vol. I, p. 135.

331 State of the Union Address, 6 February 1985, *Public Papers of the Presidents of the United States, Ronald Reagan, 1985*, vol. I, p. 135.

332 Plischke, *Contemporary U.S. Foreign Policy: Documents and Commentary*, pp. 180–1; 202–5.

333 Remarks at a Joint German–American Military Ceremony at Bitburg Air Base in the Federal Republic of Germany, 5 May 1985, *Public Papers of the Presidents of the United States, Ronald Reagan, 1985*, vol. I, p. 567; State of the Union Address, 4 February

Security Strategy of the United States published in 1988, which also contains a comprehensive explanation of the principles of US foreign policy.[334]

3.6.2 *Principles of the Reagan Doctrine for the use of force*

In continuation of the Truman Doctrine, the Reagan Doctrine makes reference to the Cold War conflict. It is unclear whether it extended the principles for the use of force by the United States beyond those established in the Truman Doctrine. Statements which may contain statements of law in connection with the Reagan Doctrine are extremely vague, just as such statements were in the case of the Truman Doctrine.[335]

3.6.2.1 Statements on the legality of the use of force in the context of the Reagan Doctrine

The core statement of Reagan's speech, 'Support for freedom fighters is self-defence and totally consistent with the OAS and UN Charters', seems *prima facie* like a statement on the circumstances which would allow the justified use of force in self-defence. As, however, only general 'support' is mentioned, it is not possible to derive the means which would be employed in order to enforce the principles of the speech and which means are considered justified from the statement.

In statements explaining the Reagan Doctrine, the right of self-defence was also drawn on in order to justify support for actions which would not necessarily violate the prohibition of force in Article 2(4) of the UN Charter.[336] Secretary of State Shultz, for example, in a speech on 22 February 1985 justified logistical support ('material assistance') as consistent with the right of self-defence: 'The UN and OAS Charters reaffirm the inherent right of self-defence against aggression – aggression of the kind committed by the Soviets in Afghanistan, by Nicaragua in Central America, and by Vietnam in Cambodia. Material assistance to those opposing such aggression can be a lawful form of collective self-defence . . . '[337]

1986, Public Papers of the Presidents of the United States, Ronald Reagan, 1985, vol. II, p. 129.

334 R. Reagan, *National Security Strategy of the United States* (Washington: Pergamon–Brassey's, 1988).

335 See above, section 3.1.1.1.

336 *Military and Paramilitary Activities in and against Nicaragua* (*Nicaragua* v. *United States of America*), Merits, Judgment, I.C.J. Rep. 1986, p. 119, No. 228.

337 *Department of State Bulletin*, 85 (1985), 20.

This statement does not contain a precise statement of the US understanding of the legality of the use of force in self-defence, according to which the use of force going beyond the principles of the Truman Doctrine is considered legal. Rather, this statement is regarded by scholars as a political explanation using legal idiom.[338] Yet this statement on the Reagan Doctrine makes clear that the doctrine gave a high priority to logistical support. To what degree are these types of supporting actions permissible without violating the prohibition on the use of force in Article 2(4)?[339] And to what extent does the Reagan Doctrine intend the use of force to go beyond that? Different authors attributed varying contents to the Reagan Doctrine. The doctrine was either considered a mere repetition and continuation of already existing principles of US security policy, or as a dramatic break from its hitherto existing principles.[340]

3.6.2.2 Criteria of the Reagan Doctrine for the use of force

A description of the Reagan Doctrine by the State Department considers the doctrine as signifying a break from the policy of 'containment',[341] and as a return to the concept of 'roll-back' of John Foster Dulles. This concept intended to actively push back communist regimes.[342] However, the adoption of a policy of 'roll-back' in the Reagan Doctrine was explicitly denied by Kirkpatrick and Gerson.[343] As both the strategic concepts of 'containment' and 'roll-back' do not contain a precise definition of their principles for the use of force, and the relationship between the two is disputed, no clarity can be gained by characterising the Reagan Doctrine as 'roll-back'. Indeed, it is unclear whether 'roll-back' was seen as the opposite of, or merely as a certain type of 'containment'.[344]

338 M. Reisman, 'Old Wine in New Bottles: The Reagan and Brezhnev Doctrines in Contemporary International Law and Practice', Y.J.I.L., 13 (1988), 186.

339 On this see: Randelzhofer, 'Art. 2(4)', in Simma (ed.) *The Charter of the United Nations*, pp. 119–20, in particular No. 26.

340 C. DeMuth *et al.* (eds.), *The Reagan Doctrine and Beyond* (Washington, DC: The American Enterprise Institute, 1987).

341 On this: Evans and Newnham, *International Relations*, pp. 95–97.

342 Department of State, *Reagan Doctrine*, available at: www.state.gov/r/pa/ho/time/dr/17741pf.htm; likewise see: Smith, *The Last Years of the Monroe Doctrine, 1945–1993*, p. 164.

343 Kirkpatrick and Gerson, 'The Reagan Doctrine, Human Rights and International Law', in Henkin *et al.* (ed.), *Right v. Might. International Law and the Use of Force*, pp. 55–6.

344 See, for example, Kissinger, *Diplomacy*, pp. 450–2.

Publications by scholars trying to prove a break between the Reagan Doctrine and the preceding doctrines of US security policy imply a certain understanding of prior doctrines in the course of their comparison. The following summary of Gaddis Smith's views illustrates this opinion: 'The Truman Doctrine had said it should be the policy of the United States to help free people under attack from armed minorities. The Reagan Doctrine said it should be the policy of the United States "to assist armed minorities in their attacks on Communist governments."'[345] Other authors, however, by contrast consider the Reagan Doctrine to be a repetition of the principles of the Truman Doctrine.[346] Others cite a revival of the Roosevelt Corollary to the Monroe Doctrine.[347]

Just like the Johnson Doctrine, the Reagan Doctrine was compared and contrasted to the Brezhnev Doctrine.[348] A similarity between the Reagan and Brezhnev doctrines is that both intended interventions in order to promote a certain ideology.[349] Both are considered to be doctrines of 'selective intervention'.[350]

On the other hand, it is assumed that a considerable difference exists between these two doctrines because the principles of the Reagan Doctrine for the use of force went beyond those of the Brezhnev Doctrine. While the Brezhnev Doctrine intended the use of force in order to avoid regime change and, hence, was aimed at the preservation of the status quo, the Reagan Doctrine aimed at supporting the use of force in order to bring about regime change – a change in the status quo.[351] In this respect the Reagan Doctrine did not match the Brezhnev Doctrine, but the Khrushchev Doctrine.[352]

345 Smith, *The Last Years of the Monroe Doctrine*, p. 164.

346 Kirkpatrick and Gerson, 'The Reagan Doctrine, Human Rights and International Law', in Henkin *et al.* (ed.), *Right v. Might. International Law and the Use of Force*, p. 31.

347 F. Boyle, *World Politics and International Law* (Durham, NC: Duke University Press, 1985), pp. 268–72.

348 For example, ASIL Proceedings, 81st Annual Meeting, 1987, pp. 561–78.

349 K. Thompson, 'The Reagan Doctrine', in Tucker (ed.), *Intervention & the Reagan Doctrine*, pp. 29–30.

350 W. Reisman, 'International Law After the Cold War', A.J.I.L., 84 (1990), 860. Yet Reisman makes a distinction of the Reagan Doctrine into two elements. According to Reisman the doctrine contains a defensive and an offensive element: a claim for a defensive perimeter, a zone of influence and furthermore a claim (like the Brezhnev Doctrine) that a right to support selected insurgencies exists. Reisman, 'Old Wine in New Bottles: The Reagan and Brezhnev Doctrines in Contemporary International Law and Practice', pp. 171–98.

351 Tucker, 'Intervention & the Reagan Doctrine', in Tucker (ed.), *Intervention & the Reagan Doctrine*, p. 15.

352 T. Franck, *Judging the World Court* (New York: Priority Press Publication, 1986), p. 64.

In line with this interpretation, the Reagan Doctrine was also called a counterdraft and negation of the Brezhnev Doctrine,[353] with its principle of the impossibility of a change of regime within a state once it became socialist.[354] Secretary of State Shultz interpreted the principle of open support of anti-communist insurgents as an explicit rejection of the Brezhnev Doctrine.[355]

The different correlation of the right of self-determination to each doctrine is also given as a reason for the essential difference of objectives: whereas the Brezhnev Doctrine specifically aimed at maintaining influence over a foreign state, the Reagan Doctrine aimed at realising the right of self-determination of the local people.[356]

The Reagan Doctrine has been considered a revival and enhancement of the hypothesis advanced during the process of decolonisation, that it shall be legal for national liberation movements to use force in order to enforce the right of self-determination.[357] Despite the fact that this hypothesis has developed beyond a postulate of policy of law *de lege ferrenda*[358] to a conviction of law *de lege lata*,[359] it has to be noted that the Reagan Doctrine refers to the participation of an external, foreign state in such a conflict, waged in order to establish a certain type of government. Thus, in a reference to the right of self-determination, the principle of the so-called 'pro-democratic intervention' was developed.[360] According to this theory, a state has the right to use force in order to remove a government in another state which is not democratically legitimated.[361] Indeed, the

353 W. Bode, 'The Reagan Doctrine', Strategic Rev., 14 (1986), 22.

354 On this see further above, section 3.3.4.

355 'we would be conceding the Soviet notion, that communist revolutions are irreversible while everything else is up for grabs; we would be, in effect, enacting the Brezhnev Doctrine into American Law'. G. Shultz, 'New Realities and New Ways of Thinking', For.Aff., 63/4 (1984), 713.

356 Kirkpatrick and Gerson, 'The Reagan Doctrine, Human Rights and International Law', in Henkin *et al.* (ed.), *Right v. Might. International Law and the Use of Force*, p. 31. Similarly see: Reisman, ASIL Proceedings, 81st Annual Meeting, 1987, p. 568.

357 Reisman, 'Old Wine in New Bottles: The Reagan and Brezhnev Doctrines in Contemporary International Law and Practice', pp. 188 *et seq.*

358 Still supported by W. Kewenig, 'Gewaltverbot und zulässige Machteinwirkung', in W. Schaumann (ed.), *Völkerrechtliches Gewaltverbot und Friedenssicherung*, pp. 208–9.

359 K. Doehring, 'Self-Determination', in Simma (ed.), *The Charter of the United Nations*, p. 61, No. 55.

360 On this see: M. Byers and S. Chestermann, '"You the People": pro-Democratic Intervention in International Law', in G. Fox and B. Roth (eds.), *Democratic Governance and International Law* (Cambridge University Press, 2000), pp. 259–92, in particular pp. 262–71.

361 M. Reisman, 'Coercion and self-determination: Construing Charter Art. 2(4)', A.J.I.L., 78 (1984), 643–5, with a rejecting remark by O. Schachter, 'The Legality of Pro-Democratic Invasion', A.J.I.L., 78 (1984), 645–50. On this see further below, section 3.6.2.3.2.

Reagan Doctrine did link support by the United States to resistance against a government not legitimised by its people, but whether this includes cases of pro-democratic use of force is unclear.[362]

Hence, these comparisons of the Reagan Doctrine with other political concepts do not allow for a secure conclusion *ex negativo*, under which circumstances the Reagan Doctrine intends the use of force by the United States and which other activities the Reagan Doctrine targets.

Attempts to reach further precision in establishing the principles of the Reagan Doctrine by taking a closer look at interventions considered as ideal implementations of the Reagan Doctrine do not lead to clear conclusions either. President Reagan himself considered cases of very different types of US engagement as ideal implementations of the Reagan Doctrine.[363]

The supporting of the Contras in Nicaragua and the Mujahideen in Afghanistan are usually cited as particular examples of the implementation of the Reagan Doctrine.[364] In addition to these examples, a number of other cases of use of force during Reagan's term of office were considered by academics to be implementations of the Reagan Doctrine: among which were the intervention in Lebanon in 1982;[365] the intervention in Grenada in 1983;[366] and the bombing of Tripoli and Benghazi in 1986.[367] Different justifications were brought forward by members of the US administration, which did not, however, characterise these interventions as implementations of the Reagan Doctrine.[368]

There is a general consensus that the Reagan Doctrine comprised the open support of anti-communist resistance movements. Each of the

362 R. Turner, 'International Law, the Reagan Doctrine, and World Peace: Going Back to the Future', Wash.Q., 11/4 (1988), 126–7.

363 'Around the world, in Afghanistan, Angola, Cambodia, and yes, Central America, the United States stands today with those who would fight for freedom. We stand with ordinary people who have the courage to take up arms against communist tyranny. This stand is at the core of what is called the Reagan Doctrine.' Speech on 31 October 1988, quoted after: D. Moynihan, *On the Law of Nations* (Cambridge, MA: Harvard University Press, 1990), p. 122.

364 For example, E. Luard, 'Western Europe and the Reagan Doctrine', Int.Aff. 63 (1987), 563–74.

365 D. Nuechterlein, 'The Reagan Doctrine in Perspective', P.P.Sci., 19/1 (1990), 43–9.

366 S. Malawer, 'Reagan's Law and Foreign Policy, 1981–87: The "Reagan Corollary" of International Law', Harv.I.L.J., 29/1 (1988), 93–4.

367 E. Schoonbroodt, *La Doctrine Reagan* (Bruxelles: Groupe de recherches et d'information sur la paix, 1987), pp. 14–16.

368 Kirkpatrick and Gerson, 'The Reagan Doctrine, Human Rights and International Law', in Henkin *et al.* (ed.), *Right v. Might. International Law and the Use of Force*, p. 19; K. Zielkowski, *Gerechtigkeitspostulate als Rechtfertigung von Kriegen* (Baden-Baden: Nomos, 2006), p. 89.

different views of the Reagan Doctrine outlined above has to be taken into account when evaluating the reconcilability of the principles of the Reagan Doctrine with the law on the use of force in place at the time.

3.6.2.3 Evaluation of the principles of the Reagan Doctrine for the use of force under international law

Based on different principles for the use of force, attributed to the Reagan Doctrine, statements on the reconcilability of the Reagan Doctrine with international law differ widely.

3.6.2.3.1 Evaluation of the Reagan Doctrine under international law when interpreting it restrictively It is assumed by some scholars that the Reagan Doctrine does not contain any principles for the use of force which deviate substantially from those of the Truman Doctrine. According to this view, the Reagan Doctrine merely represents a renewed confirmation of the willingness to use force in exercise of collective self-defence – a 'Stimson Doctrine with Teeth' – which, aside from diplomatic protests, intends the use of force in exercise of collective self-defence in response to an armed aggression in breach of international law.[369]

Some assume that the Reagan Doctrine did not intend the use of force by the United States, at least not through the participation of its own troops. Rather, the Reagan Doctrine is limited to providing logistical support which is entirely in accordance with the prohibition of force in Article 2(4).[370] But this does not answer the question of whether supporting action of that type itself constitutes a violation of the prohibition of force. This matter was subsequently dealt with by the ICJ in 1986 in the *Nicaragua* case.[371]

If use of force according to the principles of the Reagan Doctrine is considered to be limited to the use of force in self-defence under Article 51,[372] then there is no conflict with Article 2(4). The United Sates does not

369 Turner, 'International Law, the Reagan Doctrine, and World Peace: Going Back to the Future', pp. 126–7.

370 Kirkpatrick, *Legitimacy and Force*, vol. I, p. 428: 'It should be emphasized that the sympathy, solidarity and assistance offered by Reagan do *not* include U.S. participation in combat. [The] Reagan Doctrine is sharply distinguished from "containment" or "rollback" approaches.'

371 *Military and Paramilitary Activities in and against Nicaragua* (*Nicaragua* v. *United States of America*), Merits, Judgment, I.C.J. Rep. 1986, p. 119, Nos. 228 *et seq.* On this see further below, section 3.6.2.3.3.

372 Of this opinion: J. Moore, 'The Secret War in Central America and the Future of World Order', A.J.I.L., 80 (1986), 111–16.

give a specific explanation on the understanding of the legality of the use of force in self-defence within the framework of the Regan Doctrine. The Reagan Doctrine does not, however, provide any explanation as to the US understanding of whether a right of self-defence existing prior to the UN Charter continues to exist.[373] However, in this context this question can remain unanswered, as the assumption of a continuing existence of a customary right of self-defence can only result in an extension of the right of self-defence, and not in a further limitation of the right of self-defence.[374]

A restrictive interpretation of the Reagan Doctrine concerning the use of force can, therefore, also be considered as complying with international law, even if adhering to the narrow interpretation of the use of force admissible under Article 51 of the UN Charter. Moreover, this narrow view of the Reagan Doctrine does not foresee the bringing about of forceful regime change. Especially with regard to Nicaragua, some have argued that this was never the aim of US policy.[375]

Indeed, while several members of the Reagan administration might have tended towards supporting a right to pro-democratic intervention,[376] cases of the use of force during Reagan's term of office were never justified by reference to that right. Instead, far less controversial justifications were given.[377] The United States did not claim in the Nicaragua case that forcible pro-democratic intervention was legal and did not otherwise claim the existence of such a right.[378]

The controversy about the legality of the principles of the Reagan Doctrine under international law, however, refers to the wide interpretation of the Reagan Doctrine which leaves far more room for the use of force than the restrictive interpretation which limits it to cases of the use of force in self-defence. Even though the wide view acknowledges the

373 On this see further below, Chapter 4, section 4.2.2.2.

374 Brownlie, *International Law and the Use of Force by States*, pp. 272–4; Bowett, *Self-Defence in International Law*, pp. 184–5.

375 Moore, 'The Secret War in Central America and the Future of World Order', pp. 111–12.

376 Turner, 'International Law, the Reagan Doctrine, and World Peace: Going Back to the Future', pp. 126–7.

377 Likewise: Gray, *International Law and the Use of Force*, pp. 105–7; M. O'Connell, *The Myth of Preemptive Self-Defense*, ASIL Task Force Papers, p. 15, fn.74.

378 P. Kahn, 'From Nuremberg to the Hague: The United States Position in Nicaragua v. United States and the Development of International Law', Y.J.I.L., 12 (1987), 1–62 at 17–27; B. Roth, 'Governmental Illegitimacy Revisited: "Pro-Democratic" Armed Intervention in the Post-Bipolar World', T.L.C.P., 3 (1993), 485–6.

defensive character of the doctrine,[379] the scope of 'self-defence' to be allowed under the wide view of the doctrine seems wider than that allowed by international law for the use of force then in force.

3.6.2.3.2 Evaluation of the wide interpretation of the Reagan Doctrine

The wide view of the Reagan Doctrine assumes that the doctrine considered that it promoted the United States' willingness to use force in order to intervene in states with governments considered not to be democratically legitimated.[380] Some authors even go as far as to state that the Reagan Doctrine would prefer a 'military variant' of foreign policy in order to implement a concept of hegemony 'which no national interest of other states could resist without going unpunished'.[381] Such an extensive (actually limitless) interpretation of the Reagan Doctrine which, rather imprecisely, considers the doctrine to be a denial of any limitation of the use of force by international law cannot be read into the US statements considered as authoritative representations of the Reagan Doctrine, even when interpreting them broadly. Consequently, this view is not met with approval by the literature dealing with the Reagan Doctrine.[382]

Accordingly, authors who interpret the Reagan Doctrine broadly for the most part do not assume that the Reagan Doctrine advocates a general right to intervention for the United States. They consider that the Reagan Doctrine does not aim at the forcible removal of governments considered as illegitimate, but instead intended to support already existing resistance movements against governments that do not have the approval of the population and rely on external support in order to maintain their power.[383]

379 Reisman, 'Old Wine in New Bottles: The Reagan and Brezhnev Doctrines in Contemporary International Law and Practice', pp. 175–80.

380 S. Malawer, 'Reagan's Law and Foreign Policy, 1981–87: The "Reagan Corollary" of International Law', Harv.I.L.J., 28/1 (1988), 86, fn. 6; J. Miller, 'International Intervention – The United States Invasion of Panama', Harv.I.L.J., 31 (1990), 639; Byers and Chestermann, '"You the People" Pro-Democratic Intervention in International Law', in Fox and Roth (eds.), *Democratic Governance and International Law*, p. 262, fn. 17; Kolb, *Ius contra bellum*, p. 231, No. 557; similarly: M. Janis, *An Introduction to International Law*, 3rd edn. (New York: Aspen Law & Business, 1999), p. 188.

381 Author's translation of: 'dem sich keine nationalen Interessen anderer Staaten ungestraft widersetzen sollten.' Paech and Stuby, *Machtpolitik und Völkerrecht in den internationalen Beziehungen*, p. 239.

382 For example, Tucker, 'Intervention & the Reagan Doctrine', in Tucker (ed.), *Intervention & the Reagan Doctrine*, pp. 13 *et seq.*

383 Kirkpatrick and Gerson, 'The Reagan Doctrine, Human Rights and International Law', in Henkin *et al.* (ed.), *Right v. Might. International Law and the Use of Force*, pp. 19–20.

This course of action is usually described as 'counterintervention'.[384] Accordingly, the proponents of the wide interpretation of the Reagan Doctrine also assume that the doctrine aims at responsive actions, rather than 'first strikes' by the United States. The decisive factor, however, for this responsive action is not the occurrence of an armed aggression or an armed attack, but the existence of an armed insurgency against a regime considered by the US to be non-democratic. This is regarded as a situation similar to that of self-defence of the population of the respective state.[385] It is in this crucial respect that the wide view of the Reagan Doctrine deviates from the restrictive view. The starting point of the Reagan Doctrine, according to the wide view, is not an action of any kind by a state against the United States, but the political and ideological conviction of the respective regime which poses a hidden threat to it.

Besides an endorsement of the right to pro-democratic intervention, the Reagan Doctrine is also considered to be an attempt to extend the right of collective self-defence to include the preservation of a certain political system among the goods to be defended.[386] This interpretation of the right to self-defence in the context of the Reagan Doctrine – a right of self-defence to repel ideological rescheduling[387] – cannot be reconciled with the international law in force at the time, even when interpreting it as broadly as possible.[388] This issue has also been discussed in connection with prior doctrines.[389]

Despite the fact that a right to pro-democratic intervention was considered by the vast majority of international lawyers as clearly unlawful under international law,[390] was rejected by the ICJ in the *Nicaragua*

384 D. Scheffer, 'Use of Force After the Cold War: Panama, Iraq, and the New World Order', in Henkin *et al.* (ed.), *Right v. Might. International Law and the Use of Force*, p. 119.

385 Kirkpatrick and Gerson, 'The Reagan Doctrine, Human Rights and International Law', in Henkin *et al.* (ed.), *Right v. Might. International Law and the Use of Force*, pp. 28–30.

386 Kohen, 'The Use of Force by the United States After the End of the Cold War, and its Impacts on International Law', in Byers and Nolte (eds.), *United States Hegemony and the Foundations of International Law*, p. 199; C. Joyner and M. Grimaldi, 'The United States and Nicaragua: Reflections on the Lawfulness of Contemporary Intervention', Va.J.I.L., 25 (1985), 678–81.

387 Schoonbroodt, *La Doctrine Reagan*, p. 22.

388 Franck, *Recourse to Force*, pp. 69–75.

389 See above, section 3.3.5.

390 O. Schachter, 'The Legality of Pro-Democratic Invasion', A.J.I.L., 78 (1984), 645–50; Byers and Chestermann, '"You the People": pro-Democratic Intervention in International Law', in Fox and Roth (eds.), *Democratic Governance and International Law*, pp. 262–70 with further evidence.

judgment[391] and by contemporary state practice,[392] some continued to argue for a separate model of justifications for these types of interventions under the Reagan Doctrine. Michael Reisman argued in 1984 that in case of failure by the United Nations, a unilateral use of force without Security Council authorisation or on invitation had to be possible. He thus considered an interpretation of the prohibition of force in Article 2(4) of the UN Charter to that end as necessary. His central argument in doing so was the advancement of current international law.[393] Yet Reisman did not consider that such a right was actually in existence, nor that it accorded with the prevailing opinion among scholars. He promoted it as desirable *de lege ferenda*.[394]

Even though Kirkpatrick and Gerson assume that the Reagan Doctrine did not envisage the use of force by the United States, they go along with Reisman and consider these type of interventions to be justified. According to their view the prohibition on the use of force in Article 2(4) of the UN Charter has to be read in the context of the whole of the UN Charter. They argue further that in spite of the principle of sovereign equality, the UN Charter is not free of a commitment to certain values and shows a preference for democratic types of government, and for this reason pro-democratic interventions ought to be justified.[395]

Some also argued for the legitimacy of the Reagan Doctrine on the basis of reciprocity with the Brezhnev Doctrine. Even though both doctrines are at odds with the UN Charter, they would constitute 'survival norms' indispensable for avoiding conflicts, hence, serving the primary purpose of international law to maintain a minimum order. However, this assumption is based on a specific broad understanding of international law which includes non-legal 'rules' in its considerations. The creation of these rules does not comply with the recognised processes of the creation

391 *Military and Paramilitary Activities in and against Nicaragua* (*Nicaragua* v. *United States of America*), Merits, Judgment, I.C.J. Rep. 1986, pp. 109–10, No. 209; pp. 132–3, Nos. 262–3.

392 On this see: S. Chestermann, *Just War or Just Peace? Humanitarian intervention in International Law* (Oxford University Press, 2001), pp. 106–8 with further evidence.

393 Reisman, 'Coercion and self-determination: Construing Charter Art. 2(4)', pp. 643–5.

394 Byers and Chestermann, '"You the People": pro-Democratic Intervention in International Law', in Fox and Roth (eds.), *Democratic Governance and International Law*, pp. 261–4.

395 Kirkpatrick and Gerson, 'The Reagan Doctrine, Human Rights and International Law', in Henkin *et al.* (ed.), *Right v. Might. International Law and the Use of Force*, pp. 25 *et seq*.

of public international law. Accordingly, proponents of this theory write about the 'rules of the game'.[396]

Irrespective of whether one considers pro-democratic intervention as being in compliance or non-compliance with international law, it has to be noted that the Reagan Doctrine as laid out by the US authorities cannot necessarily be seen as advocating such a right. Although single voices in the Reagan Administration might have been inclined towards such a right,[397] these statements are neither decisive for determining the content of the Reagan Doctrine, nor do they reach the quality of *opinio iuris*. Accordingly, some authors do not write of adherence to the concept of pro-democratic intervention by the Reagan Doctrine, but much more accurately of an echo of this concept in the Reagan Doctrine.[398]

The ICJ addressed the question of admissibility of interventions in order to bring about a specific political system in a state in the 1986 *Nicaragua* judgment. This judgment can also be seen as an evaluation of the Reagan Doctrine under international law.

3.6.2.3.3 The Reagan Doctrine and the *Nicaragua* judgment Several passages of the *Nicaragua* judgment are considered in academic discussions as an explicit rejection of the Reagan Doctrine,[399] the following passage in particular:[400]

396 Reisman, 'Old Wine in New Bottles: The Reagan and Brezhnev Doctrines in Contemporary International Law and Practice', pp. 181–5, in particular p. 182: 'Under textual inquiry neither the Brezhnev nor the Reagan doctrine is lawful.'; Reisman, ASIL Proceedings, 81st Annual Meeting, 1987, pp. 562–7.

397 For example, Bode, 'The Reagan Doctrine', pp. 21–9; Kirkpatrick, *Legitimacy and Force*, vol. I, pp. 422 *et seq.*; Kirkpatrick and Gerson, 'The Reagan Doctrine, Human Rights and International Law', in Henkin *et al.* (ed.), *Right v. Might. International Law and the Use of Force*, pp. 19–36.

398 J. Crawford, 'Democracy and the Body of International Law', in Fox and Roth (eds.), Democratic Governance and International Law, p. 106. Similarly: Chestermann, Just War or Just Peace? Humanitarian intervention in International Law, pp. 93–4; E. Bethke, 'Just War and Humanitarian Intervention', Third Annual Grotius Lecture, ASIL Proceedings, 95th Annual Meeting, 2001, pp. 1–12.

399 S. Alexandrov, *Self-Defense Against the Use of Force in International Law* (Den Haag: Kluwer Law International, 1996), p. 140; Kohen, 'The Use of Force by the United States After the End of the Cold War, and its Impacts on International Law', in Byers and Nolte (eds.), *United States Hegemony and the Foundations of International Law*, p. 199; Kolb, *Ius contra bellum*, p. 231, No. 557; W. Nagan and C. Hammer, 'The New Bush National Security Doctrine and the Rule of Law', Berk.J.I.L., 22 (2004), 398.

400 For example, R. Mullerson, 'Self-Defense in the Contemporary World', in Damrosh Fisler and Scheffer (eds.), *Law and Force in the New International Order*, p. 16; Miller, 'International Intervention – The United States Invasion of Panama', p. 639.

> Adherence by one state to any particular doctrine... The Court cannot contemplate the creation of a new rule opening up a right of intervention by one State against another on the ground that the latter has opted for some particular ideology of political system.[401]

Yet the assumption of a rejection of the Reagan Doctrine in this passage implies a certain interpretation of the doctrine: only if one assumes that the Reagan Doctrine endorses a pro-democratic right to use force or a right to use force against states with a certain ideology[402] can one see the *Nicaragua* judgment as an explicit rejection of the doctrine.

However, neither in connection with its actions in Nicaragua,[403] nor in terms of *opinio iuris* did the United States adhere to the theory that forcible pro-democratic intervention is in accordance with international law.[404] If the Reagan Doctrine is regarded as a commitment to the right to pro-democratic intervention,[405] there is no doubt that it cannot be reconciled with the *Nicaragua* judgment and has to be considered as illegal under international law.[406] But if the Reagan Doctrine is interpreted restrictively and it is merely considered to be a declaration of willingness to provide logistical support, the question arises as to what extent that type of action is lawful or violates the prohibition on the use of force. This relates to the question of the scope of the prohibition of force, also discussed in the *Nicaragua* judgment. The ICJ made reference to a phrase in the Friendly Relations Declaration of the UN General Assembly of 24 October 1970[407] to delimit the scope of the prohibition of the use of force. The declaration states that 'encouraging', 'assisting' and 'participating' in the actions of irregular forces on the territory of another state is unlawful.[408]

The wording of the Friendly Relations Declaration has been criticised in the literature.[409] Some maintain that its vague wording would cause a

401 *Military and Paramilitary Activities in and against Nicaragua* (*Nicaragua* v. *United States of America*), Merits, Judgment, I.C.J. Rep. 1986, p. 133, No. 263.

402 On this see further above, section 3.6.2.3.2.

403 *Military and Paramilitary Activities in and against Nicaragua* (*Nicaragua* v. *United States of America*), Merits, Judgment, I.C.J. Rep. 1986, p. 109, No. 208.

404 Roth, 'Governmental Illegitimacy Revisited: "Pro-Democratic" Armed Intervention in the Post-Bipolar World', p. 485.

405 R. Charvin, 'La doctrine Américaine de la "Souveraineté Limitée" ', R.B.D.I., 20 (1987), 24.

406 See above, section 3.6.2.3.2.

407 UN. Doc. GA Res. 2625 (XXV), 24 October 1970.

408 *Military and Paramilitary Activities in and against Nicaragua* (*Nicaragua* v. *United States of America*), Merits, Judgment, I.C.J. Rep. 1986, p. 101, No. 191.

409 M. Virally, 'Art. 2(4)', in Cot and Pellet (eds.), *La Charte des Nations Unies*, p. 123.

blurring of the limits between armed force and other actions, thus resulting in a loss of clarity of the prohibition on force.[410] Mere supporting actions contravene the prohibition of intervention, but not the prohibition on the use of force.[411] While almost any kind of support can be subsumed within the wording of the Friendly Relations Declaration, the ICJ made another attempt in the *Nicaragua* judgment of a further limitation of the scope of the prohibition of force. The wording chosen by the ICJ, that not every supporting action is contrary to the prohibition of force but that this would require force or the threat of force,[412] merely repeats the question left open in the Friendly Relations Declaration instead of answering it.[413] With regard to US aid to the Contras in Nicaragua, the ICJ classified the arming and training of insurgents as being in breach of the prohibition of force, but not the granting of financial support.[414]

If the restrictive view of the Reagan Doctrine is taken that it is limited to granting logistical support there is room for supporting action in terms of the narrow view of the Reagan Doctrine. It has to be kept in mind that the granting of that type of support can nevertheless be in breach of the prohibition of force. Thus, action supporting insurgents based on the Reagan Doctrine can be considered to be in accordance with international law without drawing upon a justification based on self-defence under Article 51 of the UN Charter.

3.6.3 Conclusion

Unlike prior doctrines such as the Monroe and Truman Doctrines, the term 'Reagan Doctrine' does not refer to principles contained within a single declaration, but to the principle of supporting anti-communist insurgents which is repeated in several declarations.[415] The Reagan Doctrine contains a comprehensive concept of US security policy that is not limited to a specific region. Whether the principles of the Reagan Doctrine comply with international law depends significantly on the view one

410 Randelzhofer, 'Art. 2(4)', in Simma (ed.), *The Charter of the United Nations*, pp. 120–1
411 W. Kewening, 'Gewaltverbot und zulässige Machteinwirkung', in Schaumann (ed.), *Völkerrechtliches Gewaltverbot und Friedenssicherung*, pp. 187–8.
412 *Military and Paramilitary Activities in and against Nicaragua (Nicaragua* v. *United States of America)*, Merits, Judgment, I.C.J. Rep. 1986, p. 119, No. 228.
413 Randelzhofer, 'Art. 2(4)', in Simma (ed.), *The Charter of the United Nations*, pp. 120–1.
414 *Military and Paramilitary Activities in and against Nicaragua (Nicaragua* v. *United States of America)*, Merits, Judgment, I.C.J. Rep. 1986, p. 119, No. 228.
415 Moynihan, *On the Law of Nations*, p. 122.

takes of the content of the doctrine. There is a consensus that the Reagan Doctrine provided for the open support of anti-communist insurgents, but dispute over the scope and shape this supporting action should take under the doctrine.[416]

If the Reagan Doctrine is interpreted restrictively as a repetition of the principles of the Truman Doctrine and limited to the use of force in self-defence, actions based on the principles of the doctrine are unproblematic from the perspective of international law. Furthermore, if the Reagan Doctrine is understood as not intending the use of US troops but merely logistical support, action based on these principles may be justified without recourse to an argument based on self-defence. Only if logistical support for insurgents falls into the scope of the prohibition of force will that type of action require justification as an action in self-defence.[417] When interpreted restrictively, the Reagan Doctrine does not contain a claim that international law on the use of force has to change, but merely makes a statement *de lege lata*.

However, most authors interpret the Reagan Doctrine more widely and assume that it contains a commitment, based on an ideology of pro-democratic intervention, and is hence a statement *de lege ferenda*. Several voices developed a particular model of justification for pro-democratic intervention. This model is based on the object and purpose of the Charter according to Article 1 of the UN Charter, which is considered to make it possible to justify a pro-democratic intervention. However, this is a postulate of legal policy, not a description of the law in force. The idea that intervention can be justified because of the support of another state for another political ideology or a particular political system within a third state was rejected by the ICJ explicitly in the *Nicaragua* judgment. If one assumes that the Reagan Doctrine constitutes a commitment to that principle, the *Nicaragua* judgment can also be read as a rejection of the Reagan Doctrine.[418]

Even though individual members of the Reagan Administration might have supported such an extensive interpretation of the Reagan Doctrine, the United States never adopted this type of model of justification. Likewise, the United States justified interventions considered to be implementations of the Reagan Doctrine on far more traditional justifications, and not on justifications such as a right of pro-democratic intervention or self-defence in order to avoid an ideological rescheduling.[419]

416 See above, section 3.6.2.2. 417 See above, section 3.6.2.3.1.
418 See above, section 3.6.2.3.2. 419 See above, section 3.6.2.3.3.

In this respect it seems unfounded to see the Reagan Doctrine as a demand for a change of law in terms of recognition of a right of pro-democratic intervention. The content attributed by some legal scholars to the Reagan Doctrine goes beyond the undisputed content attributed to the doctrine by the US government.[420] The Reagan Doctrine is at least open to a restrictive interpretation in compliance with international law: the dispute about its legality refers to its wider interpretation.

Even though the Reagan Doctrine triggered a discussion of possible relaxations of the prohibition on the use of force, the discussion of US practice considered as implementation of the Reagan Doctrine offered an opportunity for further precision of the scope of the prohibition of force, such as, for example, the *Nicaragua* judgment.

A number of declarations of political principles by the United States between 1990 and 2000 labelled as 'doctrines' were in part also considered as a challenge to the prohibition on the use of force.

420 Gray, *International Law and the Use of Force*, p. 106; O'Connell, *The Myth of Preemptive Self-Defense*, ASIL Task Force Papers, August 2002, p. 15, fn. 74.

4

The doctrines since 1991

Even though the labelling of the international system after 1991 as unipolar is occasionally contested depending on the varying definitions of unipolarity,[1] the 'dissolution' of the Soviet Union in December 1991 can be seen as the conversion into international law of the transformation of the international system from a state of bipolarity to a state of unipolarity due to the loss of one of the two poles.[2] On the one hand, the influence of the United States on the development of international law – as hegemonic power in this unipolar system – has generated special interest.[3] On the other hand, the increased importance of the 'international community',[4] accompanied by a decreasing significance of power and the ability to use force, raises severe doubts with regard to the ability of a hegemonic power's ability to shape the legal regulation of the use of force.[5]

4.1 The so-called doctrines of the 1990s

The label 'doctrine' has been used for several declarations of principles between 1991 and 2000, making the use of the denomination 'doctrine' during this period of time almost inflationary. Yet it is questionable to what extent these declarations constitute doctrines of US security policy in terms of the definition on which this work is based. They may constitute

1 See in general on unipolarity: K. Mingst, *Essentials of International Relations* (New York: W. W. Norton, 1999), pp. 88–90; G. Evans and J. Newnham, *The Penguin Dictionary of International Relations* (London: Penguin Books, 1998), pp. 550–1.

2 For example, S. Sharma, 'The American Doctrine of "Pre-emptive Self-Defence"', I.J.I.L., 43/2 (2003), 215.

3 M. Byers and G. Nolte (eds.), *United States Hegemony and the Foundations of International Law* (Cambridge University Press, 2003); D. Vagts, 'Hegemonic International Law', A.J.I.L., 95 (2001), 843–8.

4 On this see: A. Paulus, *Die internationale Gemeinschaft im Völkerrecht – eine Untersuchung zur Entwicklung des Völkerrechts im Zeitalter der Globalisierung* (Munich: Beck, 2001), Ph.D. thesis, Munich, 2000.

5 W. Grewe, *Epochs of International Law* (Berlin: Walter de Gruyter, 2000), pp. 703–6.

declarations of another kind, such as, for example, military doctrines as opposed to political doctrines.[6]

4.1.1 The so-called Bush Senior Doctrine

A speech by President George Bush Senior on 5 January 1993 at the US Military Academy at West Point is generally regarded as the statement of a 'doctrine'.[7] For reasons of conceptual clarity the term 'Bush Senior Doctrine' is used here in order to avoid confusion with the Bush Doctrine treated below.

In this speech, President Bush Senior discussed criteria according to which the United States should decide about the use of force in international relations. According to these criteria, the United States should balance the costs and benefits of the use of force with each other; should pursue a clearly defined, achievable goal; and, although it should aim for multilateral support, it should be willing to use force unilaterally.[8]

It seems impossible to derive a precise strategic concept for the use of force in the international relations of the United States from the principles of this speech or the statements about it. A sufficient degree of precision is indispensable for an evaluation under international law. Besides that the term doctrine has been used only in isolated instances in the literature on political science and international law with regard to the principles of this speech.[9] Official US-American sources do not use the label 'Bush Doctrine' for these principles.[10]

6 See above, Chapter 1, section 1.6.

7 M. Kohen, 'The Use of Force by the United States After the End of the Cold War, and its Impacts on International Law', in Byers and Nolte (eds.), *United States Hegemony and the Foundations of International Law*, pp. 199–200; W. Nagan and C. Hammer, 'The New Bush National Security Doctrine and the Rule of Law', Berk.J.I.L., 22 (2004), 399.

8 'Using military force makes sense as a policy, where the stakes warrant, where and when force can be effective, where no other policies are likely to be effective, where its application can be limited in scope and time, and where the potential benefits justify the potential costs and sacrifice. Once we are satisfied that force makes sense, we must act with the maximum possible support. The United States should lead, but we will want to act in concert, where possible involving the United Nations or multinational grouping . . . Sometimes a great power has to act alone.' *Public Papers of the Presidents, George Bush, 1992–1993* (Washington, DC: Government Printing Office, 1993), vol. II, pp. 2230–1.

9 For example, Kohen, 'The Use of Force by the United States After the End of the Cold War, and its Impacts on International Law', in Byers and Nolte (eds.), *United States Hegemony and the Foundations of International Law*, p. 199.

10 Consequently, these principles are not labelled as a 'doctrine' in the public papers on the presidency of George Bush Senior, *Public Papers of the Presidents, George Bush, 1992–1993*, vol. II, pp. A1–A15.

Hence, a declaration of principles concerning the use of force in international relations considered in the opinion of the US Government to be a binding concept and labelled by it as 'doctrine', which would be required in order to consider the Bush Doctrine a doctrine of US security policy according to the definition this work is based on is lacking.[11]

The Powell Doctrine is considered by scholars as standing in the tradition of the Bush Senior Doctrine and as its enhancement.[12]

4.1.2 *The so-called Powell Doctrine*

The so-called Powell Doctrine is a declaration of principles dealing with operative questions of the use of force, in particular with the interaction between different military branches. A speech by the then Chairman of the Joint Chiefs of Staff, Colin Powell, at the National Press Club on 23 September 1993 is regarded as a declaration of the 'Powell Doctrine'.[13] Powell announced in this speech that the following guiding principle must apply with regard to sending US-American troops:

> do not embark on high risk operations that have less than [an] overwhelming chance of success; do not start something without a clear idea of how to end it; do not use force incrementally or gradually.[14]

Powell had already formulated similar principles in an article in *Foreign Affairs* prior to this speech.[15] Besides this, the 'Joint Publication 3–0 Doctrine for Joint Operations' edited by Colin Powell in his capacity as Chairman of the Joint Chiefs of Staff is considered a promulgation of the Powell Doctrine.[16]

With regard to its content, the Powell Doctrine shows considerable similarities to the Weinberger Doctrine of 1984 and repeats its core

11 See above, Chapter 1, section 1.6.

12 C. Stevenson, 'The Evolving Clinton Doctrine on the Use of Force', A.F. & S., 22/4 (1996), 514 *et seq*.

13 Kohen, 'The Use of Force by the United States After the End of the Cold War, and its Impacts on International Law', in Byers and Nolte (eds.), *United States Hegemony and the Foundations of International Law*, p. 200.

14 Printed in S. Dagget and N. Serafino (eds.), *The Use of Force: Key Contemporary Documents* (Washington, DC: Congressional Research Service, 1994), p. 34.

15 C. Powell, 'U.S. Forces: Challenges Ahead', For.Aff., 71/5 (1991–3), 32–45.

16 Stevenson, 'The Evolving Clinton Doctrine on the Use of Force', pp. 514–16.

statements.[17] Sometimes the Powell and Weinberger Doctrine are labelled uniformly as the 'Weinberger–Powell Doctrine'.[18]

The Weinberger Doctrine, which was explained in a speech by Secretary of Defense Caspar Weinberger at the National Press Club on 28 November 1984,[19] is often closely connected with the so-called 'Vietnam Syndrome' and seen as an expression of it.[20]

In this speech Secretary of Defense Caspar Weinberger outlined six criteria, which had to be met before sending US-American troops. In short they read as follows:

1. For the deployment of US-American troops a threat to vital the interests of the United States or its allies had to occur.
2. Troops should be sent only with the declared and accepted goal of winning a military confrontation.
3. The political and military aim of the use of force had to be defined precisely in advance.
4. A sufficient strength of forces in order to achieve these goals had to be available.
5. Support for the deployment of troops by the American people and Congress had to be assured.
6. The deployment of troops should be used only as a last resort in order to solve a conflict.[21]

All these criteria refer mainly to the modalities or scope, the 'how', of the use of force by the United States, but do not contain a statement concerning the situations in which the United States should use force. Hence, the question of whether force should be used or how use of force should be justified under international law is not mentioned. The intention behind these 'doctrines' is often described as an anxiety on the

17 J. Kurth, 'Boss of all Bosses', in M. Leffler and J. Legro (eds.), *To Lead the World – American Strategy after the Bush Doctrine* (Oxford University Press, 2008), p. 129.

18 K. Campbell, 'Once Burned, Twice Cautious: Explaining the Weinberger–Powell Doctrine', A.F. & S., 24/3 (1998), 357–75; Stevenson, 'The Evolving Clinton Doctrine on the Use of Force', p. 518; J. Dormont, 'The Powell Factor: Analyzing the Role of the Powell Doctrine in U.S. Foreign Policy', *Gaines Junction*, Spring 2005, pp. 22–40.

19 C. Weinberger, 'The Uses of Military Power', *Defense*, January 1985, pp. 2–11.

20 Evans and Newnham, *The Penguin Dictionary of International Relations*, pp. 563–4, 570.

21 On this see further: Campbell, 'Once Burned, Twice Cautious: Explaining the Weinberger–Powell Doctrine', pp. 357–75.

part of military leaders that political decision-makers would resort too easily to military force.[22]

The Weinberger Doctrine and the Weinberger–Powell Doctrine, respectively, hence, clearly fall into the category of 'military doctrine' or as a declaration to be categorised as 'operational',[23] aiming primarily at the national American audience. Thus, the Powell Doctrine or the Weinberger–Powell Doctrine are political declarations different from a doctrine of US security policy in terms of the definition on which this work is based. Rather, they can be attributed the term 'military doctrine'.

The Powell Doctrine in turn is considered to be a predecessor to the Clinton Doctrine.[24]

4.1.3 The so-called Clinton Doctrine

The label 'Clinton Doctrine' is used in relation to two different principles for the use of force (or for the interaction of these two principles): on the one hand, it is considered as a commitment to the concept of humanitarian intervention;[25] and, on the other hand, it is considered as a limitation on the use of force by the United States according to criteria similar to those of the Powell Doctrine.[26]

A multitude of speeches and declarations are regarded by scholars as statements of the Clinton Doctrine.[27] A section in the National Security Strategy 1994, 'A Strategy of Engagement and Enlargement' (NSS 1994),[28]

22 D. Kennedy, 'Two Concepts of Sovereignty', in Leffler and Legro (eds.), *To Lead the World*, pp. 173–4

23 On the distinction between theses different levels of planning see above, Chapter 1, pp. 6–7.

24 Kohen, 'The Use of Force by the United States After the End of the Cold War, and its Impacts on International Law', in Byers and Nolte (eds.), *United States Hegemony and the Foundations of International Law*, p. 200.

25 K. Regensburg, 'Refugee Law Reconsidered: Reconciling Humanitarian Objectives with the Protectionist Agendas of Western Europe and the United States', Corn.I.L.J., 29 (1996), 243–5; D. Brinkley, 'Democratic Enlargement: The Clinton Doctrine', For.Pol., 106 (1997), 111–27; R. P. Watson, C. Gleek and M. Grillo (eds.), *Presidential Doctrines: National Security from Woodrow Wilson to George W. Bush* (New York: Nova Science Publishers, 2003), pp. 123–4.

26 Stevenson, 'The Evolving Clinton Doctrine on the Use of Force', pp. 519–20.

27 C. Maynes, 'A Workable Clinton Doctrine', For.Pol., 93 (1993), 3–20.

28 Kohen, 'The Use of Force by the United States After the End of the Cold War, and its Impacts on International Law', in Byers and Nolte (eds.), *United States Hegemony and the Foundations of International Law*, p. 200; Stevenson, 'The Evolving Clinton Doctrine

in which the principles of the Clinton Administration on foreign policy are outlined comprehensively, is seen as the most comprehensive statement of the Clinton Doctrine.[29]

In the section entitled 'Deciding When and How to Employ US Force', when US troops should be deployed is explained. Three different situations are described in which, depending on the kind of US interests being threatened ('vital interests', 'important national interests', 'humanitarian interests'), different criteria shall be decisive for the use of force. However, preceding these specifications it is stated that these may not constitute a comprehensive delimitation as that would be 'unwise'.[30]

It has been doubted repeatedly, in particular in the international relations literature, if the security policy has shown sufficient conceptual cohesion to speak of a doctrine.[31] The Clinton Doctrine has been criticised in particular in connection with the intervention in Kosovo in 1999. The conceptual coherence of such a Clinton Doctrine has also been seriously doubted by scholars.[32] Consequently, instead of mentioning a Clinton Doctrine, they mention 'something called "Clinton doctrine"'[33] or a 'putative Clinton doctrine'.[34] However, this aspect concerns the implementation of a doctrine and questions in the field of what Herbert Kraus called 'doability' ('*Tunlichkeit*') of doctrines and is not part of an evaluation of doctrines under international law.[35]

Based on these non-judicial statements, it becomes clear that doubts arise regarding the use of the term 'Clinton Doctrine' even when used merely as a label for a rationalisation of US security policy in hindsight. The Clinton Doctrine deals only with the question 'if' force should be

on the Use of Force', pp. 525 *et seq.*; Evans and Newnham, *The Penguin Dictionary of International Relations*, pp. 68–70.

29 W. Clinton, *National Security Strategy of the United States: 1994–1995* (Washington, DC: Brassey's, 1995).

30 NSS 1994, pp. 39 *et seq.*

31 M. Mandelbaum, 'Foreign Policy as Social Work', For.Aff., 75 (1996), 16–32; M. Knapp, 'Die Macht der USA und die Moral der Staatengemeinschaft: Zur UN-Politik der Clinton Administration', in M. Berg *et al.* (eds.), *Macht und Moral – Beiträge zur Ideologie und Praxis amerikanischer Außenpolitik im 20. Jahrhundert*, FS-Krakau (Münster: Lit Verlag, 1999), pp. 295–318; Newsweek, 'The Clinton Doctrine', 28 April 1994, p. 3.

32 M. Mandelbaum, 'A Perfect Failure – NATO's War Against Yugoslavia', For.Aff., 78 (1998), 2–8, in particular 5–6.

33 J. Elshtain, 'Just War and Humanitarian Intervention', ASIL Proceedings, 95th Annual Meeting, 2001, pp. 9–10.

34 M. Dunne, 'American Judicial Internationalism in the Twentieth Century', ASIL Proceedings, 90th Annual Meeting, 1996, p. 154.

35 See above, Chapter 1, section 1.6.

used, provided it is considered a declaration of belief in humanitarian intervention. Yet the question arises if this constitutes a principle which has been considered a doctrine by US-American officials.

Just as it is the case for the Bush Senior Doctrine, a labelling of such a concept by official US-American sources as 'doctrine' is lacking in case of the Clinton Doctrine. President Clinton's National Security Advisor, Sandy Berger, rejected the labelling of specific principles as the 'Clinton Doctrine'.[36] When asked directly, President Clinton did not confirm the emergence of such a Clinton Doctrine.[37]

Hence, the labelling of single political tenets or principles for the use of force as the 'Clinton Doctrine' did not enter the language of the US Government. Thus, the Clinton Doctrine, just like the Johnson, Carter and Bush Senior doctrines, does not constitute a doctrine of US security policy in terms of the definition on which this work is based.

What the 'doctrines' of the 1990s have in common is abstaining from naming situations and conditions under which force shall be used (unless the Clinton Doctrine is perceived as a commitment to a humanitarian intervention), but being guided by the desire to outline situations in which force shall *not* be used. At best it can be assumed the Clinton Doctrine presupposes tacitly a comprehensive right of humanitarian intervention, but does not state this claim. Instead of being in favour of certain courses of action, certain courses of action are ruled out. The formulation of purely excluding criteria for the use of force, make statements about the legal admissibility of cases of foreseen use of force according to these doctrines impossible.

Thus, Kohen's evaluation seems to be apt with regard to these 'doctrines' of the 1990s: 'little if any insight can be derived from these doctrines which would shed light on the formulation or interpretation of the rules of international law relative to the use of force'.[38]

In contrast to these 1990s' 'doctrines', the Bush Doctrine, treated below, is considered a commitment to the use of force under certain legal

36 'I instinctively resist doctrine, but I think it is a principle that we have established in Kosovo: there are some activities that governments engage in, such as genocide or ethnic cleansing that we cannot ignore . . .' Quoted after: B. Brown 'Special Project: Humanitarian Intervention and Kosovo: Humanitarian Intervention at a Crossroads', W. & M.L.R., 41 (2000), 1692, fn. 27.

37 *Public Papers of the Presidents, William J. Clinton, 1999* (Washington, DC: Government Printing Office, 2000), vol. I, pp. 969–70.

38 Kohen, 'The Use of Force by the United States After the End of the Cold War, and its Impacts on International Law', in Byers and Nolte (eds.), *United States Hegemony and the Foundations of International Law*, p. 201.

prerequisites. Accordingly, the Bush Doctrine received far more attention from scholars of international law.

4.2 The Bush Doctrine

Even though the second Bush administration was eager to emphasise the differences between its foreign policy and that of the Clinton Administration,[39] it is mostly assumed that this desire did not result in immediate fundamental changes of US foreign policy.[40] The events of 11 September 11 2001 gave the prior debate about concepts for US security policy a theoretical ring to it.[41]

On 11 September 2001, nineteen persons of non-US-American nationality, who were associated with the militant Islamist terror network *Al Quaida*, hijacked four commercial aircraft of American Airlines and United Airlines. They crashed them into the Pentagon building in Washington and the twin towers of the World Trade Center in New York – both 107-storey towers collapsed as a result of that crash. One aircraft crashed into an open field in Pennsylvania. In total, more than 3,000 people of different nationalities, mainly US citizens, lost their lives.[42]

A little more than one year later, on 17 September 2002, the White House published the National Security Strategy (NSS) 2002.[43] This was a report by the US President to Congress according to 50 United States Code § 404a (2000), which the president is obligated to submit since the Goldwater–Nichols Act of 1986.[44] The principles for the use of force

39 C. Rice, 'Promoting the National Interest', For.Aff., 79 (2000), 45–62.

40 I. Wallerstein, 'The Eagle has Crash Landed', For.Pol., 81 (July/August 2002), 60–8; R. Jervis, 'Understanding the Bush Doctrine', P.S.Q., 118/3 (2003), 365–88. A return to the principles of the Reagan Administration within the Bush Doctrine is assumed by S. Rogov, 'The Bush Doctrine', Rus.P.L., 46 (2002), 47–61

41 R. Scholz, 'Der 11. September 2001: Wendepunkt in der nationalen wie internationalen Sicherheitspolitik', in E. Conze, U. Schlie and H. Seubert (eds.), *Geschichte zwischen Wissenschaft und Politik*, FS-Stürmer (Baden-Baden: Nomos, 2003), pp. 469–81. For a summary of the different conceptions of US-American security policy in discussion see: B. Posen and A. Ross, 'Competing Visions for U.S. Grand Strategy', Int.Sec., 21/3 (1996/7), 5–53.

42 Detailed description of the events of 11 September at: S. Murphy (ed.), 'Contemporary Practice of the United States Relating to International Law', A.J.I.L. 96 (2002), 237–55.

43 The National Security Strategy of the United States of America (NSS), September 2002, p. 6, available at: www.whitehouse.gov/nsc/nss.pdf; partially printed in Murphy (ed.), 'Contemporary Practice of the United States Relating to International Law', pp. 203–4; printed in its entirety in L. Korb, *A New National Security Strategy* (New York: Council on Foreign Relations, 2003), pp. 99–139.

44 B. Lombardi, 'The "Bush Doctrine" and Anticipatory Self-defence', Int.Spectator, 37 (2002), 92–3.

laid down in the NSS are generally referred to as the 'Bush Doctrine'.[45] Normally, only the term 'Bush Doctrine' is used.[46]

This designation is also used in official US-American statements.[47] Based on several such official statements it is assumed by some that the Bush Doctrine as such constitutes US-American *opinio iuris*.[48] This brings up the question of the exact content of the Bush Doctrine.

4.2.1 The Bush Doctrine according to the NSS of 17 September 2002

The NSS 2002, just as the NSS 1994, contains a comprehensive concept with regard to a multitude of aspects of US foreign and security policy. In doing so, most basic ideas which could already be found in the NSS 1994 are sustained.[49] The 'promotion of democratic values', global economic growth, free markets and free trade are explicitly mentioned as means of ensuring American and international security.[50]

The central statement with regard to the use of force reads as follows:

> We will disrupt and destroy terrorist organizations by: . . . defending the United States, the American people and our interests at home and abroad by identifying and destroying the threat before it reaches our borders . . . we will not hesitate to act alone, if necessary, to exercise our right of self-defense by acting pre-emptively against such terrorists, to prevent them from doing harm against our people and our country.[51]

45 For example, by R. Falk, 'The New Bush Doctrine: Fighting Terrorism Requires New Thinking, but not a U.S. Empire', *The Nation*, 15 July 2002; W. Lafeber, 'The Bush Doctrine', Dipl.Hist., 26 (2002), 543–58; F. Heisbourg, 'A Work in Progress: The Bush Doctrine and Its Consequences', Wash.Q., 26/2 (2003), 75–88; D. Murswiek, 'Die amerikanische Präventivkriegsstrategie und das Völkerrecht', N.J.W. (2003), 1018; H. Neuhold, 'Law and Force in International Relations – European and American Positions', ZaöRV/H.J.I.L., 64 (2004), 263–79; J. Noyes, 'American Hegemony, U.S. Political Leaders, and General International Law', Conn.J.I.L., 19 (2004), 293–313.

46 O. Dörr, 'Staats- und völkerrechtliche Aspekte des Irak-Krieges 2003', J.I.L.P.A.C./Hu.V-I, 16 (2003). 184.

47 For example, by President Bush himself (United States Embassy to India, *Bush Says Proliferation Controls Must Be Strengthened*, 25 April 2003, http://usembassy.state.gov/posts/in1/wwwhpr0428b.html) and by Secretary of State Colin Powell (United States Embassy to Australia, *Powell Hails Thailand's Support in War on Terror*, 29 July 2002, http://usembassy-australia.state.gov/hyper/2002/0729/epf.104htm).

48 J. Cohan, 'The Bush Doctrine and the Emerging Norm of Anticipatory Self-Defense in Customary International Law', PaceI.L.R., 15 (2003), 295.

49 A. Roberts, 'Law and the Use of Force After Iraq', Survival, 46 (2003), 2, 46; R. Litwak, 'The New Calculus of Pre-emption', Survival, 44 (2002/03), 4, 53–80.

50 NSS 2002, pp. 1, 3–4.

51 NSS 2002, p. 6.

In connection with a general definition of targets for US foreign policy, the concept of preventive action in order to ensure the United States' own security surfaced prior to the NSS 2002 and is repeated in several passages:

> The U.S. national security strategy will be based on a distinctly American internationalism that reflects the union of our values and our national interests . . . Our goals . . . are clear: political and economic freedom, peaceful relations with other states, and respect for human dignity . . . To achieve these goals the United States will: . . . prevent our enemies from threatening us, our allies, and our friends, with weapons of mass destruction . . .[52]

With a hint of the special danger posed by weapons of mass destruction in the hands of terrorists, the necessity of preventive action is emphasised:

> As was demonstrated by the losses on September 11, 2001, mass civilian casualties is the specific objective of terrorists and these losses would be exponentially more severe if terrorists acquired and used weapons of mass destruction.
>
> The United States has long maintained the option of pre-emptive actions to counter a sufficient threat to our national security. The greater the threat, the greater is the risk of inaction – and the more compelling the case for taking anticipatory action to defend ourselves, even if uncertainty remains as to the time and place of the enemy's attack. To forestall or prevent such hostile acts by our adversaries, the United States will, if necessary, act pre-emptively . . .[53]

President Bush had already formulated the principle of preventive self-defence as a principle of US security policy in a speech at the US Military Academy in West Point on 1 June 2002.[54] A letter by the US ambassador to the United Nations, John Negroponte, to the UN Security Council of 7 October 2001 had touched upon a reservation for a further use of force.[55]

52 NSS 2002, p. 1. 53 NSS 2002, p. 15.

54 'For much of the last century America's defense relied on the cold war doctrines of deterrence and containment. In some cases, those strategies still apply, but new threats also require new thinking. Deterrence – the promise of massive retaliation against nations – means nothing against shadowy terrorist networks with no nation or citizen to defend. Containment is not possible when unbalanced dictators with weapons of mass destruction can deliver those weapons on missiles or secretly provide them to terrorist allies . . . If we wait for threats to fully materialize, we will have waited too long . . . We must take the battle to the enemy, disrupt his plans, and confront the worst threats before they emerge . . .' George W. Bush, Commencement Address at the United States Military Academy West Point, 1 June 2002, available at: www.whitehouse.gov/news/releases/2002/06/20020601–3.html.

55 'We may find that our self-defense requires further actions with respect to other organizations and other states', UN-Doc. S/2001/946; www.un.int/usa/s-2001–946.htm.

Furthermore, the label 'Bush Doctrine' is already used with regard to President Bush's State of the Union Address in January 2002.[56]

Within the NSS 2002 it is stated that an action, guided by these principles, must be admissible according to international law in force, or at least ought to be admissible.[57] The NSS 2002 has generated far more interest among the general public and among scholars of public international law than prior strategy papers. In these discussions the principles for the use of force have been defined very differently. That results in different consequences for the evaluation of actions based on this doctrine under international law.

4.2.1.1 Criteria of the Bush Doctrine for the use of force

It is generally accepted that the Bush Doctrine contains a declaration of belief in a concept of preventive self-defence.[58] The NSS 2002 mentions the preventive exercise of the right of self-defence for which the term 'pre-emptive' is used ('to exercise our right of self-defence by acting pre-emptively . . .').[59]

In principle, a general distinction can be made between anticipated self-defence ('anticipatory self-defence') and preventive or pre-emptive self-defence ('pre-emptive self-defence'):[60] anticipated self-defence refers to the use of force in cases in which no armed attack has taken place, but

56 T. Farer, 'Beyond the UN Charter Frame: Unilateralism or Codominium', A.J.I.L., 96 (2002), 359–64; T. Farer, 'The Bush Doctrine and the UN Charter Frame', Int.Spectator, 37 (2002), 3, 91–100.

57 'For centuries, international law recognized that nations need not suffer an attack before they can lawfully take action to defend themselves against forces that present an imminent danger of attack. Legal scholars and international jurists often conditioned the legitimacy of pre-emption on the existence of an imminent threat – most often a visible mobilization of armies, navies, and air forces preparing to attack. We must adapt the concept of imminent threat to the capabilities and objectives of today's adversaries . . .' NSS, p. 15. On this see further below, section 4.2.1.2.

58 I. Brownlie, *Principles of Public International Law*, 7th edn. (Oxford University Press, 2008), p. 734; M. O'Connell, *The Myth of Preemptive Self-Defense*, ASIL Task Force Papers, August 2002, Washington, 2002, p. 2: 'This strategy is based on a conception of preemptive self-defense'; C. Schaller, 'Massenvernichtungswaffen und Präventivkrieg', ZaöRV/H.J.I.L., 62 (2002), 640–1; E. Benvenisti, 'The US and the Use of Force: Double Edged Hegemony and the Management of Global Emergencies', E.J.I.L., 15 (2004), 684.

59 NSS 2002, p. 6.

60 Instead of the term 'pre-emption' partially the term 'preventive self-defense' or 'preventive war' is used. Y. Dinstein, *War, Aggression and Self-Defence*, 4th edn. (Cambridge University Press, 2004), p. 182; I. Brownlie, *International Law and the Use of Force by States* (Oxford: Clarendon Press, 1963), p. 275.

in which an armed attack is imminent.[61] In contrast to this, preventive self-defence refers to the use of force in order to eliminate an already existing possibility of an attack by another state, even if there is no reason to assume that an armed attack is imminent.[62]

The term 'pre-emptive self-defence', as used in the Bush Doctrine, is used differently and sometimes merely as a description of the use of force in anticipated self-defence in the case of an imminent armed attack. This term is contrasted with 'preventive self-defence', which describes what has been labelled above as preventive self defence.[63]

Once more large parts of the wording of the NSS 2002 leave room for several interpretations as to which criteria for the use of force shall be determined within the doctrine.[64] In principle, there is agreement that the Bush Doctrine goes beyond the use of force in cases of anticipated self-defence described above as the use of force when an armed attack is imminent.[65] Furthermore, the United States declared that it would use force unilaterally in cases where the possibility of a terrorist attack with weapons of mass destruction should arise, without an armed attack being considered as imminent.[66]

In a logical inversion of an argument it can be concluded from the ascertainment within the NSS 2002, that the United States would not use force in *all* cases to avoid an emerging threat.[67] Hence, the NSS would

61 A. Arend and R. Beck, *International Law and the Use of Force – Beyond the UN Charter Paradigm* (London: Longman, 1993), pp. 72–3.

62 M. O'Connell, *The Myth of Preemptive Self-Defense*, p. 2.

63 That is, by Senator Edward Kennedy, Cong. Reg., 7 October 2002, vol. 148, p. 10002. Also in favour of the label 'preventive self-defense': M. Sapiro, 'Iraq: The Shifting Sands of Preemptive Self-Defense', A.J.I.L., 97 (2003), 599–607. Imprecise on terms is Cohan who writes of a 'Bush Doctrine of anticipatory self-defense, or preventive war . . .' J. Cohan, 'The Bush Doctrine and the Emerging Norm of Anticipatory Self-Defense in Customary International Law', PaceI.L.R., 15 (2003), 283–356.

64 J. Stromseth, 'Law and Force after Iraq: A Transitional Moment', A.J.I.L., 97 (2003), 635–6.

65 G. Nolte, 'Die USA und das Völkerrecht', Friedens-Warte/J.I.P.O., 78 (2003), 131; C. Tomuschat, 'Völkerrecht ist kein Zweiklassenrecht', *Vereinte Nationen*, 2/2003, p. 44; M. Shaw, *International Law*, 5th edn. (Cambridge University Press, 2003), p. 1030; M. Byers, *Expert Analysis, Iraq and the 'Bush-Doctrine' of Pre-emptive Self-Defence*, available at: www.crimesofwar.org/print/expert/bush-Byers-print.html.

66 The adoption of a strategic concept like this by the United States had already been suggested several years prior to the declaration of the Bush Doctrine. C. Krauthammer, 'The Unipolar Moment', For.Aff., 70 (1990/1), 1, 31–2; A. Carter and W. Perry, *Preventive Defense: A New Security Strategy for America* (Washington, DC: The Brookings Institution Press, 1999).

67 'The United States will not use force in all cases to preempt emerging threats, nor should nations use preemption as a pretext for aggression. Yet in an age where enemies of

include the use of force in *some* cases in order to avoid even the emergence of a threat.[68] The declaration of this doctrine has sparked off controversy among scholars of international law, in particular with regard to the arrangement of the *ius ad bellum*.

4.2.1.2 Statements on the legality of the use of force in the context of the Bush Doctrine

The NSS 2002 itself states what the United States considers as the law in force: according to this definition it shall be a recognised standard that a state is not only entitled to use force in cases where an armed attack has already taken place, but even prior to that. Furthermore, this will depend on the presence of an imminent threat:

> Legal scholars and international jurists often conditioned the legitimacy of pre-emption on the existence of an imminent threat – most often a visible mobilization of armies, navies, and air forces preparing to attack . . .[69]

Yet because no statement is made wherefrom such a right to use force without a prior armed attack shall be derived from, these statements offer only apparent clarity over which courses of action ought to be justified. At the same time it is emphasised in the subsequent sentence that the criteria of an imminent danger has to be adapted to the current circumstances, particularly taking into consideration so-called 'rogue states':[70]

> We must adapt the concept of imminent threat to the capabilities and objectives of today's adversaries. Rogue states and terrorists do not seek to attack us using conventional means.[71]

However, it is uncertain if this formulation constitutes a description of the given law *de lege lata* or a demand for a change of law *de lege ferenda*,[72] in support of which an extensive and restrictive interpretation of the NSS 2002 is advocated.

civilization openly and actively seek the world's most destructive technologies, the United States cannot remain idle while dangers gather.' NSS 2002, p. 15.

68 E. Benvenisti, 'The US and the Use of Force: Double Edged Hegemony and the Management of Global Emergencies', E.J.I.L., 15 (2004), 677–700.

69 NSS 2002, p.15.

70 On this see further: P. Minnerop, 'Classification of States and Creation of Status within the International Community', M.P.Y.U.N.L., 7 (2003), 79–182, in particular pp. 158–71; H. Neuhold, 'Law and Force in International Relations – European and American Positions', ZaöRV/H.J.I.L., 64 (2004), 265–6.

71 NSS 2002, p. 15.

72 M. Bothe, 'Terrorism and the Legality of Pre-emptive Force', E.J.I.L., 14 (2003), 232.

In part this is considered by scholars as a hint as to the context of this passage as a claim for the extension of the right of anticipated self-defence in the sense of a right of preventive self-defence.[73] According to this opinion, the NSS 2002 contains a claim to use force in cases which have so far not been covered by the right of anticipated self-defence. Hence, in cases in which no armed attack is imminent, the use of force shall not be admissible under the current law in force.[74]

In contrast to this wide interpretation of the NSS 2002, a memorandum by the Legal Advisor of the Department of State, William H. Taft IV, to the ASIL-CFR Roundtable on 18 November 2002 can be considered as an example of the restricted interpretation of the Bush Doctrine. However, as this is an internal document it is questionable if it can be considered as government opinion or an individual opinion,[75] and it cannot be considered as *opinio iuris*.[76]

According to this interpretation, the NSS 2002 merely foresees the use of force in cases already covered by the law in force. Furthermore, the NSS shall not contain a change of the legal opinion of the United States,[77] because the United States had so far reserved the right to use preventive force and had argued accordingly in connection with the British destruction of the *Caroline* in 1837 and the Israeli bombing of the Iraqi reactor Osirak in 1981. However, in case of the preventive use of force a 'clear and absolute necessity' ought to be shown and for this criterion of 'necessity' in turn sub-criteria are put forward.[78]

The question of to which degree the NSS 2002 constitutes merely a statement of the law in force or goes beyond that, and if a change of law should be brought forward through the Bush Doctrine, does not only depend upon the content attributed to the NSS 2002, but cannot be answered without discussing the question of what is considered as the law in force.

4.2.2 Evaluation of the Bush Doctrine under international law

Possible consequences of the use of force after 11 September 2001 for the *ius ad bellum* have been discussed thoroughly among international

73 R. Gardner, 'Neither Bush nor the "Jurisprudes"', A.J.I.L., 97 (2003), 586–8.

74 Bothe, 'Terrorism and the Legality of Pre-emptive Force', pp. 236–9.

75 Sapiro, 'Iraq: The Shifting Sands of Preemptive Self-Defense', p. 602.

76 W. Taft, *The Legal Basis of Preemption*, Memorandum to ASIL-CFR Roundtable, 18 November 2002, available at: www.cfr.org/pub5250/william_h_taft_iv/the_legal_basis_for_preemption.php.

77 On this see further below, section 4.2.2.3.

78 Taft, *The Legal Basis of Preemption.*

lawyers prior to the publication of the Bush Doctrine.[79] In the course of this debate, an extension of the understanding of the right of self-defence as reaction to prior terrorist use of force has been noticed in particular.[80] According to this opinion, the right of self-defence today also covers undisputedly the use of military force against states that intentionally support or host terrorist groups which have already committed acts of terror against the state exercising self-defence.[81]

Until 2001 it was disputed whether it was apt to classify supporting actions for terrorists as an armed attack or an action giving rise to the right of self-defence.[82] While the possibility of an armed, cross-border resistance against such actions was ruled out to some extent,[83] partially these types of supporting actions were, based on different reasons, considered as an armed attack entitling to the exercise of self-defence.[84]

As a result of 11 September 2001, a harmonisation of the interpretation of the term 'armed attack' has been noted by scholars. According to that opinion the right of self-defence today also covers armed action against states which actively support or harbour terrorists, if these have already committed acts of terror against the state exercising self-defence.[85] This

79 F. Mégret, '"War"? Legal Semantics and the Move to Violence', E.J.I.L., 13 (2002), 361–99; A. Cassese, 'Terrorism is also Disrupting Some Crucial Categories of International Law', E.J.I.L., 12 (2001), 993–1001; C. Tomuschat, 'Der 11. September und seine rechtlichen Konsequenzen', Eu.GRZ, (2001), 535–45; C. Stahn, 'International Law at a Crossroads? The Impact of September 11', ZaöRV/H.J.I.L., 62 (2002), 183–255; J. Frowein, 'Der Terrorismus als Herausforderung für das Völkerrecht', ZaöRV/H.J.I.L., 62 (2002), 879–905; M. Krajewski, 'Selbstverteidigung gegen bewaffnete Angriffe nicht-staatlicher Organisationen – Der 11. September und seine Folgen', AVR, 40 (2002), 183–214.

80 S. Ratner, '*Jus ad Bellum* and *Jus in Bello* After September 11', A.J.I.L., 96 (2002), 905–21; T. Franck, 'Terrorism and the Right of Self-Defense', A.J.I.L., 95 (2001), 839–43; Kohen, 'The Use of Force by the United States After the End of the Cold War, and its Impacts on International Law', in Byers and Nolte (eds.), *United States Hegemony and the Foundations of International Law*, pp. 204–31.

81 M. Byers, 'Terrorism, the Use of Force and International Law after 11 September', I.C.L.Q., 51 (2002), 409–10; F. Kirgis, 'Israel's Intensified Military Campaign Against Terrorism', ASIL Insights, December 2001, available at: www.asil.org/insights/insigh78.htm

82 On this controversy see: C. Kreß, *Gewaltverbot und Selbstverteidigung nach der Satzung der Vereinten Nationen bei staatlicher Verwicklung in Gewaltakte Privater* (Berlin: Duncker und Humblot, 1995), pp. 143–68.

83 F. Boyle, 'Remarks', ASIL Proceedings, 81st Annual Meeting, 1987, pp. 288–97.

84 Brownlie, *International Law and the Use of Force by States*, p. 373; P. Zanardi, *Indirect Military Aggression*, in Cassese (ed.), *The Current Legal Regulation of the Use of Force*, p. 113; Dinstein, *War, Aggression and Self-Defence*, pp. 201–4.

85 Occasionally the label 'Bush Doctrine' is used for the declaration by President Bush on 11 September 2001: 'We will make no distinction between terrorists who committed these

standardisation of *opinio iuris* is considered to be expressed especially clearly in the conclusion of an armed attack according to Article 5 of the NATO Treaty and Article 3(1) of the Rio Pact.[86]

The subsequent practice of the use of force by the United States is not the subject of this work, but in general the legality of the use of force based on the principles of the doctrine.[87] Thus, cases of the use of force by the United States since 11 September 2001 will be looked at only from the point of view of to what degree they possibly cause a change of the legality of the use of force.[88]

The continued validity of the general prohibition on the use of force in Article 2(4) of the UN Charter (and, consequently, the existence of a need for justification for the use of force according to the principles of the Bush Doctrine) has been questioned because of the US-American use of force since 1999.

4.2.2.1 Continued validity of the prohibition of force beyond 11 September 2001

Picking up an idea of Thomas Franck, who had in 1970 already declared the general prohibition on the use of force in Article 2(4) of the UN Charter 'dead',[89] Michael Glennon claimed in 2002 that this prohibition had lost its validity due to its continued disregard.[90]

Glennon came to this conclusion by starting with the assumed discrepancy between the limits in which Article 51 of the UN Charter permits the use of force and the cases in which states actually used force. In doing

acts and those who harbored them.'('The Bush Doctrine is the assertation that nations harboring terrorists are as guilty as terrorists themselves . . .'). B. Langille, 'It's "Instant Custom": How the Bush Doctrine Became Law After the Terrorist Attacks of September 11, 2001', B.C.I.C.L.R., 26 (2003), 145–56. However, this use of the term neither matches with the connotation of the term used by US officials, nor by other scholars of international law (see above, section 4.2).

86 B. Grady, 'Article 5 of the North Atlantic Treaty: Past, Present, and Uncertain Future', G.J.I.C.L., 31 (2002), 185 *et seq.*; F. Kirgis, *Terrorist Attacks on the World Trade Center and the Pentagon*, ASIL Insights, September 2001, available at: www.asil.org/insights/insigh77.htm.

87 See above, Chapter 1, section 1.6.

88 See further on this below, section 4.2.2.2.1.3.

89 T. Franck, 'Who killed Article 2(4)?', A.J.I.L., 64 (1970), 809–37; also in 1986, J. Combacau, 'The Exception of Self-Defence in the U.N. Practice', in Cassese (ed.), *The Current Legal Regulation of the Use of Force*, p. 32; differing, however, see: Franck, 'Terrorism and the Right of Self-Defense', pp. 839–43.

90 M. Glennon, 'The Fog of Law: Self-Defense, Inherence, and Incoherence in Article 51 of the United Nations Charter', H.J.L.P.P., 25 (2002), 539–41; similarly: A. Arend, 'International Law and the Preemptive Use of Military Force', Wash.Q,. 26 (2003), 2, 89–103.

this he argued with close reference to the use of force by the United States against the Afghan Taliban government. A result-oriented interpretation of international law, aiming at an interpretation in which politically legitimate cases of use of force may not appear to be against the law in force will have blurred the distinction between *lex lata* and *lex ferenda* beyond recognition.[91] This reproach of result-oriented interpretation can also be made towards Glennon (*tu quoque*), who chooses the assumption that the law in force states hopelessly unrealistic assumptions on how states should behave[92] as starting point of his rationale.

Just like Franck's prior reasoning,[93] Glennon's opinion has been contradicted by other academics of international law and has been proven wrong.[94] A course of action which may seem *prima facie* as a violation of law and is justified by a state as an exception to an existing rule, rather confirms the rule than questions it, no matter if the justification brought forward is apt or not.[95] As long as a violation of law is also considered as such and not as a step towards the creation of customary law, a rule persists in spite of inconsistent state practice.[96]

In spite of suggestions put forward by academics, to bring about change with regard to the legality of the use of force[97] no change of rules aimed at the abandonment of the general prohibition on the use of force has been pursued by states, in particular not by the United States. Instead, cases in which their conformity with the UN Charter seems to be particularly questionable, such as the intervention in Kosovo in 1999 and the intervention in Iraq 2003, have been justified by the United States as being covered by existing exceptions to the prohibition of force.[98]

91 Glennon, 'The Fog of Law: Self-Defense, Inherence, and Incoherence in Article 51 of the United Nations Charter', p. 549.

92 'The received interpretation of Article 51 consists in hopelessly unrealistic prescriptions as how states should behave.' Glennon, 'The Fog of Law: Self-Defense, Inherence, and Incoherence in Article 51 of the United Nations Charter', p. 541; M. Glennon, 'The Emerging Use-of-Force Paradigm', J.C.S.L., 11 (2006), 310–11.

93 L. Henkin, 'The Reports of the Death of Article 2(4) Are Greatly Exaggerated', A.J.I.L., 65 (1971), 544–8.

94 O'Connell, *The Myth of Preemptive Self-Defense*, pp. 14–15; O. Dörr, 'Staats-und Völkerrechtliche Aspekte des Irak-Krieges 2003', J.I.L.P.A.C./Hu.V-I, 16 (2003), 182.

95 *Military and Paramilitary Activities in und against Nicaragua* (*Nicaragua* v. *United States of America*), Merits, Judgment, I.C.J. Rep. 1986, p. 98, para. 198.

96 O'Connell, *The Myth of Preemptive Self-Defense*, p. 15.

97 M. Glennon, 'Why the Security Council Failed', For.Aff,. 82 (2003), 3, 30–5.

98 S. D. Murphy, 'Contemporary Practice of the United States Relating to International Law', A.J.I.L., 93 (1999), 628–35; A.J.I.L., 97 (2003), 419–32; W. Taft and T. Buchwald, 'Preemption, Iraq and International Law', A.J.I.L., 97 (2003), 557–63.

Consequently, the prohibition on the use of force in Article 2(4) of the UN Charter continues to exist as universal customary international law and as *ius cogens*.[99]

A need for the justification of the use of force results from that. With regard to the principles of the Bush Doctrine for the use of force, it is of particular interest that according to it a use of force solely by the United States is foreseen ('we will not hesitate to act alone, if necessary... by acting pre-emptively against such terrorists . . .').[100] The UN Charter recognises only one case in which the use of force without authorisation by the Security Council is justified: the exercise of the right of self-defence mentioned in Article 51.

4.2.2.2 The Bush Doctrine and the right of self-defence

By using the term 'imminent threat' the NSS 2002 takes up the *Caroline* formula.[101] In an exchange of notes following the destruction of the S/S *Caroline* on 29 December 1837 by British troops, the then US Secretary of State Daniel Webster declared that self-defence could be permitted only if there was a 'necessity of self-defence, instant, overwhelming, leaving no choice of means and no moment for deliberation'.[102] Furthermore, the action taken had to be proportionate ('The act justified by the necessity must be limited and kept clearly within it.').[103] These requirements have been accepted in the period following as customary legal limitations of the right of self-defence.[104]

However, the *Caroline* formula is treated within two different legal contexts: on the one hand, it is used in order to put in concrete form a right to self-defence derived from Article 51 of the UN Charter; on the other hand, it is used as basis of a customary right to self-defence which continues to exist with an own control mechanism under the UN Charter. This fundamentally different understanding of the right of self-defence has consequences for the evaluation of the Bush Doctrine. The question, in which context the *Caroline* formula is treated, touches upon the basic

99 Brownlie, *Principles of Public International Law*, p. 732; A. Randelzhofer, 'Art. 2(4)', in B. Simma (ed.), *The Charter of the United Nations*, 2nd edn. (Oxford University Press, 2002), pp. 133–4, paras. 52, 61–6 with further references.

100 NSS 2002, p. 6. 101 Taft, *The Legal Basis of Preemption*.

102 Quoted after: J. Moore, *A Digest of International Law* (Washington, DC: Government Printing Office, 1906), vol. II, p. 412.

103 On the *Caroline* crisis of 1837–42 see: R. Jennings, 'The *Caroline* and *McLeod* Cases', A.J.I.L., 32 (1938), 82–99.

104 See W. Meng, 'The *Caroline*', , E.P.I.L., I (1992), 537–8.

understanding of the right to self-defence according to Article 51 of the UN Charter, and the underlying opinion on the sources of the right to self-defence. Different opinions with regard to the legality of anticipated self-defence result from these different starting points.[105] The relationship between Article 51 of the UN Charter and the customary right to self-defence existing prior to the UN Charter have been the subject of much controversy since the UN Charter came into force.[106]

4.2.2.2.1 The Bush Doctrine: assuming a customary pre-Charter right no longer exists The narrowest interpretation of Article 51 of the UN Charter assumes that the right to self-defence can have only the scope which Article 51 attributes to this right. A customary right to self-defence which existed prior to the charter, from which a right to self-defence could be derived in cases other than an armed attack, no longer exists under the UN Charter.[107]

The labelling of the right of self-defence as 'inherent' merely constitutes an explanation on legal theory by the lawmaker that it constitutes a law derived from natural law and not derived from positivist law, but this label does not constitute a regulation of its own.[108] Nothing in the wording of the UN Charter or *travaux préparatoires* hints that the parties to the treaty wanted to attribute a broader scope to the right of self-defence in cases other than an armed attack.[109]

Even if a customary right of self-defence persisted after the UN Charter came into force, this right would have been modified by the UN Charter and, hence, could only have the scope which this right had in 1945.[110] That is why anticipated self-defence would have been inadmissible even then.[111] The ICJ seems to have followed this basic concept that a customary,

105 Summarising on that: S. Schwebel, 'Aggression, Intervention and Self-Defence', RdC, 136 (1972-II), 479–81.

106 B. Asrat, *Prohibition of Force Under The UN Charter, A Study of Art. 2(4)* (Uppsala: Iustus Verlag, 1991), pp. 201–8.

107 H. Kelsen, *The Law of the United Nations* (London: Stevens & Sons, 1950), pp. 797–8; H. Wehberg, *Krieg und Eroberung im Wandel des Völkerrechts* (Frankfurt: Metzner, 1953), pp. 82–5; A. Cassese, 'Art. 51', in J. Cot and A. Pellet (eds.), *La Charte des Nations Unies*, 2nd edn. (Paris: Economia, 1991), pp. 777–8.

108 Kelsen, *The Law of the United Nations*, pp. 791–2.

109 L. Henkin, *How Nations Behave – Law and Foreign Policy* (New York: Frederick A. Praeger, 1968), p. 232.

110 Brownlie, *International Law and the Use of Force by States*, p. 274, yet with the limitation that: 'Some difficult though somewhat academic cases in which preventive action on a small scale might be justified are reserved for discussion later . . .', p. 278.

111 R. Ago, 'Addendum to Eighth Report on Responsibility', ILC Yearbook, 13 (1980), 65–7.

pre-charter right of self-defence has experienced a modification through the UN Charter in the *Nicaragua* judgment.[112] In addition to that, the purpose of the rule in Article 51 of the UN Charter is to limit unilateral use of force; an inclusion of an anticipated right of self-defence would work against this purpose.[113]

The limitation of a customary right of self-defence through Article 51 of the UN Charter goes so far that also in the case of worrying, obvious military preparations of a conventional armed attack, only an appeal to the Security Council, but not a preventive use of force, shall be justified.[114]

If one adheres to such a restrictive interpretation of Article 51 of the UN Charter, which leaves no room for self-defence without the occurrence of an armed attack and, hence, anticipated self-defence, the cases of the use of force foreseen in the Bush Doctrine, no matter how the criterion of 'imminence' is evaluated, are always illegal.

It is only in cases in which a low degree of force is considered as being below the threshold of the prohibition on the use of force because it violates neither the territorial integrity nor the political independence of a state,[115] does this opinion leave room for the use of force in the sense of the Bush Doctrine. However, even the supporters of this opinion recognise that there might be a necessity for a state to use force first if an armed attack cannot be awaited due to its consequences.[116]

In this context supporters of this opinion draw on the *Caroline* formula. To what extent a regulatory content of its own is attributed to the *Caroline* formula is disputed within this opinion.[117] To some extent it is assumed that this formula refers only to a customary pre-Charter right and, hence, no independent meaning is attributed to it.[118] On the other hand, it is assumed that the *Caroline* formula also has an independent

112 *Military and Paramilitary Activities in and against Nicaragua* (*Nicaragua* v. *United States of America*), Merits, Judgment, I.C.J. Rep.1986, pp. 14, 94 *et seq.*, paras. 176 *et seq.*; just as: Krisch, *Selbstverteidigung und kollektive Sicherheit*, pp. 139–40 with further evidence.

113 Randelzhofer, 'Art. 51', in Simma (ed.), *The Charter of the United Nations*, pp. 803–4, para. 39; Dinstein, *War, Aggression and Self-Defence*, pp. 183–4.

114 P. Jessup, *A Modern Law of Nations*, 4th edn. (New York: Macmillan, 1952), p. 166.

115 L. Henkin, *How Nations Behave* (1979), p. 145; A. D'Amato, 'Israel's Air Strike Upon the Iraqi Nuclear Reactor', A.J.I.L., 77 (1983), 584; Arend and Beck, *International Law and the Use of Force*, p. 108.

116 S. Schwebel, 'Aggression, Intervention and Self-Defence', RdC, 136 (1972-II), 481; O'Connell, *The Myth of Preemptive Self-Defense*, p. 8.

117 C. Gray, *International Law and the Use of Force* 3rd edn. (Oxford University Press, 2008), pp. 117–20.

118 Cassese, 'Art. 51', in Cot and Pellet (eds.), *La Charte des Nations Unies*, p. 772.

meaning under the UN Charter, because the criteria of 'necessity' and 'immediacy' determined within it constitute criteria for the exercise of self-defence recognised by customary international law. These criteria may be consulted in order to determine whether the requirement of an armed attack is fulfilled.[119]

This also touches upon the highly disputed question of the right of self-defence: namely, when an armed attack can be considered as begun.[120] The ICJ abstained in 1986 from answering this question explicitly in the *Nicaragua* case.[121]

Also according to this opinion, which considers the occurrence of an armed attack as compellingly necessary for the justification of the use of force in self-defence, a narrow scope for the application of the *Caroline* formula as an aid for answering the question when an armed attack occurs persists.[122] Starting with the notion that the parties to the treaty when signing the UN Charter in 1945 did not intend to limit the right of self-defence, already narrowly constrained by the *Caroline* formula, any further,[123] the wording 'in case of an armed attack' should at least not be understood as '*after* an armed attack'.[124] Hence, a state shall be entitled to self-defence in case of a not yet advanced armed attack if the occurrence of an armed attack is considered as a compellingly necessary prerequisite for the exercise of self-defence. This stream of argument goes back to Sir Humphrey Waldock, on whose central statement on this interpretation of the armed attack is drawn repeatedly.[125] Sir Humphrey argued that:

> where there is convincing evidence not merely of threats and potential danger but of an attack being actually mounted, then an armed attack may be said to have begun to occur, though it has not passed the frontier.[126]

119 Dinstein, *War, Aggression and Self-Defence*, p. 191; Bothe, 'Terrorism and the Legality of Pre-emptive Force', p. 231.

120 Randelzhofer, 'Art. 51', in Simma (ed.), *The Charter of the United Nations*, pp. 796 *et seq.*, paras. 20 *et seq.*

121 *Military and Paramilitary Activities in and against Nicaragua* (*Nicaragua* v. *United States of America*), Merits, Judgment, I.C.J. Rep. 1986, p. 93, para. 194.

122 O'Connell, *The Myth of Preemptive Self-Defense*, p. 9.

123 H. Waldock, 'The Regulation of the Use of Force by Individual States in International Law, RdC, 81 (1952-II), 497–8.

124 S. Alexandrov, *Self-Defense Against the Use of Force in International Law* (The Hague: Kulwer Law International, 1996), pp. 99–100.

125 O'Connell, *The Myth of Preemptive Self-Defense*, pp. 8–9; Dinstein, *War, Aggression and Self-Defence*, p. 191; Alexandrov, *Self-Defense Against the Use of Force in International Law*, p. 99.

126 Waldock, 'The Regulation of the Use of Force by Individual States in International Law', p. 498.

The term 'incipient self-defence' is also used for this concept.[127] Clearly recognisable preparations for an armed attack are, according to this opinion, regarded as an equivalent to an armed attack. For the determination of this equivalent to an armed attack, the *Caroline* formula shall be consulted, just as presented above.[128]

4.2.2.2.1.1 The reference to the Caroline *formula in the Bush Doctrine when rejecting a pre-Charter right* If the use of the term 'imminent threat' within the NSS 2002 as a reference to the *Caroline* formula is seen in this context, the Bush Doctrine would merely refer to the situation when an armed attack has begun, or when a situation may be considered as equivalent to an armed attack and consequently entitles the United States to a right of self-defence.

Therefore, the Bush Doctrine would merely consider preventive use of force prior to the actual exercise of an imminent armed attack as justified. Yet such a narrow interpretation of the Bush Doctrine would contradict the other arguments and principles of the NSS 2002. The NSS 2002 emphasises in particular that the use of force by the United States could not be limited to the repulsion of imminent traditional attacks because terrorists would not limit themselves to attacks in the conventional military sense of the term. The NSS mentions instead defence against what is considered by the United States as a 'sufficient threat to our national security'.[129]

4.2.2.2.1.2 Abandonment of the requirement of an 'armed attack' within the Bush Doctrine The question arises, if the principles of the Bush Doctrine could not be interpreted in a way, that the doctrine foresees the use of force only in case of an armed attack. However, if the principles of the doctrine do not leave room for such an interpretation, this must be considered as a rejection of this criterion by the United States. Hence, the principles of the Bush Doctrine would be, according to this opinion, *contra legem* and the Bush Doctrine would make a statement *de lege ferenda.*

The use of force prior to the actual occurrence of an armed attack, also according to this opinion possible within narrow limits, requires a prognosis with regard to the likelihood and size of the threat.[130] Exactly

127 Dinstein, *War, Aggression and Self-Defence*, p. 191.
128 Bothe, 'Terrorism and the Legality of Pre-emptive Force', pp. 231 *et seq.*
129 NSS 2002, p. 15.
130 Waldock, 'The Regulation of the Use of Force by Individual States in International Law', p. 498; Dinstein, *War, Aggression and Self-Defence*, p. 172.

this principle (the inclusion of size and likelihood of the threat) is also contained in the Bush Doctrine, as described in the NSS 2002.[131]

The danger which lies in this purely subjective prediction is also recognised in the NSS 2002 ('nor should nations use pre-emption as a pretext for aggression').[132] The wording, which seems to foresee the use of force a long time before the actual occurrence of an armed attack, reads: 'to preempt emerging threats'.[133] Narrowly interpreted, an 'emerging threat' can be understood – with a lot of good will – merely as an imminent armed attack.

From the basic concept of avoiding an emerging threat, some scholars derive that, hence, it is a declared principle of US foreign policy to support the promotion and installation of governments well-disposed towards the United States, if necessary by force: a policy of forcefully brought about 'regime changes'.[134] The strategic utility of the Bush Doctrine is questioned mainly due to this concept.[135] 'Regime change' is, furthermore, understood as a corollary to the idea of the preventive use of force, because a disarming of weapons of mass destruction could not prevent a government from acquiring them, but would instead create an incentive to boost its efforts in order to acquire them.[136] Yet no explicit declaration of belief in 'regime change' can be found in the NSS 2002 or other documents describing the Bush Doctrine.[137] Rather, this term is used in texts which deal with the implementation of the doctrine.[138] This concept also deals with range, sustainability and consequences of the use of force, but not the prerequisites for the use of force and, hence, cannot be considered as an element of the Bush Doctrine as a doctrine of US security policy.[139]

131 'The greater the threat, the greater the risk of inaction, – and the more compelling the case for taking anticipatory action to defend ourselves . . .' NSS 2002, p. 15.

132 NSS 2002, p. 15. 133 NSS 2002, p. 15.

134 J. Alvarez, 'Hegemonic International Law Revisited', A.J.I.L., 97 (2003), 873–88; J. Ikenberry, 'America's Imperial Ambition', For.Aff., 81 (2002), 5, 44–60.

135 IISS (ed.), 'The Bush National Security Strategy', Strategic Comments, 8 (2002), 2.

136 M. Reisman, 'Assessing Claims to Revise the Laws of War', A.J.I.L., 97 (2003), 87.

137 For example, George W. Bush, Commencement Address at the United States Military Academy, West Point, 1 June 2002; Taft, *The Legal Basis of Preemption*; C. Rice, *Dr. Condolezza Rice Discusses President's National Security Strategy*, 1 October 2002.

138 Reisman, 'Assessing Claims to Revise the Laws of War', p. 87; R. Wedgwood, 'The Fall of Saddam Hussein: Security Council Mandates and Preemptive Self-Defense', A.J.I.L., 97 (2003), 582; R. Falk, 'What Future for the UN Charter System of War Prevention?', A.J.I.L., 97 (2003), 596; T. Farer, 'The Prospect for International Law and Order in the Wake of Iraq', A.J.I.L., 97 (2003), 628; J. Stromseth, 'Law and Force after Iraq: A Transitional Moment', p. 636.

139 See on this term above, Chapter 1, section 1.6.

The aforementioned formulations of the NSS 2002 concerning the principles of the Bush Doctrine for the use of force, may be open to a restrictive interpretation that the doctrine can also be interpreted as being in conformity with the UN Charter as *contra legem*. Yet this is not possible for the explicit abandonment of the criterion of temporary imminence of an armed attack in the NSS 2002:

> The greater the threat, the greater the risk of inaction, and the more compelling the case for taking anticipatory action to prevent ourselves, *even if uncertainty remains as to the time and place of the enemy's attack.*[140]

By no stretch of the imagination can an affirmation of the requirement of an armed attack be read into the announcement of the intention to use force in cases of uncertainty with regard to the time and the place of the attack. Yet a temporary proximity of the armed attack is, according to this opinion, rejecting a pre-Charter right of self-defence compellingly required for the preventive use of force.[141]

Hence, the principles for the use of force contained in the Bush Doctrine are according to this opinion illegal and the statement of the NSS 2002 on the criterion of an 'imminent threat' a statement *de lege ferenda*, which must be considered with regard to the rules for the use of force as ('*potentiell systemsprengend*')[142] 'potentially blasting the system'.[143]

4.2.2.2.1.3 Possible justification of the Bush Doctrine due to an extension of the term 'armed attack' after 11 September 2001 When evaluating the use of force according to the principles of the Bush Doctrine, it has to be taken into account that the legal term 'armed attack' in Article 51 of the UN

140 NSS 2002, p. 15 (added emphasis).

141 Dinstein, *War, Aggression and Self-Defence*, p. 191; Alexandrov, *Self-Defense Against the Use of Force in International Law*, p. 99.

142 Nolte, 'Die USA und das Völkerrecht', p. 132; G. Nolte, *Le droit international face au défi américain*, Université Panthéon-Assas, Paris II – Cours et travaux No. 6 (Paris: Pedone, 2005), pp. 28–31; likewise: C. Eick, '"Präemption", "Prävention" und die Weiterentwicklung des Völkerrechts', ZRP, 6 (2004), 200–3.

143 T. Schweisfurth, 'Aggression', in K. Ambos and J. Arnold (eds.), *Der Irak-Krieg und das Völkerrecht* (Berlin: BWV, 2004), pp. 359–65; O. Dörr, 'Das völkerrechtliche Gewaltverbot am Beginn des 21. Jahrhunderts – Was bleibt von Art. 2(4) UN-Charta?', in O. Dörr (ed.), *Ein Rechtslehrer in Berlin – Symposium für Albrecht Randelzhofer* (Berlin: Springer, 2004), pp. 43 *et seq.*; G. Seidel, 'Quo vadis Völkerrecht?', AVR, 41 (2003), 475, 478; P. Minnerop, 'Classifcation of States and Creation of Status within the International Community', M.P.Y.U.N.L., 7 (2003), 158–71; O. von Lepel, 'Die präemptive Selbstverteidigung im Lichte des Völkerrechts', J.I.L.P.A.C./Hu.V-I, 16 (2003), 77–81; G. Nolte, 'Preventive Use of Force and Preventive Killings', T.Inq.L., 5 (2004), 126–7.

Charter exceeds conventional cross-border use of armed forces,[144] even though the general wording suggests such a narrow interpretation.[145] If the term 'armed attack' is interpreted so broadly that it already contains a mere supporting activity of an act of terror, this would leave room for preventive use of force just as the Bush Doctrine foresees.

Yet to what degree supporting actions for terrorists or their toleration can be considered as an armed attack is unclear.[146] To some extent it is assumed that in case of a close connection between the terrorist and the 'basing' state, an armed attack can be attributed to the state as its own attack.[147] Partially this evaluation is based on the matter of whether the supporting state is responsible for not preventing the acts of terror.[148] For the most part scholars of international law assume that the right of self-defence does not depend on the presence of an armed attack by the harbouring state, because Article 51 of the UN Charter also contains a non-state armed attack.[149] However, it is disputed whether a non-state armed attack entitles the attacked state to the cross-border use of force in self-defence.[150] This opinion in principle leaves room for the use of force against states supporting terrorist groups if the state promotes their actions.

Yet it is questionable which level of support this promotion must have acquired, and which state the preparation of an armed attack must have achieved in the particular case in order to consider an 'armed attack' as begun, that a right of self-defence exists. With regard to this matter it has been argued by some scholars that it is ultimately irrelevant if the acts of terror committed on 11 September 2001 constitute an 'armed attack'. As the United States have ensured prior to the use of force against the Taliban regime the recognition of this course of action by the UN

144 C. Greenwood, 'International Law and the "War against Terrorism"', Int.Aff., 78/2 (2002), 307 with further reference. On the narrower, outdated opinion that the use of regular armed forces alone may constitute an armed attack: Q. Wright, 'United States Intervention in the Lebanon', A.J.I.L., 53 (1959), 112–25. See above, Chapter 3, section 3.1.4.

145 Brownlie, *International Law and the Use of Force by State*, p. 278.

146 In detail on this discussion: Kreß, *Gewaltverbot und Selbstverteidigung nach der Satzung der Vereinten Nationen bei staatlicher Verwicklung in Gewaltakte Privater*, pp. 149–53.

147 Dinstein, *War, Aggression and Self-Defence*, pp. 204–6; P. Zanardi, *Indirect Military Aggression*, in Cassese (ed.), *The Current Legal Regulation of the Use of Force*, p. 113.

148 Y. Blum, 'State Responses to Acts of Terrorism', G.Y.I.L., 19 (1976), 236.

149 Dinstein, *War, Aggression and Self-Defence*, pp. 207–8; J. Combacau, 'The Exception of Self-Defence in the U.N. Practice', in Cassese (ed.), *The Current Legal Regulation of the Use of Force*, p. 26.

150 Rejecting: L. Stuesser, 'Active Defense: State Military Response to International Terrorism'; Cal.W.I.L.J., 17 (1987), 20.

Security Council, NATO and OAS as acting in self-defence, the right of self-defence shall now also cover military action against states supporting terrorist groups which have already attacked this state.[151] As Michael Byers phrased this matter generally: 'State sponsored terrorism on this scale now also constitutes an "armed attack".'[152]

This statement can hardly refer to state-supported terror in its entirety, because if this permanent phenomenon were to be considered wholly as an armed attack this would, hence, result in a permanent right of self-defence.[153] Furthermore, an exact determination is required as to what can be considered, particularly after 11 September 2001, with regard to acts of terror as an armed attack triggering the right of self-defence.

The narrow limits within which commencing self-defence ('incipient self-defence') in case of clearly recognisable acts of preparation is considered legal[154] require a clear prognosis with regard to the armed attack. However, it is questionable to what this prognosis refers depending on the decision of the supporting act: the act of terror as such or a connection of both make up for the 'armed attack'. The ICJ considers the support of acts of force by private persons to be part of the term 'armed attack'.[155] Yet this term of 'substantial involvement' has to be interpreted restrictively when it comes to answering the question: to what extent does such an involvement constitute an armed attack?[156]

151 Ratner, '*Jus ad Bellum* and *Jus in Bello* After September 11', p. 914. Narrower: Gray, who only assumes a right of self-defence after prior acts of terror by private persons if the Security Council has confirmed the entitlement to such a right according to chapter VII. C. Gray, 'The US National Security Strategy and the New "Bush Doctrine" on Preemptive Self-Defense', Chin.J.I.L., 2 (2002), 441; M. Schmitt, 'Responding to Transnational Terrorism under the *Jus ad bellum*', in M. Schmitt and J. Pejic (eds.), *International Law and Armed Conflict: Exploring the Faultlines* (Leiden: Nijhoff, 2007), pp. 159–95 at 174–5.

152 Byers, 'Terrorism, the Use of Force and International Law after 11 September', p. 409; similar: Alvarez, 'Hegemonic International Law Revisited', pp. 879–82; C. Henderson, 'The Bush Doctrine: From Theory to Practice', J.C.S.L., 9 (2004), 3–4; F. Kirgis, 'Israel's Intensified Military Campaign Against Terrorism', ASIL Insights, December 2001, available at: www.asil.org/insights/insigh78.htm.

153 On this see: T. Bruha, 'Gewaltverbot und humanitäres Völkerrecht nach dem 11. September 2001', AVR, 40 (2002), 383 at 421; H. Dederer, 'Krieg gegen Terror', JZ, (2004), 421–31.

154 Dinstein, *War, Aggression and Self-Defence*, p. 191.

155 *Military and Paramilitary Activities in und against Nicaragua* (*Nicaragua* v. *United States of America*), Merits, Judgment, I.C.J. Rep. 1986, pp. 93–4, para. 195.

156 Randelzhofer, 'Art. 51', in Simma (ed.), *The Charter of the United Nations*, p. 801, para. 33.

The reasoning, building on the already committed act of terror in order to determine the presence of an armed attack, contains a temporary paradox. As a methodical aid – for the purpose of illustration and not as a normative statement – following the categories of 'act's wrong' ('*Erfolgsunwert*') and 'action's wrong' ('*Handlungsunrecht*') of German criminal law can be of use. This applies even though this theory of personal wrongs ('*personale Unrechtslehre*') is referring to individuals and has beyond any doubt no validity in international law for actions of states and can only be partially transferred to them. 'Act's wrong' ('Erfolgsunwert') describes the legally disapproved success, 'action's wrong' ('*Handlungsunwert*') describes the legally disapproved action. The evaluation of the result *ex post facto* is in this connection independent from the evaluation of the legality of the action itself.[157] However, the concept that in case of an already committed act of terror self-defence may be justified[158] bases the judgement about the legal evaluation of an action merely on the results of the action. If one exaggerates this thought, an action by a terrorist group would be logically possible, that is, the use of nuclear-armed middle-range missiles ('action's wrong' / 'Handlungsunrecht') which, if it fails, say, because the rockets go down due to a technical failure over state-free territory (lacking 'result's wrong'/'Erfolgsunrecht') cannot be considered an armed attack.

According to this logic the support of the Taliban regime for the terror network Al Quaida prior to 11 September 2001 would not have to be categorised as an 'armed attack' if the World Trade Center had been missed, if the hijackers had been overpowered and the aircraft had been landed safely. An action, *ex ante* indistinguishable from an action with different results would be re-evaluated *ex post facto* as an 'armed attack'. Yet the success of an act of terror is not solely crucial for the decision as to whether a supporting action may constitute an 'armed attack',[159] which the case law of the ICJ seems to support.[160]

In an inversion of the argument this also emphasises that the supporting action alone does not suffice in order to constitute an 'armed attack', even

157 C. Roxin, *Strafrecht-Allgemeiner Teil*, 3rd edn. (Munich: C. H. Beck, 1997), pp. 264–72.

158 See Byers, 'Terrorism, the Use of Force and International Law after 11 September', p. 409.

159 Y. Daudet, 'International Action against State Terrorism', in R. Higgins and M. Flory (eds.), *Terrorism and International Law* (London: Routledge, 1997), pp. 203–6.

160 *Military and Paramilitary Activities in und against Nicaragua* (*Nicaragua* v. *United States of America*), Merits, Judgment, I.C.J. Rep. 1986, p. 94, para. 195.

though a supporting action may constitute a violation of the prohibition of force.[161] Interpreting the term 'armed attack' that broadly would mean beyond any doubt pushing the term towards being limitless. Hence, the prediction has to refer to the interaction of supporting action and the act of terror to be expected, which both constitute an element of the armed attack.

In the case of the attacks of 11 September 2001, which are different from, for example, the bombing of Tripoli and Benghazi in 1986 and Iraq in June 1993 as reaction to prior or planned acts of terror, it has actually been accepted that these attacks entitle the United States to exercise the right of self-defence.[162] Yet this does not constitute an extension of the term 'armed attack', as referring to the supporting action alone.[163]

Hence, the term 'armed attack' at least has not experienced an extension to the effect that supporting actions by states for terrorist groups without the imminence of an act of terror fall under that term.[164] The resolutions of the UN Security Council and the NATO Council do not even give information as to whether it is assumed that an armed attack necessarily has to be brought forward by a state.[165] On top of that, the ICJ seems to tend in its opinion on the *Legal Consequences of the Construction of a Wall in the Occupied Palestinian Territory* of 9 July 2004 to the view that an armed attack may only emerge from a state.[166] Yet the wording of the opinion[167] leaves room for a different interpretation that an armed attack may not be launched exclusively by another state.[168]

161 Alexandrov, *Self-Defense Against the Use of Force in International Law*, p. 120 with further references.

162 UN Doc. SC/Res/1373, UN Doc. SC/7158; on this: Gray, *International Law and the Use of Force*, pp. 198 *et seq.*

163 J. Delbrück, 'The Fight Against Global Terrorism: Self-Defense or Collective Security as International Police Action? Some Comments on the International Legal Implications of the "War Against Terrorism"', G.Y.I.L., 44 (2001), 18–19; C. Stahn, 'International Law at a Crossroads? The Impact of September 11', ZaöRV/H.J.I.L., 62 (2002), 232–4.

164 Alvarez, 'Hegemonic International Law Revisited', p. 879.

165 G. Gaja, 'In What Sense was There an "Armed Attack?"', E.J.I.L. Discussion Forum, available at: www.ejil.org/forum_WTC/ny-gaja.html.

166 *Legal Consequences of the Construction of a Wall in the Occupied Palestinian Territory*, Advisory Opinion, I.C.J. Rep. 2004, p. 136, No. 139.

167 'in case of an armed attack by a state . . .' and not '*exclusively* in case of an armed attack by a state, *the only entity which can launch an armed attack* . . .'

168 Like this: Separate Opinion of Judge Higgins, *Wall in the Occupied Palestinian Territory*, No. 33; Declaration of Judge Buergenthal, *Wall in the Occupied Palestinian Territory*, Nos. 5–6.

Hence, a possible extended interpretation of the term 'armed attack' after 11 September 2001 does not change the classification of the principles of the Bush Doctrine for the use of force as (according to this opinion rejecting a pre-Charter right) as illegal and of the statement in the NSS 2002 on the criterion of imminent threat as a statement *de lege ferenda.*[169]

4.2.2.2.2 The Bush Doctrine: assuming the continued existence of a customary right of self-defence Another opinion, however, assumes that a customary right of self-defence continues to exist under the UN Charter. The member states of the UN shall not just befit the rights which are attributed to them by the UN Charter, but also the rights which befit them according to general international law. These rights have merely been modified by the Charter, but do not lose their own regulatory value.[170] Partially this is geared to the word 'inherent'.[171]

The wording of Article 51 of the UN Charter, according to which nothing in the Charter shall impair the right of self-defence in case of an armed attack, would not allow for the conclusion that self-defence is admissible only against an armed attack. 'In case of an armed attack' should not mean '*exclusively* in case of an armed attack'.[172] The *travaux préparatoires* would not suggest another conclusion, because within them merely the prevention, but not the limitation of the right of self-defence is mentioned.[173] In this way, state practice after the coming into force of the UN Charter, due to repeated claiming of the exercise of self-defence, does not allow for a conclusion that the right of self-defence existing prior to the charter has been limited.[174] If one adheres to this opinion and the occurrence of an armed attack is not considered a compellingly

169 Similar also: R. Wolfrum, 'The Attack of September 11, 2001, the Wars Against the Taliban and Iraq: Is there a Need to Reconsider International Law on the Recourse to Force and *ius in bello*', M.P.Y.U.N.L., 7 (2003), 33.

170 Bowett, *Self-Defence in International Law*, p. 187.

171 L. Casey and D. Rivkin, '"Anticipatory" Self-Defense against Terrorism is Legal', Legal Opinion Letter, 14 December 2001, available at: www.wlf.org/upload/casey.pdf.

172 L. Goodrich and E. Hambro, *Charter of the United Nations*, 2nd edn. (London: Stevens & Sons, 1949), p. 301; Dissenting Opinion of Judge Schwebel, *Military and Paramilitary Activities in und against Nicaragua* (*Nicaragua* v. *United States of America*), Merits, Judgment, I.C.J. Rep. 1986, pp. 347–8, Nos. 172–3.

173 Bowett, *Self-Defence in International Law*, p. 188; J. Stone, *Aggression and World Order, A Critique of United Nations Theories of Aggression* (London: Stevens & Sons, 1958), pp. 43–4.

174 Bowett, *Self-Defence in International Law*, pp. 187–93.

necessary prerequisite for the exercise of self-defence, the question for the solution of the basic dilemma of self-defence, accurately phrased by William H. Taft, IV, comes to mind: how long does a state have to wait before pre-emptive measures can be taken to prevent serious harm?[175]

This question is answered differently by the supporters of the opinion that an armed attack is not necessary for the exercise of self-defence. This influences the response to the question: to what extent is the use of force based on the principles of the Bush Doctrine considered to be in accordance with the law in force?

4.2.2.2.2.1 The Bush Doctrine: interpreting a pre-Charter right restrictively

To some extent a customary law of self-defence, which is assumed to continue to exist under the UN Charter, is interpreted narrowly. According to this opinion, the *Caroline* formula describes the prerequisites which have to be fulfilled for the use of force in self-defence: according to this, the use of force in self-defence shall be justified only if an armed attack is imminent. In this context 'imminent' is understood in the sense of a temporarily proximate armed attack for which secure signs are known.[176]

Considerations of legal policy, such as the unreasonable endurance of a first attack since the existence of nuclear weapons and the necessity of a limitation on the unilateral use of force, are included in the reasoning of this opinion.[177] These considerations are also expressed in the *travaux préparatoires* of the Charter, which mirror, on the one hand, the desire of the member states to preserve the right of self-defence, but, on the other hand, also the desire to bring about a limitation on the use of force.[178]

The wording 'in case of an armed attack' should not be understood as sole description of the prerequisites of the right of self-defence, but as an expression of a general conviction of law that at least clear signs of a temporarily proximate armed attack must be known.

It was the intention of the signatory states to the UN Charter to prevent cases in which a situation of self-defence was merely claimed as a

175 Taft, *The Legal Basis of Preemption.*

176 O. Schachter, 'International Law: The Right of States to Use Armed Force', Mich.L.Rev. 82 (1984), 1634–6; O. Schachter, *International Law in Theory and Practice* (Dordrecht: Martin Nijhoff Publishers, 1991), pp. 150–2.

177 Bowett, *Self-Defence in International Law*, pp. 191–2; R. Higgins, *Problems and Process, International Law and How We Use It* (Oxford: Clarendon Press, 1994), pp. 242–3.

178 Goodrich and Hambro, *Charter of the United Nations*, p. 301; Schachter, 'International Law: The Right of States to Use Armed Force', p. 1635.

pretext.[179] In consequence, the cases in which the use of force in self-defence is regarded as justified according to this opinion, though based on dogmatically fundamentally different starting points, deviate only marginally from the opinion presented above, according to which an armed attack is necessarily required.[180] The danger emphasised by this opinion of claiming a situation of self-defence as a pretext is also mentioned in the NSS 2002, where it states: 'The United States will not use force in all cases to pre-empt emerging threats, nor should nations use pre-emption as a pretext for aggression . . .'[181]

Decisive for the decision if the NSS makes a statement *de lege lata* or *de lege ferenda* is, according to this opinion, if the interpretation of the term 'imminent' abandons or maintains the requirement of a temporarily proximate attack. Supporters of this opinion assume, like supporters of the aforementioned opinion, that the NSS 2002 abandons entirely the temporarily proximate armed attack for the use of force. Thus, they classify the use of force according to the principles of the Bush Doctrine as *contra legem.*[182] The question for the requirement of a temporarily proximate armed attack also poses itself when extensively interpreting a customary right of self-defence.

4.2.2.2.2.2 The Bush Doctrine: interpreting a pre-Charter right extensively
According to an opinion which also assumes the continued existence of a customary right of self-defence, it can be derived from the wording of Article 2(4) of the UN Charter that 'all members shall refrain in their international relations from the threat or use of force . . . in any other manner inconsistent with the Purpose of the United Nations', that the Charter is not a value-free document and not just direct itself against the use of force in general, but only against the use of force, which contradicts the aim and purpose of the UN Charter.[183] It is also argued by supporters of this opinion with a hint to the *telos* of this rule that the inherent right of self-defence must contain a right to take preventive measures. Otherwise

179 Bowett, *Self-Defence in International Law*, pp. 182–4.
180 See above, section 4.2.2.2.1.
181 NSS 2002, p. 15. On this see further above, section 4.2.2.2.1.2.
182 Henderson, 'The Bush Doctrine: From Theory to Practice', pp. 1, 7–10; M. Byers, 'Der Irak und der Fall Caroline', in Ambos and Arnold (eds.), *Der Irak-Krieg und das Völkerrecht*, pp. 240–1; M. Byers, *Iraq and the "Bush-Doctrine" of Pre-emptive Self-Defence*, available at: www.crimesofwar.org/print/expert/bush-Byers-print.html; similarly: N. Shah, 'Self-defence, Anticipatory Self-defence and Pre-emption: International Law's Response to Terrorism', J.C.S.L., 12 (2007), 95–126 at 100.
183 M. McDougal, 'The Soviet–Cuban Quarantine and Self-Defense', A.J.I.L., 57 (1963), 600.

such a right would contradict the aim and purpose of the UN Charter and force states if the worst happens to endure their own annihilation. For this reason the legality of the use of force ought to undergo a comprehensive examination for which individual criteria are developed.[184]

A narrow interpretation of the *Caroline* formula to the effect that an armed attack has to be temporarily imminent, is considered to constitute merely a fictitious limitation of the use of force assumed by scholars of international law. Yet it does not find any backing in the practice of states,[185] because a literal understanding of the criteria of the *Caroline* formula would result in a paralysis of single states. In order to determine whether the necessary factual prerequisites for the exercise of self-defence are present, the general, customarily recognised criteria of necessity and proportionality are applied instead.[186]

The objection that this opinion faces, that, compared with the criterion of an 'armed attack', such an extremely subjective standard of reasonable necessity finally results in no limitation on the use of force at all,[187] is met with the reply that certain political conflicts are not, or only to a certain degree, litigable.[188]

Starting with this basic thought, the *Caroline* formula is merely consulted as a means in order to determine the criterion of 'necessity'. The Bush Doctrine and its reference to the criterion of 'imminence' are also looked at from this point of view. In doing so, supporters of this opinion particularly emphasise that state practice since the *Caroline* crisis of 1837–41 has caused an evolution in the concept of 'imminence'. Today, this concept has had to be evaluated differently from that time. Consequently, 'imminence' is not interpreted in the sense of an impending attack, but based on other matters.[189]

184 McDougal and Feliciano, *Law and Minimum World Public Order*, pp. 217–43, in particular p. 238; A. Sofaer, 'On the Necessity of Preemption', E.J.I.L., 14 (2003), 221–5.

185 Sofaer, 'On the Necessity of Preemption', pp. 212–20; J. Yoo, 'International Law and the War in Iraq', A.J.I.L., 97 (2003), 573.

186 McDougal and Feliciano, *Law and Minimum World Public Order*, p. 217.

187 For example, K. Krakau, *Missionsbewußtsein und Völkerrechtsdoktrin in den Vereinigten Staaten von Amerika* (Frankfurt a.M.: Metzner, 1967), pp. 505–14.

188 A. Chayes, 'A Common Lawyer Looks at International Law', H.L.R., 78 (1965), 1409–13, different however: A. Chayes, *The Cuban Missile Crisis* (Oxford University Press, 1974), pp. 65–6.

189 Yoo, 'International Law and the War in Iraq', p. 572; W. Slocombe, 'Force, Pre-emption and Legitimacy', *Survival*, 45 (2003) 1, 117–30, in particular at p. 125, yet without specific reference to a customary right of self-defence. Similarly: A. C. Arend, 'International Law and the Preemptive Use of Military Force', Wash.Q., 26 (2003), 89–103, in particular pp. 96 *et seq.*

With a hint to new developments in international law, it is stressed that 'imminence' does not refer only to a temporary proximity of the realisation of a threat, but also includes the likelihood of the realisation of a threat.[190] In addition to that, the extent of expected damages in case of inaction are taken into account.[191]

The action of the United States during the Cuban Missile Crisis in October 1962, during which the deployment of nuclear-armed long-range missiles on Cuba was considered an 'immediate threat', is called upon as an example for that kind of understanding of imminent threats.[192] Yet an argument like this overlooks the fact that in the case of the Cuban Missile Crisis the United States specifically refrained from resorting to action in exercise of self-defence.[193] That is why their declarations in this context cannot be drawn upon in order to determine when a threat has been considered as 'imminent' in the sense of the *Caroline* formula, and, hence, entitles states to use of force.

Yet according to this opinion, even when the threat is posed by weapons of mass destruction, a temporarily close realisation of a threat is not considered as being entirely dispensable for the determination of 'imminence'. This is considered to be lacking, for example, in the case of the Israeli bombing of the Iraqi reactor in Osirak in 1981.[194]

Furthermore, after the declaration of the Bush Doctrine another limitation on the scope of application of the *Caroline* formula has been advocated. If one takes into consideration the circumstances of the *Caroline* case, it becomes clear that the *Caroline* formula refers to situations in which a state, from the territory of which the threat emerges, is willing and able to prevent the realisation of the threat and does not support the threat and not to cases of preventive self-defence.

190 Stahn wrote in this regard of favouring a replacement of the current criterion of an 'imminent threat' by a 'sufficient threat'. C. Stahn, 'Enforcement of the Collective Will after Iraq', A.J.I.L., 97 (2003), 820.

191 Yoo, 'International Law and the War in Iraq', p. 572 with a hint to the judgment of the ICJ in the *Gabcykovo-Nagymaros* case, *Gabcikovo-Nagymaros Project (Hungary/Slovakia)*, Judgment, I.C.J. Rep. 1997, p. 7, in which 'imminence' is, however, treated without reference to the *Caroline* case, but with regard to the meaning of 'imminent peril' in Art. 33 of the ILC's Draft Articles on the International Responsibility of States (ILC Yearbook, 2.2 (1980), 34).

192 McDougal, 'The Soviet–Cuban Quarantine and Self-Defense', pp. 600–3.

193 On the US-American justification for the blockade of Cuba see above, Chapter 2, section 2.2.3.6.

194 Yoo, 'International Law and the War in Iraq', p. 574.

According to this opinion the narrow limitations of the *Caroline* formula for self-defence do not refer to cases in which the state is not willing and not able to suppress attacks brought forward from its territory.[195] Consequently, the *Caroline* formula is not considered in such cases to be a suitable aid to determining if the criterion of 'necessity' of the use of force is fulfilled.[196]

Even though this dismissal of the *Caroline* formula seems highly questionable in view of the continued reference of states to its wording,[197] the temporarily close occurrence of an armed attack is deemed by this opinion to be a requirement for necessity and, consequently, for the legality of the use of force.[198]

The NSS 2002 mentions preventive action in order 'to pre-empt emerging threats'. It is not specified what shape this threat must have taken. However, a right to use force in case of an 'imminent danger of attack'[199] is mentioned, and this could be seen as the inclusion of the criterion of temporary proximity of an imminent armed attack. Yet if one takes a closer look at the context of this formulation, it can be understood only as the total abandonment of an imminent armed attack as the NSS 2002 claims and by the same token a right to take forceful measures at any time against a state which is subjectively perceived as a threat.[200]

The announcement of an intention to act preventively and unilaterally also suggests this interpretation,[201] just like the chosen wide formulation 'to pre-empt emerging threats'.[202] In particular, the declaration that the threat of weapons of mass destruction must be prevented[203] is seen by some authors as a renunciation of the requirement of an imminent armed

195 A. Sofaer, 'On the Necessity of Preemption', p. 214. Yet in favour of the application of the *Caroline* formula on such cases: A. Sofaer, 'Terrorism and the Law', For.Aff., 65 (1985), 920; Yoo, 'International Law and the War in Iraq', pp. 572–4.

196 Sofaer, 'On the Necessity of Preemption', p. 214. Similarly: Greenwood, 'International Law and the "War against Terrorism"', pp. 2, 308.

197 W. Meng, The *Caroline*, pp. 537–8; Taft also makes reference to the *Caroline* formula in his interpretation of the NSS 2002. Taft, *The Legal Basis of Preemption.*

198 Sofaer, 'On the Necessity of Preemption', p. 221.

199 NSS 2002, p. 15.

200 Nolte, 'Preventive Use of Force and Preventive Killings', pp. 112–17; M. Byers, *Expert Analysis, Iraq and the 'Bush-Doctrine' of Pre-emptive Self-Defence.*

201 T. Franck, 'What Happens Now? The United Nations After Iraq', A.J.I.L., 97 (2003), 619–20; Stromseth, 'Law and Force after Iraq: A Transitional Moment', p. 636.

202 NSS 2002, p. 15.

203 'We must be prepared to stop rogue states and their terrorist clients before they are able to threaten or use weapons of mass destruction against the United States or our allies and friends . . .' NSS 2002, p. 14.

attack.[204] The assurance of taking action, even if uncertainty remains as to the time and place of the attack, ultimately makes it clear that a temporary proximity of an armed attack is not considered a requirement for the use of force.[205]

If the Bush Doctrine is understood as entirely free of the requirement of temporary proximity of an armed attack, the doctrine could not be reconciled with the law in force no matter how wide this requirement may be interpreted. The phrase 'We must adapt the concept of imminent threat . . .' is hence to be understood as a claim *de lege ferenda*.

Only if one renounces the requirement of temporary proximity of an imminent attack entirely when it comes to determining the criterion of 'imminence' and takes instead a general customary criterion of necessity into account,[206] is there room for use of force based on a wide interpretation of the Bush Doctrine (against states which are subjectively perceived as a threat without an armed attack being temporarily imminent). If one follows this opinion, the principles of the Bush Doctrine for the use of force would be, also in case of a wider interpretation of these principles, in accordance with a pre-Charter right. According to such an opinion, the Bush Doctrine would make no statement, aiming for an extension of the hitherto in force right of self-defence, but make merely a statement *de lege lata*.

Even though the scope this opinion leaves for the preventive use of force is wider than that of the aforementioned opinions, according to this opinion the Bush Doctrine can be seen as a statement *de lege lata*, as well as a statement *de lex ferenda*. Yet such a wide and general interpretation of 'necessity' is not advocated by the supporters of this opinion.[207]

The explanations on the Bush Doctrine within the NSS 2002 and the statements referring to the NSS hint that the Bush Doctrine, as outlined in the NSS 2002, is considered merely as a repetition of the hitherto legal opinion of the United States. Within the NSS 2002 itself it is stated that the United States had reserved the option of preventive measures for a

204 Stromseth, 'Law and Force after Iraq: A Transitional Moment', p. 635.

205 NSS 2002, p. 15.

206 McDougal and Feliciano, *Law and Minimum World Public Order*, pp. 217–43; W. Bradford, 'The Duty to Defend Them: A Natural Law Justification for the Bush Doctrine of Preventive War', N.D.L.R., 79 (2004), 1462 *et seq.*; Similarly: Murphy, *The United States and the Rule of Law in International Affairs*, pp. 176–7; J. Darby, 'Self-Defense in Public International Law: the Doctrine of Pre-emption and Its Discontents', in J. Bröhmer *et al.* (eds.), *Internationale Gemeinschaft und Menschenrechte*, FS-Ress (Cologne: Carl Heymanns Verlag, 2005), pp. 29–33.

207 Sofaer, 'On the Necessity of Preemption', p. 221.

long time.[208] Thus, the Legal Advisor of the Department of State saw no change in the US legal position in the NSS 2002.[209]

Hence, an ascertainment of the previous US legal opinion admits of conclusions of the content of the NSS 2002. To what extent, according to the previous US opinion, a right of preventive self-defence has been recognised, can thus possibly give information as to which statement the Bush Doctrine is making about the legality of preventive use of force.

4.2.2.3 The Bush Doctrine and the previous legal opinion of the United States on preventive self-defence

Two alternative evaluations of the relation between the Bush Doctrine and previous US legal opinion on preventive self-defence are possible: on the one hand, the Bush Doctrine is considered as corresponding to a long tradition of the United States;[210] and, on the other hand, the Bush Doctrine is seen as a clear break with previous US legal opinion in this regard.[211] Within the NSS itself, in anticipation of possible criticism, it is hinted that 'for centuries international law recognised that nations need not suffer an attack before they can lawfully take action . . .'[212]

The fact that no precise statement is made on the part of the United States on the source of the right of self-defence, makes a precise determination of US legal opinion before the publication of the NSS impossible. Instead, certain actions are categorised as justified by a right of self-defence, not described in detail, of which the source has not been determined. This lack of dogmatic commitment runs like a thread through US-American statements on the right of self-defence since the coming into force of the UN Charter:

Already in 1946, it had been stated in an internal US Government memorandum that in view of the development of nuclear weapons the term 'armed attack' in Article 51 of the UN Charter had to be interpreted at least widely enough so that not only dropping a bomb, but preparatory steps prior to such an action must be considered as an 'armed attack'.[213] Such a wide interpretation of the term 'armed attack', which brings the

208 'The USA has long maintained the option of preemptive actions to counter a sufficient threat to our national security', NSS 2002, p. 15.

209 Taft, *The Legal Basis of Preemption.*

210 L. Feinstein and A-M. Slaughter, 'A Duty to Prevent', For.Aff., 83 (2004), 1, 147.

211 Gray, 'The US National Security Strategy and the New "Bush Doctrine" on Preemptive Self-Defense', pp. 440–3; Roberts, 'Law and the Use of Force After Iraq', pp. 2, 46.

212 NSS 2002, p. 15.

213 Quoted after: Jessup, *A Modern Law of Nations*, pp. 166–7.

justification of preventive action close to the concept of 'incipient self-defence' advocated by Dinstein,[214] does not, however, allow for the conclusion that this goes together with an abandonment of a pre-Charter right.

A case frequently referred to as evidence for the argument that the Bush Doctrine matches previous US legal opinion is the Cuban Missile Crisis and US-American justifications. However, in doing so no account is taken of the fact that imposing the sea blockade on Cuba was specifically not justified as an action in exercise of self-defence.[215] Hence, the United States refrained intentionally from claiming Article 51 of the UN Charter.[216] Instead, President Kennedy listed the defence of the security of the United States and the whole western hemisphere as reasons for the blockade.[217] Even though this reasoning brings the measure close to anticipated self-defence, the United States did not base this measure on such a right. If the situation on which the American 'quarantine' was based sufficed for the criteria of the *Caroline* formula, it was doubted in the Security Council debate.[218] Yet this was from the very beginning an idling debate, as the United States had consciously avoided the term 'self-defence'. Furthermore, the justification was based on an authorisation by the OAS and Article 53 of the UN Charter. Specific references to the right of self-defence or the Monroe Doctrine were abstained from.[219]

Several interventions of US-American practice have been explained as being undertaken with the intention of eliminating possible future threats to the security of the United States (in Grenada 1983 and Libya in 1986). Yet the United States never claimed when justifying these interventions to be exercising preventive self-defence, and refused to support approaches based on an interpretation of Article 51 of the UN Charter pointing towards anticipated self-defence. Instead, such interventions were justified through different reasoning, such as, for example,

214 See above, section 4.2.2.2.1.1.

215 Taft, *The Legal Basis of Preemption*; Different: C. Tomuschat, 'Völkerrecht ist kein Zweiklassenrecht', Vereinte Nationen, 2/2003, 42, who assumes a reference to Article 51 of the UN Charter, and Yoo, 'International Law and the War in Iraq', p. 573, who assumes less specifically an action with reference to the right of self-defence.

216 On this see further above, Chapter 2, section 2.1.3.5.

217 *Department of State Bulletin*, 47 (1962), 715.

218 Ghana made an explicit reference to the *Caroline* formula, UN Yearbook 1962, pp. 101 *et seq*. Partially reproduced at: Arend and Beck, *International Law and the Use of Force*, p. 74.

219 Henkin, *How Nations Behave – Law and Foreign Policy*, pp. 231–6. In detail on this see: Chayes, *The Cuban Missile Crisis*, pp. 62–6.

intervention by invitation in the case of the intervention in Grenada in 1983.[220]

Furthermore, a wide interpretation of 'armed attack' has been drawn upon: for example, with regard to the use of force by the United States against Libya it was assumed on the part of the United States that an armed attack by Libya had taken place. It was emphasised, in particular by the Legal Advisor of the State Department, Abraham Sofaer, that the behaviour of Libya constituted not just an 'armed attack', but even matched the narrower definition of an 'aggression', and thus the actions by the United States were in accordance with the Friendly Relations Declaration.[221] On the United States' part, the occurrence of an armed attack was assumed likewise in the case of air strikes against Iraq on 26 June 1993,[222] and against Sudan and Afghanistan on 20 August 1998.[223] So far the United States has never claimed to be using force in self-defence without assuming that an armed attack has already occurred. Israel, on the other hand, has repeatedly considered preventive self-defence (in particular in 1967 and 1981[224]) to be in accordance with Article 51 of the UN Charter. The United States has refrained in the Security Council debates dealing with these cases from considering more closely the legal basis of such actions.[225]

The Legal Advisor of the State Department, William Taft, emphasised in November 2002 that the principles of the Bush Doctrine are grounded on the same legal basis as the Israeli action in 1981, and that condemnation of the Israeli action was based on the fact that Israel had not exhausted all peaceful means for the settlement of the dispute prior to the action.[226]

The basic problem for establishing US legal opinion springs up here too: an action is considered as a justified exercise of self-defence, but a dogmatic commitment from which such a right of self-defence is derived is not made. Hence, even if the quality of *opinio iuris* could be attributed to this statement, no precise legal opinion of the United States could be derived from Taft's statement.

Though this comparison of preventive use of force (based on the principles of the Bush Doctrine) with the Israeli bombing in 1981 does not

220 Nolte, *Eingreifen auf Einladung*, pp. 261–95.
221 Sofaer, 'Terrorism and the Law', pp. 920–1.
222 UN Yearbook, 1993, p. 431.
223 UN Doc. S/1998/780.
224 UN Yearbook, 1967, p. 176; UN Yearbook 1981, p. 277.
225 UN Yearbook 1981, p. 276; Arend and Beck, *International Law and the Use of Force*, pp. 77–9.
226 Taft, *The Legal Basis of Preemption.*

take into account that in this case a temporary proximity of the realisation of the threat had been put forward,[227] from which the Bush Doctrine specifically abstains. That is the reason why this case is usually treated with regard to matters of anticipated self-defence.[228] The United States has, however, hitherto abstained from claiming to act in exercise of anticipated self-defence or condoning such an action,[229] yet no declaration can be found in which such a right has been explicitly denied. However, the Bush Doctrine exceeds a turn towards anticipated self-defence, because the criterion of a temporarily proximate realisation of the threat is abandoned.

This abandonment of not just the occurrence of an armed attack, but also of the temporary close realisation of an armed attack, or the imminent realisation of a threat in favour of general considerations of urgency as prerequisite for the exercise of self-defence bring the Bush Doctrine close to an extensive interpretation of a pre-Charter right,[230] even though no statement about the dogmatic foundation of a justification for these cases of use of force is made. Taking into account that the principles of the Bush Doctrine for the use of force can be justified only when interpreting a pre-Charter right extensively, this stresses that this constitutes a turn away from the previous US legal position.

The Bush Doctrine performs this turn away in two steps: first, the criterion of the compellingly required (broadly interpreted) armed attack for the exercise of self-defence is abandoned; second, a right of anticipated self-defence is extended by abandoning the criterion of temporary proximity of the realisation of a threat, extending it towards the right of preventive self-defence.

Just as in case of anticipated self-defence, the United States itself never claimed to act in exercise of preventive self-defence, and has been sceptical towards this type of approach to justification,[231] but has at no point in time rejected such a justification in principle.

It seems doubtful to what extent the United States is willing in practice to build on such a justification. This resembles the discrepancy between the principles of the Reagan Doctrine and the justifications brought

227 UN Doc. S/PV.2289, 12 June 1981, Nos. 52–5.

228 Alexandrov, *Self-Defense Against the Use of Force in International Law*, pp. 154–65; Arend and Beck, *International Law and the Use of Force*, pp. 71–81.

229 L. Henkin, 'The Use of Force: Law and U.S. Policy', in L. Henkin *et al.* (eds.), *Right v. Might – International Law and the Use of Force*, 2nd edn. (New York: Council on Foreign Relation Press, 1991), pp. 46, 50–1.

230 See above, section 4.2.2.2.2.2.

231 Roberts, 'Law and the Use of Force After Iraq', pp. 2, 46–7.

forward for the use of force during Reagan's time in office.[232] Consequently, the United States abstained from justifying the occupation of Iraq in March 2003 as exercising preventive self-defence,[233] even though some scholars assume an orientation of the NSS 2002 towards an intervention in Iraq from the start.[234]

Even though the US Congress also authorised the President to use force in self-defence according to the principles of the Bush Doctrine in the resolution in which it authorised him to use force against Iraq,[235] President Bush did not make use of this authorisation. Instead, he referred to the unilateral enforcement of UN Security Council resolutions,[236] also included in the authorisation by Congress.[237] However, by the same token the justification put forward instead can be considered as a refusal of the United States to be bound by the limits of Article 51 of the UN Charter when using force unilaterally.[238]

The deviation from previous US legal opinion, as expressed in the Bush Doctrine, leaves the question unanswered as to the degree to which this changed legal opinion constitutes an attempt at changing law.

4.2.3 Law-changing elements of the Bush Doctrine

The statements of the Bush Doctrine concerning the legality of the use of force are considered almost unanimously not as a reproduction of the

232 See above, Chapter 3, sections 3.6.2.3.3 and 3.6.3.

233 UN Doc. S/2003/351; O. Dörr, 'Das völkerrechtliche Gewaltverbot am Beginn des 21. Jahrhunderts – Was bleibt von Art. 2(4) UN-Charta?', in Dörr (ed.), *Ein Rechtslehrer in Berlin – Symposium für Albrecht Randelzhofer*, p. 43; C. von Buttlar, 'Rechtsstreit oder Glaubensstreit?', in Bröhmer *et al.* (eds.), *Internationale Gemeinschaft und Menschenrechte*, FS-Ress, pp. 18–19; on the justification brought forward by the United States see further: S. Sharma, 'The American Doctrine of "Pre-emptive Self-Defence"', I.J.I.L., 43 (2003), 2, 215–30. On the British justification see: C. Warbrick and D. McGoldrick, 'Current Developments – Public International Law', I.C.L.Q., 51 (2003), 811–14; T. Gazzini, 'The Rules on the Use of Force at the Beginning of the XXI Century', J.C.S.L., 11 (2006), 319–42 at 325.

234 Murphy, *The United States and the Rule of Law in International Affairs*, pp. 169–76; Gray, 'The US National Security Strategy and the New "Bush Doctrine" on Preemptive Self-Defense', p. 443; B. Lombardi, 'The "Bush Doctrine" and Anticipatory Self-defence', Int.Spectator, 37 (2002), 105; R. Litwak, 'The New Calculus of Pre-emption', Survival, 44 (2002), 4, 60.

235 M. Schmitt, 'Preemptive Strategies in International Law', Mich.J.I.L., 24 (2003), 528.

236 Authorization for the Use of Military Force Against Iraq, Resolution of 2002, Public Law No. 107–243, 116 Stat., pp. 1498–99, 1501.

237 UN Doc. S/2003/35. On the justification for the intervention in Iraq in 2003, see W. Taft and T. Buchwald, 'Preemption, Iraq and International Law', A.J.I.L. 97 (2003), 557–63.

238 C. Tomuschat, 'Iraq – Demise of International Law?', Friedens-Warte/J.I.P.O., 78 (2003), 141–60, 154 *et seq.*

law in force, but as a claim to change the law in force.[239] The assent of the other states required for such a change of law has hitherto been lacking. A right of preventive self-defence has also been rejected by the other states after the US intervention in Iraq in 2003.[240] The states of the European Union have spoken out against preventive use of force in their June 2003 declaration of strategy against the proliferation of weapons of mass destruction, and emphasised that they give precedence to multilateral approaches.[241] Even though single statements by the Australian Prime Minister, John Howard, in December 2002 can be understood as an acceptance of preventive, unilateral use of force,[242] the community of other states has spoken out (for example, within the UN General Assembly) specifically against legalising that type of use of force.[243] UN Secretary General, Kofi Annan, explained clearly his rejection of unilateral, preventive use of force,[244] as did the group of experts appointed by him in December 2004 in their final report, the High Level Panel Report on Threats, Challenges and Change.[245]

However, the question arises as to which change of law in detail should be promoted by the Bush Doctrine and how international law could be organised in a way that would allow the use of force based on the principles of the Bush Doctrine to be admissible.

4.2.3.1 Attempt at establishing unilateral authority to act through the Bush Doctrine?

Supporters of the opinion that there is a necessity to adjust the current law to the principles for the use of force in the Bush Doctrine usually emphasise the hint at multilateral solutions in the NSS 2002, which express

239 See above, section 4.2.2.2.

240 Henderson, 'The Bush Doctrine: From Theory to Practice', pp. 1, 10–12.

241 *Basic Principles for an EU Strategy against Proliferation of WMD*, 16 June 2003, available at: http://europa-eu-un.org/articles/lt/article_2478_lt.htm. On this see: D. Daniel, P. Dombrowski and R. Payne, 'The Bush Doctrine: Rest in Peace?', Defence Studies, 4 (2004), 1, 18–39, who use the label 'Solana Doctrine' for the EU strategy (p. 21).

242 N. Frankland, 'Australia Supports Pre-emptive Strikes', *The Guardian*, 2 December 2002.

243 Henderson, 'The Bush Doctrine: From Theory to Practice', pp. 1, 12, with further references.

244 UN Secretary General, Address to General Assembly, 23 September 2003, available at: www.un.org/webcast/ga/58/statements/sg2eng030923.htm.

245 UN Report of the Secretary General's High-level Panel on Threats, Challenges and Change, 'A More Secure World: Our Shared Responsibility, p. 63, para. 191, available at: www.un.org/ secureworld/report2.pdf.

the subordinate meaning of the unilateral use of force foreseen only as *ultima ratio*.[246]

On the other hand, followers of the opinion that the principles of the NSS 2002 for the use of force are against international law and that the creation of corresponding rules of international law are not desirable, tend to emphasise the low importance that the NSS 2002 attributes to international mechanisms for solving conflicts.[247] Unilateral action is not only seen as an inferior option for action. Yet from the political context in which the doctrine has been declared, it follows that the legality of preventive use of force as stated within it does not at all constitute a claim for a universal right. Rather, this is seen as standing for an attempt to establish a unilateral authority to act solely for the United States.[248]

Prior to the declaration of the Bush Doctrine the question had already been brought up as to what extent US state practice constitutes an attempt at creating rules *sui generis* for the use of force. In view of the long existence of customary rules on the use of force, there seems to be hardly any room for the creation of special rules of this kind, for example, by assuming the role of a persistent objector.[249]

If, however, the deeper dogmatic rooting of this desire to establish rules *sui generis* is taken into consideration, changes of that kind seem possible. If, prior to that change, the rules for the creation of law experience a change in that special rules for the creation of law (different from those governing the creation of law by other states) are in force for the sole superpower as hegemon, change seems possible.[250]

In 1995, Brownlie wrote in this context about a 'hegemonial approach to international law-making'.[251] The judicial consequences of hegemony, or a unipolar international system, have received special attention within

246 Wedgwood, 'The Fall of Saddam Hussein: Security Council Mandates and Preemptive Self-Defense', p. 583.

247 Franck, 'What Happens Now? The United Nations After Iraq', pp. 619–20.

248 T. Farer, 'Beyond the UN Charter Frame: Unilateralism or Codominium', A.J.I.L., 96 (2002), 360; D. Murswiek, 'Die amerikanische Präventivkriegsstrategie und das Völkerrecht', NJW, (2003), 1019; D. Murswiek, 'Das exklusive Recht zum Angriff', in Ambos and Arnold (eds,), *Der Irak-Krieg und das Völkerrecht*, pp. 282–4.

249 M. Byers, 'The Shifting Foundations of International Law: A Decade of Forceful Measures against Iraq', E.J.I.L., 13 (2002), 1, 30.

250 G. Symes, 'Force without Law, Seeking a Legal Justification for the September 1996 U.S. Military Intervention in Iraq', Mich.J.I.L., 19 (1998), 616.

251 I. Brownlie, 'International Law at the Fiftieth Anniversary of the United Nations', RdC, 255 (1995), 32–3.

the scholarship of international law under the heading 'hegemonic international law'.[252] The consequences for international law were under discussion among scholars well before 11 September 2001.[253]

As hegemony is the expression of a considerable difference in power, a tension exists between the normative claim of sovereign equality, as laid down in Article 2(1) of the UN Charter, and the factual state of hegemony, because hegemony describes relations between states based on superordination and subordination rather than on equality and mutuality.[254]

These tensions between international legal order and the possible courses of action of a hegemon in a unipolar system (expressed particularly clearly by reference to the principle of sovereign equality) have been subject to intense scrutiny in political science.[255] The alternating behaviour of the hegemon between compliance with the law and breaking the law is described in the course of this as 'the paradox of hegemony'.[256]

Even though the unparalleled scope of power of the hegemon and other states may have found gradual recognition in international law (for example, by granting the right of veto in the Security Council), it has been assumed hitherto by the vast majority of scholars that hegemonic policy lacks a foundation in international law.[257]

Hegemonic international law describes a state of public international law in which the position of the hegemon has received recognition in international law by achieving special rights. Providing that such a hegemonic international law is considered desirable, supporters of this idea even deem a hierarchy of norms between the domestically determined intention of the hegemon – more precisely the US Constitution – and

252 D. Vagts, 'Hegemonic International Law', A.J.I.L., 95 (2001), 843–8.

253 For example, ASIL Proceedings, 94th Annual Meeting, 2000, pp. 64–70.

254 K. Ginther, 'Hegemony', E.P.I.L., II (1995), 685–8; A. Alvarez, 'Hegemonic International Law Revisited', pp. 873–88; H. Triepel, *Die Hegemonie: ein Buch von führenden Staaten* (Stuttgart: Kohlhammer, 1938), pp. 125 *et seq.*

255 B. Kubbig, 'The US Hegemony in the "American Century": The State of the Art and the German Contributions', American Studies, 46 (2001), 4, 1–22.

256 According to this theory, a hegemon is forced to alternate between unilateralism and multilateralism, in order not to endanger (due to his wider options for action than other states) the rules favouring his hegemony through his behaviour. On this see further: B. Cronin, 'The Paradox of Hegemony: America's Ambiguous Relationship with the United Nations', Eu.J.I.R., 7 (2001), 1, 103–30; Similarly: N. Krisch, 'Amerikanische Hegemonie und Liberale Revolution im Völkerrecht', Der Staat, 43 (2004), 267–97; N. Krisch, 'International Law in Times of Hegemony: Unequal Power and the Shaping of the International Legal Order', E.J.I.L., 16 (2005), 369–408 at 378–80.

257 Ginther, 'Hegemony', E.P.I.L., II (1995), 687–8.

the international legal order to be desirable.[258] A tendency of the United States since the mid-1980s to accept new treaties of international law only if they merely re-state US domestic law,[259] supports the assumption of a US-American desire for the creation of a hegemonic international law.

A hegemonic international law of that kind obviously contravenes the prohibition of intervention in Article 2(1) of the UN Charter, just as the prohibition of force in Article 2(4) of the UN Charter provided a right to use force vested within it. The Roosevelt Corollary to the Monroe Doctrine,[260] containing the claim of a right to use force in the western hemisphere, can be considered a classic example of a hegemonic-designed international law. There is an obvious parallel between the Roosevelt Corollary[261] and the demand not to limit the opportunity of the United States to use force unilaterally, as advanced by the supporters of a hegemonic international law.[262] Authors who believe in the conformity of the Bush Doctrine with the UN Charter, or at least the political necessity that preventive use of force as laid out by the Bush Doctrine should be admissible under the Charter, consequently draw upon a statement by Elihu Roots in 1914 on the Monroe Doctrine as a reasoning:[263]

> the exercise of the right of self-protection may and frequently does extend in its effect beyond the limits of the territorial jurisdiction of the state exercising it . . . the very same principle which underlies the Monroe Doctrine; that is to say, upon the right of every sovereign state, to protect itself by preventing a condition of affairs in which it will be too late to protect itself.[264]

Root described aptly the basic dilemma of the legal regulation of the use force, which is also considered under the UN Charter, as a weakness of the opinion which deems an armed attack as compelling necessity – that a state which will possibly be the victim of an armed attack may

258 J. Bolton, 'Is There Really "Law" in International Affairs?', T.L.C.P., 10 (2000), 48.

259 N. Krisch, 'Weak as Constraint, Strong as Tool: The Place of International Law in U.S. Foreign Policy', in Y. F. Khong and D. M. Malone (eds.), *Unilateralism and U.S. Foreign Policy* (Boulder, CO: Rienner, 2003), p. 61.

260 On this see further above, Chapter 2, section 2.1.2.2.

261 Vagts, 'Hegemonic International Law', p. 846.

262 Bolton, 'Is There Really "Law" in International Affairs?', p. 48.

263 R. Wedgwood, 'The Fall of Saddam Hussein: Security Council Mandates and Preemptive Self-Defense', p. 585; Yoo, 'International Law and the War in Iraq', p. 572, who quotes a Memorandum of the Assistant Attorney General of 30 August 1962, in which in turn the aforementioned statement by Root is quoted.

264 E. Root, 'The Real Monroe Doctrine', A.J.I.L., 8 (1914), 432.

not choose the most favourable moment in order to use counterforce.[265] This is also the starting point for the critique of the supporters of a wide interpretation of the term 'imminence' (as requiring no temporary proximity of the realisation of the threat) against the opposing opinion, which in consequence considers the principles of the Bush Doctrine as *contra legem*.[266]

Even though Root emphasised the unilateral character of the Monroe Doctrine,[267] his description of the doctrine contradicts what is today described as hegemonic international law. He instead stressed that the doctrine does not foresee rights of the United States towards other states and also does not limit the sovereignty of other states, but that these limitations result only from the sovereignty of other states.[268]

Actually it was certainly not the intention of the United States to promote the concept of 'pre-emptive strikes' formulated in the NSS 2002 as a general rule of law,[269] yet this can be derived only from its context, not from the chosen type of declaration.

For Michael Reisman, it lies vested in the nature of a political doctrine that it contains a claim for exception.[270] By its function the doctrine is a declaration of political principles of US security policy. However, as it contains at the same time an assertion of law, it also stipulates an abstract principle when the use of force is deemed legal.

Just like the description of the Bush Doctrine in the NSS 2002, a right to which all are entitled is described in the interpretation of the Monroe Doctrine by Root. By declaring such a principle in the shape of a doctrine, this does not constitute a claim for breaking the principle of sovereign equality to the extent of a change of law. The claim for a special right can be derived at best from the context due to the special means of action for the United States. The hint at the circumstance that a demand for such a unilateral authorisation for action can be derived only from these

265 K. Hailbronner, 'Die Grenzen des völkerrechtlichen Gewaltverbots', DGVR-Berichte, 26 (1986), 80–4.

266 See above, section 4.2.2.2.2.2.

267 See above, Chapter 2, section 2.1.3.3.1.

268 Root, 'The Real Monroe Doctrine', pp. 436, 439.

269 Gray, 'The US National Security Strategy and the New "Bush Doctrine" on Preemptive Self-Defense', pp. 446–7; Tomuschat, 'Völkerrecht ist kein Zweiklassenrecht', p. 45; J. Rose, 'Die Schlacht zum Feind tragen', in D. S. Lutz and H. Gießmann (eds.), *Stärke des Rechts oder das Recht des Stärkeren* (Baden-Baden: Nomos, 2003), pp. 146–7; C. Kegley and G. Raymond, 'Preventive War and Permissive Normative Order', I.S.P., 4 (2003), 391–3.

270 M. Reisman, 'Assessing Claims to Revise the Laws of War', p. 90.

interests[271] includes the concession that the NSS 2002 itself does not ask for such a right.[272] Hence, such an intention only constitutes a motive irrelevant for the creation of law, but does not count as *opinio iuris.*[273]

If the Bush Doctrine as formulated in the NSS 2002 is interpreted as a demand for a far-reaching change of law, a breach of the principle of sovereign equality and a special right to the use of force, the principles of the Bush Doctrine for the use of force consequently seem at odds not only with the current rules for the use of force, but also with the principle of sovereign equality. (One could also say that this applies only if it is interpreted to the disadvantage of the United States.)

The Bush Doctrine, however, contains according to the NSS, in spite of the almost unanimously assumed statement *de lege ferenda* due to the abandonment of temporal proximity of the realisation of a threat,[274] no demand for the creation of a rule of international law *sui generis.* No existence of such a rule is claimed by the United States in the sense of *opinio iuris.*[275] Nor does a possibility of locking up the basic concept of the NSS 2002 as a general rule of law exist due to the fundamental contradiction with the principle of sovereign equality such a rule would exhibit.[276]

Even though the statement by Root, quoted as evidence for the legitimacy of the Bush Doctrine, was stipulated during the phase of the Monroe Doctrine as an instrument of US hegemony, Root explicitly pays allegiance to the principle of sovereign equality:

> The fundamental principle of international law is the principle of independent sovereignty. Upon that all other rules of international law rest . . . The Monroe Doctrine does not infringe upon that right. It asserts the right.[277]

271 D. Murswiek, 'Die amerikanische Präventivkriegsstrategie und das Völkerrecht', NJW, (2003), 1019.

272 Gray, *International Law and the Use of Force*, pp. 218 *et seq.*; N. Wheeler, 'The Bush Doctrine: The Dangers of American Exceptionalism in a Revolutionary Age', Asian Perspective, 27 (2003), 183–216.

273 Byers, *Custom, Power and the Power of Rules: International Relations and Customary International Law*, pp. 147–51.

274 See above, section 4.2.3.2.

275 This interpretation of the NSS would match the interests of a hegemon according to the theory of the paradox of hegemony. On this in general see: B. Cronin, 'The Paradox of Hegemony: America's Ambiguous Relationship with the United Nations', pp. 103–30; C. Kupchan, 'After Pax Americana: Benign Power, Regional Integration, and the Sources of Stable Multipolarity', Int.Sec., 23 (1998), 3, 63–83; with close reference to the Bush Doctrine: A. Hurrell, '"There are no Rules" (George W. Bush): International Order after September 11', Int.Rel. 16 (2002), 188–9.

276 Tomuschat, 'Völkerrecht ist kein Zweiklassenrecht', p. 45.

277 Root, 'The Real Monroe Doctrine', p. 434.

Regardless of the question as to what extent the practice of interventions by the United States at the time of the statement by Root matched with the principle formulated in his statement, and regardless of whether this matter constitutes an adequate description of the Monroe Doctrine under the Roosevelt Corollary (which seems highly doubtful), this emphasises that the basic principle is upheld. However, Root emphasises that duties derive from sovereignty and the United States could insist on compliance with these duties.[278] This included in context with the Roosevelt Corollary the forceful enforcement of this compliance.[279]

Obligations flowing from sovereignty are emphasised within the NSS 2002 in close connection with the declaration of the Bush Doctrine: the announcement of an intention to act if necessary by exercising preventive self-defence against terrorists is followed by the announcement of the necessity of compelling states to fulfil their responsibilities.[280]

It is, however, questionable if possible limitations of sovereignty go so far that a right to use force against other states follows from this, let alone a right that leaves room for use of force according to principles of the Bush Doctrine.

4.2.3.2 The Bush Doctrine as a demand for sovereignty reinforced by sanctions?

Not only rights but also duties flow from sovereignty.[281] The duty of a state to protect another state from damaging actions emerging from its territory, like acts of terror directed against the other state, is one of those.[282]

Yet it is questionable if such a duty is reinforced by sanctions, so that a violation of this duty entitles other states to enforce the compliance with this duty by force. The fact that a state failed to comply with its obligations towards other states does not at the same time confer a right upon other states to become active against this breach of duty, let alone

278 'the sovereign rights of every other American republic would have been limited by the equal sovereign rights of every other American republic, including the United States. The United States would have the right to demand from every other American State observance of treaty obligations and of the rules of international law . . . The United States would have the right to demand from every other American State to object to acts which the United States might deem injurious to its peace and safety . . .' Root, 'The Real Monroe Doctrine', p. 436.

279 On this see further above, Chapter 2, section 2.1.3.1.

280 NSS 2002, p. 6: 'We will disrupt and destroy terrorist organizations by: . . . compelling states to accept their sovereign responsibilities . . .'

281 PCA, *Island of Palmas Case* (*U.S.* v. *Netherlands*), R.I.A.A. 1928, pp. 829, 839.

282 Frowein, 'Der Terrorismus als Herausforderung für das Völkerrecht', p. 883.

a justification to use force.[283] The declaration in the NSS 2002 to force states if necessary to fulfil their duties, suggests, that the United States favours an understanding of sovereignty reinforced by sanctions.[284]

Illuminating with regard to the US-American opinion on this matter according to the Bush Doctrine, is a statement by Richard Haas, then Policy Planning Director in the State Department, in *The New Yorker* in April 2002:

> What you are seeing in this administration is the emergence of a new principle or body of ideas . . . about what we might call the limits of sovereignty. Sovereignty entails obligations. One is not to massacre your own people. Another is not to support terrorism in any way. If a Government fails to meet these obligations, then it forfeits some of the normal advantages of sovereignty, including the right to be left alone inside your own territory . . .[285]

The idea of creating an opportunity to enforce duties following from sovereignty through the international community has received a boost due to the ethnic conflicts after 1990. Thus, the Evans–Sahnoun Commission, established by the Canadian Government, assumed the emergence of a 'responsibility to protect' of states towards their own population flowing from sovereignty. In case a state should not tend to this duty, the international community shall be obligated to take care of the fulfilment of this 'responsibility to protect', and interference in internal affairs in that case would not be contrary to the prohibition on intervention.[286]

In turn, this thought has been supplemented by voices among scholars of international law with the demand that the international community should also be collectively obliged to prevent regimes without internal democratic control from obtaining weapons of mass destruction ('duty to prevent').[287]

The NSS 2002 adheres to this claim with regard to the underlying understanding of sovereignty, in as much as it claims an authorisation to intervene in cases where a state is either unwilling or unable to eliminate

283 M. Reisman, 'Legal Responses to International Terrorism', Hous.J.I.L., 22 (1999), 54.

284 On changes of the US-American understanding of sovereignty see further: A. Cronin, 'Rethinking Sovereignty: American Strategy in the Age of Terrorism', Survival, 44 (2002), 2, 119–39. On this in general see: G. Nolte, 'Zum Wandel des Souveränitätsbegriffs', *Frankfurter Allgemeine Zeitung*, 6 April 2005, p. 8.

285 Quoted after: J. Ikenberry, 'America's Imperial Ambition', pp. 5, 52.

286 Canadian Department of Foreign Affairs and International Trade (ed.), *The Responsibility to Protect: Report of the International Commission on Intervention and State Sovereignty* (Ottawa: International Development Research Centre, 2002)

287 L. Feinstein and A-M. Slaughter, 'A Duty to Prevent', For.Aff., 83 (2004), 1, 136–50.

the danger of use of weapons of mass destruction emerging from its territory.[288] However, the Bush Doctrine goes beyond this proposition by considering preventive self-defence as justified in principle, thus promoting an extension of the unilateral authority to use force.[289]

The idea of limitations of sovereignty, from which a right to use force follows, can be found likewise in the Soviet Brezhnev Doctrine. In this respect the Bush Doctrine also shows a parallel with the Roosevelt Corollary to the Monroe Doctrine, as within it a right to use force was claimed by referring to duties flowing from sovereignty.[290] Just as the Brezhnev Doctrine and its subsequent practice challenge the principle of sovereign equality, so the Bush Doctrine challenges the principle of sovereign equality.

Yet the Bush Doctrine does not contain a claim for a special rule of international law which would permit the use of force for the United States alone as a hegemon, because this only follows from the context of the declaration.[291] The formulation in the NSS building on sovereignty ('compelling states to accept their sovereign responsibilities') does not allow for the conclusion that a special right for the United States is requested.

Furthermore, a clear difference has to be made between the principle of sovereign equality and the prohibition on intervention in Article 2(1) of the UN Charter (resulting from it) and the prohibition on force in Article 2(4) of the UN Charter, because no right to use force can be derived from limitations on sovereignty or a waiving of sovereignty alone.[292] Neither can the prohibition of force as a common good of the community be 'waived' by a single state by making concessions to another state,[293] and this principle has not been challenged by the United States.[294]

288 W. Nagan and C. Hammer, 'The New Bush National Security Doctrine and the Rule of Law', Berk.J.I.L., 22 (2004), 428–33.

289 See above, section 4.2.1.

290 B. Meissner, *Die 'Breshnew-Doktrin' – Das Prinzip des proletarisch-sozialistischen Internationalismus und die Theorie von den 'verschiedenen Wegen zum Sozialismus'* (Cologne: Verlag Wissenschaft und Politik, 1969), pp. 34–38; D. Schröder, 'Die Idee der kollektiven Regionalintervention – Rechtsvergleichende Betrachtungen zur Breshnew-Doktrin', Recht in Ost und West, 13 (1969), 203 *et seq.*

291 See above, section 4.2.3.1.

292 T. Schweisfurth, 'Breschnjew-Doktrin als Norm des Völkerrechts?', Aussenpolitik, 21 (1970), 523

293 Randelzhofer, 'Art. 2(4)', in Simma (ed.) *The Charter of the United Nations*, p. 129. paras. 51–52.

294 Higgins, 'The Attitude of Western States Towards Legal Aspects of the Use of Force', in Cassese (ed.), *The Current Legal Regulation of the Use of Force*, pp. 436–40.

Only if certain types of anti-terrorist use of force are not covered by the prohibition on force would a unilateral use of force according to the principles of the Bush Doctrine be admissible. In particular, with regard to 'failed states' it is questionable whether a lower threshold for preventive action when using force against terrorists in these states may exist. It has been claimed that the prohibition on force in Article 2(4) of the UN Charter should at least not possess full validity with regard to anti-terror use of force in 'failed states' and has to be constrained to that effect, that at least the use of force against terrorists has to be considered as legal.[295] Yet, as the hitherto prevailing practice of states proves, it has to be assumed that in spite of the loss of effective state authority the territory of a 'failed state' still enjoys the comprehensive protection of the prohibition on force.[296] Hence, preventive use of force in terms of the Bush Doctrine cannot be justified by a limited validity of the prohibition of force.

Instead, the question arises whether the general prohibition on force has undergone an extension to the end that a state is increasingly obliged to actively suppress terrorist groups within its territory or to enable a suppression of their activity.[297] Only if inaction towards terrorist groups can be considered as 'substantial involvement' and, hence, as an 'armed attack' would a right of self-defence follow from that.[298] Yet preventive self-defence in terms of the Bush Doctrine cannot be justified based on a changed understanding of sovereignty or a sovereignty reinforced by sanctions.

Even though the NSS 2002 does emphasise the duties deriving from sovereignty and announces the enforcement of complying with these duties, it is not possible to conclude from this that such enforcement will inevitably take the shape of unilateral use of force.

4.2.4 Conclusion

Just like prior doctrines, the Bush Doctrine is considered by the United States as basically a reference to an already existing legal position and not

295 Reisman, 'International Legal Responses to Terrorism', pp. 41 *et seq.*

296 On this see in detail: D. Thürer, 'The "Failed State" and International Law', I.R.R.C., 836 (1999), 731–61.

297 Frowein, 'Der Terrorismus als Herausforderung für das Völkerrecht', pp. 883 *et seq.*

298 *Military and Paramilitary Activities in und against Nicaragua* (*Nicaragua* v. *United States of America*), Merits, Judgment, I.C.J. Rep. 1986, pp. 93–4, No. 195. See further above, section 4.2.2.2.1.3.

as a demand for the creation of a new legal position. However, the Bush Doctrine, in contrast to prior doctrines, contains an explicit claim for the adjustment of the given law to a strategic concept. This requirement is vested in the demand for an adjustment of the interpretation of the term 'imminence'. The result of the abandonment of a temporary proximate realisation of a threat as prerequisite for the use of force in self-defence declared in the doctrine, is the illegality of the use of force according to the principles of the Bush Doctrine.

No matter in which legal context one places the *Caroline* formula, whether it is understood as an aid in order to determine the occurrence of an armed attack or as a description of the factual prerequisites for the exercise of self-defence, the reference in the NSS 2002 to the criterion of imminence or the imminent realisation of a threat remains a claim for a change of law.[299]

The Bush Doctrine abandons the criterion of an 'armed attack' as prerequisite for the exercise of self-defence. Also, a possible extension of the term 'armed attack' after 11 September 2001 does not change the categorisation of the principles of the Bush Doctrine for the use of force as illegal. As the term 'armed attack' in case of acts of terror refers to the combination of supporting action and act of terror, a supporting action alone does not suffice in order to consider an armed attack as having begun in the sense of the theory of 'incipient self-defence'.

Even if the occurrence of an armed attack is considered as not necessary due to the continued existence of a customary right of self-defence, the principles of the doctrine for the use of force have to be considered as illegal under international law due to the abandonment of the temporary proximity of the realisation of a threat.

Only if the *Caroline* formula is considered merely as an aid for the determination of a generally described necessity, can the general abandonment of temporary proximity of the realisation of a threat be considered as a restatement of the law in force. However, even supporters of an extensive interpretation of a customary right of self-defence do not favour this interpretation. Even though large parts of the wording of the Bush Doctrine, as described in the NSS 2002 ('sufficient threat', 'pre-emptive action', 'emergence of a threat'), are terms in need of interpretation which leave room for an interpretation of conformity with the Charter, such an

299 Likewise: T. D. Gill, 'The Temporal Dimension of Self-defense: Anticipation, Pre-emption, Prevention and Immediacy', in Schmitt and Pejic (eds.), *International Law and Armed Conflict: Exploring the Faultlines*, pp. 113–55 at 154–5.

interpretation is impossible for the explicitly declared abandonment of a temporary proximity.[300]

Since the declaration of the Roosevelt Corollary to the Monroe Doctrine in 1904,[301] this is the first doctrine of US security policy in which the principles cannot be brought in accord with the law in force, even when making an effort to find an interpretation of these principles in conformity with international law.[302]

In spite of declaring in the NSS 2002 that the United States had historically reserved a right to take preventive action, the Bush Doctrine breaks with previous US legal opinion on anticipated and preventive self-defence. The Bush Doctrine turns away from previous US legal opinion in two ways: (1) the abandonment of armed attack as a compulsory necessary prerequisite for the exercise of self-defence; and (2) the extension of the right of anticipated of self-defence to the end that no temporary proximate realisation of a threat is necessary. Due to the lack of determination with regard to the sources of the right of self-defence in the past, as within the Bush Doctrine itself, such a limitlessly wide interpretation of this right has, however, never been explicitly denied by the United States.

The attempt to establish in international law a unilateral authorisation to act in the shape of rules *sui generis* for the use of force for the United States is not made by the Bush Doctrine. Only by including factual considerations and the special options for action by the United States can a striving for extended freedom of action for the United States be derived from the context. However, rules *sui generis* are neither claimed nor aspired to in the sense of *opinio iuris*.

Just as it has been the case in connection with the Roosevelt Corollary to the Monroe Doctrine, duties resulting from sovereignty are emphasised in connection with the Bush Doctrine. That a violation of these duties will give other states a right to take action against these violating states is also expressed in the NSS 2002. Even though duties resulting from sovereignty are emphasised in the NSS 2002 and the enforcement of

300 See above, section 4.2.1. 301 See above, Chapter 2, section 2.1.2.3.

302 On the similarities between the Bush Doctrine and the Monroe Doctrine see: J. de Wilde, 'Mondialisering van de Monroe Doctrine', International Spectator, 57 (2003), 346–52; N. Paech, 'Interventionsimperialismus – Von der Monroe – zur Bush-Doktrin', *Blätter für deutsche und Internationale Politik*, 48 (2003), 1258–68. Similarly: A. Kreutzer, *Preemptive Self-Defense, Die Bush-Doktrin und das Völkerrecht* (Munich: M-Press, 2004), pp. 138–46, who assumes on top of that a parallel between Bush Doctrine and 'Großraumtheorie' (without discussing the later concept).

compliance with these duties is announced, due to linguistic ambiguities of this declaration it cannot be concluded that this enforcement shall necessarily take the shape of the unilateral use of force according to the Bush Doctrine.

Certainly, 2009 is too early to evaluate in full what impacts on international law the Bush Doctrine has had. Provided that the legality of the use of force has changed through the Bush Doctrine or the subsequent practice of the United States, changes of rules are still in the process of creation and subject to intense discussion.[303] Changes in the debate among scholars will be discussed in Chapter 5.[304]

Due to the failure of the United States to argue along the lines of the Bush Doctrine when justifying the occupation of Iraq in March 2003,[305] it may be assumed that the United States followed advice to interpret the Bush Doctrine restrictively.[306] Yet this would require an acceptance of the criterion of temporary proximity of the realisation of a threat. This would mean such a fundamental deviation from the principles of the Bush Doctrine that it could be viewed as at least partially abandoned. However, in the NSS 2006 the Bush Administration basically reaffirmed the principles of this controversial doctrine for the use of force.[307] Whether the Obama Administration has abandoned the Bush Doctrine will be discussed in section 4.3 below.

4.3 The 'Obama Doctrine'?

The Bush Doctrine was announced at a point in time regarded as the heyday of a generally hostile approach by the United States towards international law.[308] Just like the Roosevelt Corollary to the Monroe Doctrine

303 Byers, 'Terrorism, the Use of Force and International Law after 11 September', pp. 413–14; L. Damrosh and B. Oxman 'Agora: Future Implications of the Iraq Conflict, Editors' Note', A.J.I.L., 97 (2003), 553–7, 803–4.

304 See below, section 4.3.2.

305 J. Murphy, 'Is US Adherence to the Rule of Law in International Affairs Feasible?', in Schmitt and Pejic (eds.), *International Law and Armed Conflict: Exploring the Faultlines*, pp. 197–227 at 204–11.

306 Stromseth, 'Law and Force after Iraq: A Transitional Moment', p. 636; Gray, *International Law and the Use of Force*, pp. 218 *et seq.*

307 V. Lowe, *International Law* (Oxford University Press, 2007), pp. 277–8; on the NSS 2006 see further below, section 4.3.2.

308 J. Ikenberry, 'The End of the Neo-Conservative Moment', Survival, 46 (2004), 7–22; A. Hurrell, *On Global Order* (Oxford University Press, 2007), pp. 280–1; C. Greenwood,

100 years earlier,[309] this doctrine challenged terms of the *ius ad bellum* which thus far were considered to be firmly established.

The scholarly, as well as the political, debate have undergone some changes since the Bush Doctrine was announced in the NSS 2002. Even before the end of the Bush Administration's term of office in 2009, the focus of the debate had shifted considerably. During the presidential campaign in 2007/8, 'change' became a popular watchword in the debate on US security policy and US policy in general.[310] Most commentators emphasise the remarkable changes in style and rhetoric of the US administration, considered as already being underway during the last years of the Bush Administration.[311] Since international law attributes rather little, if any, attention to matters of political style, and is not just about substance but the incarnation of the very essence of the interest of states,[312] changes of that kind will hardly be noted rapidly in the arena of international law. This applies even more so to the core of the legal regulation on the use of force. The slow mechanisms for change and the creation of international law are naturally averse to quick changes. Nevertheless, perceptions matter – in international relations even more so than is the case for the creation and interpretation of international law.[313]

In the following section an attempt will be made to analyse whether these noted changes of style are matched by substantial changes in US security policy and attitudes towards the legality of the use of force under international law. This raises the question of whether these changes could possibly amount to the announcement of a new doctrine. Doctrinal statements stand out by their very nature; they mark turning points, real paradigmatic shifts in the focus of US security policy. But was the change of government in 2009 one of these paradigmatic shifts?

'International Law and the Pre-emptive Use of Force: Afghanistan, Al-Qaida and Iraq', in C. Greenwood (ed.), *Essays on War in International Law* (London: Cameron May, 2006), pp. 667–700 at 668.

309 See above, Chapter 2, section 2.1.6.

310 Obama for America (ed.): *Change We Can Believe In* (New York: Three Rivers Press, 2008).

311 D. Vagts, 'American International Law: A Sonderweg?', in K. Dicke *et al.* (eds.), *Weltinnenrecht – Liber amicorum Jost Delbrück* (Berlin: Duncker & Humblot, 2005), pp. 835–47 at 842–3.

312 Krisch, 'International Law in Times of Hegemony: Unequal Power and the Shaping of the International Legal Order', pp. 369–408.

313 V. Lowe, *International Law* (Oxford University Press, 2007), pp. 50 *et seq.*

4.3.1 Changes in the political debate: an emerging 'Obama Doctrine'?

Oblivious to critique by scholars and most notably the ICJ, in March 2006 the United States published the NSS 2006.[314] Though less heavy-handed in its rhetoric, it basically restated the concept of pre-emptive self-defence outlined in the NSS 2002.[315] Some explicit hints at the legal regulation of the use of force, such as the quote reminiscent of the *Caroline* formula still present in the NSS 2002, were notably dropped from the NSS 2006. Broad criteria for the use of force were at least moderated by repeated references to multilateralism,[316] unless one considers this dropping of specific references to international law an even further departure from the UN Charter.[317] Pre-emptive military action appeared to be foreseen only as used against a 'hard core of terrorists' impossible to deter by other means.[318] The discussion of pre-emption also occurs primarily in the section on weapons of mass destruction.[319] Nonetheless, pre-emptive use of force was still considered a possible course of action in the NSS 2006. However, the NSS 2006 added an explicit reference to the right of self-defence in connection with pre-emptive action, thus at least making clear that the basis for pre-emption can be found in self-defence.[320] The relevant passage for this gradual move away from explicit defiance of the recognised criteria for the use of force in self-defence reads as follows: 'To forestall or prevent such hostile acts by our adversaries, the United States will, if necessary act pre-emptively *in exercising our inherent right of self-defense*.'[321]

314 (NSS) 2006, available at: http://merln.ndu.edu/whitepapers/USnss2006.pdf; partially printed in J. Crook, 'Contemporary Practice of the United States Relating to International Law', A.J.I.L., 100 (2006), 690–724 at 690–1.

315 On this see: Crook, 'Contemporary Practice of the United States Relating to International Law', pp. 690–1; Gray, 'The Bush Doctrine Revisited: the 2006 National Security Strategy of the USA', pp. 555–78.

316 See M. Reisman and A. Armstrong, 'The Past and Future of the Claim of Preemptive Self-Defense', A.J.I.L., 100 (2006), 525–50 at 531–2.

317 M. O'Connell, 'Defending the Law against Preemptive Force', in Fischer-Lescano *et al.* (eds.), *Frieden in Freiheit – Peace in liberty – Paix en liberté, Festschrift für Michael Bothe zum 70. Geburtstag* (FS-Bothe), p. 245.

318 NSS 2006, p. 12

319 Schmitt, 'Responding to Transnational Terrorism under the *Jus ad bellum*', in Schmitt and Pejic (eds.), *International Law and Armed Conflict: Exploring the Faultlines*, pp. 159–95 at 190–1.

320 Gray, 'The Bush Doctrine Revisited: the 2006 National Security Strategy of the USA', pp. 555–78 at 563.

321 NSS 2006, p. 18 (added emphasis).

With the coming into office of a new US administration which has repeatedly voiced its intention to set a new tone in Washington, it remains to be seen what doctrinal developments the near future may hold. Two questions have to be distinguished: (1) was the Bush Doctrine abandoned?; and (2) was a new doctrine declared?

This leads to the problem that no criteria exist for doctrines or apply to them as does *desuetudo* for the creation and replacement of a rule of customary international law. Some commentators consider an explicit, outspoken declaration of abandonment of the doctrine as necessary in order to consider the doctrine abandoned.[322] Even if one adheres to this high standard for the abandonment of a doctrine and does not let a mere abstaining from arguing along the lines of a doctrine suffice, the Bush Doctrine and the principle of pre-emptive self-defence can no longer be considered a declared policy of the United States.

During the presidential campaign of 2007/8, virtually all candidates were eager to outline their foreign policy agenda[323] and tried to put some space between their concepts and the Bush Administration's foreign policy. Writing in July 2008 in *Foreign Affairs*, a statement by Barack Obama outlining the criteria for the uses of force almost seems to echo a phrase in the NSS 2002: 'I will not hesitate to use force, unilaterally if necessary, to protect the American people or our vital interests . . .'[324] The similar phrase in the NSS 2002 reads 'we will not hesitate to act alone, if necessary, to exercise our right of self-defence . . .' However, the way the phrase continues constitutes a decisive turn. While the NSS 2002 continues 'by acting pre-emptively against such terrorists, to prevent them from doing harm against our people and our country . . .',[325] Obama wrote: 'whenever we are attacked or imminently threatened'. At least this statement suggests adherence to the criterion of 'imminence' (or 'immediacy'), though its very existence has been recently doubted by some scholars.[326]

322 D. Fleck, 'Meiertöns, Heiko: Die Doktrinen U.S.-Amerikanischer Sicherheitspolitik', ZaÖRV/H.J.I.L., 67 (2007), 1391–3 (review of the German edition of this book).

323 H. Clinton, 'Security and Opportunity for the Twenty-First Century', For.Aff., 86/6 (2007), 2–18; J. Edwards, 'Reengaging with the World', For.Aff., 86/5 (2007), 19–37; R. Giuliani, 'Towards a Realistic Peace', For.Aff., 85/5 (2007), 1–18; J. McCain, 'An Enduring Peace Built on Freedom', For.Aff., 86/6 (2007), 19–39; B. Richardson, 'A New Realism', For.Aff., 87/1 (2008), 142–54; M. Huckabee, 'America's Priorities in the War on Terror', For.Aff., 87/1 (2008), 155–68.

324 B. Obama, 'Renewing American Leadership', For.Aff., 86/4 (2007), 2–16.

325 NSS 2002, p. 5.

326 M. Glennon, 'The Emerging Use-of-Force Paradigm', J.C.S.L., 11 (2006), 310–11.

A number of specific statements on intended changes in security policy have emerged from the new Obama Administration since coming into office in January 2009. In the first month of his term of office, President Obama called for 'a world without nuclear weapons',[327] reached out to Iran[328] and Russia,[329] and called for substantial improvement in relations between the United States and the Muslim world.[330] However, the most specific statements on matters of political doctrine and use of force have so far been made by Vice President Joe Biden. When asked in the Vice Presidential debate at Washington University on 2 October 2008 how a Biden Administration would differ from an Obama Administration in case he should ever accede to power, Vice President Biden announced that he would carry out Barack Obama's policy. One element of this would be 'a policy that would reject the Bush Doctrine of pre-emption and regime change and replace it with a doctrine of prevention and cooperation'.[331] In his capacity as newly elected Vice President, Joe Biden made a statement at the Munich Security Conference in February 2009 very much along the lines of his prior statement:

> we will strive to act preventively, not pre-emptively to avoid wherever possible choice of last resort between risks of war and the dangers of inaction.[332]

Though this constitutes a quite explicit abandonment of the Bush Doctrine, the substance of this statement should not be overestimated. When

327 The White House, Office of the Press Secretary, 3 April 2009, 'Remarks by President Obama at Strasbourg Town Hall', Strasbourg France, available at: www.whitehouse.gov/the_press_office/Remarks-by-President-Obama-at-Strasbourg-Town-Hall.

328 The White House, 19 March 2009, 'A New Year, A New Beginning', available at: www.whitehouse.gov/nowruz.

329 The White House, Office of the Press Secretary, 7 July 2009, 'Remarks by the President at the New Economic School Graduation, Gostinny Dvor, Moscow, Russia', available at: www.whitehouse.gov/the_press_office/REMARKS-BY-THE-PRESIDENT-AT-THE-NEW-ECONOMIC-SCHOOL-GRADUATION.

330 The White House, Office of the Press Secretary, 4 June 2009, 'Remarks by the President on a New Beginning', Cairo University, Egypt, available at: www.whitehouse.gov/the_press_office/Remarks-by-the-President-at-Cairo-University-6–04–09.

331 *The New York Times*, 2 December 2008, 'Transcript: The Vice-Presidential Debate', Senator Biden's opponent, Governor Palin (Rep., Alaska), did not voice any comparable statement on the Bush Doctrine, but was mainly noted for her staggering lack of knowledge of the Bush Doctrine, 'Transcript of Interview with Charlie Gibson on ABC, 11 September 2008', available at: http://abcnews.go.com/Politics/Vote2008/Story?id=5782924&page=1.

332 J. Biden, Speech at the 45th Munich Security Conference, 7 February 2009, available: www.securityconference.de/konferenzen/rede.php.

seen in the context of his speech, Vice President Biden left a backdoor open for the unilateral use of force by the United States, which is not necessarily in accordance with the strict criteria of the UN Charter. Before stating this explicit move away from the Bush Doctrine, Vice President Biden stated: 'we will work in partnership whenever we can, alone only when we must'. Yet a different focus is undeniable. Even though weapons of mass destruction still featured prominently in Biden's Munich speech, they were not mentioned in direct connection with terrorism and the use of force on the part of the United States. And in line with former doctrines, these statements are clearly open to interpretation in accordance with the UN Charter.

However, as outlined above the issue of whether a new doctrine has already emerged has to be distinguished from the question of whether the Bush Doctrine can be considered as abandoned. By the same token, a negative abandonment of an old doctrine does not necessarily put a new doctrine in its place. Publications by scholars and think-tanks were certainly not short of suggestions for 'blue prints' for the security policy of a US administration after 2009.[333] In this context, the term 'Obama Doctrine' has been used frequently by journalists and scholars.[334] It refers to different concepts which contain little reference to the *ius ad bellum* and instead serves to highlight the aforementioned changes in rhetoric. They do not necessarily treat criteria for the use of force in international relations with sufficient precision in order to evaluate them under international law. Thus, this so-called 'Obama Doctrine' does not constitute a doctrine in terms of the criteria for a doctrine on which this work is based.[335]

When questioned directly during the second presidential debate on 7 October at Belmont University, Nashville, Tennessee about what an 'Obama Doctrine' would look like,[336] Barack Obama gave the following answer:

333 D. Forsythe *et al.* (eds.), *American Foreign Policy in a Globalized World* (New York: Routledge, 2006); Leffler and Legro (eds.), *To Lead the World – American Strategy after the Bush Doctrine*; M. Fullilove, 'Hope or Glory? The Presidential Election and U.S. Foreign Policy', Brookings, Policy Paper No. 9, October 2008; J. Chin, 'Promoting Democracy: A Blueprint for the Next Administration', Policy Matters J. Spring 2008, 33–9.

334 S. Ackerman, 'The Obama Doctrine', *The American Prospect*, 24 March 2008; D. Klaidman, 'Defining the Obama Doctrine', Newsweek, 28 December 2009/4 January 2010, p. 8.

335 See above, Chapter 1, section 1.6.

336 Reply to a question by interviewer Tom Brokaw: 'What is the Obama Doctrine for use of force that the United States would send when we don't have national

> Well, we may not always have national security issues at stake, but we have moral issues at stake. If we could have intervened effectively in the Holocaust, who among us would say that we had a moral obligation not to go in? If we could've stopped Rwanda, surely, if we had the ability, that would be something that we would have to strongly consider and act. So when genocide is happening, when ethnic cleansing is happening somewhere around the world and we stand idly by, that diminishes us.
>
> And so I do believe that we have to consider it as part of our interests, our national interests, in intervening where possible.... We're not going to be able to be everywhere all the time. That's why it's so important for us to be able to work in concert with our allies...

Instead of outlining abstract criteria for when to use force, this statement begins by emphasising moral obligations and then outlines the limitations to the use of force. The focus and technique of this statement (not outlining when to use force but when *not* to use force) bear similarity to the so-called Powell and Clinton doctrines of the 1990s.[337] Just like President Clinton, President Obama emphasised the preservation of elements of the security policy of his predecessor. In his speech on the State of the Nation on 24 February 2009, President Obama pointed out that fighting terrorism is still one of the top priorities of US security policy:

> with our friends and allies, we will forge a new and comprehensive strategy for Afghanistan and Pakistan to defeat al Qaeda and combat extremism. Because I will not allow terrorists to plot against the American people from safe havens half a world away.

A changed attitude towards the use of force can thus be found instead in the subtext and context of the speech, and are therefore well below the threshold of a legally relevant statement in terms of *opinio iuris.*

The most notable point is probably what Obama and Biden abstained from saying. President George W. Bush started out his letter introducing the NSS 2006 with the controversial statement 'America is at war.'[338] The fixation on the term 'war' by non-lawyers is not a new experience for international lawyers, who are more prone to use the more apt term 'armed conflict'. In particular, the inflationary use of the term 'war' has repeatedly aggrieved scholars of international law.[339] Christine Gray, for

security issues at stake?', Debate Transcript, The Second McCain–Obama Presidential Debate, 7 October 2008, Commission on Presidential Debates, available at: www.debates.org/pages/trans2008c.html.

337 See above, sections 4.1.2 and 2.1.3.

338 NSS 2006, p.1.

339 B. Ackerman, 'This is Not a War', Y.L.J., 13 (2004), 1871–907; Mégret, '"War"? Legal Semantics and the Move to Violence', pp. 361–99; A. Cassese, 'Terrorism is also Disrupting Some Crucial Categories of International Law', E.J.I.L., 12 (2001), 993–1001.

example, aptly puts the label 'war on terror' in brackets.[340] Even without adhering to the critical international law school of thought and without aiming at 'deconstructing' international law,[341] it is worthwhile examining the subconscious changes and adjustments which may result from this in the future.

The term 'war on terror' highlights a rhetorical lopsidedness: 'terror' is – in spite of all the problems of finding a concise definition of the term[342] – in the first place merely a strategic concept which cannot be fought irrespective of its political aims.[343] Just as it is impossible to declare war on 'area bombing' or 'tank warfare', it is impossible to declare war on 'terror' as such.[344] 'War on terror' is actually an anti-strategic label.[345] This label ignores a principle already outlined in 1830 by Carl von Clausewitz – an often quoted but unfortunately rarely read author.[346] According to this principle, political purpose and strategic means cannot be discussed separately.[347] Clausewitz's well known and frequently misunderstood dictum 'War is the continuation of politics by other means',[348] thus actually describes the way things ought to be (*Sollvorschrift*), not the way they actually are. This term ('war on terror') may be only the most obvious example of the sneaky dilution of terminology and challenges for the clarity of the *ius ad bellum* rooted, *inter alia*, in the Bush Doctrine.[349]

It is currently (2009) too early to say how a possibly emerging 'Obama Doctrine' or the NSS 2010 will differ from the NSS 2006. Yet what is

340 Gray, *International Law and the Use of Force*, pp. 234 *et seq.*

341 M. Koskenniemi, *From Apology to Utopia, the Structure of International Legal Argument* (Helsinki: Lakimiesliiton, 1989), pp. 458–501.

342 P. Wilkinson, 'Liberal State Responses to Terrorism and Their Limits', in A. Bianchi and A. Keller (eds.), *Counterterrorism: Democracy's Challenge* (Oxford: Hart Publishing, 2008), pp. 71–5.

343 J. Kiras, *Terrorism and Irregular Warfare*, in J. Baylis *et al.* (eds.), *Strategy in the Contemporary World – An Introduction to Strategic Studies* (Oxford University Press, 2002), pp. 208–32.

344 J. Goldsmith, *The Terror Presidency – Law and Judgment inside the Bush Administration* (New York: W. W. Norton, 2009), p. 103.

345 C. Gray, 'What is War? A View from Strategic Studies', Oxford–Leverhulme Programme on the Changing Character of War, available at: http://ccw.politics.ox.ac.uk/events/archives/ht04_gray_a.pdf.

346 H. Münkler, *Clausewitz' Theorie des Krieges* (Baden-Baden: Nomos, 2003), p. 1.

347 M. Howard, *Clausewitz – A Very Short Introduction* (Oxford University Press, 2002), pp. 36–7.

348 Author's translation of: 'Der Krieg ist eine bloße Fortsetzung der Politik mit anderen Mitteln.' C. von Clausewitz, *Vom Kriege* (Augsburg: Weltbildverlag, 1998), p. 34.

349 This may apply even more so to the field of international humanitarian law. J. Paust, *Beyond the Law – The Bush Administration's Unlawful Responses to the 'War' on Terror* (Cambridge University Press, 2007), pp. 48–50.

clear is that a less dogmatic approach towards the use of force will be taken by the Obama Administration. It is no surprise that the presidents that Obama is usually placed in line with, and likes to draw upon in his speeches (Kennedy and Clinton),[350] both failed to come up with a concise doctrine for the use of force in terms of the definition on which this work is based.[351] In accordance with this, most senior foreign policy officials of the Obama Administration are regarded as not particularly ideological or dogmatic.[352]

Just as the focus of US foreign policy officials has shifted, the focus of debate among scholars of international law has also undergone noticeable changes since the Bush Doctrine was initially announced in the NSS 2002.

4.3.2 Changes in the legal debate

It would certainly be wrong to assume with hindsight that the debate stirred by the Bush Doctrine has unfolded into three neat, easily separable steps: (1) the United States claimed a right of preventive self-defence; (2) this claim was generally rejected; and (3) no changes were caused by this declaration. First, this 'claim' on the part of the United States did not constitute a claim in terms of *opinio iuris* or in favour of a general alteration in the law towards a general permission of pre-emptive self-defence.[353] However, the declaration of the Bush Doctrine added a new dimension to the debate surrounding the use of force. Though in general it may be apt to say that the principles of the Bush Doctrine for this use of force were rejected, this would also be an essentially oversimplified, flawed distortion of the actual debate. At the very least, in spite of vocal protests a gradual and subtle change of rules for the use of force may have been brought about, but this cannot yet be fully fathomed, however. Subconsciously, limitations on the use of force, considered almost self-evident, seem to have become matters for debate. The just war theory, which prior to the Bush Doctrine was a rather theological, historical (and from a legal point of view primitive) aspect of the discussion on the legality of the use of force, has experienced a revival in the scholarly debate.[354] This discussion

350 See above, Chapter 3, section 3.3.2 and Chapter 4, section 4.1.3.

351 See above, Chapter 1, section 1.6.

352 'A Cast of 300 Advises Obama on Foreign Policy', *The New York Times*, 18 July 2008.

353 See above, section 4.2.4.

354 K. Ziolkowski, *Gerechtigkeitspostulate als Rechtfertigung von Kriegen*, (Nomos: Baden-Baden, 2006), pp. 30–3, Ph.D. thesis, Berlin, 2006.

even amounts to turning to heralding in general terms a more flexible interpretation of the limitations of Article 2(4).[355]

In the first instance, the Bush Doctrine has lifted the always contentious debate on the legality of self-defence to another level. In particular, one achievement was that it brought certain issues on to the agenda of scholars of international law: 'imminence' or 'immediacy'. Whether 'immediacy' has to be reinterpreted in the light of new threats in order to accommodate terrorist attacks has become a contentious issue. However, this criterion is regularly discussed without placing it in a specific dogmatic context ('armed attack' or the *Caroline* formula), thus rendering these arguments difficult to evaluate.[356]

The Bush Doctrine provoked some explicit statements on the range of self-defence that UN bodies had been reluctant to issue until then.[357] Though the Report of the High-Level Panel on Threats, Challenges and Change rejects the notion of 'pre-emptive' self-defence, it states that 'imminent threats are fully covered by Article 51 . . . Lawyers have long recognised that this covers an imminent attack as well as one that has already happened.'[358] Yet agreements or clarifications on interpretation and changes in the debate among scholars cannot be equated with material changes in the law. Aside from the Bush Doctrine, several other events of legal relevance prior to 11 September 2001 (like the UN Security Council's Resolutions 1368 and 1373) have sparked creative suggestions and controversies enabling states to act earlier against terrorist threats,[359] but they have not materialised in terms of actual changes in the law but remain in the field of suggestions *de lege ferenda*. Anticipated self-defence has certainly not been stretched to encompass self-defence against 'latent threats' in addition to the danger of an imminent armed attack as is occasionally claimed.[360]

355 I. Shearer, *A Revival of the Just War Theory?* in Schmitt and Pejic (eds.), *International Law and Armed Conflict: Exploring the Faultlines*, pp. 1–20.

356 See above, section 4.2.2.2.

357 N. Ronzitti, 'The Expanding Law of Self-Defence', J.C.S.L., 11 (2006), 343–59 at 345–6.

358 UN Report of the Secretary General's High-level Panel on Threats, Challenges and Change, 'A More Secure World: Our Shared Responsibility', para. 124, available at: www.un.org/ secureworld/report2.pdf.

359 A. Guiora, 'Anticipated Self-Defence and International Law – A Re-Evaluation', J.C.S.L., 13 (2008), 3–24. Guiora suggests a 'strict scrutiny' test; on this see: T. Gazzini, 'A Response to Amos Guiora: Pre-Emptive Self-Defence Against Non State Actors?', J.C.S.L., 13 (2008), 25–32; M. Kiancioglu, 'A Response to Amos Guiora: Reassessing the Parameters of Use of Force in the Age of Terrorism', J.C.S.L., 13 (2008), 33–48.

360 Ronzitti, 'The Expanding Law of Self-Defence', pp. 343–59 at 357.

Though the United States have now abandoned the 'claim' of preventive self-defence in the NSS 2002, some other states have adopted the claim of being entitled to pre-emptive self-defence for themselves. Several governments have openly debated the possibility of a right to pre-emptive self-defence, and in this respect, the United States has found some unlikely supporters: North Korea and Iran.[361] For the most part, other states, whether supportive or opposed to the US-led attack on Iraq in 2003, have straightforwardly rejected the claim of pre-emptive self-defence.[362]

The ICJ has now made it very clear in its judgment in the *Case Concerning Armed Activities on the Territory of the Congo* (*Democratic Republic of Congo* v. *Uganda*) that Article 51 of the Charter 'does not allow the use of force by a State to protect perceived security interests . . .'[363] Though the ICJ did not explicitly extend its discussion in this case to the question of 'imminent threat',[364] this is generally understood as a rejection of the Bush Doctrine and the principle of pre-emptive self-defence.[365] Judge Simma was even more outspoken in his differing opinion and mentioned the Bush Doctrine explicitly.[366] The Bush Doctrine can thus be considered as a premature normative conclusion produced as a reaction to the terrorist attacks on 11 September. [367]

The legitimate willingness on the part of the United States to question the adequacy of the *ius ad bellum* has certainly caused changes in the focus of legal debates. It remains to be seen which other aspects will draw new attention and form new centres of interest. In the field of *ius ad bellum*, several aspects come to mind and all could serve as potential *nuclei* for future doctrines: self-defence against terrorists in possession

361 This is sometimes explained as being one consequence of the policy of 'regime change', sending out the clear message that no state can be safe unless militarily protected against a US invasion. R. Haas, 'Regime Change and Its Limits', For.Aff., 84/4 (2005), 66–78.

362 For example, the 118 states of the Non-Aligned Movement, UN Doc. S/2006/780, 29 September 2006; Reisman and Armstrong, 'The Past and Future of the Claim of Pre-emptive Self-Defense', pp. 525–50 at 538 *et seq.*; Gray, *International Law and the Use of Force*, pp. 213–14 with further evidence.

363 ICJ, *Case Concerning Armed Activities on the Territory of the Congo* (*Democratic Republic of Congo* v. *Uganda*), Judgment, 10 December 2005, para. 148.

364 N. Shah, 'Self-defence, Anticipatory Self-defence and Pre-emption: International Law's Response to Terrorism', J.C.S.L., 12 (2007), 95–126 at 100.

365 Gray, *International Law and the Use of Force*, p. 164.

366 1 ICJ, *Case Concerning Armed Activities on the Territory of the Congo* (*Democratic Republic of Congo* v. *Uganda*), Judgment, 10 December 2005, Separate Opinion by Judge Simma, No. 11.

367 G. Nolte, 'Vom Weltfrieden zur menschlichen Sicherheit? Zu Anspruch, Leistung und Zukunft des Völkerrechts', in H. Münkler (ed.), *Sicherheit und Risiko* (forthcoming 2010) (inaugural lecture at Humboldt-University Berlin, 26 January 2009).

of weapons of mass destruction;[368] human security;[369] responsibility to protect (R2P).[370]

Dominant power on the part of the United States was for almost two decades (since 1989) the defining feature of international order and at the centre of debates. At least the focus of the debate among scholars of international law has moved away slightly from this issue. However, since the law is naturally reacting only slowly to political changes, it would certainly be premature to speak in terms of Grewe's 'post-American' epoch of international law.

The same can be said for the focus of debate among scholars of international relations, but unlike international lawyers they do not shy away from taking the debate one step further: scholars of international relations discuss the prospect of a 'post-American' era. Whether this is also merely a premature conclusion or could herald a political change about to affect the plain of international law remains to be seen.

4.3.3 *Changes in the debate among international relations scholars*

While the evaluation of the Bush Doctrine under international law is a contentious issue, ultimately there is basic agreement on its illegality among scholars of international law. In contrast, its political evaluation is a more diversified and far more controversial issue. Quite a number of publications discuss the so-called 'war on terror' in connection with the Bush Doctrine.[371] The effects and applications of this particular doctrine on and to certain regions have been the subject of close scrutiny among political scientists.[372] Evaluations range from commending it for its proactive approach[373] to deeming it to be counterproductive.[374]

368 G. Guillaume, 'Terrorism and International Law', I.C.J.Q., 53/3 (2004), 537–48.

369 M. Kaldor, M. Martin and S. Selchow, 'Human Security: a New Strategic Narrative for Europe', Int.Aff., 83 (2007), 273–88.

370 C. Stahn, 'Responsibility to Protect: Political Rhetoric or Emerging Legal Norm?', A.J.I.L., 110 (2007), 99–120; R. Thakur, *The United Nations, Peace and Security – From Collective Security to the Responsibility to Protect* (Cambridge University Press, 2006), pp. 244–64.

371 M. Buckley and R. Singh (eds.), *The Bush Doctrine and the War on Terrorism: Global Responses, Global Consequences* (London: Routledge, 2006).

372 G. Prevost and C. Oliva (eds.), *The Bush Doctrine and Latin America* (New York: Palgrave Macmillan, 2007); M. Gurtov, 'The Bush Doctrine in Asia', in Forsythe *et al.* (eds), *American Foreign Policy in a Globalized World*, pp. 287–311.

373 A. Wall, 'International Law and the Bush Doctrine', I.Y.H.R., 37 (2004), 193–229 at 229. M. Owens, 'The Bush Doctrine: The Foreign Policy of a Republican Empire', Orbis, 53 (2009), 23–40.

374 J. Habermas, 'Interpreting the Fall of a Monument', G.L.J., 7 (2003), 701–8.

Though virtually all candidates during the presidential race in 2008 were eager to outline their foreign policy agenda,[375] and tried to highlight the differences between their conceptions and the Bush Administration's foreign policy, structural features of the relationship between the United States and the rest of the world can hardly be considered as altered merely by a change of administration. When thinking in terms of the distribution of power, US predominance remains a defining element of the international order in spite of gradual policy changes. There has been no shortage of suggestions of how to conduct future US foreign policy following the Bush Doctrine.[376]

However, it is undeniable that another notion prevails in the discussion of US security policy. Since about 2006, it is no longer a doctrinal statement that is top of the list when discussing US security policy. Some authors tend to put more emphasis on the 'rise of the rest' instead of emphasising US dominance, and write of a post-American world.[377] Others reassign the label 'second world' to developing states and consider their rise as causing a change towards a non-American world.[378] Due to this effect, Fareed Zakaria considers the discussion that took place during the presidential campaign of 2007/8 on the need to lessen the perceived anti-Americanism to be beside the point. In his terms, the world is moving 'from anger to indifference, from anti-Americanism to post-Americanism'.[379] This evaluation can be considered as symptomatic of a changed perception of the role of the United States in the international system: from challenger to being the most challenged power. Following on from this perception, it seems apt to consider the unilateral attack on Iraq as the apogee or turning point of unilateralism. This estimation on the part of political scientists confirms the evaluations that it cannot be underestimated in terms of law that the United States abstained from justifying this intervention along the lines of the Bush Doctrine.[380]

375 Clinton, 'Security and Opportunity for the Twenty-First Century', pp. 2–18; Edwards, 'Reengaging with the World', pp. 19–37; Giuliani, 'Towards a Realistic Peace', pp. 1–18; McCain, 'An Enduring Peace Built on Freedom', pp. 19–39; Obama, 'Renewing American Leadership', pp. 2–16; Richardson, 'A New Realism', pp. 142–54; Huckabee, 'America's Priorities in the War on Terror', pp. 155–68.

376 Leffler and Legro (eds.), *To Lead the World – American Strategy After the Bush Doctrine.*

377 F. Zakaria, *The Post-American World* (New York: W. W. Norton, 2008).

378 P. Khanna, *The Second World – Empires and Influence in the New Global Order* (London: Penguin Books, 2008), pp. 321–41.

379 Zakaria, *The Post-American World*, p. 36.

380 Stahn, 'Enforcement of the Collective Will after Iraq', pp. 822–3; H. Meiertöns, 'Das *ius ad bellum* zwischen Menschenrechten und Souveränität – Die Bush-Doktrin, neokonservative Sicherheitspolitik und das Dilemma zwischen Sicherheit und Gerechtigkeit',

Yet this may merely mean a change in perception by putting the focus on a different aspect of hegemony without substantially altering the situation on the ground. Theories of post-Americanism sound repetitive – though political scientists may eagerly point out the difference in the debate – in many ways of the debates of the late 1980s on a possible 'imperial overstretch'.[381] Yet most commentators agree that the United States will not fall victim to the fate of past hegemons. Consequently, they assume instead a gradual loss of hegemonic power and are lacking the apocalyptic connotations of similar previous theories.

From the point of view of an international lawyer, one should not overestimate these changed *perceptions* of US power and mistake them for actual *changes* in substance and structure. A 'weaker unilateralism'[382] is still unilateralism, but, as the term itself indicates, is simply a softened, mushy form. International law is only one of many institutions playing a role in these considerations. Replies to terrorist threats and terrorism as an unusual military strategy, defined by the response of the onlooker, can possibly be found in totally different fields than that of international law. Some authors argue that the best reply of a society may be resilience.[383] Though an evaluation of these considerations of policy is well beyond the positivist approach chosen in this work,[384] they may reflect the subconscious damage that the Bush Doctrine has done to the perceived utility of international law.

4.3.4 Conclusion

The *ius ad bellum* has turned out to be remarkably resistant against premature normative over-reactions like the Bush Doctrine. Regulations of the *ius ad bellum* never yielded to this onslaught of the Bush Administration, parts of which at a certain point in time displayed an almost certain pride in its little interest in international limitations,

in D. Weingärtner (ed.), *Streitkräfte und Menschenrechte* (Baden-Baden: Nomos, 2008), pp. 175–83.

381 P. Kennedy, *The Rise and Fall of Great Powers: Economic and Military Conflict from 1500 to 2000* (New York: Random House, 1987). For a critique see: J. Nye, *Bound to Lead: The Changing Nature of American Power* (New York: Basic Books, 1990); S. Strange, 'The Persistent Myth of Lost Hegemony', Int.Org., 41/4 (1987), 551–74.

382 Zakaria, *The Post-American World*, p. 47.

383 H. Münkler, 'Asymmetrie und Kriegsvölkerrecht. Die Lehren des Sommerkrieges 2006', Friedens-Warte/ J.I.P.O., 81 (2006), 59–65. Likewise: Zakaria, *The Post-American World*, p. 16.

384 See above, Chapter 1, section 1.6.

condescendingly labelled as 'lawfare'.[385] In spite of numerous shortcomings, particularly in the field of international humanitarian law,[386] the Bush Administration soon realised that obedience to international law was a course of action without any alternatives.[387] The slow mechanisms for changing international law make it averse to changes based on short-term policy considerations. International lawyers witnessed a gradual evolution of a normative framework, not its dismantling.

The Bush Doctrine and other attempts by the United States to reshape international law have gained no traction in the international community and have been firmly rejected.[388] This highlights a failure in the confrontational approach to try to alter the law on war and this approach in general.[389] In this respect, the performance of the Bush Administration can serve as a perfect illustration for the sheer necessity of legitimacy in order to exercise control. This legitimacy may have become even more important as power becomes more diversified.[390] Exercising control over an increasingly complex and pluralist international legal order may be far more complicated now than it might have been for dominant powers in the past.[391] Consequently, the concept of 'legitimacy in international society' has also been attracting more attention recently.[392]

On the crucial point of imminence, exactly the point where the Bush Doctrine breaks with the law in force, the Obama Administration has reversed the position of the Bush Administration, rendering the Bush Doctrine obsolete. The very spot picked to outline this new principle, the Munich Security Conference, was considered noteworthy it might have provoked concerns about being 'soft on terror' for the most ardent supporters of unilateralist security policy. (Ironically, the Munich Security Conference is the very place where the then Russian President, Vladimir

385 Goldsmith, *The Terror Presidency*, pp. 58–64.

386 D. Forsythe, 'The United States and International Humanitarian Law', in Fischer-Lescano *et al.* (eds.), *Frieden in Freiheit – Peace in liberty – Paix en liberté, Festschrift für Michael Bothe zum 70. Geburtstag* (FS-Bothe), pp. 409–16.

387 F. Moustakis and R. Chaudhuri, 'The Rumsfeld Doctrine and the Cost of US Unilateralism: Lessons Learned', Defence Studies, 7 (2007), 358–75.

388 R. Kagan, 'America's Crisis of Legitimacy', For.Aff., 83/2 (2004), 65–88; T. Gazzini, *The Changing Rules on the Use of Force in International Law* (Manchester University Press, 2005), pp. 203–4.

389 Zakaria, *The Post-American World*, p. 222.

390 Zakaria, *The Post-American World*, p. 39.

391 A. Hurrell, *On Global Order – Power, Values, and the Constitution of International Society* (Oxford University Press, 2007), pp. 279–82.

392 I. Clark, *Legitimacy in International Society* (Oxford University Press, 2007).

Putin, had two years earlier harshly distanced himself from expansive claims to the right to use force pre-emptively.[393]) Many other factors hint at a 'return of international law' to US foreign policy:[394] within days of entering office, President Obama issued a series of executive orders reversing legal opinions of the Bush Administration on international law. As a result, the difference between the American and European conceptions of fighting terrorism has been reduced considerably.[395]

During its first month in office, the Obama Administration had not announced any principles for the use of force on the part of the United States, which would count as a doctrine in terms of the definition on which this work is based.[396] Statements during the first year of Obama's term of office also make it seem rather unlikely that his administration will declare a concise doctrine.

393 V. Putin, Speech at the 43rd Munich Security Conference, 10 February 2007, available at: www.securityconference.de/konferenzen/rede.php.

394 S. Power, 'Legitimacy and Competence', in Leffler and Legro (eds.), *To Lead the World – American Strategy after the Bush Doctrine*, pp. 133–56 at 140 *et seq.*

395 On this see: A. Dworkin, 'Beyond the "War on Terror": Towards a New Transatlantic Framework for Counterterrorism', ECFR Policy Brief, May 2009.

396 See above, Chapter 1, section 1.6.

5

Conclusion

Since 1823 the United States has declared seven doctrines in which principles for the use of force have been outlined. These principles were considered by the US Government as binding concepts for the use of force in its international relations and were subsequently labelled 'doctrines'.

Moreover, the label 'doctrine' is used for several political declarations and principles of US security policy. These so-called 'doctrines' either contain no principles for the use of force, like the so-called Ford Doctrine,[1] or have not been considered by the US Government as 'doctrine', like the so-called Johnson,[2] Carter[3] or Clinton doctrines.[4] However, these half- and pseudo-doctrines, and the statements by scholars of international law in relation to them, reveal information about the characteristics of doctrines.

5.1 Consistency of doctrines with the respective international law in force

The degree to which the principles for the use of force contained in specific doctrines are consistent with the respective international law in force is evaluated differently by scholars.

5.1.1 The subjectivity of the evaluation of doctrines under international law

The consistency of the principles for the use of force as explained in doctrines with the respective international law in force is evaluated differently depending on two factors: on the one hand, these different evaluations result from the differing contents attributed to doctrines; on the other

1 See above, Chapter 3, section 3.4.3.
2 See above, Chapter 3, section 3.3.
3 See above, Chapter 3, section 3.5.
4 See above, Chapter 4, section 4.1.3.

hand, from different opinions with regard to the legality of the use of force.

5.1.2 Differences in evaluation due to a differing understanding of the content of doctrines

Often a differing evaluation of doctrines under international law results from a different understanding of the content attributed to a doctrine and not from a different interpretation of the respective *ius ad bellum* in force.

While it is possible to clearly delimit the issues of international law that are referred in the 'doctrines' of other states, such as the Federal German Hallstein Doctrine on the matter of recognition of the GDR under international law,[5] or the doctrines of Latin American states on specific questions of diplomatic protection and the prohibition of intervention,[6] the doctrines of US security policy are worded in more general terms and touch upon several problematic areas of international law.[7] The content of the Stimson Doctrine can be delimited most clearly among the doctrines treated to the matter of the recognition of the illegal acquisition of territory under international law. Yet even the Stimson Doctrine is connected with statements on matters of the *ius ad bellum* and assumes a certain understanding of the legality of the use of force.[8]

An essential problem for the evaluation of doctrines under international law results from this: the content attributed to a doctrine allows for a multitude of interpretations. As a result, different political constellations are often referred to when speaking of a specific doctrine.[9]

US doctrines often contain merely the explicit declaration and repetition of principles which have been declared or discussed in American politics before. Scholars assume even of the Monroe Doctrine that it repeats the principles Thomas Jefferson and George Washington had

5 In detail on this see: C. von Wrede, 'Der Rechtsanspruch der Deutschen Bundesregierung auf völkerrechtliche Alleinvertretung Gesamtdeutschlands und die Hallstein-Doktrin', Ph.D. thesis, Freiburg/Switzerland, 1966.
6 See on this see: K. Krakau 'Lateinamerikanische Doktrinen zur Realisierung staatlicher Unabhängigkeit und Integrität', VRÜ, 8 (1975), 117–44.
7 H. Kissinger, *Diplomacy* (New York: Simon & Schuster, 1994), p. 731.
8 See above, Chapter 2, section 2.2.3.1.
9 For example, the different interpretations of the Reagan Doctrine, see above, Chapter 3, section 3.6.2.2.

already formulated.[10] Such a political principle becomes a doctrine just by being labelled a doctrine unilaterally. The central problem when determining whether a principle is a doctrine, however, is that for doctrines as political principles (different from a rule of international law) no set of rules exists to determine who is entitled to exercise the power of defining a binding doctrine. A doctrine is a construct which is not set out comprehensively in one single document, but this construct and the underlying idea have to be deduced from several documents. This task is complicated by the fact that often even various levels of the US administration do not agree[11] on what a doctrine is stating specifically. This is particularly clear, for example, in the case of the Reagan Doctrine.[12]

The analysis of the legality of a doctrine under international law thus offers only the illusion of conceptual clarity, whereas a closer description of the single principles contained in a doctrine and an evaluation of these single principles allows for greater intelligibility. This enormous flexibility of doctrines makes it questionable if the subject of doctrines allows for sufficient certainty in order to deliver a precise legal evaluation. Ultimately this evaluation has to be based on the temporary aid of an assumed definition of a doctrine. The question of the conformity of a doctrine with international law is in this regard a question that offers only apparent conceptual clarity, as the legal evaluation depends on the answer to the prior non-legal question for the content of a doctrine. When interpreting a doctrine widely (for example, the Monroe Doctrine in terms of a right of intervention by the United States in Latin America, or the Reagan Doctrine in terms of a right of pro-democratic intervention), the scope of foreseen cases of use of force in need of justification becomes wider. Hence, this leaves more space for a discussion of the legality of such actions

10 J. Clark, *Memorandum on the Monroe Doctrine: December 17, 1928* (Washington, DC: Government Printing Office, 1930), p. XI.

11 For example, J. Kirkpatrick and A. Gerson, 'The Reagan Doctrine, Human Rights and International Law', in L. Henkin *et al.* (ed.), *Right v. Might. International Law and the Use of Force*, 2nd edn. (New York: CFR, 1991), pp. 19 *et seq.*; J. Kirkpatrick, *Legitimacy and Force* (New Brunswick, NJ: Transaction Books, 1988), vol. I, pp. 422–46; W. Bode, 'The Reagan Doctrine', Strategic Rev., 14 (1986), 22.

12 Lacking certainty of doctrines also poses problems with regard to the evaluation of doctrines under US constitutional law. See on this see: L. Henkin, *Foreign Affairs and the U.S. Constitution*, 2nd edn. (Oxford: Clarendon Press, 1996), pp. 5, 44–5; L. Damrosh; 'The Interface of National Constitutional Systems with International Law and Institutions on Using Military Forces: Changing Trends in Executive and Legislative Powers', in C. Ku and H. Jacobson (eds.), *Democratic Accountability and the Use of Force in International Law* (Cambridge University Press, 2003), pp. 39–60.

under international law. Discussions among scholars of international law, based on different interpretations of doctrines, do not necessarily hint at a differing understanding of the admissibility of the use of force.

The assumption of Alejandro Alvarez, for example, that the Monroe Doctrine is a rule of American international law and, hence, action based on its principles in accordance with international law does not refer to a right of intervention in terms of the Roosevelt Corollary. Rather, Alvarez places such a right of intervention under the term 'Politique de Hégémonie', which is used as a counterpart to the Monroe Doctrine, whereas other authors do not consider the Roosevelt Corollary as opposed to the Monroe Doctrine but as a sub-category of the Monroe Doctrine.[13]

Opposing statements on the compliance of the Reagan Doctrine with international law can be put down to the drastically differing principles that single authors see vested in the Reagan Doctrine: either it is understood restrictively as a repetition of the principles of the Truman Doctrine, or it is understood extensively as a deviation from its principles. This, in turn, has an impact on the evaluation of the conformity with international law of the cases of use of force foreseen in the doctrine.[14]

5.1.3 Differences in the evaluation of doctrines based on a differing understanding of the legality of the use of force

For the most part, different evaluations of the conformity of cases of use of force as intended in doctrines with international law can be traced back to different contents attributed to single doctrines. However, the conformity of the doctrines with international law is sometimes evaluated differently, even when an almost congruent content is attributed to a doctrine. These differences result in turn from a different understanding of the legality of the use of force.

5.1.3.1 Conformity of doctrines with international law prior to the UN Charter

Prior to the general prohibition of force and the codification of this prohibition in the UN Charter, the use of force according to the Monroe Doctrine was in accordance with international law in force at the time. This legality resulted from a lack of need for justification.

The emergence of limitations of use of force diminishes the compatibility of the Monroe Doctrine with international law with regard to its

13 See above, Chapter 2, section 2.1.3.2.5.

14 See above, Chapter 3, section 3.6.2.3.

content, exceeding the mere defence of the territorial integrity of the United States. In its moulding through the Roosevelt Corollary (stating a general right of intervention of the United States in Latin America), a content in accordance with international law cannot be attributed to the doctrine by means of restrictive interpretation. This is because it did not comply with the limitations for the use of force in force at that time in the form of the pre-requisites for the right of self-defence or a broader right of self-help.[15] The inclusion of the Monroe Doctrine in Article 21 of the League of Nations Covenant did nothing to change that incompatibility. At no point in time did the Monroe Doctrine assume the quality of a rule of international law which would justify separate actions according to the Roosevelt Corollary. After abandoning the Roosevelt Corollary, however, it became possible to interpret the Monroe Doctrine in accordance with international law.[16]

The Stimson Doctrine differs from the Monroe Doctrine and the subsequent doctrines of US security policy with regard to the fact that it not only formulates principles for the use of force on the part of the United States, but also contains generally binding principles for the use of force. The interpretation of the Briand–Kellogg Pact in terms of a general prohibition on the use of force, on which the Stimson Doctrine is based, was controversial at the point of its declaration, but was subsequently generally accepted. Thus, the criteria for the use of force as laid down in the Stimson Doctrine can be considered as being in accordance with international law.[17]

With exception of the Monroe Doctrine in its moulding through the Roosevelt Corollary, the doctrines of US security policy before the coming into force of the UN Charter can be interpreted in accordance with international law. Hence, they were in accordance with the rules of international law for the use of force at that time.

5.1.3.2 Conformity of doctrines with the UN Charter

The codification of the general prohibition on the use of force in Article 2(4) of the UN Charter constitutes a fundamental break with regard to the evaluation of the legality of doctrines under international law.

5.1.3.2.1 Conformity of doctrines with the prohibition on the use of force in Article 2(4) of the UN Charter The Monroe Doctrine leaves room for

15 See above, Chapter 2, section 2.1.6.
16 See above, Chapter 2, section 2.1.3.3.
17 See above, Chapter 2, section 2.2.4.

a restrictive interpretation, which makes it possible to limit the cases of use of force foreseen within it in a way that can be justified through the right of self-defence in Article 51 of the UN Charter.[18] A so-called multilateralised Monroe Doctrine, as expressed in the rules of Articles 6 and 8 of the Rio Pact and Article 25 of the OAS Charter, is also in accordance with Articles 2(4), 51 and 53 of the UN Charter.[19]

Equally, the doctrines of US security policy declared during the Cold War, the Truman, Eisenhower and Nixon doctrines, leave room for an interpretation to the effect that cases of intended use of force are limited to cases which can be justified as an exercise of self-defence or as intervention by invitation.[20]

The Eisenhower Doctrine merely repeats the principles of the Truman Doctrine for the use of force with regard to a specific region.[21] The Nixon Doctrine adds to this, on the one hand, the limitation of actions by the United States and mentions, on the other hand, the use of nuclear weapons which, however, is not *per se* against international law.[22]

Most scholars interpret the Reagan Doctrine broadly and consider it as being contrary to international law. However, some consider the Reagan Doctrine merely a repetition of the principles of the Truman Doctrine. Thus, the Reagan Doctrine also leaves room for an interpretation in accordance with international law.[23]

Though some scholars claimed with regard to prior doctrines (such as the Johnson Doctrine and Reagan Doctrine) that they represent a revival of the right of intervention of the Roosevelt Corollary,[24] this statement was not apt for these doctrines as they left room for a restrictive interpretation, according to which they can be considered as being in accordance with international law. By contrast, no such interpretation in accordance with international law is possible in the case of the Bush Doctrine. The reference in the NSS 2002 to the *Caroline* formula is treated within different contexts, depending on the respective understanding of the right of self-defence according to Article 51 of the UN Charter and a customary right of self-defence. Yet to a large extent there is a consensus: the Bush Doctrine does not leave room for an interpretation in accordance with the UN Charter based on a restrictive interpretation of the doctrine.[25] Hence, the Bush Doctrine is intended to apply to cases of

18 See above, Chapter 2, section 2.1.3.4.
19 See above, Chapter 2, section 2.1.3.6.
20 See above, Chapter 3, sections 3.1.4, 3.2.4 and 3.4.4.
21 See above, Chapter 3, section 3.4.2.2.
22 See above, Chapter 3, section 3.4.4.
23 See above, Chapter 3, sections 3.6.2.3.1 and 3.6.3.
24 See above, Chapter 3, sections 3.3.3 and 3.6.2.3.2.
25 See above, Chapter 4, section 4.2.2.1 and 4.2.4.

use of force which are illegal under international law. This represents a clear break with the doctrines of US security policy declared up to that point.

5.1.3.2.2 Conformity of doctrines with the prohibition on the threat of force according to Article 2(4) of the UN Charter All doctrines have a threatening aspect in common. By announcing the use force in case of non-compliance, they aim at directing the behaviour of other states in a certain way.[26] However, this does not constitute a breach of the prohibition on the threat of force in Article 2(4) of the UN Charter.[27]

In order to constitute a threat of force in terms of Article 2(4) of the UN Charter, this demand would have to aim for a specific reaction of a threatened state.[28] A connection to certain courses of action with regard to certain states or regions, however, only results from the circumstances in which a doctrine was declared and not explicitly from the explanation of the doctrine itself.

Besides lacking a sufficient degree of certainty of the reactions demanded, an indispensable degree of temporary proximity of the threatened use of force is lacking.[29] The use of force threatened in doctrines refers to uncertain, possibly arising situations in the future, of which the emergence shall be particularly avoided by declaring the doctrine.[30] Therefore, the declaration of a doctrine does not constitute a breach of the prohibition on the threat of force according to Article 2(4) of the UN Charter due to the low degree of specification of the threat.

5.2 Law-creating effects of doctrines

It is possible to interpret the majority of the doctrines of US security policy in a way that they are in accordance with the UN Charter. Yet it is also possible to attribute to doctrines a content *de lege ferenda* beyond the law in force. Impulses for the development of international

26 See above, Chapter 3, sections 3.1.2.1 and 3.2.2.1.
27 The same conclusion is reached by J. Alvarez, 'Hegemonic International Law Revisited', A.J.I.L., 97 (2003), 882.
28 A. Randelzhofer, 'Art. 2(4)', in B. Simma (ed.), *The Charter of the United Nations*, 2nd edn. (Oxford University Press, 2002), No. 38, p. 124.
29 R. Sadurska, 'Threats of Force', A.J.I.L., 82 (1988), 242–3.
30 See above, Chapter 3, section 3.4.2.2.2.

law have emanated from this content of doctrines beyond the law in force.[31]

In order to justify political principles for the use of force beyond the law in force as they are contained in doctrines, scholars and states drew upon constructs which have been largely rejected by scholars of international law as well as state practice. Such constructs include the idea of an 'American international law', a 'Großraumordnung' and a 'right of pro-democratic intervention'. However, these constructs mainly constitute political demands of law *de lege ferenda.* They call for an adjustment of international law in terms of an international law considered desirable, but do not constitute statements referring to a given law *de lege lata.* Yet changes of law in terms of these constructs have had no, or only very limited, inroads into the legal opinion of the United States.

5.2.1 *Limits of legalisation of doctrines*

A contradiction exists between the nature of a doctrine as a unilateral political declaration – subject only to the will of a single state – and the nature of a rule of international law as a principle removed from the will of a single state. John Spencer wrote in 1936 that it was impossible to frame a political doctrine into international law, as a doctrine itself could not adjust to such a transformation.[32]

A limit of the possible legalisation of doctrines is that when these principles are enacted as a rule of international law, the unilateral power of the United States to define which principles a doctrine contains and what they state specifically cannot be upheld. Besides that, the legalisation of doctrines hits a further limit: according to Max Huber it is a starting point of the international legal order that it is based directly on the will of the subjects of law.[33] Yet as the drastically differing interpretations of doctrines (as outlined above) emphasise, doctrines of US security policy lack an unambiguous articulation of the will of a single subject of law. Hence, this 'will' cannot have an efficient impact on the level of a legal

31 H. Kraus, *Die Monroedoktrin in ihren Beziehungen zur Amerikanischen Diplomatie und zum Völkerrecht* (Berlin: Guttenag, 1913), pp. 352–3.

32 J. Spencer, 'The Monroe Doctrine and the League Covenant', A.J.I.L., 30 (1936), 413: 'an attempt to legislate into international law a political doctrine, which cannot adapt itself to such a transformation'. Agreeing with a hint to this passage: C. Walter, *Vereinte Nationen und Regionalorganisationen* (Berlin: Springer, 1996), Ph.D. thesis, Heidelberg, 1995, p. 14.

33 M. Huber, *Die soziologischen Grundlagen des Völkerrechts* (Berlin: Verlag Dr. Walther Rothschild, 1928), p. 9.

order, unless this very ambiguity of the statement itself is considered as being in the interest of the declaring state. The discipline of strategic studies calls this type of behaviour in relation to the use of force in international relations 'strategic ambiguity'.[34] The assumption of such an interest of a hegemon matches with the hypothesis that vagueness of legal regulations constitutes a key to hegemonial power, because the hegemon reserves the right to interpret the law in case there should be doubts.[35] Narrower, but similar, is the opinion which considers it a characteristic feature of hegemonic exercise of power to claim a privileged position in the development of an informed opinion of a group of states.[36]

5.2.2 Doctrines and the power of defining the legality of an action

Doctrines state unilaterally if and when the use of force is considered – politically as well as legally – permissible. Hence, they mark an attempt to sustain or attain the unilateral power to define the legality of the use of force.

This attempt can be considered as partially successful in the early phases of doctrines of US security policy. This is highlighted by the opinion, advocated by some scholars, that a subsidiary influence results from the mentioning of the Monroe Doctrine in Article 21 of the LNC as inferior to the (unilaterally to be determined) Monroe Doctrine.[37] Opinions opposed to this view, according to which the Monroe Doctrine has become subject to authentic interpretation due to it being mentioned in Article 21 of the LNC were not accepted.[38] At least after the UN Charter came into force, this assumed unilateral authority to decide when an action violates the Monroe Doctrine and is, thus, illegal under international law is partially lost.[39]

The doctrines of the Cold War period (unlike the Monroe Doctrine) do not relate to the question of formulating a specific right under international law for the use of force, but concern the interpretation of

34 On this see: K. Payne and C. Dale Walton, 'Deterrence in the Post-Cold War World', in J. Baylis *et al.* (eds.), *Strategy in the Contemporary World – An Introduction to Strategic Studies* (Oxford University Press, 2002), p. 164.

35 C. Schmitt, 'Völkerrechtliche Formen des modernen Imperialismus', in C. Schmitt (ed.), *Positionen und Begriffe* (Hamburg: Hanseatische Verlagsanstalt, 1940), pp. 163–84. See also: D. Vagts, 'Hegemonic International Law', A.J.I.L., 95 (2001), 845–6.

36 H. Triepel, *Die Hegemonie: ein Buch von führenden Staaten* (Stuttgart: Kohlhammer, 1938), pp. 218 *et seq.*

37 See above, Chapter 2, section 2.1.3.3.2.4.

38 See above, Chapter 2, section 2.1.3.3.2.2.

39 See above, Chapter 2, sections 2.1.3.3.2.2 and 2.1.4.

existing norms of the UN Charter. They refer to the interpretation of the limits of Article 2(4) of the UN Charter and the interpretation of self-defence according to Article 51 of the UN Charter.[40] A certain interpretation of the Briand–Kellogg Pact had already been assumed in the earlier Stimson Doctrine. This interpretation was generally accepted by states.[41]

Thus, after coming into force the doctrines of the UN Charter represent by and large unilateral interpretations of Articles of the UN Charter. Consequently, since the UN Charter came into force doctrines can be considered as claims for an interpretation of the right of self-defence according to Article 51 of the UN Charter in terms of an extension of the circumstances entitling states to act in self-defence.[42]

However, this is a narrow way of looking at a political matter of fact, which can be measured only partially by legal means. A doctrine is an abstract construction of thought, an idea. Just like *opinio iuris*, doctrines are in need of articulation. The same is true for declarations of interpretations on treaties in international law. A minimum standard for *opinio iuris*, however, is that it claims to describe a certain law which requires a minimum of a sufficiently certain, legal position or of the action considered legal.[43] This type of certainty is lacking for the most part in doctrines of US-American security policy.[44] Merely specific statements, considered declarations of doctrines, also meet the standard of a declaration of *opinio iuris*.

In addition, the doctrines are also lacking a clearly articulated will of a party necessary for a unilateral declaration of interpretation to a treaty. Hence, doctrines represent political principles which do not attain to the level of *opinio iuris*. Instead, the legitimacy of an aim or action is articulated in doctrines on a rather pre- or sub-legal level.[45]

Choosing a doctrine as a type of action has numerous benefits: unlike a rule of international law, the authority of interpretation of a doctrine is not removed from the United States. Principles are formulated in doctrines as a domestic act in order to ensure that they are not removed from the

40 See above, Chapter 2, section 2.1.3.4. 41 See above, Chapter 2, section 2.2.3.3.

42 For example, Q. Wright, 'United States Intervention in the Lebanon', A.J.I.L., 53 (1959), 117.

43 M. Byers, *Custom, Power and the Power of Rules* (Cambridge University Press, 1999), p. 208; I. McGibbon, 'Customary International Law and Acquiescence', B.Y.I.L., 33 (1957), 115–45, on this see further above, Chapter 1, section 1.6.

44 See above, sections 5.1.2 and 5.2.1.

45 On this see further below, sections 5.2.4 and 5.3.

authority of the United States to interpret these principles. No obligation and no right follow from the mere declaration of a doctrine.[46]

However, it is inevitable when implementing a doctrine to undertake deeds relevant for international law.[47] Political doctrines as political declarations of principles resist a transformation into a rule of international law due to their nature.[48] Yet this is not the case for specific principles outlined within such doctrines. If a single principle contained in a doctrine is detached from the unilateral authority of definition of the state declaring the doctrine, it is possible to enact this principle as a rule of international law. Principles contained in doctrines have found their way into treaties of international law and have thus resulted in obligations of the United States under treaties.

5.2.3 Doctrines and treaty obligations of the United States

A state is not bound by a self-declared political doctrine *eo ipso*, but is free to change this political maxim. Doctrines serve to signal a willingness to use force below the threshold of being obligated to take a certain action under international law.[49] A legal obligation to adhere to the principle of a doctrine can, however, be caused indirectly by including the principles of a doctrine in a treaty. This has happened several times in the case of the doctrines of US security policy.

Even though the Monroe Doctrine can be considered only to a certain extent as 'multilateralised' and is still open to unilateral modifications by the United States, single regulations in treaties of international law which enact these principles in a legally-binding way for the United States can be considered as an expression of basic principles of the Monroe Doctrine. Article 6 in connection with Article 8 of the Rio Pact and Article 25 of the OAS Charter also belong to these rules.[50]

The principle of the Truman Doctrine of supporting states considered 'free' has experienced at least a gradual legalisation, because the United States has with Article 5 of the NATO Treaty and Article 4 of the SEATO

46 On this see further below, section 5.2.4. See also: von Wrede, 'Der Rechtsanspruch der Deutschen Bundesregierung auf völkerrechtliche Alleinvertretung Gesamtdeutschlands und die Hallstein-Doktrin', pp. 35–6.

47 L. Focsaneanu, 'La "Doctrine Eisenhower" Pour Le Proche Orient', A.F.D.I. (1958), 105–7.

48 See above, section 5.2.1.

49 B. Kuniholm, 'The Carter Doctrine, the Reagan Corollary and the Prospects for United States Policy in Southwest Asia', Int.J., 41 (1986), 344.

50 See above, Chapter 2, section 2.1.3.5.

Treaty entered into obligations under international law, which oblige them in a legally-binding way to undertake supporting actions in terms of the Truman Doctrine. However, the scope of support is left to the United States.[51] The repetition of this principle in the Eisenhower Doctrine with regard to a certain region has, in turn, been enacted in several different bilateral treaties.[52]

Actually, the United States is still free to strive politically to liberate itself from these obligations, yet this would require not just a unilateral declaration, but also getting rid of obligations under international law. In this respect, doctrines constitute a paradox: while, on the one hand, doctrines aim to indemnify from responsibility, on the other hand, the attempts made to enact principles contained in doctrines into international law result in obligations under international law.

5.2.4 Doctrines as claims for rules sui generis

A characteristic feature of 'hegemonial doctrines' ('*Hegemonialdoktrinen*'),[53] such as the doctrines of US security policy, is the fact that they resemble a legal rule or are the law-like fitting out of a political maxim for action. This maxim is, thus, presented as a principle of a generally valid rule of law and constitutes at the same time a claim for an exception.[54]

Whereas political pre-dominance has in single cases found entry into legal regulations – as in the case of the right of veto according to Article 27(3) of the UN Charter[55] – doctrines resist that type of legalisation.[56] A demand for a special right of a unilateral authority to act can be derived merely from the political context in which a doctrine is declared. However, it does not reach the level of a 'claim', which would be required for the capacity as *opinio iuris*.[57] Hence, doctrines emphasise

51 See above, Chapter 3, section 3.1.3. 52 See above, Chapter 3, section 3.2.3.

53 G. Nolte, *Eingreifen auf Einladung* (Berlin: Springer, 1999), p. 167.

54 'In modern International Law, a doctrine – such as Brezhnev, Carter, and Reagan doctrines – consists of a formal and credible statement by a significant international actor of a firm policy and the resolve to implement it upon certain contingencies. Doctrines are positioned at the interface of law and power. They are based on a general right that is theoretically available to other states. By their nature, they constitute a demand for an exception.' M. Reisman, 'Assessing Claims to Revise the Laws of War', A.J.I.L., 97 (2003), 90. Similarly: D. Murswiek, 'Die amerikanische Präventivkriegsstrategie und das Völkerrecht', N.J.W., (2003), 1019.

55 K. Ginther, 'Hegemony', E.P.I.L., (1995), 685–8. 56 See above, section 5.2.1.

57 On this see above, Chapter 1, section 1.6 and section 5.2.2.

that the formation of hierarchies and systems of rules among states do not result only from rules of international law, but also from the context of these rules.[58]

Every state is formally entitled to a right stated in a doctrine. Due to a hegemon's greater options for action, exercising that right is possible only for the politically dominant state. At the same time, the right cannot be enforced against him.[59] It is conspicuous in this context, that the two doctrines which stipulate illegal cases of the use of force (the Monroe Doctrine in its moulding through the Roosevelt Corollary and the Bush Doctrine) use an argument which is based on obligations derived from sovereignty.[60] This argument, camouflaged as an extension of sovereignty, however, is ultimately aiming at a limitation of sovereignty, due to the concession to the hegemon of a special 'right' to use force.

With regard to the doctrines' objectives of aiming for limitations of sovereignty, an idea going back to Dieter Schröder has been taken up and sharpened aptly by Theodor Schweisfurth:

> [a] common feature of all doctrines . . . [stipulating the use of force] is, that the holder of the [claimed] right to intervention projects the image of being the bearer of an 'epoch making idea'; from his point of view 'an international law', which chooses states as central topos and makes the sovereignty of single states the central term of the legal order, is plainly wrong, as it is not based on the moving, decisive element of foreign policy, the big idea. In the first place it does not do justice to the imagined essential situation of a fight. The state of emergency is drawn upon in order to justify any type of limitation of sovereignty. International law is made void under this permanent international state of emergency and power hence becomes the only decisive factor of international relations.[61]

58 N. Krisch, 'Amerikanische Hegemonie und Liberale Revolution im Völkerrecht', Der Staat, 43 (2004), 291.

59 On the limits of obligation international law see: E. Kaufmann, *Das Wesen des Völkerrechts und die Clausula Rebus Sic Stantibus* (Tübingen: J. C. B. Mohr, 1911), pp. 204 *et seq.*, who finishes with the phrase 'only he who can, is allowed to' (author's translation of 'nur wer kann, der darf') (p. 231). Critical on that: M. Koskenniemi, *The Gentle Civilizer of Nations: The Rise and Fall of International Law 1870–1960* (Cambridge University Press, 2001), pp. 249–61.

60 See above, Chapter 4, section 4.2.3.2.

61 T. Schweisfurth, *Sozialistisches Völkerrecht?* (Berlin: Springer, 1979), p. 569 with reference to D. Schröder, 'Die Idee der kollektiven Regionalintervention – Rechtsvergleichende Betrachtungen zur Breshnew-Doktrin', Recht in Ost und West, 13 (1969), 209–10. Author's translation of: 'ist ein Völkerrecht, das den Staat zum zentralen Topos und die Souveränität des einzelnen Staates zum zentralen Begriff der Rechtsordnung wählt, schlichtweg falsch, da es nicht an dem bewegenden, entscheidenden Element der auswärtigen Politik, nämlich der großen Idee orientiert ist, vor allem nicht der gedachten

The danger which ultimately lies in such an understanding of public international law, limiting sovereignty,[62] has also been aptly pointed out by Theodor Schweisfurth: 'Ultimately one reaches an understanding of international law, which separates the world into big empires and subjects the sovereignty of states to the right of existence of the empires.'[63]

What specifically constitutes this 'epoch-making' idea as the instrument of which doctrines of US security policy will serve, has experienced considerable changes over time since the declaration of the first doctrine in 1823; even the basic idea of a US 'exceptionalism', a sense of mission, a 'manifest destiny' may be an element[64] which has been preserved from doctrine to doctrine. The epoch-making idea underlying the Bush Doctrine may be best described as 'fundamental liberal re-shaping of the world'.[65]

One essential feature of the limitations of sovereignty and the justifications for the use of force resulting from these limitations is that they are not only justified by pursuing US-American interests, but are presented by the United States as action for the sake of a bigger community of states. This claim for authority is derived from the conviction of being the bearer of a 'moral' idea.[66] Whereas this bigger community of states was regionally limited in the case of the Monroe Doctrine where the doctrine referred to a certain region, the other doctrines of US security policy

existenziellen Kampfsituation gerecht wird. Die Notlage wird zur Rechtfertigung jeder Einschränkung der Souveränität herangezogen, das Völkerrecht wird in einem permanenten internationalen Ausnahmezustand aufgehoben und die Macht damit zum allein bestimmenden Faktor der internationalen Beziehungen erhoben.'

62 In general on this see: G. Nolte, 'Zum Wandel des Souveränitätsbegriffs', *Frankfurter Allgemeine Zeitung*, 6 April 2005, p. 8.

63 Schweisfurth, *Sozialistisches Völkerrecht?*, p. 569: author's translation of: 'Am Ende gelangt man zu einer Völkerrechtsauffassung, die Welt in mehrere große Reiche aufteilt und die Souveränität der Staaten dem Existenzrecht der Reiche unterordnet.'

64 On this see: K. Krakau, *Missionsbewußtsein und Völkerrechtsdoktrin in den Vereinigten Staaten von Amerika* (Frankfurt a.M.: Metzner, 1967), Ph.D. thesis, Hamburg, 1967, pp. 122 *et seq.*; E. Luck, 'American Exceptionalism and International Organization: Lessons from the 1990s', in R. Foot, S. MacFarlane and M. Mastanduno (eds.), *US Hegemony and International Institutions* (Oxford University Press, 2003), pp. 25–48; J. Hathaway, 'America, Defender of Democratic Legitimacy?', E.J.I.L., 11 (2000), 121–34.

65 Krisch, 'Amerikanische Hegemonie und Liberale Revolution im Völkerrecht', p. 275 ('grundlegende liberale Umgestaltung der Welt').

66 Similar with regard to the Monroe Doctrine: H. Kraus, 'Interesse und zwischenstaatliche Ordnung', N.Z.I.R., 49 (1934), 37–42; on the current shape of this characteristic of US policy N. Krisch, 'More Equal than the Rest? Hierarchy, Equality and US Predominance in International Law', in M. Byers and G. Nolte (eds.), *United States Hegemony and the Foundations of International Law* (Oxford University Press, 2003), pp. 148–55; N. Krisch, 'Unilateral Enforcement of the Collective Will: Kosovo, Iraq, and the Security Council', M.P.Y.U.N.L., 3 (1999), 59–103.

(with the exception of the Eisenhower Doctrine)[67] claim global influence. They thus make the use of force subject to their principles as unilateral enforcement of the collective will of an international community. The state and its sovereignty are understood as being instrumental in this process in order to give influence to a higher idea on the basis of natural law,[68] whereas traditional, positivist international law is considered as impairing this idea. Corresponding to this fact, the principles for the use of force outlined in doctrines of US security policy are considered to be in accordance with international law by supporters of the New Haven School[69] (which also bases its understanding of international law on an aim-based approach),[70] whereas positivists among international lawyers assume an illegality of these principles under international law.[71] From a US-American point of view, the tensions arising from isolated contradictions between doctrines and the UN Charter may express that the UN Charter if 'in the dilemma between security and justice, intentionally prefers the first'.[72]

Doctrines of US security policy since 1945 are marked in particular by the desire to give influence to single criteria of domestic orders, described as 'values',[73] on the international level.[74] This constitutes, among other factors, the force of this approach with the potential of 'blasting the

67 See above, Chapter 3, section 3.2.

68 For example, W. Bradford, 'The Duty to Defend Them: A Natural Law Justification for the Bush Doctrine of Preventive War', N.D.L.R., 79 (2004), 1365–492, in particular 1426–41. On the influence of considerations of natural law on US-American thought on international law see: A. Nussbaum, *Geschichte des Völkerrechts* (Munich: C. H. Beck, 1960), pp. 179 *et seq.*

69 For example, M. McDougal, 'Law and Power', A.J.I.L., 46 (1952), 102–4; M. Reisman, 'Critical Defense Zones and International Law: The Reagan Codicil', A.J.I.L., 76 (1982), 589–91; M. Reisman, 'Assessing Claims to Revise the Laws of War', A.J.I.L., 97 (2003), 82–90.

70 On this see further: R. Beck, 'International Law and International Relations: The Prospects for Interdisciplinary Collaboration', in A. Arend, R. Beck and R. Vander Lugt (eds.), *International Rules – Approaches from International Law and International Relations* (Oxford University Press, 1996), pp. 6–7 and Chapter 1, section 1.4.

71 For example, L. Gross, 'The Charter of the United Nation and the Lodge Reservations', A.J.I.L., 41 (1947), 531–54; J. Stromseth, 'Law and Force after Iraq: A Transitional Moment', A.J.I.L., 97 (2003), 628–42.

72 F. Berber, *Lehrbuch des Völkerrechts* (Munich: C. H. Beck, 1960), vol. II, p. 43, author's translation of 'in dem Dilemma zwischen Sicherheit und Gerechtigkeit bewußt erstere vorzieht'.

73 R. Watson, C. Gleek and M. Grillo, 'Conclusion', in R. Watson, C. Gleek and M. Grillo (eds.), *Presidential Doctrines: National Security From Woodrow Wilson to George W. Bush* (New York: Nova Science Publishers, 2003), pp. 113–18.

74 Krisch, 'Unilateral Enforcement of the Collective Will: Kosovo, Iraq, and the Security Council', pp. 102–3.

system'.[75] In this respect, the doctrines discussed above may be considered as an expression of an anti-formal, instrumental reasoning, which refers to the assumed *ratio* of a certain rule and does not see an intrinsic value in an existing rule itself. This reasoning, in turn, favours with regard to the use of force in international relations, politically dominant protagonists due to their more wide-ranging options of action.[76]

Yet this debate also raises a number of questions that are beyond the scope of this work: namely, to what degree actions of the United States have resulted in a change of the rules for the creation of rules of law which, in turn, created the possibility of the creation of rules *sui generis* or may facilitate their creation.[77] At the same time, doctrines mark the limits of hegemonic exercise of power, because they lay down commandments for action and prohibitions, of which the enforcement is beyond the actual options for action of the declaring state. In this regard doctrines also serve as an 'ersatz-instrument of the politically weak'.[78] This becomes especially clear in the case of the Stimson Doctrine and its predecessor, the Open Door Principle.[79]

Doctrines, thus, express two different interests or standpoints: on the one hand, a position of the stronger party, based on an instrumental understanding of international law, and, on the other hand, a position of the weaker party, based on a formalistic understanding of international law.[80] Since the end of the Cold War an anti-formalistic approach has prevailed on the part of the United States,[81] as the Bush Doctrine highlights.

75 G. Nolte, 'Die USA und das Völkerrecht', Friedens-Warte/J.I.P.O., 79 (2003), 132, who uses the German words: 'potentiell systemsprengend'.

76 M. Koskenniemi, 'What is International Law For?', in M. Evans (ed.), *International Law*, 2nd edn. (Oxford University Press, 2006), pp. 63–4 with direct reference to the Bush Doctrine in fn. 14; Koskenniemi, *The Gentle Civilizer of Nations: The Rise and Fall of International Law 1870–1960*, p. 34.

77 M. Byers, 'The Shifting Foundations of International Law: A Decade of Forceful Measures against Iraq', E.J.I.L., 13 (2002), 21 *et seq.*; G. Symes, 'Without Law, Seeking a Legal Justification for the September 1996 U.S. Military Intervention in Iraq', Mich.J.I.L., 19 (1998), 581.

78 K. Krakau, 'Lateinamerikanische Doktrinen zur Realisierung staatlicher Unabhängigkeit und Integrität', VRÜ, 8 (1975), 117 ('Ersatz-Instrument des politisch Schwachen'). See also: W. Grewe, *Spiel der Kräfte in der Weltpolitik* (Düsseldorf: Econ Verlag, 1970), p. 634.

79 See above, Chapter 2, sections 2.2.2 and 2.2.4.

80 Koskenniemi, 'What is International Law For?', in Evans (ed.), *International Law*, pp. 67–9.

81 G. Nolte, 'Remarks', ASIL Proceedings, 94th Annual Meeting, 2000, p. 66; G. Nolte, 'Guantanamo und Genfer Konventionen: Eine Frage der lex lata oder de lege ferenda?', in H. Fischer *et al.* (eds.), *Krisensicherung und Humanitärer Schutz*, FS-Fleck (Berlin: Berliner Wissenschafts-Verlag, 2004), pp. 393–404, in particular p. 403.

Based on the distinctive interests expressed in doctrines (as described above), and after analysing the law-creating impacts of doctrines, a uniform statement on the legal nature of doctrines of US security policy can be made.

5.3 The legal nature of the doctrines of US security policy

A doctrine is the law-like smokescreen of a political maxim for action. With regard to the legal nature of doctrines, it would be inadequate to attribute to this type of action a particular quality under international law or even the status of a rule of law. The fact that the United States regards the treatment of doctrines partially as being not merely a matter of politics but also a matter of law,[82] is of no importance for their legal nature. Merely by 'pretending to be international law' a political doctrine does not assume a particular status in international law.[83]

On top of that, the United States itself does not have an interest in considering doctrines as rules of international law, as the continued change of doctrines proves. This would also be at odds with their function.[84] Besides that, recognition by other states of doctrines as a type of action of particular quality is lacking, as it would be necessary for the process of law creation under international law.[85]

This result supports the conclusion drawn in earlier works that doctrines, due to a lack of general recognition, cannot be considered as 'general principles of law' in terms of Article 38(I)(c) of the ICJ Statute.[86] Also, no self-binding effect for the declaring state results *eo ipso* from declaring a doctrine.[87] A desire to be legally bound, necessary for such a self-binding effect, is lacking[88] as well as a clearly recognisable desire of

82 C. Schmitt, *Völkerrechtliche Großraumordnung mit Interventionsverbot für raumfremde Mächte*, 4th edn. (Berlin: Deutscher Rechtsverlag, 1941), p. 25 *et seq.*

83 Berber, *Lehrbuch des Völkerrechts*, vol. I, p. 73; M. Dixon, *Textbook on International Law*, 6th edn. (Oxford University Press, 2007), p. 328.

84 For example, Kraus, *Die Monroedoktrin in ihren Beziehungen zur amerikanischen Diplomatie und zum Völkerrecht*, pp. 398–400.

85 P. Allott, 'The Concept of International Law', in M. Byers (ed.), *The Role of Law in International Politics* (Oxford University Press, 2000), pp. 76 *et seq.*

86 Berber, *Lehrbuch des Völkerrechts*, vol. I, p. 73.

87 On this see section 5.2.3. See also: von Wrede, *Der Rechtsanspruch der Deutschen Bundesregierung auf völkerrechtliche Alleinvertretung Gesamtdeutschlands und die Hallstein-Doktrin*, pp. 35–6.

88 ICJ, *Nuclear Tests* (*New Zealand* v. *France*), Judgment, 20 December 1974, I.C.J. Rep.1974, pp. 472–3, paras. 46–7.

the state declaring the doctrine.[89] For the most part statements considered by some authors as descriptions of the doctrine cannot be considered as *opinio iuris*.[90]

Even though it is partially assumed by scholars that a specific change of law is promoted in doctrines, the evaluation of doctrines among scholars of international law and in state practice does not confirm this assumption. Doctrines lack a sufficiently determined demand for a certain change of law required to confirm this assumption.[91] Instead, doctrines represent merely a declaratory repetition of the law in force and are mostly considered by the United States as such.[92] The Roosevelt Corollary to the Monroe Doctrine and the Bush Doctrine alone cannot be understood as a purely declaratory repetition of existing law and contain strategic and legal concepts exceeding it.[93]

The idea of a doctrine is engaged when political means of power do not suffice in order to prevent action against the principles of the doctrine, or when exercise of political force is covered by the appearance of legal correctness as being in conformity with international law.[94] Doctrines represent the appeal to a quasi-legal concept, or at least the use of an international legal idiom, in order to justify the exercise of power or claim to power.[95] They illustrate an effort by the United States to confer symbolic legitimacy upon its actions, which may also contribute to the acceptance of an action,[96] by claiming motives beyond national interest.

A prior or sub-legal desire is articulated in doctrines. The doctrines discussed constitute political declarations of belief to use force when certain factual, but not legal prerequisites are met.

5.4 Doctrines under different polarities of the international system

One possibility of distinguishing between different factual circumstances of the international system is to consider it with regard to its polarity.

89 ICJ, *Case concerning the Temple of Preah Vihear* (*Cambodia* v. *Thailand*), Preliminary Objections, Judgment, 26 May 1961, I.C.J. Rep. 1961, p. 31.
90 On this see further above, Chapter 4, section 4.2.2.
91 See above, Chapter 1, section 1.6 and Chapter 4, section 4.2.2.
92 For example, Chapter 3, sections 3.1.4, 3.2.4 and 3.3.4.
93 See above, Chapter 4, section 4.2.4.
94 W. Kubitz, *Die Stimson-Doktrin* (Würzburg: Konrad Triltsch, 1938), p. 2.
95 M. Reisman, 'Remarks', ASIL Proceedings, 81st Annual Meeting, 1987, p. 562.
96 T. Franck, *The Power of Legitimacy among Nations* (Oxford University Press, 1990), pp. 111 *et seq.*

Polarity of the system has been used in this work as a supporting criterion for its organisation, alongside a chronological way of proceeding in discussing doctrines.[97]

Different theories within the realist school of thought assumed that the international system shows different stabilities under different polarities: partly it is assumed that a bipolar system possesses the greatest stability, because each dominant state exercises a mitigating influence on the respective other state.[98] Compared with that, supporters of a hegemonic stability theory[99] consider a unipolar system as the most stable, because the hegemon is willing to guarantee unilaterally the persistence of the state of the system favourable to it.[100] However, the connection between the polarity and the stability of the international system is a contentious issue among realists.[101]

The rules of international law concerning the legality of the use of force as part of the international system and, hence, their change as change of the system, have been discussed in this work under three different polarities of the system. This is the case as a global perspective has been chosen as frame of reference for the respective polarity. The categorisation of doctrines under international law as in conformity with international law or at odds with it, may serve in this process as evidence of whether US security policy was aiming at supporting or changing the structures of the international system.

The result, that the principles for the use of force contained in doctrines of the Cold War period – hence, during a phase of bipolarity – can be reconciled with the respective law in force, whereas doctrines during phases of multipolarity and unipolarity (the Roosevelt Corollary to the Monroe Doctrine and the Bush Doctrine) are at odds with the respective law in force, seems to support the theory that a bipolar system possesses the greatest stability.

Yet the questions as to how the practice of US security policy followed the principles of doctrines, and which changes of the system in terms of

97 See above, Chapter 1, section 1.5.

98 For example, K. Waltz, 'International Structure, National Force, and the Balance of World Power', J.I.A., 21 (1967), 215–31.

99 For a summary of this see: G. Evans and J. Newnham, *The Penguin Dictionary of International Relations* (London: Penguin Books, 1998), pp. 220–1.

100 For example, R. Keohane, *After Hegemony: Cooperation and Discord in the World Political Economy* (Princeton University Press, 1984).

101 K. Mingst, *Essentials of International Relations* (New York: W. W. Norton, 1999), pp. 90–1.

shifts of polarity may have resulted from this practice remain unanswered. The response to this question is further left to political science, not to the study of international law. This constitutes a possible starting point for a further reaching exploration of doctrines by the political sciences and the interdisciplinary use of this work.

5.5 Final remarks

With the exception of the Monroe Doctrine in its moulding through the Roosevelt Corollary and the Bush Doctrine, the cases of use of force stipulated in the doctrines of US security policy were, or are, in accordance with international law. The other doctrines are at least open to an interpretation under which they stipulate actions only in accordance with the valid *ius ad bellum*. This similarity between the Bush Doctrine and Roosevelt Corollary to the Monroe Doctrine can be seen as an expression of an increased, often assumed renewed, willingness of the United States to define international order in terms of ideological content, whereas it has intentionally avoided emphasising ideological differences during the Cold War period for the sake of détente.[102]

By contrast, other doctrines merely make reference to the existing situation of the law. Thus, it would be incorrect to assume that a doctrine always contains a dramatic break with the law in force. Some authors assume the biggest possible break with the valid law up to that point in a doctrine, and use it as a starting point for the examination of the conformity of doctrines under international law. Such examinations must lead inevitably, due to the understanding of the doctrine on which they are based, to the result that a doctrine deviates drastically from the given law. This means answering academic questions on the legality of the use of force, which do not pose themselves in the reality of law and occasionally assume Don Quixote-like features.

Yet besides making reference to the law in force, doctrines also have a law-shaping effect, even though the mere announcement of a doctrine has no impact on the legality of the use of force.[103] There is, however, room for the announcement of doctrines as political principles aimed at

102 L. Freedman, 'Prevention, Not Pre-emption', Wash.Q., 26/2 (2003), 110–11; Krisch, 'Amerikanische Hegemonie und Liberale Revolution im Völkerrecht', p. 278.

103 ICJ, *Military and Paramilitary Activities in and against Nicaragua* (*Nicaragua* v. *United States of America*), Merits, Judgment, 27 June 1986, I.C.J. Rep. 1986, p. 133, para. 263.

changes of law, but not causing a change of international law in itself.[104] Besides, the mere declaration of a doctrine does not constitute a breach of the prohibition on the threat of force in Article 2(4) of the UN Charter.[105] Specific principles described in doctrines have found their way into norms of international law which also apply to the United States. Thus, these principles have been enacted by international law and removed from unilateral changeability by the United States.[106]

The political reality of international relations may in the same way resist being formally captured by doctrines,[107] just as some attempts at capturing the legitimacy of the use of force in precise terms of international law may appear as attempts at an exaggerated simplification of a complex problem.[108] In this respect the formulation of doctrines provides the same challenges as the determination of rules of international law: there is a necessity to base one's work on an explanation for the reasons for the use of force considered as fitting in order to derive from it general rules of behaviour for the future regulation of the use of force. However, doctrines may possess a greater proximity to state practice and, hence, may have more direct effect on the shaping of actions of the declaring state than rules of law.[109] The main focus of the content of doctrines lies in the outlining of political aims and not in outlining procedures of how to reach these aims. This circumstance places doctrines in the realm of ideology and not that of international law.[110] Even though doctrines

104 'States may declare such policies and support them by diplomatic representations and other peaceful methods. But such policies do not constitute a part of the "self" of a state, and do not of themselves justify armed intervention in foreign territory. They justify such intervention only insofar as they are declaratory of the justifications recognized by international law.' Q. Wright, 'United States Intervention in the Lebanon', p. 117; E. Zivier, 'Pax Americana – Bellum Americanum', RuP, 39 (2003), 196–7.

105 See above, section 5.1.3.2.2.

106 See above, sections 5.2.2 and 5.2.3.

107 Kissinger, *Diplomacy*, p. 708.

108 D. W. Bowett, *Self-Defence in International Law* (Manchester University Press, 1958), p. 192; W. Abendroth, 'Großmächte', in H. Schlochauer (ed.), *Wörterbuch des Völkerrechts*, 2nd edn. (Berlin: Walter de Gruyter, 1962), p. 717.

109 M. Reisman: 'Unilateral pronouncements such as the Monroe Doctrine, the Brezhnev Doctrine and the Carter Doctrine may be prescriptive if they are accompanied by sufficient authority signals and control intention.' ASIL Proceedings, 75th Annual Meeting, 1981, p. 120; R. MacDonald, 'Foreign Policy, Influence of Legal Considerations Upon', E.P.I.L., II (1992), 442–6.

110 On this see: Q. Wright, 'International Law and Ideologies', A.J.I.L., 30 (1954), 616–26; S. Scott, 'International Law as Ideology: Theorizing the Relationship between International Law and International Politics', E.J.I.L., 5 (1994), 313–25.

in their capacity as declarations of political maxims for action have no law-shaping effect and though they can be legalised only to a certain extent, it is impossible to implement doctrines without taking actions of relevance under international law.[111]

To what extent US foreign policy, and single interventions in particular, may be considered as a subsequent implementation of doctrines is a possible starting point for the examination of doctrines beyond the question of their impact on international law. What repercussions single cases of the use of force by the United States based on doctrines have had on the rules of international law concerning the use of force, is in turn a question of international law reaching far beyond the objective of this work.

In comparing the US practice of the use of force and the justifications brought forward for those actions, one may reach the conclusion that doctrines merely present a special type of rhetoric in foreign policy.[112] In line with this, for example, the US justification under international law for the use force in Iraq in 2003 does not build on the justification of unilateral use of force in terms of the Bush Doctrine.[113]

Statements during the first year of President Obama's term of office make it seem rather unlikely that the Obama Administration will declare a concise doctrine.[114] However, for the future it can be assumed that the United States will not abandon the instrument of declaring political doctrines.[115] Even though political doctrines under international law are merely the engaging of a quasi-legal rhetoric in order to make a political claim appear as a rule of law, this rule-of-law-like outfit of principles of security policy is exactly in line with a particular tradition of US security policy.[116] Doctrines are subject to constant changes: 'Every day a new side of their contents may come to bear, an old one may vanish.'[117]

111 Similarly: L. Focsaneanu, 'La "Doctrine Eisenhower" Pour Le Proche Orient', A.F.D.I., (1958), 105–7.

112 Similar, for example, M. Reisman, 'Old Wine in New Bottles: The Reagan and Brezhnev Doctrines in Contemporary International Law and Practice', Y.J.I.L., 13 (1988), 186–7.

113 See above, Chapter 4, section 4.2.2.3.

114 See above, Chapter 4, section 4.3.4.

115 Already correct in this regard in 1986: Crabb, *The Doctrines of American Foreign Policy – Their Meaning, Role and Future*, 3rd edn. (Baton Rouge, LA: Louisiana State University Press, 1990), pp. 428–9: 'there will be a future doctrine'.

116 M. Dunne, 'American Judicial Internationalism in the Twentieth Century', ASIL Proceedings, 90th Annual Meeting, 1996, pp. 148–54, in particular p. 154.

117 Kraus, *Die Monroedoktrin in ihren Beziehungen zur amerikanischen Diplomatie und zum Völkerrecht*, p. 401. Author's translation of: 'im vollen Flusse ständiger Umgestaltung. Jeden Tag kann eine neue Seite ihres Inhalts sich entfalten, eine alte entschwinden.'

The choice of doctrines as a type of action highlights the limited utility of international law as a means of hegemonic policy, for which it is only of limited value due to its formalised procedures for the creation of law.[118] International law does not mirror the single interest of a hegemon but the permanent collective interests of states.[119]

Unlike other types of actions, elevating a political principle to the status of a doctrine gives the hegemon the opportunity to claim a higher, quasi-legal authority for its own actions without having undergone a formalised process of creating law. This constitutes the special value of doctrines for hegemonic policy.

The results of this study can be summed up in the following hypothesis:

(1) All doctrines of US security policy – with the exception of the Monroe Doctrine in its shape as the Roosevelt Corollary and the Bush Doctrine – can be interpreted in a way that the principles for the use of force as set out in these doctrines are in accordance with the actually valid *ius ad bellum.*
(2) Different opinions with regard to the compatibility of the principles for the use of force as contained in the doctrines of US security policy with the actually valid *ius ad bellum* are mainly rooted in different understandings of the content attached to single doctrines, not in different interpretations of the valid *ius ad bellum.*
(3) The mere declaration of a doctrine does not violate the prohibition on the threat of the use of force according to Article 2(4) of the UN Charter, because the doctrines are lacking a threat of temporarily close use of force. The force which is threatened in the doctrines is referring to uncertain situations in the future. The occurrence of exactly such situations is be avoided by declaring a doctrine.
(4) Only to a certain degree can a doctrine as a unilateral political declaration be codified as a rule of public international law, because an unsolvable contradiction exists between the nature of a doctrine as a unilateral political declaration, which is subject only to the will of a

118 Alvarez, 'Hegemonic International Law Revisited', pp. 886–8; Krisch, 'Amerikanische Hegemonie und Liberale Revolution im Völkerrecht', pp. 295–7; N. Krisch, 'Imperial International Law', Global Law Working Paper 01/04, Hauser Global Law School Program, NYU School of Law, pp. 9–11; 48–9, available at: www.nyulawglobal.org/workingpapers/krisch˙appd˙0904.pdf.

119 Kraus, 'Interesse und zwischenstaatliche Ordnung', p. 52; N. Krisch, 'International Law in Times of Hegemony: Unequal Power and the Shaping of the International Legal Order', E.J.I.L., 16 (2005), 369–408.

single state, and a rule of public international law, which is not subject of the freedom of will of a single state.

(5) One common feature of doctrines in the realm of security policy which foresees unilateral use of force is that the declaring state is acting as if it was the representative of an epoch-making idea. As public international law is not centred around this idea, which is considered as the decisive element of foreign policy, a tension inevitably arises between such a doctrine and a public international law, which depends on the agreement of other states and does not choose this epoch-making idea as central feature of the legal order.

(6) The declaration of a doctrine does not constitute a type of action of a special legal quality in public international law. Just like *opinio iuris*, a doctrine constitutes a concept which can be changed at any time by the unilateral declaration of a state. Most doctrines of US security policy are lacking a statement of sufficiently fixable legal opinion required to constitute *opinio iuris*. A pre- or sub-legal will is expressed in doctrines.

BIBLIOGRAPHY

Abendroth, Wolfgang, 'Großmächte', in Hans-Jürgen Schlochauer (ed.), *Wörterbuch des Völkerrechts*, pp. 713–7

Abbott, Kenneth, 'Modern International Relations Theory: A Prospectus for International Lawyers', Y.J.I.L., 14 (1989), 335–411

'International Law and International Relations Theory: Building Bridges – Elements of a Joint Discipline', *ASIL Proceedings*, 86th Annual Meeting (1992), 167–72

Robert Keohane, Andrew Moravcsik, Anne-Marie Slaughter and Duncan Snidal, 'The Concept of Legalization', Int.Org., 54/3 (2000), 401–19

Ackerman, Bruce, 'This Is Not a War', Y.L.J., 13 (2004), 1871–907

Ackerman, Spencer, 'The Obama Doctrine', *The American Prospect*, 24 March 2008

Ago, Robert, Addendum to Eighth Report on State Responsibility, *ILC Yearbook*, 13 (1980), 65–7

Ahrens, Dieter, *Der Karibische Raum als Interessensphäre der Vereinigten Staaten von Amerika – Eine völkerrechtlich-politische Studie* (Stuttgart: Kohlhammer, 1965), Ph.D. thesis, Hamburg, 1964

Akehurst, Michael, 'Enforcement Action by Regional Agencies with Special Reference to the Organization of American States', B.Y.I.L., 42 (1967), 175–227

'Custom as a Source of International Law', B.Y.I.L., 47 (1974–5), 1–53

Alexandrov, Stanimir A., *Self-Defense Against the Use of Force in International Law*, (The Hague: Kluwer Law International, 1996)

Allott, Philip, 'The Concept of International Law', in Michael Byers (ed.), *The Role of Law in International Politics* (Oxford University Press, 2000), pp. 69–89

Alvarez, Alejandro, *Le Droit International Américain* (Paris: A. Pedone, 1910)

The Monroe Doctrine – Its Importance in the International Life of the States of the New World (Oxford University Press, 1924)

Alvarez, José, 'Hegemonic International Law Revisited', A.J.I.L., 97 (2003), 873–88

Ambos, Kai and Arnold, Jörg (eds.), *Der Irak-Krieg und das Völkerrecht* (Berlin: BWV, 2004)

Anderson, Chandler P., 'The Monroe Doctrine Distinguished in Principle From Mutual Protective Pacts', A.J.I.L., 30 (1936), 477–9

Anzilotti, Dionisio, *Lehrbuch des Völkerrechts* (Berlin: Walter de Gruyter, 1929)

Arend, Anthony Clark, 'International Law and the Preemptive Use of Military Force', Wash.Q., 26/2 (2003), 89–103

Arend, Anthony Clark and Beck, Robert J., *International Law and the Use of Force – Beyond the UN Charter Paradigm* (London: Longman, 1993)

Asrat, Belatchew, *Prohibition of Force Under The UN Charter, A Study of Art. 2(4)* (Uppsala: Iustus Verlag, 1991)

Aust, Anthony, *Modern Treaty Law and Practice*, 2nd edn. (Cambridge University Press, 2007)

Ball, Margaret, 'Recent Developments in Inter American Relations', Y.B. WorldAff., 3 (1943), 105–31

Barberis, Julio A., 'International Law, American', E.P.I.L., II (1992), 1178–83

Barcia Trelles, Camilo, 'La Doctrine de Monroe dans son développement historique particulièrement en ce qui concerne les relations inter-américaines', RdC, 32 (1930-II), 390–604

Baylis, John *et al.* (eds.), *Strategy in the Contemporary World – An Introduction to Strategic Studies* (Oxford University Press, 2002)

Beck, Robert J., Arend, Anthony Clark and Vanderlugt, Robert (eds.), *International Rules, Approaches from International Law and International Relations* (Oxford University Press, 1996)

Bennouna, Mohamed, *Le consentment a l'ingérence militaire dans les conflits internes* (Paris: Librarie Generale, 1974)

Benvenisti, Eyal, 'The US and the Use of Force: Double Edged Hegemony and the Management of Global Emergencies', E.J.I.L., 15 (2004), 677–700

Berber, Friedrich, *Der Mythos der Monroe-Doktrin* (Essen: Essener Verlagsanstalt, 1942)

Lehrbuch des Völkerrechts, 2 vols. (Munich: C. H. Beck, 1960)

Berg, Manfred *et al.* (eds.), *Macht und Moral – Beiträge zur Ideologie und Praxis amerikanischer Außenpolitik im 20. Jahrhundert, Festschrift für Knud Krakau zu seinem 65. Geburtstag*, FS-Krakau (Münster: Lit Verlag, 1999)

Bernhardt, Rudolf (ed.), *Encyclopedia of Public International Law* (E.P.I.L.), 5 vols. (Amsterdam: North-Holland, 1992–2002)

Berry, Nicholas O., 'The Conflict between United States Intervention and Promoting Democracy in the Third World', TempleL.Q., 60 (1987), 1015–21

Bianchi, Andrea and Keller, Alexis (eds.), *Counterterrorism: Democracy's Challenge* (Oxford: Hart Publishing, 2008)

Bilfinger, Carl, *Das wahre Gesicht des Kelloggpaktes, Angelsächsischer Imperialismus im Gewande des Rechts* (Essen: Essener Verlagsanstalt, 1942)

Die Stimsondoktrin (Essen: Essener Verlagsanstalt, 1943)

Bingham, Hiram, *The Monroe Doctrine, An Obsolete Shibboleth* (New Haven, CT: Yale University Press, 1913)

Blakeslee, George H., 'The Japanese Monroe Doctrine', For.Aff., 11 (1933), 671–81

Blix, Hans, 'Contemporary Aspects of Non-Recognition', RdC, 130 (1970-II), 593–700

Blum, Yehuda Z., 'State Responses to Acts of Terrorism', G.Y.I.L., 19 (1976), 223–37

Blumenwitz, Dieter and Wehner, Gerd (eds.), *Schritte in eine neue Rechtsordnung* (Munich: Hans Seidel Stiftung, 2003)

Bode, William R., 'The Reagan Doctrine', Strategic Rev., 14 (1986), 21–9

Bolton, John R., 'Is There Really "Law" in International Affairs?', T.L.C.P., 10 (2000), 1–48

Borchard, Edwin M., 'The Multilateral Treaty for the Renunciation of War', A.J.I.L., 23 (1929), 116–20

'The Kellogg Treaties Sanction War', ZaöRV/H.J.I.L., 1/1 (1929), 126–31

'Intervention – The Truman Doctrine and the Marshall Plan', A.J.I.L., 41 (1947), 885–8

Bothe, Michael, 'Terrorism and the Legality of Pre-emptive Force', E.J.I.L., 14 (2003), 227–40

Bowett, Derek W., *Self-Defence in International Law* (Manchester University Press, 1958)

Boyle, Francis, *World Politics and International Law* (Durham, NC: Duke University Press, 1985)

Bradford, William C., 'The Duty to Defend Them: A Natural Law Justification for the Bush Doctrine of Preventive War', N.D.L.R., 79 (2004), 1365–492

Braim, Paul F., 'General James A. Van Fleet and the U.S. Military Mission to Greece', in Rossides (ed.), *The Truman Doctrine of Aid to Greece*, pp. 117–27

Brierly, James Leslie B., *The Law of Nations – An Introduction to the International Law of Peace*, 6th edn. (Oxford: Clarendon Press, 1963)

'Some Implications of the Pact of Paris', B.Y.I.L., 10 (1929), 208–10

Brilmayer, Lea, *American Hegemony* (New Haven, CT: Yale University Press, 1997)

Brinkley, Douglas, 'Democratic Enlargement: The Clinton Doctrine', For.Pol., 106 (1997), 111–27

Bröhmer, Jürgen *et al.* (eds.), *Internationale Gemeinschaft und Menschenrechte, Festschrift für Georg Ress zum 70. Geburtstag*, FS-Ress (Cologne: Carl Heymanns Verlag, 2005)

Brown, Bartram S., 'Special Project: Humanitarian Intervention and Kosovo: Humanitarian Intervention at a Crossroads', W. & M.L.R., 41 (2000), 1683–741

Brown, Philip Marshall, 'The Monroe Doctrine and the League of Nations Covenant', A.J.I.L., 14 (1920), 207–10

'Mexico and the Monroe Doctrine', A.J.I.L., 26 (1932), 117–21

Brown, Jr., William Adams and Opie, Redvers, *American Foreign Assistance* (Washington, DC: The Brookings Institution, 1954)

Brownlie, Ian, 'International Law and the Activities of Armed Bands', I.C.L.Q., 7 (1958), 712–35

International Law and the Use of Force by States (Oxford: Clarendon Press, 1963)
'The Reality and Efficacy of International Law', B.Y.I.L., 52 (1981), 1–8
'International Law at the Fiftieth Anniversary of the United Nations', RdC, 255 (1995), 9–227
Principles of International Law, 7th edn. (Oxford University Press, 2008)
Brüel, Erik, 'Die juristische Bedeutung des Atlantikpaktes', AVR, 4 (1953/4), 288–300
Bruha, Thomas, 'Gewaltverbot und humanitäres Völkerrecht nach dem 11. September', AVR, 40 (2002), 383–421
Buckley, Mary and Singh, Robert (eds.), *The Bush Doctrine and the War on Terrorism: Global Responses, Global Consequences* (London: Routledge, 2006)
Buttlar, Christian von, 'Rechtsstreit oder Glaubensstreit? Anmerkung zur Debatte um die präventive Selbstverteidigung im Völkerrecht', in Bröhmer *et al.* (eds.), *Internationale Gemeinschaft und Menschenrechte*, FS-Ress, pp. 15–28
Byers, Michael, 'Response: Taking the Law out of International Law: A Critique of the "Iterative Perspective"', Harv.I.L.J., 38/1 (1997), 201–5
Custom, Power and the Power of Rules: International Relations and Customary International Law (Cambridge University Press, 1999)
(ed.) *The Role of Law in International Politics: Essays in International Relations and Law* (Oxford University Press, 2000)
'The Shifting Foundations of International Law: A Decade of Forceful Measures against Iraq', E.J.I.L., 13 (2002), 21–41
'Terrorism, the Use of Force and International Law after 11 September', I.C.L.Q., 51 (2002), 401–14
'Der Irak und der Fall Caroline', in Ambos and Arnold (eds.), *Der Irak-Krieg und das Völkerrecht*, pp. 235–41
and Chestermann, Simon, '"You the People": pro-Democratic Intervention in: International Law', in Fox and Roth (eds.), *Democratic Governance and International Law*, pp. 259–92
and Nolte, Georg (eds.), *United States Hegemony and the Foundations of International Law* (Oxford University Press, 2003)
Caflisch, Lucius, 'Monroe-Doktrin', in Ignaz Seidl-Hohenveldern (ed.), LdR/VR, pp. 285–7
Calliess, C., Nolte, G. and Stoll, P. (eds.), *Von der Diplomatie zum kodifizierten Recht – 75 Jahre Institut für Völkerrecht der Universität Göttingen (1930–2005)* (Cologne: Heymanns, 2006)
Campbell, Kenneth J., 'Once Burned, Twice Cautious: Explaining the Weinberger–Powell Doctrine', A.F.& S., 24/3 (1998), 357–75
Canadian Department of Foreign Affairs and International Trade (ed.), *The Responsibility to Protect: Report of the International Commission on Intervention and State Sovereignty*, Ottawa, 2002

Carey, Roger, 'The Contemporary Nature of Security', in Trevor C. Salmon (ed.), *Issues in International Relations* (London: Routledge, 2000), pp. 55–75

Carter, Ashton B. and Perry, William J., *Preventive Defense: A New Security Strategy for America* (Washington, DC: The Brookings Institution Press, 1999)

Carto, David D., 'The Monroe Doctrine in the 1980s: International Law, Unilateral Policy, or Atavistic Anachronism?', Cas.W.Res.J.I.L., 13 (1981), 203–29

Carty, Anthony, 'Critical International Law: Recent Trends in the Theory of International Law', E.J.I.L., 2 (1991), 66–96

'Schmitt's Critique of Liberal International Legal Order Between 1933 and 1945', L.J.I.L., 14 (2001), 25–76

Cassese, Antonio (ed.), *The Current Legal Regulation of the Use of Force* (Dordrecht: Martin Nijhoff Publishers, 1986)

'Art. 51', in Cot and Pellet (eds.), *La Charte des Nations Unies*, pp. 769–94

'Terrorism is also Disrupting Some Crucial Categories of International Law', E.J.I.L., 12 (2001), 993–1001

Charvin, Robert, 'La doctrine Américaine de la "Souveraineté Limitée"', R.B.D.I., 20 (1987), 5–27

Chayes, Abram, 'Law and the Quarantine of Cuba', For.Aff., 40 (1963), 550–7

'A Common Lawyer Looks at International Law', H.L.R., 78 (1965), 1396–413

The Cuban Missile Crisis (Oxford University Press, 1974)

Ehrlicher, Thomas and Lowenfeld, Andreas F. (eds.), *International Legal Process – Materials for an Introductory Course*, 2 vols. (New York: Little, Brown, 1968)

Chestermann, Simon, *Just War or Just Peace? Humanitarian Intervention in International Law* (Oxford University Press, 2001)

Chin, John, 'Promoting Democracy: A Blueprint for the Next Administration', Policy Matters J., Spring 2008, 33–9

Churchill, Sir Winston Spencer, *Memoirs of the Second World War (An Abridgement of the Six Volumes of the Second World War* (Boston, MA: Houghton Mifflin, 1990)

Clark, Ian, *Legitimacy in International Society* (Oxford University Press, 2007)

Clark, Joshua Reuben, *Memorandum on the Monroe Doctrine: December 17, 1928* (Washington, DC: Government Printing Office, 1930)

Clausewitz, Carl von, *Vom Kriege* (Augsburg: Weltbildverlag, 1998)

Clinton, Hillary, 'Security and Opportunity for the Twenty-First Century', For.Aff., 86/6 (2007), 2–18

Clinton, William Jefferson, *National Security Strategy of the United States: 1994–1995* (Washington: Brassey's, 1995)

Clyde, Paul H., 'The Diplomacy of "Playing No Favorites": Secretary Stimson and Manchuria, 1931', Miss.V.H.Rev., 35/2 (1948), 187–202

Cohan, John Alan, 'The Bush Doctrine and the Emerging Norm of Anticipatory Self-Defense in Customary International Law', PaceI.L.R., 15 (2003), 283–356

Combacau, Jean, 'The Exception of Self-Defence in the U.N. Practice', in Cassese (ed.), *The Current Legal Regulation of the Use of Force*, pp. 9–38

Constantopoulos, Dimitri S. (ed.), *Grundprobleme des internationalen Rechts: Festschrift für Jean Spiropoulus*, FS-Jean Spiropoulus (Bonn: Schimmelbusch, 1957)

'The Significance of the Truman Doctrine for Greece and the Free World', Rev.Hell.d.Int., 25 (1972), 234–48

Conze, Eckart, Schlie, Ulrich and Seubert, Harald (eds.), *Geschichte zwischen Wissenschaft und Politik, Festschrift für Michael Stürmer zum 65. Geburtstag*, FS-Stürmer (Baden-Baden: Nomos, 2003)

Cot, Jean Pierre and Pellet, Alain, *La Charte des Nations Unies*, 2nd edn. (Paris: Economia, 1991)

Crabb, C., *Nations in a Multipolar World* (New York: Harper & Row, 1968)

Crabb, Cecil Vandermeer, *The Doctrines of American Foreign Policy – Their Meaning, Role and Future*, 3rd edn. (Baton Rouge, LA: Louisiana State University Press, 1990)

Crawford, James, 'Democracy and the Body of international Law', in Fox and Roth (eds.), *Democratic Governance and International Law*, pp. 91–120

Creifelds, Carl (founder), *Rechtswörterbuch*, 18th edn. (Munich: C. H. Beck, 2004)

Cronin, Audrey Kurth, 'Rethinking Sovereignty: American Strategy in the Age of Terrorism', Survival, 44/2 (2002), 119–39

Cronin, Bruce, 'The Paradox of Hegemony: America's Ambiguous Relationship with the United Nations', Eu.J.I.R., 7 (2001), 103–30

Crook, John R., 'Contemporary Practice of the United States Relating to International Law', A.J.I.L., 100 (2006) 690–724

Current, Richard N., 'The Stimson Doctrine and the Hoover Doctrine', Am.H.Rev., 59/3 (1954), 513–42

Dagget, Stephen and Serafino, Nina (eds.), *The Use of Force: Key Contemporary Documents* (Washington, DC: Congressional Research Service, 1994)

Dahm, Georg, *Völkerrecht*, 3 vols. (Stuttgart: Kohlhammer, 1958–61)

Damrosh, Lori Fisler and Scheffer, David J. (eds.), *Law and Force in the New International Order* (Boulder, CO: Westview Press, 1991)

'The Interface of National Constitutional Systems with International Law and Institutions on Using Military Forces: Changing Trends in Executive and Legislative Powers', in Ku and Jacobson (eds.), *Democratic Accountability and the Use of Force in International Law* (Cambridge University Press, 2003), pp. 39–60

and Bernard H. Oxmann, 'Agora: Future Implications of the Iraq Conflict, Editors Note', A.J.I.L., 97 (2003), 553–7; 803–4

Daniel, Donald C. F., Dombrowski, Peter J. and Payne, Roger A., 'The Bush Doctrine: Rest in Peace?', Defence Studies, 4/1 (2004), 18–39

Danilenko, Gennady M., *Law-Making in the International Community* (Dordrecht: Martin Nijhoff Publishers, 1993)

D'Amato, Anthony, *The Concept of Custom in International Law* (Ithaca, NY: Cornell University Press, 1971)

'Israel's Air Strike Upon the Iraqi Nuclear Reactor', A.J.I.L., 77 (1983), 584–8

Darby, Joseph J., 'Self-Defense in Public International Law: the Doctrine of Preemption and Its Discontents', in Bröhmer *et al.* (eds.), *Internationale Gemeinschaft und Menschenrechte*, FS-Ress, pp. 29–33

Daudet, Yves, 'International Action Against State Terrorism', in Higgins and Flory (eds.), *Terrorism and International Law*, pp. 201–16

Davis, Norman, 'Wanted: A Consistent Latin-American Policy', For.Aff., 9 (1931), 567–80

Dederer, Hans-Georg, 'Krieg gegen Terror', JZ, 59 (2004), 421–31

Delbrück, Jost, 'Collective Security', E.P.I.L., I (1992), 646–56

'The Fight Against Global Terrorism: Self-Defense or Collective Security as International Police Action? Some Comments on the International Legal Implications of the "War Against Terrorism"', G.Y.I.L., 4 (2001), 9–24

DeMuth, Christopher C. *et al.* (eds.), *The Reagan Doctrine and Beyond* (Washington, DC: The American Enterprise Institute, 1987)

Dent, David, *The Legacy of the Monroe Doctrine* (Westport, CT: Greenwood Press, 1999)

Deutsch, Karl W. and Hoffmann, Stanley (eds.), *The Relevance of International Law: Essays in Honor of Leo Gross* (Cambridge, MA: Schenkmann, 1968)

Desjardins, Arthur, 'La Doctrine de Monroe', R.G.D.I.P., 3 (1896), 137–65

Dicke, Klaus *et al.* (eds.), *Weltinnenrecht – Liber amicorum Jost Delbrück* (Berlin: Duncker & Humblot, 2005)

Dinstein, Yoram, *War, Aggression and Self-Defence*, 4th edn. (Cambridge University Press, 2004)

Dixon, Martin, *Textbook on International Law*, 6th edn. (Oxford University Press, 2007)

Doehring, Karl, 'Kollektive Sicherheit', in Wolfrum (ed.), *Handbuch Vereinte Nationen* (Munich: C. H. Beck, 1991), pp. 405–10

'Self-Determination', in Simma (ed.), *The Charter of the United Nations*, vol. I, pp. 47–63

Völkerrecht, 2nd edn. (Heidelberg: C. F. Müller, 2004)

Dolzer, Rudolf, 'Enforcement of International Obligations through Regional Arrangements: Structures an Experience of the OAS', ZaöRV/H.J.I.L., 47 (1987), 113–33

Dore, Isaak I., 'The U.S. Invasion of Grenada: Resurrection of the "Johnson Doctrine?"', StanfordJ.I.L., 20 (1984), 173–90

Dormont, Josh, 'The Powell Factor: Analyzing the Role of the Powell Doctrine in U.S. Foreign Policy', *Gaines Junction, Spring* 2005, 22–40

Dörr, Oliver, 'Staats- und völkerrechtliche Aspekte des Irak-Krieges 2003', Hu.V-I/J.I.L.P.A.C., 16 (2003), 181–8

'Das völkerrechtliche Gewaltverbot am Beginn des 21. Jahrhunderts – Was bleibt von Art. 2(4) UN-Charta?', in Oliver Dörr (ed.), *Ein Rechtslehrer in Berlin – Symposium für Albrecht Randelzhofer* (Berlin: Springer, 2004), pp. 33–54

Dozer, Donald, *The Monroe Doctrine: Its Modern Significance* (New York: Alfred A. Knopf, 1965)

Dunn, Lynne K. and Waren F. Kuehl, *Keeping the Covenant – American Internationalists and the League of Nations, 1920–1939* (Kent, OH: The Kent State University Press, 1997)

Dunne, Michael, 'American Judicial Internationalism in the Twentieth Century', ASIL Proceedings, 90th Annual Meeting (1996), pp. 148–54

Dupuis, Charles, *Le principe d'équilibre et le concert européen de la paix de Westphalie à l'acte d'Algeciras* (Paris: Perrin, 1900)

Dworkin, Anthony, 'Beyond the "War on Terror": Towards a New Transatlantic Framework for Counterterrorism', ECFR Policy Brief, May 2009

Edwards, John 'Reengaging with the World', For.Aff, 86/5 (2007), 19–37

Eick, Christophe, '"Präemption", "Prävention" und die Weiterentwicklung des Völkerrechts', ZRP, 6 (2004), 200–3

Eisenhower, Dwight D.. *Waging Peace 1956–1961* (Garden City, NY: Doubleday, 1965)

Elliott, Charles Burke, 'The Monroe Doctrine Exception in the League of Nations Covenant', I.L.A. Rep., 30 (1921), 74–109

Elstain, Jean Bethke, 'Just War and Humanitarian Intervention', Third Annual Grotius Lecture, ASIL Proceedings, 95th Annual Meeting, 2001, pp. 1–12

Erler, Georg, 'Marshallplan', in Hans-Jürgen Schlochauer (ed.), *Wörterbuch des Völkerrechts*, vol. II, pp. 480–4

Evans, Graham and Newnham, Jeffrey, *The Penguin Dictionary of International Relations* (London: Penguin Books, 1998)

Evans, Malcolm D. (ed.), *International Law*, 2nd edn. (Oxford University Press, 2006)

Fairbank, John K., *The United States and China* (New York: Viking, 1958)

Falk, Richard A., 'International Law and the United States Role in the Viet Nam War, The Vietnam War and International Law', Y.L.J., 75 (1966), 1122–60

'What Future for the UN Charter System of War Prevention?', A.J.I.L., 97 (2003), 590–98

Faluhelyi, Ferenc, 'Entwicklungslinien des Völkerrechts nach dem Weltkrieg', ZfV, 23 (1939), 393–410

Farer, Tom J., 'Beyond the UN Charter Frame: Unilateralism or Codominium', A.J.I.L., 96 (2002), 359–64

'The Bush Doctrine and the UN Charter Frame', *International Spectator*, 37/3 (2002), 91–100

'The Prospect for International Law and Order in the Wake of Iraq', A.J.I.L., 97 (2003), 621–8

Fassbender, Bardo, 'Stories of War and Peace – On Writing the History of International Law in the "Third Reich" and After', E.J.I.L., 13 (2002), 479–512

Fauchille, Paul, *Traité de Droit International Public*, 8th edn. (Paris: Rousseau & Cie, 1922–6)

Fawcett, James E. S., 'Intervention in International Law', RdC, 103 (1961-II), 343–423

Feinstein, Lee and Anne Marie Slaughter, 'A Duty to Prevent', For.Aff., 83/1 (2004), 136–50

Fenwick, Charles G., *International Law* (London: Allan & Unwin, 1924)

International Law, 2nd edn. (New York: Appleton-Century, 1934)

'The Question of Canadian Participation in Inter-American Conferences', A.J.I.L., 31 (1937), 473–6

'Canada and the Monroe Doctrine', A.J.I.L., 32 (1938), 782–5

'The Monroe Doctrine and the Declaration of Lima', A.J.I.L., 33 (1939), 257–68

'The Third Meeting of Ministers of Foreign Affairs at Rio de Janeiro', A.J.I.L., 36 (1942), 169–203

The Organization of American States (Washington, DC: The Organization of American States, 1963)

'The Organization of American States: The Transition from an Unwritten Constitution', A.J.I.L., 59 (1965), 315–20

Ferencz, Benjamin B., *Enforcing International Law – A Way to World Peace, A Documentary History and Analysis*, 2 vols. (London: Oceana Publications, 1983)

Fiedler, Wilfried, 'Unilateral Acts in International Law', E.P.I.L., (2000), IV, 1018–23

Fischer, Horst, Froissart, Ulrike, Heintschel von Heinegg, Wolff and Raap, Christian (eds.), *Krisensicherung und Humanitärer Schutz – Festschrift für Dieter Fleck*, FS-Fleck (Berlin: Berliner Wissenschafts-Verlag, 2004)

Fischer-Lescano, Gasser, Andreas, Gasser, Hans-Peter, Marauhn Thilo, and Ronzitti, Natalino (eds.), *Frieden in Freiheit – Peace in liberty – Paix en liberté, Festschrift für Michael Bothe zum 70. Geburtstag*, FS-Bothe (Baden-Baden: Nomos, 2008)

Fitzmaurice, Gerald, 'The General Principles of International Law', RdC, 92 (1957-II), 1–227

Fitzsimons, Louise, *The Kennedy Doctrine* (New York: Random House, 1972)

Fleck, Dieter, 'Meiertöns, Heiko: Die Doktrinen U.S.-Amerikanischer Sicherheitspolitik', ZaöRV/H.J.I.L., 67 (2007), 1391–3

Fleming, Denna Frank, *The United States and the League of Nations 1918–1920* (New York: Russell & Russell, 1968)

Focsaneanu, Lazar, 'La "Doctrine Eisenhower" Pour Le Proche Orient', A.F.D.I., (1958), 33–111

Foot, Peter, 'America and the Origins of the Atlantic Alliance: a Reappraisal', in Joseph Smith (ed.), *The Origins of NATO* (University of Exeter Press, 1990), pp. 82–94

Foot, Rosemary, MacFarlane, S. Neil and Mastanduno, Michael (eds.), *US Hegemony and International Institutions* (Oxford University Press, 2003)

Forsythe, David P., McMahon, Patrice C. and Wedeman, Andrew (eds.), *American Foreign Policy in a Globalized World* (New York: Routledge, 2006)

Fox, Gregory H. and Roth, Brad R. (eds.), *Democratic Governance and International Law* (Cambridge University Press, 2000)

Fraenkel, Ernst, 'Regionalpakte und Weltfriedensordnung – zur Völkerrechtsentwicklung der Nachkriegszeit', Vierteljahreshefte für Zeitgeschichte, 2 (1954), 34–54

Franck, Thomas, 'Who killed Article 2(4)?', A.J.I.L., 64 (1970), 809–37

'Regional Intervention by the Superpowers: A Study of Words and Acts as Inchoate Law Making', in Nawaz (ed.), *Essays in Honour of Krishna Rao*, pp. 241–51

Judging the World Court (New York: Priority Press, 1986)

The Power of Legitimacy among Nations (Oxford University Press, 1990)

'Terrorism and the Right of Self-Defense', A.J.I.L., 95 (2001), 839–43

Recourse to Force (Cambridge University Press, 2002)

'What Happens Now? The United Nations After Iraq', A.J.I.L., 97 (2003), 607–20

and Weisband, Edward, 'The Johnson and Brezhnev Doctrines: The Law You Make May be Your Own', StanfordL.Rev. (1969–70), 979–1014

'The Johnson–Brezhnev Doctrines: Verbal Behaviour Analysis of Superpower Confrontations', New York University, Center for International Studies Policy Papers, vol. 3/2 (New York: New York University, 1970)

Frankland, Mark, 'Australia Supports Pre-emptive Strikes', *The Guardian*, 2 December 2002

Freedman, Sir Lawrence, 'Prevention, Not Pre-emption', Wash.Q., 26/2 (2003), 105–14

Freytag-Loringhoven, Axel Freiherr von, *Die Satzung des Völkerbundes* (Berlin: Georg Stilke, 1926)

'Die Regionalverträge', *Schriften der Akademie für Deutsches Recht*, 4 (1937)

Friede, Wilhelm, 'Die VII. Panamerikanische Konferenz (Montevideo, Dezember 1933)', ZaöRV/H.J.I.L., 4 (1934), 330–9

'Die Erklärung Japans über seine Politik in Ostasien (17.April–4. Mai 1934) und die Stellungnahme der Mächte', ZaöRV/H.J.I.L., 4 (1934), 597–608

Friedmann, Wolfgang, 'United States Policy and the Crisis of International Law', A.J.I.L., 59 (1965), 857–71

Frowein, Jochen Abraham, 'Völkerrechtliche Aspekte des Vietnam-Konflikts', ZaöRV/H.J.I.L., 27 (1967), 1–23

'Konstitutionalisierung des Völkerrechts, Völkerrecht und Internationales Privatrecht in einem sich globalisierenden internationalen System –

Auswirkungen der Entstaatlichung transnationaler Rechtsbeziehungen', DGVR-Berichte, 39 (1999), 427–45

'Der Terrorismus als Herausforderung für das Völkerrecht', ZaöRV/H.J.I.L., 62 (2002), 879–905

Fullilove, Michael, 'Hope or Glory? The Presidential Election and U.S. Foreign Policy', Brookings, Policy Paper No. 9, October 2008

Gardner, Richard N., 'Neither Bush nor the "Jurisprudes"', A.J.I.L., 97 (2003), 585–90

Gattini, Andrea, 'Sense and Quasi-sense of Schmitt's Großraum Theory in International Law: a Rejoinder to Carty's Critique of Liberal International Legal Order', L.J.I.L., 15 (2002), 53–68

Gazzini, Tarcisio, *The Changing Rules on the Use of Force in International Law* (Manchester University Press, 2005)

'The Rules on the Use of Force at the Beginning of the XXI Century', J.C.S.L., 11 (2006), 319–42

'A Response to Amos Guiora: Pre-Emptive Self-Defence Against Non State Actors?', J.C.S.L., 13 (2008), 25–32

Geib, Ekkehard, '*Das Verhältnis der Völkerbundssatzung zum Kelloggpakt*', Ph.D. thesis, Kiel, 1934

Gholz, Eugene, Press, Daryl G. and Sapolsky, Harvey M., 'Come Home America', Int.Sec., 21/4 (1997), 5–48

Gibert, Stephen P., 'Implications of the Nixon Doctrine for Military Aid Policy', Orbis, 16 (1972), 660–81

Gill, Terry D., 'The Temporal Dimension of Self-defense: Anticipation, Preemption, Prevention and Immediacy', in Schmitt and Pejic (eds.), *International Law and Armed Conflict: Exploring the Faultlines* (Leiden: Nijhoff, 2007), pp. 113–55

Ginther, Konrad, 'Hegmony', E.P.I.L., II (1995), 685–8

Giuliani, Rudolph, 'Towards a Realistic Peace', For.Aff., 85/5 (2007), 1–18

Glahn, Gerhard von, *Law Among Nations*, 6th edn. (New York: Macmillan, 1986)

Glazer, Stephen G., 'The Brezhnev Doctrine', Int.L., 5/1 (1971), 169–79

Glennon, Michael J., *Limits of Law, Prerogatives of Power – Interventionism after Kosovo* (New York: Palgrave, 2001)

'The Fog of Law: Self-Defense, Inherence, and Incoherence in Article 51 of the United Nations Charter', H.J.L.P.P., 25 (2002), 539–58

'Why the Security Council Failed', For.Aff., 82/2 (2003), 16–35

'The United States: Democracy, Hegemony and Accountability', in Ku and Jacobson (eds.), *Democratic Accountability and the Use of Force in International Law*, pp. 323–47

'The Emerging Use-of-Force Paradigm', J.C.S.L., 11 (2006), 309–17

Göppert, Otto, *Der Völkerbund* (Stuttgart: Kohlhammer, 1938)

Goldsmith, Jack, *The Terror Presidency – Law and Judgment inside the Bush Administration* (New York: W. W. Norton, 2009)

Goodhart, Arthur Lehmann, 'The North Atlantic Treaty of 1949', RdC, 79 (1951-II), 183–236

Goodrich, Leland M. and Hambro, Edvard, *Charter of the United Nations*, 2nd edn. (London: Stevens & Sons, 1949)

Gottberg, Otto von, 'Die Entwicklung eines amerikanischen Völkerrechts', Ph.D. thesis, Königsberg, 1928

Graber, Doris A., 'The Truman and Eisenhower Doctrines in the Light of the Doctrine of Non-Intervention', P.S.Q., 73/3 (1958), 321–34

Grady, Broderick C. 'Article 5 of the North Atlantic Treaty: Past, Present and Uncertain Future', G.J.I.C.L., 31 (2002), 167–98

Gray, Christine, 'The US National Security Strategy and the New "Bush Doctrine" on Preemptive Self-Defense', Chin.J.I.L., 2 (2002), 437–47

The Bush Doctrine Revisited: the 2006 National Security Strategy of the USA', Chin.J.I.L., 5 (2006), 555–78

International Law and the Use of Force, 3rd edn. (Oxford University Press, 2008)

Gray, Colin S.. *Modern Strategy* (Oxford University Press, 1999)

Grafton Wilson, George. 'Regional Understandings', A.J.I.L., 27 (1933), 310–11

Green, Marshall, 'The Nixon Doctrine: A Progress Report', *Department of State Bulletin*, 64 (1971), 161–5

Greenwood, Christopher, *Essays on War in International Law* (London: Cameron May, 2006)

'International Law and the "War against Terrorism"', Int.Aff., 78/2 (2002), 301–14

Grewe, Wilhelm Georg, *Spiel der Kräfte in der Weltpolitik* (Düsseldorf: Econ Verlag, 1970)

Epochs of International Law, trans. Michael Byers (Berlin: Walter de Gruyter, 2000)

Grommes, Klaus-Peter, '*Der Verteidigungsfall im interamerikanischen Bündnissystem und nach der Satzung der Vereinten Nationen*', Ph.D. thesis, Cologne, 1966

Gross, Leo, 'The Charter of the United Nation and the Lodge Reservations', A.J.I.L., 41 (1947), 531–54

Gruchmann, Lothar, 'Nationalsozialistische Großraumordnung – Die Konstruktion einer "deutschen Monroe-Doktrin"', *Schriftenreihe der Vierteljahreshefte für Zeitgeschichte*, No. 4 (Stuttgart: Deutsche Verlags-Anstalt, 1962)

Guillaume, Gilbert, 'Terrorism and International Law', I.C.J.Q., 53/3 (2004), 537–48

Guiora, Amos N., 'Anticipated Self-Defence and International Law – A Re-Evaluation', J.C.S.L., 13 (2008), 3–24

Haas, Richard, 'Regime Change and Its Limits', For.Aff., 84/4 (2005), 66–78

Habermas, Jürgen, 'Interpreting the Fall of a Monument', G.L.J., 7 (2003), 701–8

Habig, Helmut, 'Die SEATO und das Völkerrecht', Ph.D. thesis, Würzburg, 1973

Hackworth, Green H., *Digest of International Law*, 8 vols. (Washington, DC: Government Printing Office, 1940–4)

Hagemann, Max, 'Der Atlantikpakt und die Satzung der Vereinten Nationen', AVR, 2 (1950), 385–403

Hailbronner, Kai, 'Die Grenzen des völkerrechtlichen Gewaltverbots', DGVR-Berichte, 26 (1986), 49–111

Hall, A. Rupert, *Isaac Newton: Adventurer in Thought* (Cambridge University Press, 1996)

Hathaway, James C., 'America, Defender of Democratic Legitimacy?', E.J.I.L., 11 (2000), 121–34

Haßmann, Heinz, *Der Kellogg-Pakt und seine Vorbehalte* (Würzburg: Werkbund-buchdruckerei, 1930), Ph.D. thesis, Würzburg, 1931

Heisbourg, Francois, 'A Work in Progress: The Bush Doctrine and Its Consequences', Wash.Q., 26/2 (2003), 75–88

Heller, Francis H. and Gillingham, John R. (eds.), *NATO: The Founding of the Atlantic Alliance and the Integration of Europe* (New York: St Martin's Press, 1992)

Henderson, Christian, 'The Bush Doctrine: From Theory to Practice', J.C.S.L., 9 (2004), 3–24

Henkin, Louis, *How Nations Behave – Law and Foreign Policy* (New York: Frederick A. Praeger, 1968)

Foreign Affairs and the U.S. Constitution 2nd edn. (Oxford: Clarendon Press, 1996)

'The Reports of the Death of Article 2(4) Are Greatly Exaggerated', A.J.I.L., 65 (1971), 544–8

'The Use of Force: Law and U.S. Policy', in Henkin *et al.* (eds.), *Right v. Might – International Law and the use of Force*, 2nd edn. (New York: Council on Foreign Relation Press, 1991)

Heydte, Friedrich August Freiherr von der, *Völkerrecht*, 3 vols. (Cologne: Kiepenheuer & Wietsch, 1960)

Higgins, Rosalyn, 'The Attitude of Western States Towards Legal Aspects of the Use of Force', in Cassese (ed.), *The Current Legal Regulation of the Use of Force*, pp. 435–52

Problems and Process, International Law and How We Use It (Oxford: Clarendon Press, 1994)

and Flory, Maurice (ed.), *Terrorism and International Law* (London: Routledge 1997)

Hilaire, Max, *International Law and the United States Military Intervention in the Western Hemisphere* (The Hague: Kulwer Law International, 1997)

Hoffmann, Stanley, 'The Study of International Law and the Theory of International Relations', ASIL Proceedings, 57th Annual Meeting (1963), pp. 26–35

Holmes, Richard (ed.), *The Oxford Companion to Military History* (Oxford University Press, 2001)

Hoover, Herbert, *The Memoirs of Herbert Hoover: The Cabinet and the Presidency, 1920–1933*, vol. II (New York: Macmillan, 1952)

Hoppenstedt, Björn, 'Die Entwicklung des Gewaltverbots in der U.S.-amerikanischen Außenpolitik – Monroe Doktrin, Wilsons 14 Punkte, Kellogg Pakt', in Blumenwitz and Wehner (eds.), *Schritte in eine neue Rechtsordnung*, pp. 59–72

Housten, John A., *Latin America in the United Nations* (Westport, CT: Greenwood Press, 1956, reprinted 1978)

Howard, Michael, *Clausewitz – A Very Short Introduction* (Oxford University Press, 2002)

Huber, Max, *Die soziologischen Grundlagen des Völkerrechts* (Berlin: Verlag Dr Walther Rothschild, 1928)

Huckabee, Mike, 'America's Priorities in the War on Terror', For.Aff., 87/1 (2008), 155–68

Hughes, Charles Evans, 'Observations on the Monroe Doctrine', A.J.I.L., 17 (1923), 611–28

Hull, Cordell, *The Memoirs of Cordell Hull*, 2 vols. (New York: Macmillan, 1948)

Hurrell, Andrew, '"There are no Rules" (George W. Bush): International Order after September 11', Int.Rel., 16 (2002), 185–204

On Global Order – Power, Values, and the Constitution of International Society (Oxford University Press, 2007)

Hyde, Charles Cheney, *International Law – Chiefly as Interpreted and Applied by the United States*, 3 vols., 2nd edn. (Boston: Little, Brown, 1947)

'Legal Aspects of the Japanese Pronouncement in Relation to China', A.J.I.L., 28 (1934), 431–43

Iatrides, John O. and Rizopoulos, Nicholas X., 'The International Dimension of the Greek Civil War', WorldP.J., 17/1 (2000), 87–103

Ikenberry, John, 'Institutions, Strategic Restraint, and the Persistence of American Postwar Order', Int.Sec., 23/3 (1998/9), 43–78

'America's Imperial Ambition", For.Aff., 81/5 (2002), 44–60

'The End of the Neo-Conservative Moment', Survival, 46 (2004), 7–22

International Institute for Strategic Studies (ed.) *The Military Balance, 1969–1970*, (Basingstoke: Taylor and Francis, 1970)

'The Bush National Security Strategy', *Strategic Comments*, 8/8 (2002)

Ipsen, Knut, *Rechtsgrundlagen und Institutionalisierung der Atlantisch-Europäischen Verteidigung* (Hamburg: Hanseatischer Gildenverlag, 1967), Ph.D. thesis, Kiel, 1967

'Die rechtliche Institutionalisierung der Verteidigung des atlantisch-westeuropäischen Raumes', JöR, 2 (1970), 1–53

et al. (eds), *Völkerrecht*, 5th edn. (Munich: C. H. Beck, 2004)

Jacobini, H. B., *A Study of the Philosophy of International Law as Seen in the Works of Latin American Writers* (Westport, CT: Hyperion Press, 1954, reprinted 1979)

Jahrreiß, Hermann, *Die Hoover-Doktrin und die Heiligkeit der 'Verträge'* (Leipzig: Robert Noske, 1933)

Janis, Mark, *An Introduction to International Law*, 3rd edn. (New York: Aspen Law & Business, 1999)

Jennings, Sir Robert Yewdall, 'The *Caroline* and *McLeod* Cases', A.J.I.L., 32 (1938), 82–99

Jervis, Robert. 'Understanding the Bush Doctrine', P.S.Q., 118/3 (2003), 365–88

Jessup, Philipp, *International Security – The American Role in Collective Action for Peace* (New York: Council on Foreign Relations, 1935)

'The Generalization of the Monroe Doctrine', A.J.I.L., 29 (1935), 105–9

'The Inter-American Conference for Maintenance of Peace', A.J.I.L., 31 (1937), 85–91

'The Monroe Doctrine in 1940', A.J.I.L., 34 (1940), 704–11

A Modern Law of Nations, 4th edn. (New York: Macmillan, 1952)

Johnson, James Turner, 'Just War, the Nixon Doctrine and the Future Shape of American Military Policy', Y.B.WorldAff. (1975), 137–54

Joyner, Christopher C. and Grimaldi, Michael A., 'The United States and Nicaragua: Reflections on the Lawfulness of Contemporary Intervention', Va.J.I.L., 25 (1985), 621–89

Kagan, Robert, *Paradise & Power – America and Europe in the New World Order* (London: Atlantic Books, 2003)

'America's Crisis of Legitimacy', For.Aff., 83/2 (2004), 65–88

Kahle, Günther, *Die Rolle der politischen Doktrinen in den Beziehungen zwischen den USA und Lateinamerika 1823–1933*, Kleine Arbeitsreihe zur Europäischen und vergleichenden Rechtsgeschichte, Issue 13 (1980)

Kahn, Paul W., 'From Nuremberg to The Hague: The United States Position in Nicaragua v. United States and the Development of International Law', Y.J.I.L., 12 (1987), 1–62

Kaiser, Karl 'Völkerrecht und Internationale Beziehungen, Zum Verhältnis zweier Wissenschaften', Friedens-Warte/ J.I.P.O., 58 (1976), 197–209

Kaldor, Mary, Martin, Mary and Selchow, Sabine, 'Human Security: a New Strategic Narrative for Europe', Int.Aff., 83 (2007), 273–88

Kaplan, Lawrence S., 'NATO and the Nixon Doctrine Ten Years Later', Orbis, 24 (1980), 149–64

'After Forty Years: Reflection on NATO as a Research Field', in Heller and Gillingham (eds.), *NATO: The Founding of the Atlantic Alliance and the Integration of Europe*, pp. 15–23

Kaplan, Morton A. and Katzenbach, Nicholas de Belleville, *The Political Foundations of International Law* (New York: John Wiley, 1961)

Kaufmann, Erich, *Das Wesen des Völkerrechts und die Clausula Rebus Sic Stantibus* (Tübingen: J. C. B. Mohr, 1911)
Kegley, Charles W. and Raymond, Gregory A., 'Preventive War and Permissive Normative Order', I.S.P., 4 (2003), 385–94
Kelsen, Hans, *Reine Rechtslehre* (Leipzig: Hans Deuticke, 1934)
General Theory of Law and State, trans. Anders Wedberg (Cambridge, MA: Harvard University Press, 1945)
The Law of the United Nations (London: Stevens & Sons, 1950)
Principles of International Law, 2nd edn. (New York: Holt, Rinehart and Winston, 1967)
Kennan, George F. ('X'), 'The Sources of Soviet Conduct', For.Aff., 25/4 (1947), 566–82
American Diplomacy: 1900–1950 (New York: New American Library, 1952)
Kennedy, David, 'Theses about International Law Discourse', G.Y.I.L., 23 (1980), 353–5
'Two Concepts of Sovereignty', in Leffler and Legro (eds.), *To Lead the World*, pp. 133–56
Kennedy, Paul, *The Rise and Fall of Great Powers: Economic and Military Conflict from 1500 to 2000* (New York: Random House, 1987)
Kennedy, S. M., 'The Monroe Doctrine *Clause of the League of Nations Covenant*', Graduate Studies Texas Tech University, No. 20, May 1979
Keohane, Robert, *After Hegemony: Cooperation and Discord in the World Political Economy* (Princeton University Press, 1984)
Kersting, Klaus, 'Bündnisfall und Verteidigungsfall', Ph.D. thesis, Bochum, 1979
Kewenig, Wilhelm, 'Gewaltverbot und zulässige Machteinwirkung', in Schaumann (ed.), *Völkerrechtliches Gewaltverbot und Friedenssicherung*, pp. 175–218
Khanna, Paragh, *The Second World – Empires and Influence in the New Global Order* (London: Penguin Books, 2008)
Khong, Yuen Foong and Malone, David M. (eds.), *Unilateralism and U.S. Foreign Policy* (Boulder, CO, Lynne Rienner, 2003)
Kimminich, Otto, 'Der Stand der Friedensforschung', Universitas, 26 (1971), 289–302
Kinacioglu, Muge, 'A response to Amos Guiora: Reassessing the Parameters of Use of Force in the Age of Terrorism', J.C.S.L., 13 (2008), 33–48
Kiras, James D., 'Terrorism and Irregular Warfare', in Baylis *et al.* (eds), *Strategy in the Contemporary World – An Introduction to Strategic Studies*, pp. 208–32
Kirkpatrick, Jeane, *Legitimacy and Force*, 2 vols. (New Brunswick, NJ: Transaction Books, 1988)
and Gerson, Allen, 'The Reagan Doctrine, Human Rights, and International Law', in Henkin *et al.* (eds.), *Right v. Might – International Law and the Use of Force*, pp. 19–36
Kissinger, Henry, *Diplomacy* (New York: Simon & Schuster, 1994)

Klaidman, Daniel, 'Defining the Obama Doctrine', *Newsweek*, 28 December 2009/4 January 2010, p. 8

Knapp, Manfred, 'Die Macht der USA und die Moral der Staatengemeinschaft: Zur UN-Politik der Clinton Administration', in Berg *et al.* (eds.), *Macht und Moral – Beiträge zur Ideologie und Praxis amerikanischer Außenpolitik im 20. Jahrhundert*, pp. 295–318

Kohen, Marcelo, 'The Use of Force by the United States After the End of the Cold War, and its Impacts on International Law', in Byers and Nolte (eds.), *United States Hegemony and the Foundations of International Law*, pp. 197–231

Kolb, Robert, *Ius contra bellum* (Basel: Helbing & Lichtenhahn, 2003)

Kolbeck, Anton, *Völkerbund und Monroedoktrin* (Ebersberg: Buch- und Verlagsdruckerei Karl Schmidle, 1933), Ph.D. thesis, Würzburg, 1933

Kondis, Basil, 'The United States Role in the Greek Civil War', in Rossides (ed.), *The Truman Doctrine of Aid to Greece*, pp. 144–55

Koos, Heinrich 'Völkerrechtliche Würdigung der Blockademaßnahmen der USA gegen Kuba', Ph.D. thesis, Würzburg, 1967

Korb, Lawrence J. (ed.), *A New National Security Strategy* (New York: Council on Foreign Relations, 2003)

Koskenniemi, Martti, *From Apology to Utopia, the Structure of International Legal Argument* (Helsinki: Lakimiesliiton, 1989)

The Gentle Civilizer of Nations: The Rise and Fall of International Law 1870–1960, (Cambridge University Press, 2001)

'Carl Schmitt, Hans Morgenthau, and the Image of Law in International Relations', in Byers (ed.), *The Role of Law in International Politics*, pp. 17–34

'What is International Law For?', in Evans (ed.), *International Law*, pp. 57–81

Krajewski, Markus 'Selbstverteidigung gegen bewaffnete Angriffe nicht-staatlicher Organisationen – Der 11. September und seine Folgen', AVR, 40 (2002), 183–214

Krakau, Knud, *Missionsbewußtsein und Völkerrechtsdoktrin in den Vereinigten Staaten von Amerika* (Frankfurt a.M.: Metzner, 1967), Ph.D. thesis, Hamburg, 1967

Die kubanische Revolution und die Monroedoktrin: Eine Herausforderung der Außenpolitik der Vereinigten Staaten (Frankfurt a.M.: Metzner Verlag, 1968)

'Lateinamerikanische Doktrinen zur Realisierung staatlicher Unabhängigkeit und Integrität', VRÜ, 8 (1975), 117–44

Kratochwil, Friedrich, 'Thrasymmachos Revisited: On the Relevance of Norms and the Study of Law for International Relations', J.I.A., 37 (1984), 343–56

Kraus, Herbert, *Die Monroedoktrin und ihre Beziehungen zur Amerikanischen Diplomatie und zum Völkerrecht*, (Berlin: Guttentag 1913)

Die Krise des zwischenstaatlichen Denkens: eine Bilanz (Göttingen: Vandenhoek & Ruprecht, 1933), p. 26

'Interesse und zwischenstaatliche Ordnung', N.Z.I.R., 49 (1934), 22–65

'Carl Schmitt, Nationalsozialismus und Völkerrecht', N.Z.I.R., 50 (1935), 151–61

Der völkerrechtliche Status der deutschen Ostgebiete innerhalb der Reichsgrenzen nach dem Stande vom 31. Dezember 1937 (Göttingen: Schwartz, 1964)

Krauthammer, Charles, 'The Reagan Doctrine', *Time*, 1 April 1985

'The Poverty of Realism: The Newest Challenge of the Reagan Doctrine', *The New Republic*, 17 February 1986, pp. 14–22

'The Unipolar Moment', For.Aff., 70/1 (1990/1), 23–33

'The Unipolar Moment Revisited', Nat.Int., 70 (2002–3), 5–17

Kreß, Claus, *Gewaltverbot und Selbstverteidigung nach der Satzung der Vereinten Nationen bei staatlicher Verwicklung in Gewaltakte Privater* (Berlin: Duncker und Humblot, 1995), Ph.D. thesis, Cologne, 1994

Kreutzer, Arthur R., *Preemptive Self-Defense, Die Bush-Doktrin und das Völkerrecht* (Munich: M-Press, 2004)

Krisch, Nico, 'Unilateral Enforcement of the Collective Will: Kosovo, Iraq, and the Security Council', M.P.Y.U.N.L., 3 (1999), 59–103

Selbstverteidigung und kollektive Sicherheit (Berlin: Springer, 2001), Ph.D. thesis, Heidelberg, 2001

'Weak as Constraint, Strong as Tool: The Place of International Law in U.S. Foreign Policy', in Khong and Malone (eds.), *Unilateralism and U.S. Foreign Policy*, pp. 41–70

'More equal than the Rest? Hierarchy, equality and US predominance in international law', in and Nolte (eds.), *United States Hegemony and the Foundations of International Law*, pp. 135–75

'Amerikanische Hegemonie und Liberale Revolution im Völkerrecht', Der Staat, 43 (2004), 267–97

'International Law in Times of Hegemony: Unequal Power and the Shaping of International Legal Order', E.J.I.L., 16 (2005), 369–408

Kruse, Hans, 'Monroe-Doktrin', in Schlochauer (ed.), *Wörterbuch des Völkerrechts*, vol. 2, pp. 548–50

Ku, Charlotte and Jacobson, Harold K., (eds.), *Democratic Accountability and the Use of Force* (Cambridge University Press, 2003)

Kubbig, Bernd W., 'The US Hegemony in the "American Century": The State of the Art and the German Contributions', American Studies, 46/4 (2001), 1–22

Kubitz, Werner, *Die Stimson-Doktrin* (Würzburg: Konrad Triltsch, 1938), Ph.D. thesis, Wroclaw, 1938

Kuhn, Arthur K. 'The Lytton Report on the Manchurian Crisis', A.J.I.L., 27 (1933), 96–100

Kühner, Rolf, *Vorbehalte zu multilateralen Verträgen* (Berlin: Springer, 1986)

Kuniholm, Bruce, 'The Carter Doctrine, the Reagan Corollary and the Prospects for United States Policy in Southwest Asia', Int.J., 41 (1986), 342–61

Kunz, Josef L., 'Individual and Collective Self-Defense in Article 51 of the Charter of the United Nations', A.J.I.L., 41 (1947), 872–9

Kupchan, Charles, 'After Pax Americana: Benign Power, Regional Integration, and the Sources of Stable Multipolarity', Int.Sec., 23/3 (1998), 63–83

Kurth, James, 'Boss of Bosses', in Leffler and Legro (eds.), *To Lead the World*, pp. 109–32

Kutzner, Gerhard, *Die Organisation Amerikanischer Staaten* (Hamburg: Hansischer Gildenverlag, 1970)

Lafeber, W., 'The Bush Doctrine', Dipl.Hist., 26 (2002), 543–58

Lagon, Mark P., *The Reagan Doctrine – Sources of American Conduct in the Cold War's Last Chapter* (Westport, CT: Frederick A. Praeger, 1994)

Laing, Lionel H., 'Does the Monroe Doctrine cover Canada?', A.J.I.L., 32 (1938), 793–6

Langille, Benjamin, 'It's "Instant Custom": How the Bush Doctrine Became Law After the Terrorist Attacks of September 11, 2001', B.C.I.C.L.R., 26 (2003), 145–56

Larenz, Karl, *Methodenlehre*, 3rd edn. (Berlin: Springer, 1975)

Lauterpacht, Sir Hersch, 'The Pact of Paris and the Budapest Articles of Interpretation', Trans. Grotius Soc., 20 (1934), 178–9

Oppenheim's International Law, 7th edn. (London: Longman, Green, 1952)

Leffler, Melvyn P., and Legro, Jeffrey W. (eds.), *To Lead the World – American Strategy after the Bush Doctrine* (Oxford University Press, 2008)

Leopold, Richard W., *The Growth of American Foreign Policy: A History* (New York: Alfred A. Knopf, 1962)

Lepel, Oskar M. Freiherr von, 'Die präemptive Selbstverteidigung im Lichte des Völkerrechts', Hu.V-I/J.I.L.P.A.C., 17 (2003), 77–85

Leutert, Jürg, *Einseitige Erklärungen im Völkerrecht* (Diessenhoffen: Verlag Rügger, 1979)

Levitt, Geoffrey M., 'Review: International Law and the Superpowers', A.J.I.L., 81 (1987), 496–500

Lillich, Richard (ed.), *Humanitarian Intervention and the United Nations* (Charlottesville, VA: University of Virginia Press, 1973)

Litwak, Robert S., *Détente and the Nixon Doctrine* (Cambridge University Press, 1984)

'The New Calculus of Pre-emption', Survival, 44/4 (2002–03), 53–80

Lombardi, Ben, 'The "Bush Doctrine" and Anticipatory Self-defence', International Spectator, 37/4 (2002), 91–105

Lowe, Vaughan, *International Law* (Oxford University Press, 2007)

Luard, Evan, 'Western Europe and the Reagan Doctrine', Int.Aff., 63 (1987), 563–74

Luck, Edward C., 'American Exceptionalism and International Organization: Lessons from the 1990s', in Foot, MacFarlane and Mastanduno (eds.), *US Hegemony and International Institutions*, pp. 25–48

Luttwak, Edward N., *Strategy – The Logic of War and Peace*, 2nd edn. (Cambridge, MA: The Belknap Press of Harvard University Press, 2001)

Lutz, Dieter S. and Gießmann, Hans J. (eds.), *Die Stärke des Rechts gegen das Recht des Stärkeren* (Baden-Baden: Nomos, 2003)

MacDonald, Ronald St. John, 'Foreign Policy, Influence of Legal Considerations Upon', E.P.I.L., II (1992), 442–6

Malanczuk, Peter, *Akehurst's Modern Introduction to International Law*, 7th edn. (London: Routledge, 1997)

'Monroe Doctrine', E.P.I.L., III (1997), 460–64

Malawer, Stuart S., 'Reagan's Law and Foreign Policy, 1981–87: The "Reagan Corollary" of International Law', Harv.I.L.J., 29/1 (1988), 85–110

Mandelbaum, Michael, 'Foreign Policy as Social Work', For.Aff., 75 (1996), 16–32

'A Perfect Failure – NATO's War Against Yugoslavia', For.Aff., 87/5 (1999), 2–8

Mandelsloh, Asche Graf von, 'Die Auslegung des Kelloggpaktes durch den amerikanischen Staatssekretär Stimson', ZaöRV/H.J.I.L., 3/1 (1932/3), 617–27

Martens, Friedrich von, *Völkerrecht*, 2 vols. (Berlin: Weidmannsche Buchhandlung, 1883)

Marinin, M., *Die 'Truman-Doktrin' und der 'Marshall-Plan'* (Berlin: SWA-Verlag, 1947)

Martinez, José and Prill, Florian, 'Geschichte der Völkerrechtsforschung und – lehre and der Georg-August-Universität Göttingen', in Calliess, Nolte and Stoll (eds.), *Von der Diplomatie zum kodifizierten Recht – 75 Jahre Institut für Völkerrecht der Universität Göttingen (1930–2005)*, pp. 51–67

Mastronardi, Philippe, *Juristisches Denken. Eine Einführung* (Bern: Haupt, 2001)

Maynes, Charles William, 'A Workable Clinton Doctrine', For.Pol., 93 (1993), 3–20

McCain, John S., 'An Enduring Peace Built on Freedom', For.Aff., 86/6 (2007), 19–39

McDougal, Myers Smith, 'Law and Power', A.J.I.L., 46 (1952), 102–14

'International Law, Power, and Policy: A Contemporary Conception', RdC, 82 (1953-I), 133–258

'The Soviet–Cuban Quarantine and Self-Defense', A.J.I.L., 57 (1963), 597–604

and Feliciano, Florention P., *Law and Minimum World Public Order* (New Haven, CT: Yale University Press, 1967)

McGibbon, Ian C., 'Customary International Law and Acquiescence', B.Y.I.L., 33 (1957), 115–45

McNair, Lord Arnold, *Law of Treaties* (Oxford: Clarendon Press, 1961)

'The Stimson Doctrine of Non-Recognition', B.Y.I.L., 14 (1933), 65–74

Meeker, Leonard C., 'Defensive Quarantine and the Law', A.J.I.L., 57 (1963), 515–24

'The Dominican Situation in the Perspective of International Law', *Department of State Bulletin*, 53 (1965), 60–5

'The Legality of the United States Participation in the Defense of Viet-Nam', *Department of State Bulletin*, 54 (1966), 474–89

Mégret, Frederic, '"War"? Legal Semantics and the Move to Violence', E.J.I.L., 13 (2002), 361–99

Meier, Gert, *Der bewaffnete Angriff – Begriff und rechtliche Bedeutung in der Satzung der Vereinten Nationen, im Brüsseler Vertrag und im NATO-Vertrag* (Munich: Charlotte Schön, 1963), Ph.D. thesis, Göttingen, 1963

Meiertöns, Heiko, *Die Doktrinen U.S.-amerikanischer Sicherheitspolitik – Völkerrechtliche Bewertung und ihr Einfluss auf das Völkerrecht* (Baden-Baden: Nomos, 2006)

'Das ius ad bellum zwischen Menschenrechten und Souveränität – Die Bush-Doktrin, neokonservative Sicherheitspolitik und das Dilemma zwischen Sicherheit und Gerechtigkeit', in Weingärtner (ed.), *Streitkräfte und Menschenrechte*, pp. 175–83

Meissner, Boris, *Die 'Breshnew-Doktrin' – Das Prinzip des 'proletarisch-sozialistischen Internationalismus' und die Theorie von den 'verschiedenen Wegen zum Sozialismu'* (Cologne: Verlag Wissenschaft und Politik, 1969)

Meng, Werner, 'The *Caroline*', E.P.I.L., I (1992), 537–8

'Stimson Doctrine', E.P.I.L., IV (2000), 690–3

Merrill, Dennis, *Documentary History of the Truman Presidency, Vol. 8: The Truman Doctrine and the Beginning of the Cold War, 1947–1949* (Bethesda, MD: University Publications of America, 1996)

Miller, David Hunter, *The Drafting of the Covenant*, 2 vols. (New York: Putnam, 1928, reprinted 1969)

The Peace Pact of Paris (New York: Putnam, 1928)

Miller, Jennifer, 'International Intervention – The United States Invasion of Panama', Harv.I.L.J., 31 (1990), 633–46

Mingst, Karen, *Essentials of International Relations* (New York: W. W. Norton, 1999)

Minnerop, Petra, 'Classification of States and Creation of Status within the International Community', M.Y.P.U.N.L., 7 (2003), 79–182

Paria-Staaten im Völkerrecht? (Berlin: Springer, 2004), Ph.D. thesis, Göttingen, 2003/4

Moore, John Basset, *A Digest of International Law*, 8 vols. (Washington, DC: Government Printing Office, 1906)

Moore, John Norton, 'Legal Dimensions of the Decision to Intercede in Cambodia', A.J.I.L., 65 (1971), 38–75

'The Secret War in Central America and the Future of World Order', A.J.I.L., 80 (1986), 43–127

and Turner, Robert F., *International Law and the Brezhnev Doctrine* (Lanham, MD: University of America Press, 1987)

Morgenthau, Hans J., *Die internationale Rechtspflege, ihr Wesen und ihre Grenzen*, (Leipzig: Universitätsverlag Robert Noske, 1929), Ph.D. thesis, Leipzig, 1929

Politics Among Nations, 2nd edn. (New York: Alfred Knopf, 1954)

'Emergent Problems of United States Foreign Policy', in Deutsch and Hoffmann (eds.), *The Relevance of International Law*, pp. 47–56

Morrison, Fred L., 'The Role of Regional Organizations in the Enforcement of International Law', in Delbrück (ed.), *Allocation of Law Enforcement Authority in the International System*, pp. 39–56

Mosler, Hermann, 'Die Großmachtstellung im Völkerrecht', *Schriften der Süddeutschen Juristenzeitung*, Issue 8, Heidelberg, 1949

Moulin, Henri Alexis, 'La Doctrine de Drago', R.G.D.I.P., 14 (1907), 424–37

Moustakis, Fotios and Chaudhuri, Rudra, 'The Rumsfeld Doctrine and Cost of US Unilaterlism: Lessons Learned', *Defence Studies*, 7 (2007), 368–75

Moynihan, Daniel P., *On the Law of Nations* (Cambridge, MA: Harvard University Press, 1990)

Müller, Jörg Paul and Cottier, Thomas, 'Acquiescence', E.P.I.L., I (1992), 14–16

Münkler, Herfried, *Clausewitz' Theorie des Krieges* (Baden-Baden: Nomos, 2003)

'Asymmetrie und Kriegsvölkerrecht. Die Lehren des Sommerkrieges 2006', Friedens-Warte/J.I.P.O., 81 (2006), 59–65

Mullerson, Rein, 'Self-Defense in the Contemporary World', in Damrosh Fisler and Scheffer (eds.), *Law and Force in the New International Order*, pp. 13–25

'Intervention by Invitation', in Damrosh Fisler and Scheffer (eds.), *Law and Force in the New International Order*, pp. 127–34

Murphy, John F., *The United States and the Rule of Law in International Affairs* (Cambridge University Press, 2004)

Murphy, Sean D., 'Contemporary Practice of the United States Relating to International Law', A.J.I.L., 93 (1999), 628–35, A.J.I.L., 97 (2003), 419–32

'Contemporary Practice of the United States Relating to International Law, Terrorist Attacks on World Trade Center and Pentagon', A.J.I.L., 96 (2002), 237–55

Murswiek, Dietrich 'Die amerikanische Präventivkriegsstrategie und das Völkerrecht', N.J.W. (2003), 1014–20

Musielak, Hans-Joachim, *Grundkurs BGB*, 7th edn. (Munich: C. H. Beck, 2002)

Nagan, Winston P., 'Nuclear Arsenals, International Lawyers, and the Challenge of the Millennium', Y.J.I.L., 24 (1999), 485–535

and Hammer, Craig, 'The New Bush National Security Doctrine and the Rule of Law', Berk.J.I.L., 22 (2004), 375–438

Nawaz, Mahomed K. (ed.), *Essays in Honour of Krishna Rao* (Leiden: Sijthoff, 1976)

Neff, Donald, *Warriors at Suez: Eisenhower takes America into the Middle East* (New York: Linden Press/Simon & Schuster, 1981)

Neuhold, Hanspeter, *Internationale Konflikte – verbotene und erlaubte Mittel ihrer Austragung* (Vienna: Springer, 1970)

'Law and Force in International Relations – European and American Positions', ZaöRV/H.J.I.L., 64 (2004), 263–79

Nichols, Alan, *Neutralität und amerikanische Waffenausfuhr* (Berlin: Ebering, 1931), Ph.D. thesis, Berlin, 1931

Nixon, Richard, 'U.S. Foreign Policy for the 1970s – A New Strategy for Peace', *Department of State Bulletin*, 62 (1970), 273–332

'U.S. Foreign Policy for the 1970s – Building for Peace', *Department of State Bulletin*, 64 (1971), 341–432

'U.S. Foreign Policy for the 1970s – Shaping a Durable Peace', *Department of State Bulletin*, 68 (1973), 716–834

Nolte, Georg, *Eingreifen auf Einladung* (Berlin: Springer, 1999)

'Die "neuen Aufgaben" von NATO und WEU', ZaöRV/H.J.I.L., 54 (1999), 95–123

'Weg in eine andere Rechtsordnung', in Lutz and Gießmann (eds.), *Die Stärke des Rechts gegen das Recht des Stärkeren*, pp. 187–96

'Die USA und das Völkerrecht', Friedens-Warte/J.I.P.O., 78 (2003), 119–40

'Preventive Use of Force and Preventive Killings: Moves into a Different Legal Order', T.Inq.L., 5/1 (2004), 111–29

'Guantanamo und Genfer Konventionen: Eine Frage der lex lata oder de lege ferenda?', in Fischer *et al.* (eds.), *Krisensicherung und Humanitärer Schutz*, FS-Fleck, pp. 393–404

'Zum Wandel des Souveränitätsbegriffs', *Frankfurter Allgemeine Zeitung*, 6 April 2005, p. 8

Le droit international face au défi américain, Université Panthéon-Assas, Paris II – Cours et travaux No. 6 (Paris: Pedone 2005)

'Vom Weltfrieden zur menschlichen Sicherheit? Zu Anspruch, Leistung und Zukunft des Völkerrechts', in Münkler (ed.), *Sicherheit und Risiko* (forthcoming 2010), Inaugural lecture at Humboldt-University Berlin, 26 January 2009

and Byers, Michael (eds.), *United States Hegemony and the Foundations of International Law* (Oxford University Press, 2003)

Noyes, John E., 'American Hegemony, U.S. Political Leaders, and General International Law', Conn.J.I.L., 19 (2004), 293–313

Nuechterlein, Donald E., 'The Reagan Doctrine in Perspective', P.P.Sci., 19/1 (1990), 43–9

Nussbaum, Arthur, *Geschichte des Völkerrechts* (Munich: C. H. Beck, 1960)

Nye, Joseph S., *Bound to Lead: The Changing Nature of American Power* (New York: Basic Books, 1990)

The Paradox of American Power – Why the World's only Superpower can't go it Alone (Oxford University Press, 2002)

Obama, Barack H., 'Renewing American Leadership', For.Aff., 86/4 (2007), 2–16

Obama for America (ed.) *Change We Can Believe In* (New York: Three Rivers Press, 2008)

O'Connell, Mary Ellen, *The Myth of Preemptive Self-Defense*, ASIL Task Force Papers, August 2002, Washington 2002

'Defending the Law against Preemptive Force', in Fischer-Lescan *et al.* (eds.), *Frieden in Freiheit – Peace in liberty – Paix en liberté, Festschrift für Michael Bothe zum 70. Geburtstag*, FS-Bothe, pp. 237–48

Oppenheim, Lasa, *International Law*, 2 vols. (New York: Longmans, Green, 1905)

Osgood, Robert E. *et al.* (eds.), *America and the World – From the Truman Doctrine to Vietnam* (Baltimore, MD: The Johns Hopkins Press, 1970)

Owens, Mackubin Thomas, 'The Bush Doctrine: The Foreign Policy of a Republican Empire', Orbis, 53 (2009), 23–40

Paech, Norman and Stuby, Gerhard, *Machtpolitik und Völkerrecht in den internationalen Beziehungen* (Baden-Baden: Nomos, 1994)

'Interventionsimperialismus, Von der Monroe – zur Bush-Doktrin', Blätter für deutsche und internationale Politik, 48 (2003), 1258–68

Paulus, Andreas, *Die internationale Gemeinschaft im Völkerrecht – eine Untersuchung zur Entwicklung des Völkerrechts im Zeitalter der Globalisierung* (Munich: C. H. Beck, 2001), Ph.D. thesis, Munich, 2000

Paust, Jordan J., *Beyond the Law – The Bush Administration's Unlawful Responses to the 'War' on Terror* (Cambridge University Press, 2007)

Payne, Keith B. and Walton, C. Dale, 'Deterrence in the Post-Cold War World', Baylis *et al.* (eds.), *Strategy in the Contemporary World*, pp. 161–82

Pearce-Higgins, Alexander, 'The Monroe Doctrine', B.Y.I.L., 4 (1924), 103–18

Perkins, Dexter, *The Monroe Doctrine, 1823–26* (Cambridge, MA: Harvard University Press, 1927)

The Monroe Doctrine, 1826–1867 (Baltimore, MD: The Johns Hopkins University Press, 1933)

The Monroe Doctrine, 1867–1907 (Baltimore, MD: The Johns Hopkins University Press, 1937)

A History of the Monroe Doctrine (Boston: Little, Brown, 1955)

Petrochilos, Georgios C., 'The Relevance of the Concepts of War and Armed Conflict to the Law of Neutrality', Van.J.T.L., 31 (1998), 575–612

Pirronne, Pasquale, 'The Use of Force in the Framework of the Organization of American States', in Cassese (ed.), *The Current Legal Regulation of the Use of Force*, pp. 223–40

Planas-Suarez, Simon, 'L'extension de la Doctrine de Monroe en Amérique du Sud', RdC, 18 (1924-IV), 267–365

Plischke, Elmer, *Contemporary U.S. Foreign Policy: Documents and Commentary* (New York: Greenwood Press, 1991)

Pohl, Heinrich, 'Der Monroe-Vorbehalt', in Bonner Juristische Fakultät (ed.), *Festschrift für Paul Krüger*, FS-Krüger (Berlin: Weidmann, 1913), pp. 447–72

Posen, Barry R. and Ross, Andrew, 'Competing Visions for U.S. Grand Strategy', Int.Sec., 21/3 (1996–7), 5–53

Powell, Colin, 'U.S. Forces: Challenges Ahead', For.Aff., 71/5 (1992–3), 32–45

Power, Samantha, 'Legitimacy and Competence', in Leffler and Legro (eds.), *To Lead the World – American Strategy after the Bush Doctrine*, pp. 133–56

Prados, Alfred B., *Saudi Arabia: Current Issues and U.S. Relations* (Washington, DC: Congressional Research Service, 2002)

Prevost, Gary and Campos, Carlos Oliva (eds.), *The Bush Doctrine and Latin America* (New York: Palgrave Macmillan, 2007)

Purvis, Nigel, 'Critical Legal Studies in Public International Law', Harv.I.L.J., 32/1 (1991), 81–127

Randelzhofer, Albrecht, 'Art. 2(4)', in Simma (ed.), *The Charter of the United Nations*, vol. I, pp. 112–36

'Art. 51', in Simma (ed.), *The Charter of the United Nations*, vol. I, pp. 788–806

Ratner, Steven, '*Jus ad Bellum* and *Jus in Bello* After September 11', A.J.I.L., 96 (2002), 905–21

Rauschning, Dietrich, *Der Streit um den Suezkanal* (Hamburg: Forschungsstelle für Völkerrecht und Ausländisches Öffentliches Recht, 1956)

'Herbert Kraus (1884–1965)', in Rauschning and Nerée (eds.), *Die Albertus-Universität zu Königsberg und ihre Professoren*, pp. 371–81

and Nerée, Donata V. (eds.), *Die Albertus-Universität zu Königsberg und ihre Professoren* (Berlin: Duncker & Humblot, 1994)

Ravenal, Earl C., 'The Nixon Doctrine and our Asian Commitments', For.Aff., 49 (1970–1), 201–17

Large-Scale Foreign Policy: The Nixon Doctrine as History and Portent (Berkeley, CA: Institute of International Studies, 1989)

Reagan, Ronald, *National Security Strategy of the United States* (Washington, DC: Pergamon–Brassey's, 1988)

An American Life (New York: Hutchinson, 1990)

Regensburg, Kenneth, 'Refugee Law Reconsidered: Reconciling Humanitarian Objectives with the Protectionist Agendas of Western Europe and the United States', Corn.I.L.J., 29 (1996), 225–62

Reibstein, Ernst, *Völkerrecht*, 2 vols. (Freiburg: Alber, 1963)

Reinhold, Waldemar, *Monroedoktrin und Völkerbundssatzung* (Emsdetten (Westf.): Dissertationsdruckerei Heinr. & J. Lechte, 1937), Ph.D. thesis, Halle-Wittenberg, 1937

Reisman, W. Michael, 'Critical Defense Zones and International Law: The Reagan Codicil', A.J.I.L., 76 (1982), 589–91

'Coercion and self-determination: Construing Charter Art. 2(4)', A.J.I.L., 78 (1984), 642–5

'Old Wine in New Bottles: The Reagan and Brezhnev Doctrines in Contemporary International Law and Practice', Y.J.I.L., 13 (1988), 171–98

'International Law After the Cold War', A.J.I.L., 84 (1990), 859–66
'Legal Responses to International Terrorism', Hous.J.I.L., 22 (1999), 3–61
'The United States and International Institutions', Survival, 41/4 (1999–2000), 63–80
'Assessing Claims to Revise the Laws of War', A.J.I.L., 97 (2003), 82–90
and Armstrong, Andrea, 'The Past and Future of the Claim of Preemptive Self-Defense', A.J.I.L., 100 (2006), 525–50
and McDougal, Myers, 'Humanitarian Intervention to Protect the Ibos', in Lillich (ed.), *Humanitarian Intervention and the United Nations*, pp. 167–95
Ress, Georg and Bröhmer, Jürgen, 'Art. 53', in Simma (ed.), *The Charter of the United Nations*, vol. II, pp. 854–90
Richardson, Bill, 'A New Realism', For.Aff., 87/1 (2008), 142–54
Roberts, Adam, 'Law and the Use of Force After Iraq', Survival, 45/2 (2003), pp. 31–56
Roberts, Anthea Elizabeth, 'Traditional and Modern Approaches to Customary International Law. A Reconciliation', A.J.I.L., 95 (2001), 757–91
Röder, Matthias, 'Die Eisenhower-Doktrin vom 9. März 1957 und ihre Anwendung im Libanon im Juli 1958', Master's thesis, Hamburg, 1986, on file in the Staats- und Universitätsbibliothek Hamburg
Rogov, Sergej, 'The Bush Doctrine', Rus.P.L., 46 (2002), 47–61
Ronfeldt, David F., *Rethinking the Monroe Doctrine*, The Rand Paper Series, P-7090, April 1985
Ronzitti, Natalino, 'The Expanding Law of Self-Defence', J.C.S.L., 11 (2006), 343–59
Root, Elihu, 'The Real Monroe Doctrine', A.J.I.L., 8 (1914), 427–42
Roscher, Bernhard, *Der Briand–Kellogg-Pakt von 1928* (Baden-Baden: Nomos, 2004), Ph.D. thesis, Hamburg, 2004
Rose, Jürgen, 'Die Schlacht zum Feind tragen', in Lutz and Gießmann (eds.), *Stärke des Rechts oder das Recht des Stärkeren*, pp. 142–7
Rosenfeld, Stephen S., 'The Guns of July', For.Aff., 64/2 (1986), 698–714
Rossides, Eugene T. (ed.), *The Truman Doctrine of Aid to Greece* (Washington, DC: American Hellenic Institute Foundation, 2001)
Roth, Brad R., 'Governmental Illegitimacy Revisited: 'Pro-Democratic' Armed Intervention in the Post-Bipolar World', T.C.L.P., 3 (1993), 481–513
Rousseau, Charles, *Droit International Public*, 5 vols. (Paris: Sirey, 1970–83)
Roxin, Claus, *Strafrecht – Allgemeiner Teil*, vol. I, 3rd edn, (Munich: C. H. Beck, 1997)
Rubin, Alfred P., 'SEATO and American Legal obligations concerning Laos and Cambodia', I.C.L.Q., 20 (1970), 500–18
'The International Legal Effects of Unilateral Declarations', A.J.I.L., 71 (1977), 1–30
Rumpf, Christian, 'Central Treaty Organization', E.P.I.L., I (1992), 554–5
Russell, Ruth B., 'Review: Intervention and Negotiation', A.J.I.L., 65 (1971), 875

Salmon, Trevor C. (ed.), *Issues in International Relations* (London: Routledge, 2000)

Sapiro, Miriam, 'Iraq: The Shifting Sands of Preemptive Self-Defense', A.J.I.L., 97 (2003), 599–607

Sauer, Ernst *Grundlehre des Völkerrechts*, 2nd edn. (Cologne: Balduin Pick-Verlag, 1948)

Sauer, Heiko, 'Die NATO und das Verfassungsrecht: neues Konzept – alte Fragen', ZaöRV/H.J.I.L., 62 (2002), 317–46

Sack, Alexander N., 'The Truman Doctrine in International Law', L.G.Rev., VII (1947), 141–78

Sadurska, Romana, 'Threats of Force', A.J.I.L., 82 (1988), 239–68

Savelberg, Mathieu, *Le Problème du droit international Américain* (S'Gravenhage: A. A. M. Stols, 1946)

Sa Vianna, Manuel A. *de, De la non-existence d'un droit international américain* (Rio de Janeiro: Figueredo, 1912)

Schachter, Oscar, 'The Legality of Pro-Democratic Invasion', A.J.I.L., 78 (1984), 645–50

'International Law: The Right of States to Use Armed Force', Mich.L.Rev., 82 (1984), 1620–46

International Law in Theory and Practice (Dordrecht: Martin Nijhoff Publishers, 1991)

Schaller, Christian, 'Massenvernichtungswaffen und Präventivkrieg', ZaöRV/H.J.I.L., 62 (2002), 641–68

Schatzschneider, Hellmut, *Die neue Phase der Monroedoktrin angesichts der kommunistischen Bedrohung Lateinamerikas – Unter Berücksichtigung des Falles Guatemala vor der Organisation Amerikanischer Staaten und der Vereinten Nationen* (Göttingen: Vandenhoeck & Ruprecht, 1957)

Schaumann, Wilfried (ed.), *Völkerrechtliches Gewaltverbot und Friedenssicherung* (Baden-Baden: Nomos, 1971)

Scheffer, David J., 'Use of Force After the Cold War: Panama, Iraq, and the New World Order', in Henkin *et al.* (ed.), *Right v. Might. International Law and the Use of Force*, pp. 109–72

Scheuner, Ulrich, 'Die Sicherheitszone des amerikanischen Kontinents (Die Erklärung von Panama vom 3. Oktober 1939)', ZfV, 24 (1941), 180–226

'Der Gedanke der Sicherheit Amerikas auf den Konferenzen von Panama und Habana und die Monroedoktrin', ZfV, 24 (1941), 273–92

Schlochauer, Hans-Jürgen (ed.), *Wörterbuch des Völkerrechts,* 3 vols., founded by Karl Strupp, 2nd edn. (Berlin: Walter de Gruyter, 1962)

Schmidl, Matthias, *The Changing Nature of Self-Defense in International Law* (Baden-Baden: Nomos, 2009)

Schmidt, Helmut, 'The Brezhnev Doctrine', Survival, 11 (1969), 307–13

Schmitt, Carl, 'Nationalsozialismus und Völkerrecht', *Schriften der Deutschen Hochschule für Politik*, Issue 9, Berlin (1934)

'Großraum gegen Universalismus. Der völkerrechtliche Kampf um die Monroedoktrin', ZAkDR, 6 (1939), 333–7

'Reich und Raum – Elemente eines neuen Völkerrechts', ZAkDR, 7 (1940), 201–203

'Völkerrechtliche Formen des modernen Imperialismus', in Carl Schmitt (ed.), *Positionen und Begriffe* (Hamburg: Hanseatische Verlagsanstalt, 1940), pp. 163–84

Völkerrechtliche Großraumordnung mit Interventionsverbot für raumfremde Mächte, 4th edn. (Berlin: Deutscher Rechtsverlag, 1941)

'Raum und Großraum im Völkerrecht', ZfV, 24 (1941), 145–79

Der Nomos der Erde im Völkerrecht des Ius Publicum Europaeum (Cologne: Greven Verlag, 1950)

Schmitt, Michael N., 'Preemptive Strategies in International Law', Mich.J.I.L., 24 (2003), 513–48

'Responding to Transnational Terrorism under the Jus ad Bellum', in Schmitt and Pejic (eds.), *International Law and Armed Conflict: Exploring the Faultlines* (Leiden and Boston: Nijhoff, 2007)

and Pejic, Jelena (eds.), *International Law and Armed Conflict: Exploring the Faultlines – Essays in Honour of Yoram Dinstein* (Leiden: Nijhoff, 2007)

Schmoeckel, Mathias, *Die Großraumtheorie. Ein Beitag zur Geschichte der Völkerrechtswissenschaft im Dritten Reich, insbesondere der Kriegszeit* (Berlin: Duncker & Humblot, 1994), Ph.D. thesis, Munich, 1993

Scholz, Rupert, 'Der 11. September 2001: Wendepunkt in der nationalen wie internationalen Sicherheitspolitik', in Conze, Schlie and Seubert (eds.), *Geschichte zwischen Wissenschaft und Politik*, FS-Stürmer, pp. 469–81

Schoonbroodt, Etienne, *La Doctrine Reagan* (Brussels: Groupe de recherches et d'information sur la paix, 1987)

Schreuer, Christoph, 'Regionalism v. Universalism', E.J.I.L., 6 (1995), 477–99

Schröder, Dieter, Die Idee der kollektiven Regionalintervention – Rechtsvergleichende Betrachtungen zur Breshnew-Doktrin', *Recht in Ost und West*, 13 (1969), 203–10

Schücking, Walter, *Die Revision der Völkerbundssatzung im Hinblick auf den Kelloggpakt* (Berlin: Verlag Dr. Emil Ebering, 1931)

Schücking, Walter and Wehberg, Hans, *Die Satzung des Völkerbundes*, 2nd edn. (Berlin: Franz Vahlen, 1924)

Schwabe, Klaus, 'The Origins of the United States Engagement in Europe, 1946–1952', in Heller and Gillingham (ed.), *NATO: The Founding of the Atlantic Alliance and the Integration of Europe*, pp. 161–92

Schwebel, Stephen M., 'Aggression, Intervention and Self-Defence', RdC, 136 (1972-II), 411–97

'The Brezhnev Doctrine Repealed and Peaceful Co-Existence Enacted', A.J.I.L., 66 (1972), 816–9

Schweisfurth, Theodor, 'Breschnew-Doktrin als Norm des Völkerrechts?', *Aussenpolitik*, 21 (1970), 523–38

Sozialistisches Völkerrecht? Darstellung – Analyse – Wertung der sowjetmarxistischen Theorie von Völkerrecht 'neuen Typs' (Berlin: Springer, 1979)

'Diskussionsbeitrag', *DGVR-Berichte*, 26 (1986), pp. 133–5

'Aggression', in Ambos and Arnold (eds.), *Der Irak-Krieg und das Völkerrecht*, pp. 359–65

Schweitzer, Michael, 'Erleidet das Gewaltverbot Modifikationen im Bereich von Einflußzonen', in Schaumann (ed.), *Völkerrechtliches Gewaltverbot und Friedenssicherung*, pp. 219–44

Scobbie, Iain, 'Towards the Elimination of International Law: Some Radical Scepticism about Sceptical Radicalism', B.Y.I.L., 61 (1990), 339–62

Scott, James M., *Deciding to Intervene – The Reagan Doctrine and American Foreign Policy* (Durham, NC: Duke University Press, 1996)

Scott, Shirley V., 'International Law as Ideology: Theorizing the Relationship between International Law and International Politics', E.J.I.L., 5 (1994), 313–25

'Is There Room for International Law in Realpolitik?: Accounting for the US "Attitude" towards International Law', R.I.S., 30 (2004), 71–88

Seidel, Gerd, '*Quo vadis* Völkerrecht ?', AVR, 41 (2003), 449–83

Seidl-Hohenveldern, Ignaz (ed.) *Lexikon des Rechts/Völkerrecht*, LdR/VR, 3rd edn. (Neuwied: Luchterhand, 2001)

Shah, Niaz, 'Self-defence, Anticipatory Self-defence and Pre-emption: International Law's Response to Terrorism', J.C.S.L., 12 (2007), 95–126

Sharma, Suraya P., 'The American Doctrine of "Pre-emptive self-defence"', I.J.I.L., 43/2 (2003), 215–30

Sharp, Samuel L., 'Review: Herbert Kraus, Osteuropa und der deutsche Osten, vol. I: Die Oder-Neisse-Linie. Eine völkerrechtliche Studie', A.J.I.L., 49 (1955), 284

Shaw, Malcolm N. *International Law*, 5th edn. (Cambridge University Press, 2003)

Shearer, Ivan A., 'South-East Asia Treaty Organisation', E.P.I.L., III (2000), 483–6

A Revival of the Just War Theory? in Schmitt and Pejic (eds.), *International Law and Armed Conflict: Exploring the Faultlines*, pp. 1–20

Shotwell, James T., *War as an Instrument of National Policy* (New York: Harcourt, Brace, 1929)

Shultz, George P., 'New Realities and New Ways of Thinking', For.Aff., 63/4 (1984), 705–21

Silagi, Michael, 'Preferential Claims Against Nicaragua', E.P.I.L., III (2000), 1098–9

Simma, Bruno, 'Bemerkungen zur Methode der Völkerrechtswissenschaft', in Herma von Bonin (ed.), *Festschrift für Ernst Kolb zum 60. Geburtstag*, FS-Kolb (Innsbruck: Österreichische Kommissionsbuchhandlung, 1971), pp. 339–49

'Völkerrechtswissenschaft und Lehre von den internationalen Beziehungen: Erste Überlegungen zur Interdependenz zweier Disziplinen', ÖZföR, 23 (1972), 293–324

'Völkerrecht und Friedensforschung', *Friedens-Warte*/J.I.P.O., 57 (1974), 65–83

(ed.), *The Charter of the United Nations*, 2nd edn. (Oxford University Press, 2002)

Stefan Brunner, Stefan and Kaul, Hans-Peter, 'Art. 27', in Simma (ed.) *The Charter of the United Nations*, pp. 476–523

Slaughter, Anne-Marie, 'International Law and International Relations: A Dual Agenda', A.J.I.L., 87 (1993), 204–39

'International Law and International Relations', RdC, 285 (2000), 10–249

Tumello, Andrew S. and Wood, Stepan, 'International Law and International Relations Theory: a New Generation of Interdisciplinary Scholarship', A.J.I.L., 92 (1998), 367–97

Slocombe, Walter B., 'Force, Pre-emption and Legitimacy', Survival, 45/1 (2003), 117–30

Smith, Gaddis, *The Last Years of the Monroe Doctrine, 1945–1993* (New York: Hill and Wang, 1994)

Sofaer, Abraham D., 'Terrorism and the Law', For.Aff., 64 (1985), 901–22

'On the Necessity of Preemption', E.J.I.L., 14 (2003), 209–26

Spencer, John H., 'The Monroe Doctrine and the League Covenant', A.J.I.L., 30 (1936), 400–13

Stahn, Carsten, 'International Law at a Crossroads? The Impact of September 11', ZaöRV/H.J.I.L., 62 (2002), 183–255

'Enforcement of the Collective Will after Iraq', A.J.I.L., 97 (2003), 804–23

'Responsibility to Protect: Political Rhetoric or Emerging Legal Norm?', A.J.I.L., 110 (2007), 99–120

Steck, Peter K., *Zwischen Volk und Staat, Das Völkerrechtssubjekt in der deutschen Völkerrechtslehre (1933–1941)* (Baden-Baden: Nomos, 2003), Ph.D. thesis, Mainz, 2001

Stein, Torsten and Buttlar, Christian von, *Völkerrecht*, 12th edn. (Cologne: Heymanns, 2009)

Stevenson, Charles A., 'The Evolving Clinton Doctrine on the Use of Force', A.F. & S., 22 (1996), 511–35

Stevenson, John R., 'United States Military Actions in Cambodia: Questions of International Law', *Department of State Bulletin*, 62 (1970), 765–70

Stimson, Henry Lewis, *The Far Eastern Crisis* (New York: Howard Fertig, 1974)

Stimson, Henry Lewis and Bundy, McGeorge, *On Active Service in Peace and War* (London: Hutchinson, 1949)

Stoetzer, O. Carlos, *The Organization of American States*, 2nd edn. (Westport, CT: Praeger, 1993)

Stolleis, Michale, *History of Public Law in Germany*, trans. Thomas Dunlap (Oxford University Press, 2004)

Stone, Julius, *Aggression and World Order, A Critique of United Nations Theories of Aggression* (London: Stevens & Sons, 1958)

Stowell, Ellery C., 'The Stewardship of Secretary Stimson', A.J.I.L., 27 (1933), 102–4

Strange, Susan, 'The Persistent Myth of Lost Hegemony', Int.Org., 41/4 (1987), 551–74

Stromseth, Jane E., 'Law and Force after Iraq: A Transitional Moment', A.J.I.L., 97 (2003), 628–42

Strupp, Karl, *Wörterbuch des Völkerrechts und der Diplomatie* (Berlin: Walter de Gruyter, 1925)

Stuby, Gerhard, *Vom 'Kronjuristen' zum 'Kronzeugen'. Friedrich Wilhelm Gaus: ein Leben im Auswärtigen Amt der Wilhelmstraße* (VSA-Verlag, Hamburg, 2008)

Stürchler, Nikolas, *The Threat of Force in International Law* (Cambridge University Press, 2007)

Stuesser, Lee, 'Active Defense: State Military Response to International Terrorism', Cal.W.I.L.J., 17 (1987), 1–42

Symes, Gavin, 'Force without Law, Seeking a Legal Justification for the September 1996 U.S. Military Intervention in Iraq', Mich.J.I.L., 19 (1998), 581–622

Taft, William H., IV and Buchwald, Todd F., 'Preemption, Iraq and International Law', A.J.I.L., 97 (2003), 557–63

Takey, Ray, *The Origins of the Eisenhower Doctrine* (New York: St Martin's Press, 2000)

Thakur, Ramesh C., *The United Nations, Peace and Security – From Collective Security to the Responsibility to Protect* (Cambridge University Press, 2006)

The, Au Duong *Die Vietnampolitik der U.S.A. von der Johnson – zur Nixon–Kissinger-Doktrin* (Frankfurt: Lang, 1979)

Thomas, Ann van Wynen and Thomas Jr., A. J., *The Organization of American States* (Dallas, TX: Southern Methodist University Press, 1963)

'The Organization of American States and the Monroe Doctrine – Legal Implications', Louis.L.Rev., 30 (1970), 541–81

The Concept of Aggression in International Law (Dallas, TX: Southern Methodist University Press, 1972)

Thompson, Kenneth W., 'The Reagan Doctrine', in Tucker (ed.), *Intervention & the Reagan Doctrine*, pp. 25–30

Thompson, Sir Robert, *Revolutionary War and World Strategy: 1945–1969* (New York: Taplinger 1970)

Tocqueville, Alexis de, *De la Démocratie en Amérique, Oeuvres, papiers et correspondances*, 8th edn. (Paris: Gallimard, 1951)

Tomuschat, Christian, 'Der 11. September und seine rechtlichen Konsequenzen', Eu.GRZ, 24 (2001), 535–45

'Völkerrecht ist kein Zweiklassenrecht', VN, 51/2 (2003), 41–6

'Iraq – Demise of International Law?', *Friedens-Warte*/J.I.P.O., 78 (2003), 141–60

Tower, Charlemagne, 'The Origin, Meaning and International Force of the Monroe Doctrine', A.J.I.L., 14 (1920), 1–25

Triepel, Heinrich, *Völkerrecht und Landesrecht* (Leipzig: C. L. Hirschfeld, 1899)

Die Hegemonie: ein Buch von führenden Staaten (Stuttgart: Kohlhammer, 1938)

Truman, Harry S., *Memoirs by Harry S. Truman – Years of Trial and Hope* (New York: Smithmark Publishing, 1996)

Tucker, Robert W., 'The American Outlook', in Osgood *et al.* (eds.), *America and the World – From the Truman Doctrine to Vietnam*, pp. 27–78

(ed.), *Intervention & the Reagan Doctrine* (New York: Council on Religion and International Affairs, 1985)

Tunkin, Grigorij Ivanovic, *Theory of International Law*, trans. William E. Butler (London: George Allen & Unwin, 1974)

Turner, Robert F., 'International Law, the Reagan Doctrine, and World Peace: Going Back to the Future', Wash.Q., 11/4 (1988), 119–36

Turns, David, 'The Stimson Doctrine of Non-Recognition: Its Historical Genesis and Influence on Contemporary International Law', Chin.J.I.L., 2 (2003), 105–43

United States Congress, Senate Committee on Foreign Relations (ed.), *The Legislative Origins of the Truman Doctrine* (New York: Garland Publishing, 1979)

Unknown Author, 'Pepper Deplores Truman Doctrine', *Harvard Law Record* (1947), 16 April 1947, pp. 1–3

Unknown Author, 'Baghdad Pact', Int.Org., 11/3 (1957), 547

Unknown Author, 'Realism, Liberalism and the War Powers Resolution', H.L.R., 102-I (1989), 637–57

Vagts, Alfred and Vagts, Detlef F., 'The Balance of Power in International Law: A History of an Idea', A.J.I.L., 73 (1979), 555–80

Vagts, Detlef F., 'International Law in the Third Reich', A.J.I.L., 84 (1990), 661–704

'Hegemonic International Law', A.J.I.L., 95 (2001), 843–8

'American International Law: A Sonderweg?', in Dicke *et al.* (eds.), *Weltinnenrecht – Liber amicorum Jost Delbrück* (Berlin: Duncker & Humblot, 2005), pp. 835–47

Veeser, Cyrus, 'Inventing Dollar Diplomacy: The Roosevelt Corollary to the Monroe Doctrine', Dipl.Hist., 27/3 (2003), 301–26

Verdross, Alfred, Entstehungsweisen und Geltungsgrund des universellen völkerrechtlichen Gewohnheitsrechts', ZaöRV/H.J.I.L., 29 (1969), 635–53

Verosta, Stephan, Regionen und Perioden der Geschichte des Völkerrechts', ÖZöRV, 30 (1979), 1–21

Verwey, Wil D., 'Humanitarian Intervention', in Cassese (ed.), *The Current Legal Regulation of the Use of Force*, pp. 57–78

Vincent, R. J., *Non-Intervention and International Order* (Princeton University Press, 1974)

Virally, Michel 'Art. 2(4)', in Cot and Pellet (eds.), *La Charte des Nations Unies*, pp. 113–25

Vitzthum, Wolfgang Graf (ed.) *Völkerrecht*, 4th edn. (Berlin: Walter de Gruyter, 2007)

Voos, Sandra, *Die Schule von New Haven: Darstellung und Kritik einer amerikanischen Völkerrechtslehre* (Berlin: Duncker & Humblot, 2000), Ph.D. thesis, Berlin, 1999

Walden, Raphael M., 'The Subjective Element in the Formation of Customary International Law', Isr.L.R., 12 (1977), 344–64

Waldock, Sir Claude Humphrey Meredith, 'The Regulation of the Use of Force by Individual States in International Law', RdC, 81 (1952-II), 451–514

Wall, Adru E., 'International Law and the Bush Doctrine', I.Y.H.R., 37 (2004), 193–229

Wallerstein, Immanuel, 'The Eagle has Crash Landed', For.Pol., July/August (2002), 60–8

Walter, Christian, *Vereinte Nationen und Regionalorganisationen* (Berlin: Springer, 1996), Ph.D. thesis, Heidelberg, 1995

Waltz, Kenneth, 'International Structure, National Force, and the Balance of World Power', J.I.A., 21 (1967), 215–31

Warbrick, Colin and McGoldrick, Dominic, 'Current Developments – Public International Law', I.C.L.Q., 51 (2003), 811–4

Watson, Robert P., Gleek, Charles and Grillo, Michael (eds.), *Presidential Doctrines: National Security from Woodrow Wilson to George W. Bush* (New York: Nova Science Publishers, 2003)

Wedgwood, Ruth, 'The Fall of Saddam Hussein: Security Council Mandates and Preemptive Self-Defense', A.J.I.L., 97 (2003), 576–85

Weege, Kurt, *Panamerikanismus und Monroedoktrin (Eine völkerrechtliche und politische Arbeit)* (Schönberg: Lehmann & Bernhard, 1939), Ph.D. thesis, Kiel, 1939

Wegner, Alexis, 'Die Monroedoktrin und ihre Anwendung im 20. Jahrhundert, insbesondere in ihren Beziehungen zur Panamerikanischen Bewegung und zum Schieds-gerichtsbarkeitsgedanken', Ph.D. thesis, Breslau, 1931

Wehberg, Hans, *Die Monroedoktrin* (Mönchen-Gladbach: Volksvereins-Verlag, 1915)

'La Contribution des Conférences de la paix de la Haye au progrès du droit international', RdC, 37 (1931-III), 527–67

Krieg und Eroberung im Wandel des Völkerrechts (Frankfurt: Metzner, 1953)

'Die Stimson-Doktrin', in Constantopoulos (ed.), *Grundprobleme des internationalen Rechts: Festschrift für Jean Spiropoulus*, FS-Spiropoulus, pp. 433–43

Weingärtner, Dieter (ed.), *Streitkräfte und Menschenrechte* (Baden-Baden: Nomos, 2008)

Wheeler, Nicolas J., 'The Bush Doctrine: The Dangers of American Exceptionalism in A Revolutionary Age', *Asian Perspective*, 27 (2003), 183–216.

Whiteman, Marjorie (ed.), *Digest of International Law*, 13 vols. (Washington, DC: Government Printing Office, 1963–71)

Whitton, John B., 'Isolation: An Obsolete Principle of the Monroe Doctrine', I.Con., 290 (1933), 211–25

'La Doctrine de Monroe', R.G.D.I.P., VII (1933), 5–44, 140–80, 273–325

Wilde, Jaap de, 'Mondialisering van de Monroe Doctrine', *International Spectator*, 57/8 (2003), 346–52

Wilkinson, Paul, 'Liberal State Responses to Terrorism and Their Limits', in Bianchi and Keller (eds.), *Counterterrorism: Democracy's Challenge*, pp. 71–5

Wilson, Larman C., 'The Monroe Doctrine, Cold War Anachronism: Cuba and the Dominican Republic', J.Pol., 28 (1966), 322–46

Winfield, Percy H., 'The Grounds of Intervention in International Law', B.Y.I.L., 5 (1924), 149–62

Wolfrum, Rüdiger, 'Art. 1', in Simma (ed.), *The Charter of the United Nations*, vol. I, pp. 39–47

'The Attack of September 11, 2001, the Wars Against the Taliban and Iraq: Is there a Need to reconsider International Law on the Recourse to Force and *ius in bello*', M.P.Y.U.N.L., 7 (2003), 1–78

Woods, Carl J., 'An Overview of the Military Aspects of Security Assistance', Mil.L.Rev., 128 (1990), 71–113

Woolsey, L. H. 'Leticia Dispute between Columbia and Peru', A.J.I.L., 27 (1933), 317–24

'The Chaco Dispute', A.J.I.L., 28 (1934), 724–9

Wrede, Christoph Freiherr von, '*Der Rechtsanspruch der Deutschen Bundesregierung auf völkerrechtliche Alleinvertretung Gesamtdeutschlands und die Hallstein-Doktrin*', Ph.D. thesis, Freiburg/Switzerland, 1966

Wright, Quincy, 'The Outlawry of War', A.J.I.L., 19 (1925), 76–103

'The Stimson Note of January 7, 1932', A.J.I.L., 26 (1932), 342–8

'The Legal Foundation of the Stimson Doctrine', *Pacific Affairs*, 8 (1932) 439–46

'The Meaning of the Pact of Paris', A.J.I.L., 27 (1933), 39–61

'Some Legal Aspects of the Far Eastern Situation', A.J.I.L., 27 (1933), 509–16

'International Law and Ideologies', A.J.I.L., 30 (1954), 616–26

'United States Intervention in the Lebanon', A.J.I.L., 53 (1959), 112–25

'The Cuban Quarantine', A.J.I.L., 57 (1963), 547–67

'Legal Aspects of the Vietnam Situation', A.J.I.L., 60 (1966), 750–69

Wyllie, James H., *The Influence of British Arms – An Analysis of British Military Intervention since 1956* (London: George Allen & Unwin, 1984)

Yaqub, Salim, *Containing Arab Nationalism – The Eisenhower Doctrine and the Middle East* (Chapel Hill, NC: University of North Carolina Press, 2004)

Yepes, Jesus M., 'Les Problèmes fondamentaux du Droit des Gens en Amérique', RdC, 47 (1934-I), 1–144

Yesiboursa, Behcet Kemal, *The Baghdad Pact: Anglo-American Defence Policies in the Middle East, 1950–1959* (London: Frank Cass, 2005)

Yokota, Kisaburo, 'The Recent Development of the Stimson Doctrine', *Pacific Affairs*, 8/2 (1935), 133–43

Yoo, John, 'International Law and the War in Iraq', A.J.I.L., 97 (2003), 563–76

Zakaria, Fareed, *The Post-American World* (New York: W. W. Norton, 2008)

Zanardi, Pierluigi Lamberti, 'Indirect Military Aggression', in Cassese (ed.), *The Current Legal Regulation of the Use of Force*, pp. 111–19

Ziolkowski, Katharina, *Gerechtigkeitspostulate als Rechtfertigung von Kriegen* (Baden-Baden: Nomos,, 2006)

Zivier, Ernst R., 'Pax Americana-Bellum Americanum, Auf dem Weg zu einem neuen Völkerrecht oder einem neuen Völkerunrecht?', RuP, 39 (2003), 194–200

Worldwide web sources (accessed January 2009)

Benvenisti, Eyal, 'Expert analysis, Iraq and the "Bush Doctrine" of Pre-emptive Self-Defence', www.crimesofwar.org/print/expert/bush-Benvenisti-print.html

Byers, Michael, 'Expert analysis, Iraq and the "Bush Doctrine" of Pre-emptive Self-Defence', www.crimesofwar.org/print/expert/bush-Byers-print.html

Bush, George W., Commencement Address at the United States Military Academy, West Point, 1 June 2002, www.whitehouse.gov/news/releases/2002/06/20020601-3.html

Casey, Lee A. and Rivikin, David B., '"Anticipatory" Self-Defense against Terrorism is Legal', Legal Opinion Letter, 14 December 2001, www.wlf.org/upload/casey.pdf

Commission on Presidential Debates Debate Transcript, The Second McCain–Obama Presidential Debate, 7 October 2008, www.debates.org/pages/trans2008c.html

Department of State Reagan Doctrine, www.state.gov/r/pa/ho/time/dr/17741pf.htm

European Union, Mission to the United Nations Basic Principles for an EU Strategy against Proliferation of Weapons of Mass Destruction, 16 June 2003, europa-eu-un.org/articles/lt/article_2478_lt.htm

Franck, Thomas M., 'Expert analysis, Iraq and the "Bush-Doctrine" of Pre-emptive Self-Defence', www.crimesofwar.org/print/expert/bush-Franck-print.htm

Gaja, Giorgio, 'In What Sense was There an "Armed Attack?"', E.J.I.L. Discussion Forum, www.ejil.org/forum_WTC/ny-gaja.html

Grant, Thomas D., 'Doctrines (Monroe, Halstein, Brezhnev, Stimson)', in R. Wolfrum (ed.), *The Max Planck Encyclopedia of Public International Law* (Oxford University Press, 2008), online edition, www.mpepil.com

Gray, Colin S., 'What is War? A View from Strategic Studies', Oxford Leverhulme Programme on the Changing Character of War, http://ccw.politics.ox.ac.uk/events/archives/ht04_gray_a.pdf

Kirgis, Frederic L., 'Terrorist Attacks on the World Trade Center and the Pentagon', ASIL Insights, September 2001, www.asil.org/insights/insigh77.htm

'Israel's Intensified Military Campaign Against Terrorism, December 2001', www.asil.org/insights/insigh78.htm

Krisch, Nico, 'Imperial International Law', Global Law Working Paper 01/04, Hauser Global Law School Program, NYU School of Law, www.nyulawglobal.org/workingpapers/krisch_appd_0904.pdf

Munich Security Conference, Vladimir Putin, Speech at the 43rd Munich Conference on Security Policy, 2 October 2007, www.securityconference.de/konferenzen/rede.php

Munich, Security Conference, Joseph R. Biden, Speech at the 45th Munich Security Conference, 7 February 2009, www.securityconference.de/konferenzen/rede.php

Pellet, Alain, 'No, This is not War!', E.J.I.L., Discussion Forum, 21 October 2001, ejil.org/forum_WTC/ny-pellet.html

Rice, Condolezza Dr., Condolezza Rice Discusses President's National Security Strategy, 1 October 2002, www.whitehouse.gov/news/releases/2002/10/20021001–6.html

Taft, William, IV, 'The Legal Basis of Preemption, Memorandum to Members of ASIL-CFR Roundtable', 18 November 2002, www.cfr.org/pub5250/william_h_taft_iv/the_legal_basis_for_preemption.php

Remarks to National Association of Attorneys General, 20 March 2003, www.usinfo.state.gov/dhr/Archive/2003/Oct/09–464655.html

The White House, The National Security Strategy of the United States of America, September 2002, www.whitehouse.gov/nsc/nss.html

President Bush Announces Major Combat Operations in Iraq have Ended, http://georgewbush-whitehouse.archives.gov/news/releases/2003/05/20030501-15.html

National Security Strategy (NSS) 2006, http://merln.ndu.edu/whitepapers/USnss2006.pdf

Office of the Press Secretary, 3 April 2009, 'Remarks by President Obama At Strasbourg Town Hall', Strasbourg France, www.whitehouse.gov/the_press_office/Remarks-by-President-Obama-at-Strasbourg-Town-Hall

19 March 2009, 'A New Year, A New Beginning', www.whitehouse.gov/nowruz

Office of the Press Secretary, 4 June 2009, 'Remarks by the President on a New Beginning', Cairo University, Egypt, www.whitehouse.gov/the_press_office/Remarks-by-the-President-at-Cairo-University-6–04–09

Office of the Press Secretary, 7 July 2009, Remarks by the President at the New Economic School Graduation, Gostinny Dvor, Moscow, Russia www.whitehouse.gov/the_press_office/REMARKS-BY-THE-PRESIDENT-AT-THE-NEW-ECONOMIC-SCHOOL-GRADUATION

United Nations, The Secretary General's Address to the General Assembly, 23 September 2003 www.un.org/webcast/ga/58/statements/sg2eng030923.htm

The Secretary General's High-level Panel Report of the Secretary General's High-level Panel on Threats, Challenges and Change, 'A more secure world: our shared responsibility', www.un.org/ secureworld/report2.pdf.

United States Embassy to Australia 'Powell Hails Thailand's Support in War on Terror', 29 July 2002, usembassy-australia.state.gov/hyper/2002/0729/epf.104htm

United States Embassy to India 'Bush Says Proliferation Controls Must Be Strengthened', 25 April 2003, usembassy.state.gov/posts/in1/wwwhpr0428b.html

Zacklin, Ralph, 'The UN Secretariat and the Use of Force in a Unipolar World', Hersch Lauterpacht Memorial Lectures,2007–8, www.lcil.cam.ac.uk/Media/lectures/pdf/2008_Hersch_Lectures/2008_Lecture_3.pdf

INDEX